ACTIVITIES 1922–1929

The Collected Writings of John Maynard Keynes

At a meeting of the Liberal Industrial Inquiry, 1927.

Sir Herbert Samuel, Walter Layton, David Lloyd George,
Hubert Henderson and J.M.K.

THE COLLECTED WRITINGS OF
JOHN MAYNARD KEYNES

VOLUME XIX

ACTIVITIES 1922–1929

THE RETURN TO GOLD
AND INDUSTRIAL POLICY

IN TWO VOLUMES
PART I

EDITED BY
DONALD MOGGRIDGE

MACMILLAN
CAMBRIDGE UNIVERSITY PRESS
FOR THE
ROYAL ECONOMIC SOCIETY

Published for the Royal Economic Society
throughout the world, excluding the U.S.A. and Canada, by

THE MACMILLAN PRESS LTD
London and Basingstoke
Associated companies in Delhi   Dublin   Hong Kong   Johannesburg   Lagos
Melbourne   New York   Singapore   Tokyo

and throughout the U.S.A. and Canada by

THE SYNDICS OF THE CAMBRIDGE UNIVERSITY PRESS
32 East 57th Street, New York, NY 10022, U.S.A.

Printed in Great Britain
at the University Press, Cambridge

British Library Cataloguing in Publication Data
Keynes, John Maynard, *Baron Keynes*
The collected writings of John Maynard Keynes.
Vol. 19: Activities 1922–1929, the return to
gold and industrial policy
1. Economics
I. Moggridge, Donald Edward
II. Royal Economic Society
330.15'6   HB171
ISBN 0-333-10727-6

ISBN 0-333-10727-6
ISBN 0-521-23071-3 (the U.S.A. and Canada only)

3-19-84

CONTENTS

GENERAL INTRODUCTION

This new standard edition of *The Collected Writings of John Maynard Keynes* forms the memorial to him of the Royal Economic Society. He devoted a very large share of his busy life to the Society. In 1911, at the age of twenty-eight, he became editor of the *Economic Journal* in succession to Edgeworth: two years later he was made secretary as well. He held these offices without intermittence until almost the end of his life. Edgeworth, it is true, returned to help him with the editorship from 1919 to 1925; Macgregor took Edgeworth's place until 1934, when Austin Robinson succeeded him and continued to assist Keynes down to 1945. But through all these years Keynes himself carried the major responsibility and made the principal decisions about the articles that were to appear in the *Economic Journal*, without any break save for one or two issues when he was seriously ill in 1937. It was only a few months before his death at Easter 1946 that he was elected president and handed over his editorship to Roy Harrod and the secretaryship to Austin Robinson.

In his dual capacity of editor and secretary Keynes played a major part in framing the policies of the Royal Economic Society. It was very largely due to him that some of the major publishing activities of the Society—Sraffa's edition of Ricardo, Stark's edition of the economic writings of Bentham, and Guillebaud's edition of Marshall, as well as a number of earlier publications in the 1930s—were initiated.

When Keynes died in 1946 it was natural that the Royal Economic Society should wish to commemorate him. It was perhaps equally natural that the Society chose to commemorate him by producing an edition of his collected works. Keynes himself had always taken a joy in fine printing, and the Society, with the help of Messrs Macmillan as publishers and the Cambridge University Press as printers, has been anxious to give Keynes's writings a permanent form that is worthy of him.

The present edition will publish as much as is possible of his work in the field of economics. It will not include any private and personal correspondence or publish many letters in the possession of his family. The edition is concerned, that is to say, with Keynes as an economist.

Keynes's writings fall into five broad categories. First there are the books which he wrote and published as books. Second there are collections of articles and pamphlets which he himself made during his lifetime (*Essays in Persuasion* and *Essays in Biography*). Third, there is a very considerable volume of published but uncollected writings—articles written for newspapers, letters to newspapers, articles in journals that have not been included in his two volumes of collections, and various pamphlets. Fourth, there are a few hitherto unpublished writings. Fifth, there is correspondence with economists and concerned with economics of public affairs. It is the intention of this series to publish almost completely the whole of the first four categories listed above. The only exceptions are a few syndicated articles where Keynes wrote almost the same material for publication in different newspapers or in different countries, with minor and unimportant variations. In these cases, this series will publish one only of the variations, choosing the most interesting.

The publication of Keynes's economic correspondence must inevitably be selective. In the day of the typewriter and the filing cabinet and particularly in the case of so active and busy a man, to publish every scrap of paper that he may have dictated about some unimportant or ephemeral matter is impossible. We are aiming to collect and publish as much as possible, however, of the correspondence in which Keynes developed his own ideas in argument with his fellow economists, as well as the more significant correspondence at times when Keynes was in the middle of public affairs.

Apart from his published books, the main sources available to those preparing this series have been two. First, Keynes in his will made Richard Kahn his executor and responsible for his economic papers. They have been placed in the Marshall Library of the University of Cambridge and have been available for this edition. Until 1914 Keynes did not have a secretary and his earliest papers are in the main limited to drafts of important letters that he made in his own handwriting and retained. At that stage most of the correspondence that we possess is represented by what he received rather than by what he wrote. During the war years of 1914–18 and 1940–6 Keynes was serving in the Treasury. With the opening in 1968 of the records under the thirty-year rule, the papers that he wrote then and between the wars have become available. From 1919 onwards, throughout the rest of his life, Keynes had the help of a secretary—for many years Mrs Stephens. Thus for the last twenty-five years of his working life we have in most cases the carbon copies of his own letters as well as the originals of the letters he received.

There were, of course, occasions during this period on which Keynes wrote himself in his own handwriting. In some of these cases, with the help of his correspondents, we have been able to collect the whole of both sides of some important interchanges, and we have been anxious, in justice to both correspondents, to see that both sides of the correspondence are published in full.

The second main source of information has been a group of scrapbooks kept over a very long period of years by Keynes's mother, Florence Keynes, wife of Neville Keynes. From 1919 onwards these scrapbooks contain almost the whole of Maynard Keynes's more ephemeral writing, his letters to newspapers and a great deal of material which enables one to see not only what he wrote but the reaction of others to his writing. Without these very carefully kept scrapbooks the task of any editor or biographer of Keynes would have been immensely more difficult.

The plan of the edition, as at present intended, is this. It will total thirty volumes. Of these the first eight are Keynes's published books from *Indian Currency and Finance*, in 1913, to the *General Theory* in 1936, with the addition of his *Treatise on Probability*. There next follow, as vols. IX and X, *Essays in Persuasion* and *Essays in Biography*, representing Keynes's own collections of articles. *Essays in Persuasion* differs from the original printing in two respects: it contains the full texts of the articles or pamphlets included in it and not (as in the original printing) abbreviated versions of these articles, and it also contains one or two later articles which are of exactly the same character as those included by Keynes in his original collection. In *Essays in Biography* there have been added a number of biographical studies that Keynes wrote both before and after 1933.

There will follow two volumes, XI–XII, of economic articles and correspondence and a further two volumes, already published, XIII–XIV, covering the development of his thinking as he moved towards the *General Theory*. There are included in these volumes such part of Keynes's economic correspondence as is closely associated with the articles that are printed in them. A supplement to these volumes, XXIX, prints some further material relating to the same issues, which has since been discovered.

The remaining fourteen volumes deal with Keynes's *Activities* during the years from the beginning of his public life in 1905 until his death. In each of the periods into which we divide this material, the volume concerned publishes his more ephemeral writings, all of it hitherto uncollected, his correspondence relating to these activities, and such other material and correspondence as is necessary to the understanding of Keynes's activities. These volumes are edited by Elizabeth Johnson and Donald Moggridge, and it has been their task to trace and interpret Keynes's activities sufficiently to make the material fully intelligible to a later generation. Elizabeth Johnson has been responsible for vols. XV–XVIII, covering Keynes's earlier years and his activities down to the end of World War I reparations and reconstruction. Donald Moggridge is responsible for all the remaining volumes recording Keynes's other activities from 1922 until his death in 1946.

The record of Keynes's activities during World War II is now complete with the publication of volumes XXV–XXVII. It thus remains to fill the gap between 1922 and 1939 with three volumes of which this is the first; to print certain of Keynes's published articles and the correspondence relating to them which have not appeared elsewhere in this edition, and to publish a volume of his social, political and literary writings.

Those responsible for this edition have been: Lord Kahn, both as Lord Keynes's executor and as a long and intimate friend of Lord Keynes, able to help in the interpreting of much that would be otherwise misunderstood; the late Sir Roy Harrod as the author of his biography; Austin Robinson as Keynes's co-editor on the *Economic Journal* and successor as Secretary of the Royal Economic Society. Austin Robinson has acted throughout as Managing Editor; Donald Moggridge is now associated with him as Joint Managing Editor.

In the early stages of the work Elizabeth Johnson was assisted by Jane Thistlethwaite, and by Mrs McDonald, who was originally responsible for the systematic ordering of the files of the Keynes papers. Judith Masterman for many years worked with Mrs Johnson on the papers. More recently Susan Wilsher, Margaret Butler and Leonora Woollam have continued the secretarial work. Barbara Lowe has been responsible for the indexing. Since 1977 Judith Allen has been responsible for much of the day-to-day management of the edition as well as seeing the volumes through the press.

EDITORIAL NOTE

In this and subsequent volumes, in general all of Keynes's own writings are printed in large type. All introductory matter and all writings by others than Keynes are printed in smaller type. The only exception to this general rule is that occasional short quotations from a letter from Keynes to his parents or to a friend, used in introductory passages to clarify a situation, are treated as introductory material and printed in the smaller type.

Most of Keynes's letters included in this and other volumes are reprinted from the carbon copies remaining among his papers. In most cases he added his initials to the carbon. We have no means of knowing in most circumstances whether the top copy sent to the recipient carried a more formal signature.

Most of Keynes's journalism appeared under his own name. However, in the case of *The Nation and Athenaeum* of which he was Chairman, Keynes wrote more than he signed. In determining what unsigned material was Keynes's we have used two sources of information: the incomplete run of marked copies of the magazine that survive in the Keynes Papers[1] and the two special scrapbooks of *Nation* articles which he asked his mother to keep and for which he provided the necessary information as regards unsigned articles. Naturally the two sources overlap on some occasions, as do other fragments surviving in the Keynes Papers, thus giving us more confidence about particular items.[2]

Keynes's own footnotes, as well as those of his correspondents,

---

[1] *The Nation*'s complete set of marked copies was destroyed during the Blitz.
[2] Sir Roy Harrod was thus mistaken when he suggested that Keynes, with one exception, 'contributed nothing to the paper which was not signed or initialled' (*The Life of John Maynard Keynes*, p. 337).

are indicated by asterisks or other symbols to distinguish them from the editorial footnotes indicated by numbers.

Crown copyright material appears with the permission of the Controller of Her Majesty's Stationery Office. The Social Sciences and Humanities Research Council of Canada provided financial support.

The Editor wishes to thank Gary Dobinson for assistance with the proofs.

Chapter 1

FINANCE AND INVESTMENT, 1922–1923

Although domestic events and policies absorbed some of Keynes's attention during 1920–2, international affairs, most notably the working out of the peace treaties and post-war reconstruction, absorbed most of the time and energy he devoted to public affairs. From late 1922 onwards, however, the focus of his interests began to shift more towards Britain and her problems.

An indication of this shift in focus came with the fall of Lloyd George's Coalition Government, in the midst of talk of an election campaign, following the meeting of Conservative members of Parliament at the Carlton Club on 19 October 1922, and Bonar Law's succession as Prime Minister. Two days after Law assumed office, Keynes spoke to the 95 Club, a Liberal society, in Manchester.

Notes for a speech at the 95 Club, Manchester, 25 October 1922

I believe in the depth and reality of the great traditional divisions between parties,—that they depend on deep principles which are forever reappearing in changing circumstances.

I therefore welcome it with profound relief that the confusions which perhaps inevitably followed the suspension of political controversy during the war have been brought suddenly to an end; and that Liberals can again stand together as Liberals determined to make prevail sooner or later the principles of wise government.

But eight years have passed since we were in this position. Other preoccupations have overwhelmed us. We need therefore a greater intellectual effort than usual to get our principles clearly embodied in a programme. And when Liberals meet together on such an occasion as this, we shall spend our time best in discussing together what this programme ought to be.

We must begin with the national finance, the consolidation of which is the necessary condition of progress in most other directions.

I

I venture to lay down this proposition—that the field of possible economies is comparatively narrow.

A large part of our expenditure—service of debt, pensions—honourable and unalterable commitments.

A further part are social services which it would be wasteful to curtail. I am afraid that we must agree that all further expensive schemes of social improvement, even though they may be productive in the long run, must be postponed. But we must be equally obstinate in keeping those we have.

Beyond this there may be waste arising from mismanagement. Economies in this direction not significant in relation to the budget.

There only remain two categories of large expenditure, armaments and commitments abroad.

I think we have got to go for these two items bald-headed.

B[onar] L[aw]'s administration will do its best but not bald-headed.

We must have a change of policy so drastic that it may even involve some risks.

Beginning with overseas commitments

> Evacuation of Palestine and Mesopotamia with possible exception of Basra
>
> Appeal to Dominions to take up more fully their share of policing the Empire
>
> Reduction of the Army even to a point incompatible with our exerting agreed influence in Europe.

There is no better way of ensuring peace than by assuming it. We can only save ourselves by assuming that for 15 years we are not going to be involved in a war by land, even if the assumption is doubtful and needs courage. If no one is afraid of us, I do not think that there is anyone of whom *we* need be afraid.

We must take the lead in disarmament and not make it conditional on the action of others.

If we have a happy and prosperous people at home, we should always be equal to a great emergency if it ever arises again. This

2

is the best form of preparedness and if, as I believe it is, it is incompatible with the other forms of preparedness, this is the one to be followed.

There are no important economies to be made except in this direction. We must therefore attack these with courage and the utmost determination. So much for expenditure. (Does Mr McK.[enna] feel confident that the conservative administration will do this?) What about revenue?

It would be very nice to reduce the income tax—too high for social expediency. But very rash at present to promise reduction of any taxes at all.

Are there any new taxes which ought to be put on. What about protective import duties?

I have not the slightest doubt that B[onar] L[aw]'s administration will introduce protection sooner or later. Mr Law himself won his spurs on this subject. He is still an ardent and convinced protectionist. He has selected as his C[hancellor] of [the] E[xchequer] the parent of the Safeguarding of Industries Bill.[1] He will find it hard to balance his budget. Partly on pretext of revenue etc.

You in Manchester all know what a disastrous and deceptive prescription this would be for making both ends meet.

Nevertheless the danger is great—a wave of protective sentiment passing over Europe.

Yet every scrap of experience which accumulates emphasizes the blindness and disastrous folly of this policy. We in this country must not only hold high the banner of unfettered trade here. But everywhere where we can exert our influence in Europe we must cast it on the side of freedom.

Formerly free trade was a desirable aid to increased wealth. It has now become a necessary and essential defence against a crushing poverty. Unless we direct our resources into the directions where they are most productive, we shall not be able to gain a living at all.

There is one other tax which deserves mention. The capital

---

[1] Stanley Baldwin.

levy. Two years ago I was in favour. The collapse of values since that date has changed the situation. But circumstances may still arise from which the capital levy will be the right way out.

The circumstances for which a levy is reserved are easily indicated.

The working part of the population owes the burden of old obligations—proportion of the fruits of their toil.

If this proportion becomes unbearably high there are two remedies—one deliberate, the other undeliberate. The capital levy and depreciation of the currency.

All the continental belligerents have chosen the second alternative—Germany, France.

It is possible that we here can avoid both. But it would not be prudent to rely on this until we find by trying what economies are possible.

Even here I think there would be not much harm in a modest dose of depreciation. I believe that we should be in a better equilibrium all round if prices rose to 2 or $2\frac{1}{2}$ times pre-war. This would go a long way towards balancing the budget. But if we could not balance our budget at this level, I should prefer a capital levy, which I believe to be perfectly feasible technically (as a Manchester man Mr Sydney Arnold[2] has shown more clearly than anyone), to further depreciation.

In short I do not think that a capital levy is practical politics at present but it is not inconceivable that we may be forced to fall back on it.

My financial policy for Liberalism is therefore

(1) Drastic economies on fighting and foreign services

(2) Uncompromising free trade

(3) No promises of any reduction in taxation until the Budget has been balanced including provision for sinking funds

(4) The preservation of our existing social expenditure, especially on health and education, but no new expensive projects just at present.

[2] The reference is to S. Arnold, 'A Capital Levy: The Problems of Realisation and Valuation', *Economic Journal*, June 1918.

I believe that the Liberal Party is the only party in the state which can achieve this programme.

I do not agree with McKenna that Bonar is the one man who can do it because

(1) His economies will not be firm enough

(2) He will be led into protection

(3) If he attacks the social services he will cause a dangerous reaction.

On the other hand the Labour Party though they may make the economies and may be freetraders are likely to neutralise these virtues by premature reductions of taxation and premature social programmes

Webb's article

A word or two about Foreign Policy

Our course is plain—a sincere, open and generous policy with which we persevere. Peace, Freedom and Reconstruction. Seeking for ourselves no direct advantages. It may now be much too late to preserve Europe from past catastrophes. The moral defection of Mr L.G. at the last election and during the Peace Conference, when he more or less consciously sinned against the light, have made him an architect of almost irreparable ruin.

We can only do our best. I am not confident but I am not pessimistic. Anyway the only possible hope lies in an attempt to settle things on their merits, to tell the truth and not to talk cant and humbug to please anyone.

I do not think that any party except ours combines the wisdom and the experience with freedom from recent entanglements necessary to carry this policy to success.

One further point. In the present situation of the Liberal Party the personality of Mr L.G. has an inevitable importance. At the moment apparently he is up for auction willing to heed any party or section from Limehouse to Belgravia who makes him a good offer. At this auction I hope we shall not be bidders.

But so far as our programme is concerned does it not exhibit a policy on which all rank-and-file Liberals can combine? And is it not a policy which none but Liberals can hope to carry to success?

The next day Keynes spoke to the Manchester Luncheon Club on 'Is the Nineteenth Century Over?'. No notes for this speech survive.

Bonar Law obtained a dissolution of Parliament on 25 October, and called the general election for 15 November. Keynes was out of the country for most of the election campaign, acting as an unofficial adviser to the German Government.[3]

On the night of the election, with Sir Charles Addis a director of the Bank of England in the chair, Keynes delivered the first of four lectures to the Institute of Bankers. The lectures, which were followed by an examination for those attending, were private and, as a result, not extensively reported. A stenographer's transcript, corrected by Keynes, survives. These lectures provide a useful transition from Keynes's German preoccupations to domestic matters.

Lecture to the Institute of Bankers, 15 November 1922

MR KEYNES: Ladies and gentlemen, Sir Charles Addis, I owe you all a sincere apology for not appearing last week. I tried up to the last moment to be here, but I was unavoidably detained. But perhaps there have been two advantages from that. In the first place, you and I have the pleasure of having with us now Sir Charles Addis on his first public appearance, I think, since his recovery. In the second place, my visit to Berlin will, I hope, enable me to illustrate some of the economic theories which I shall put before you from some very recent events.

A great number of years ago now Professor Irving Fisher wrote his book, which was called *Appreciation and Interest* [1896]. He first emphasised what other economists had noted but had not emphasised, namely, the important distinction between the real rate of interest and the money rate of interest. If prices are going up or going down there is a distinction between the two. If a man lends for a year at 5 per cent £100,

[3] See *JMK*, vol. XVIII, pp. 61-3.

which is worth one hundred units of goods, and if at the end of the year that sum of money is worth one hundred and ten units of goods, he gets at the end of the year not one hundred and five but one hundred and fifteen units of goods, because he receives back the hundred units of money plus the five units of money interest; so that, while the money rate of interest is five per cent the real or commodity rate of interest is fifteen per cent. Correspondingly, when prices are rising so that the money is worth a smaller amount of commodities, at the end of the period you may have a real rate of interest which is much lower than the money rate of interest. If the £100 were worth ninety units of commodities at the end of the period instead of one hundred or one hundred and ten, as in the first example, then he would receive back at the end of the period about ninety-five units, so that the one hundred and five units of money would buy ninety-five units of commodities. Therefore, while the money rate of interest would still be five per cent, the real rate of interest would now be minus five per cent. A man who had simply kept the commodities or had bought the commodities at the beginning of the period and had held them, would be in a better position than the man who had lent out the money at five per cent because the rate of depreciation in the value of the money itself had been going on at a greater rate than was represented by the interest. Professor Fisher brought that fundamental truth to the front, and he illustrated it in connection with dear and cheap money in relation to rising and falling prices. When it is generally supposed that prices are going to rise, a much higher money rate of interest is required in order to make it the real rate of interest at a given level. Suppose that it is generally expected that prices may rise anything up to ten per cent in the period in question. If that is anticipated, clearly a higher money rate of interest will be required in order to compensate the lender for the fact that he will be repaid in a currency of smaller value than that in which he lent in the first instance. Businessmen do not look at it in that way; but they look at it in a way which comes to the same thing, because if they feel that prices are going to go up rather than down they are much more willing to buy commodities ahead and, therefore, much more prepared to pay a stiffish rate of interest for the money which they must borrow in order to enable them to do so. When a boom is in full swing and is expected to continue, businessmen think it imprudent to put off buying and, therefore, they are not deterred by the high rate of interest. That is because they believe, although they do not put it that way, that though the money rate of interest is high, the real rate of interest is not high. Correspondingly, when you have a depression in full swing, the unwillingness of people to buy, because they think that if they hold off they will get goods at a lower price, makes them particularly unwilling to borrow money in any case in which they can postpone purchase; so that when you have a depression and falling prices are anticipated there is a tendency for money to be cheap, so the dearness or cheapness of money in the boom and in the depression are attempts to keep the real rate of interest more stable than it would be if we had the same money rate of interest, whether prices were going up or were going down.

It very seldom happens that the fluctuations of the money rate of interest are nearly large enough to keep the thing stable. That is partly because people do not act sufficiently consciously in the matter, and also because, when people have a general impression that prices are going to rise or fall, they do not know it for certain and, therefore, they are not prepared to pay the same rate of interest that they would pay if they knew for certain that prices were going up. Thus you find in general that when prices are rising there is a tendency for money to be dear, but not dear enough to counteract the actual rise of prices that takes place.

That is a piece of what is now fairly familiar theory. I found in Berlin a very startling example of its operation in practice. In Germany prices have now continued to rise for so long and with such violence that, rightly or wrongly (very likely rightly, but that does not matter), the impression in everybody's mind is that they will continue to rise. Nobody has confidence in the future of the mark. Therefore everyone wishes to buy at once, and nobody wishes to put off buying. They are willing to pay what in ordinary times would be fantastic rates of interest. On all past dates in the recent history of the mark, the real rate of interest in Germany has been negative, to a very great extent; that is to say, anybody who can borrow marks and turn them into assets would at the end of any given period find that the appreciation in the value of the assets in terms of marks was far greater than the interest he had to pay for borrowing those marks. It has been good business for many months now to borrow marks and turn them into assets. Everybody is at the game. The consequence is that now the rate of interest has risen to fantastic heights with extremely interesting reactions on business enterprise of all kinds.

When I was in Berlin a week ago, what you might call the gilt-edged rate of interest for short loans was about twenty-two per cent; that is to say, the Deutsche Bank or institutions of that kind making advances to a favoured customer, on absolutely perfect collateral, would charge about twenty-two per cent. That worked out as follows: two per cent above bank rate (bank rate at that date was eight per cent: it was altered to ten per cent a day or two ago) plus a commission of one per cent a month. That is the gilt-edged rate. I daresay that today it is two per cent higher, because the Reichsbank has raised its rate to ten per cent. It is two per cent above bank rate, plus the commission of one per cent a month. Anybody who can borrow at twenty-two per cent feels extremely pleased. As a matter of fact, demands for credit at that rate are rationed. You must not only bring perfect collateral, and you must not only be a favoured customer, but you must make out a very strong case why you must have the money before your bank will lend it you, even at that rate. The open market rate for stock exchange transactions, or for anything speculative, or for dealings in exchange was from sixty to one hundred per cent per annum. In particular, anybody who had mark balances, anybody who had cash marks and was prepared to sell them for foreign exchange spot and buy them back three months forward so that he ran no exchange risk, could earn interest for that three months—and I think that he can today—at the rate of about one hundred per cent per annum. Anybody who has mark assets, anybody who has cash marks can utilise cash marks to earn interest at the rate of about one hundred per cent per annum today, by dealing spot and forward, over the exchanges. But people are not particularly willing to embark on such transactions, because the general impression is that it is much better business to sell your marks for foreign *valuta* than to buy them back three months forward. People prefer the speculation of the exchanges to the certainty of one hundred per cent per annum, that is, to the certainty of twenty-five per cent over three months. It shows the extent to which the demoralisation of opinion in the matter has now proceeded.

Professor Cassel and Mr Hawtrey and other authorities have held that the solution for a great many monetary troubles and for the maladjustment of the market consists in raising the rate of discount, the bank rate. In ordinary circumstances I agree with them that the world under-estimates the power of that instrument for bringing about a better adjustment. In such circumstances as exist in Germany that instrument has lost its power, because the lack of confidence in the money is such that people will pay these enormous rates of interest and will not be deterred. Consequently, that particular method is virtually ineffective. The scarcity of money which results from the situation, the dearness of money, is bound obviously sooner or later to have the most far-reaching effects on industry. The position has been getting more acute for some months past, but since about last August it has become really important. The ordinary manufacturing concern in Germany is now suffering acutely, not only from the higher rates of money which it has to pay, but from the inability to get funds at all to finance the productive process during the period of production. In the ordinary way a given firm can, of course, get money from its bank for that purpose. The firm is chiefly influenced by whether it sees good business. There are now cases in Germany in which a factory sees good business, that is to say, that at the prices it has to pay it anticipates that it can sell its products, after it has manufactured them, at a profit; but it cannot obtain from its bank enough credit during the productive process to finance the purchase of the raw materials and the payment of wages. I heard of many firms that were going at something less than full time, even half-time in some cases, not because business was not profitable, not because they could not sell their goods at a profit when they had manufactured them, but simply because they could not get from their banker, even at fancy rates, enough cash to enable them to buy their raw material and pay wages during the time that must elapse before their goods were ready for sale. That sort of thing is bound to happen when you get money rising to these heights. Money is bound to be at very high rates as long as the present state of lack of confidence continues to prevail. It may be—and I think that it is very likely the case—that people are now not doing it; but people always do what it has been profitable to do during the previous six months—they look back and not forward—and as everyone who has borrowed marks has done very well for a considerable time past now, that is the popular way of conducting one's affairs, and a high rate of interest, as I have explained is not as deterrent as one might have expected. That is one side of the situation.

I will now deal with more or less the same phenomenon from a slightly different angle of approach. I daresay that many of you are familiar, using Mr Fisher's name again, with his method of stating the quantity theory. There is an alternative method, not so well known, which is more illuminating, I think. I think that it is set forth in detail only by Professor Pigou. This theory puts the quantity theory thus. In ordinary circumstances it is convenient for private persons and businesses to keep a certain proportion of their total resources in the form of claims to legal tender—in the form of money, if you like, but I take rather a wider thing than [that to be] money—which will, of course, include bank deposits. If, therefore, you measure the community's resources in terms of something other than money, say in wheat, it suits the community for the purposes of convenience and the rest of it that a certain proportion, k, of their total resources should be kept in the form of titles to legal tender, that is to say, money, bank deposits and the like. That is obviously a true thing. Claims to legal tender, the amount of claims for legal tender, depend on a certain proportion of the scale of everybody's turnover and the resources of the community in general. It will fluctuate as the habits of the community fluctuate; but in a given set of habits a certain proportion of the community's resources will be kept in the form of titles to legal tender. If the number of titles to legal tender is M and the value of each unit is P, then the total value is PM, so that you have PM equal to kR. The number of claims to legal tender multiplied by the value of each claim is equal to the proportion of their resources that it suits the community to keep in the form of titles to legal tender. That is absolutely indisputable, although it may not take you very far until you have further analysed the several items. In pre-war days it was usual to concentrate on these two elements in the equation. It was assumed that the community's resources either changed slowly or were constant. It was assumed that the proportion that it suited the community to keep in the form of titles to legal tender always was a comparatively stationary thing, that if you doubled M you halved P, that PM was equal to something that did not change rapidly or in the ordinary way; so if you double the number of units of currency you halve their value, P being their value and M their number. That is the ordinary crude quantity theory. That, of course, is only the case if the other elements in the equation remain unchanged. It is only true that doubling M halves P if kR is remaining constant. The depreciation of the currencies of Central Europe began by the increase of M. The value of P began to fall because M was multiplied so largely. But we have now got to a different stage of the proceedings. People who have kept their resources in the form of titles to legal tender have come out of it so badly that they are beginning materially to alter their habits and to try to protect themselves from their losses by keeping a smaller and smaller proportion of their resources in the form of money. The great trouble in Germany now is not that M is getting so very big, though that is getting big, too, but that k is getting so very small. People are keeping a smaller and smaller proportion of their resources in money. Nobody keeps a bank balance which is going to be worth half its real value at the end of a month. Equally, people keep very little money in their pockets; so that the value of each unit of money has been falling much more than in proportion to the increase in M because that little factor k has been falling.

The depreciation of the German money could not now be cured merely by reducing the units of legal tender; it could not be cured merely by reducing M. You have to get k back to something like normal, and the extent to which people have economised in the proportion of their resources which they keep in the form of money has been something phenomenal. It is rather difficult to use figures because in the present state of the market one's figures change every day by something very material. A week ago—and I do not think that it is very different now—the value of all the notes in circulation in Germany was about one-tenth of the gold value of the pre-war German circulation; so that, though the Reichsbank has so enormously multiplied its note issue, the value of the mark has fallen ten times as fast as would be justified merely by the multiplication of the number of units of currency. Since pre-war days the territory of Germany has been reduced by about ten per cent and the scale of operations of business in Germany has also been, to a certain extent, diminished. On the other hand, gold prices, world prices, have risen fifty per cent, so I think that one can very roughly set off one of those things against the other and say that if Germany was pursuing its normal pre-war habits in the matter of the proportion of its resources which it kept in the form of money, it would require ten times as much currency at the present value of each unit as it is actually using today. That is what one means when one says that the value of the currency is a matter of confidence. The phrase is very often used very loosely. Politicians very often will tell you that it is a matter of confidence when it is really a matter of the value of M. After M has been multiplied to a certain extent there is a further reaction. k begins to fall, apart from alterations in M. That is what one scientifically means by the failure of confidence. In Germany, in order to get things straight, you have to do more than control M. You have to prevent the undue increase of M; but the main thing you have to do is to increase k. If you increased k and did not increase M, prices would have to rise a good deal further, or rather prices would have to fall a good deal, because the amount of currency would not go round if k was increased; so, unless you seek a great deflation in Germany, unless you are anxious for a very great deflation, you must allow, I think, a certain further increase in the units of currency, provided you have first of all set some definite limit to that. You must not let M increase indefinitely. If you are going to increase k by creating confidence, you must simultaneously be prepared to increase M a little. Otherwise P would have to fall to so great an extent—I think that I might have it the wrong way round, but you can easily keep me right: one always does that in lecturing—would have to increase to such an extent that you would have all the usual ill effects of deflation.

In present circumstances the attempts to economise the use of money and to do without money have reached lengths that are highly inconvenient to everybody concerned. Banks have not nearly enough cash in their tills and customers have not nearly enough deposits. Nobody has enough change. The economising of the use of money has gone to an extent which is extraordinarily inconvenient. The moment there was any revival of confidence the amount of money which people would want to have would rapidly increase. I daresay that in pre-war days people were unduly extravagant because they had more of their resources in the form of titles to legal tender than was, in fact, wise. Now they have gone very far in the other direction in Germany. There is not nearly enough money, and great practical inconveniences result. People cannot give change for ridiculously small sums of money. It happens that banks have to refuse in a most extraordinary manner on Saturday claims from their customers for cash to pay wages. When I was in Hamburg in August there was one Saturday there when the branch of the Reichsbank actually advised all the leading banks of Hamburg not to cash any cheque for a greater number of marks than at that time represented a pound. You had firms employing hundreds of men, coming for money to pay weekly wages and being told that they could not have cash for a cheque for more than a pound, simply because the banks had not enough money in their tills, and the Reichsbank branch had not enough money in its till to feed the other banks. Therefore, I say the situation is a very artificial one. A very small revival of confidence would immensely increase the amount of money which was wanted in circulation.

To a certain extent those people who economise in this way do without money at all, but in certain important respects they use foreign money. No doubt, one of the reasons why they can get along with one-tenth of the gold value of the money they used to have is the fact that for a considerable number of purposes foreign money and foreign deposits are now employed.

In that connection I would emphasise one point. There is now what everybody is very familiar with, namely, the flight from the mark. Money hoarded was speculatively employed in the hope of making profit arising from the fall in the value of the mark or, perhaps, to get out of the reach of the German tax collector, who was impelled by the Allied demands to require a great deal. There is the flight from the mark. In Germany now there is a considerable use of foreign currency. It is by no means in the full sense of the words a flight from the mark. It is merely the act of an ordinary prudent person. For example, I heard of such a case as this. A man had saved enough marks to build a house. He had been intending to do that, and he was told by his friends and by his banker and everybody—and he acted upon their advice—that the moment he let the contract to build the house he must forthwith sell his marks for dollars, because, if he did not do that, the depreciation of the mark during the period when the house was being built would mean that his marks might be utterly insufficient to pay the builder's bill. The builder, of course, would not give him a firm contract. It depended upon wages and upon the cost of materials and so forth. He was told that he ran the risk that, perhaps, the marks would fall to such an extent that they would pay only one-tenth part of his bill and that, in order to be quite sure that he really could pay for the house during the period the house was being built, he must hold his assets in the form of dollars and then, when the bills came along, he would sell the dollars and would pay the builder with the proceeds, which, in terms of marks, would have risen in proportion to the depreciation of the mark, if it had taken place in the meantime. If, on the other hand, the mark had remained stable or had appreciated, provided prices responded, he would be no loser. It was simply the act of a cautious man.

The position has now been reached that people who keep money as reserve against contingencies or against their commitments for short periods will not keep it in the form of marks any longer. It would be foolish and dangerous and rash to do so. There is, therefore, a considerable demand for foreign currency merely as a means of holding money safe for a short period. If a German has accumulated some marks for the purpose and is going abroad on business, he does not turn his marks into foreign currency as he requires it in the way that an English traveller turns his money into foreign currency as he requires it. The moment he decides to go abroad he turns the whole thing into foreign currency in order that his plans may not be completely deranged by an alteration in the value of the mark in the meantime. That is, obviously, a legitimate and sensible thing to do, and that you cannot complain of. It is a way of protecting yourself. As the result of that, the German balance of payments is burdened at the present time by the fact that people have to have foreign money to bank in. Over and above the flight from the mark strictly speaking, they have to have foreign money in which to keep their bank reserves, in which they keep the kind of money which persons in England would put on deposit with their bankers for three or six months against a commitment which was falling due at the end of that period.

There is one point of detail which it is worthwhile to introduce at this point. Many persons who have bought foreign currency, partly perhaps for security, partly in a speculative spirit, now see very big profits. Other persons who have not bought foreign currency have bought ordinary shares in order to get out of money and to be in assets. That is being very widely done in Germany. These ordinary shares have now risen, in terms of marks, to dizzy heights. Some of the shares are quoted at a thousand times what their price was a few months ago. Many such persons might be content with their profit. They might say, 'The thing has gone on a very long way. It will not go on for ever. Now, perhaps, is the moment to turn round. I will bring my foreign assets back to Germany. I will sell my dollars and pay off my banker', or 'I will get my assets in some other shape than in ordinary shares.' But there is a law in Germany now which stands very much in the way of that. Owing to the fall in the value of the mark since the law was passed, practically everybody in Germany who is not starving pays income tax at the maximum rate, because any income that is above starvation point in terms of marks is so much above what it was when the law was passed that everybody is liable for the maximum rate of income tax. According to this law, realised profits on stock exchange transactions or from dealings in foreign exchange are liable to income tax. Unrealised profits, book profits, are not so liable. Therefore the man does not pay any income tax as long as he keeps his shares or keeps his foreign exchange. If he sells them he at once has to hand over to the tax collector sixty per cent of his profit. Therefore, he has to take a very decidedly bearish view of the situation before he is prepared to sell at the cost of handing over sixty per cent to the tax collector. The effect of that tax is to prevent people from realising. That, obviously, works out in the absurdest way when the tax is so very heavy. It means that the more any security rises in price the less willing people are to sell because the bigger the sacrifice they have to make to the tax collector. On the other hand, if a security begins to fall in price everybody wants to sell it and everybody wants to have a realised loss which they can set off in their income tax returns against income or against profits. So whenever a security falls in price it becomes an extremely popular thing to unload. You have, therefore, the situation that the more prices fall the more people sell, and the more they rise the less they sell. Therefore a thing can go on rising to an absurd height.

I ought to say with regard to this income tax matter that the Germans are not yet suffering as they will suffer if no change is made from this crushing tax. Income tax in Germany, as in all other countries, is necessarily collected a little in arrear. If you are paying sixty per cent of your last year's income in today's marks, you can clear it off by selling a handkerchief; so actually at the moment the income tax paid by the Germans is not at all burdensome. But supposing that the tax went on as it is now, if the mark does not depreciate further, then, when next year the tax collector comes round and tries to collect sixty per cent of this year's income in a mark of the same value or of a high value, the burden will be a crushing one because, as I say, the maximum income is now such a very small income that everybody who is not starving has to pay it. No doubt, there will have to be some modification of the income tax, and, no doubt, when the modification comes, we shall say, 'The Germans, as usual, are evading their proper liabilities and evading the taxation that ought to be imposed upon them.' The worst of the existing situation is that you are always at one extreme or the other. At present the Germans are getting off income tax; but it is quite hopeless: you cannot prevent it. You cannot levy a tax of £10 in the pound on your last year's income, and unless you levy a tax of £10 in the pound you are bound to get very little if the tax is paid up in the mark at its present value. It is quite hopeless to budget and collect your taxes in terms of a unit which fluctuates in value to such an extraordinary extent as the mark does at present. It means that direct taxation becomes hopeless because it is either totally inadequate, as it is at this moment, or hopelessly oppressive, as it will be next year if the present situation is stabilised.

One part of the German income tax which they are getting in which is proving of the utmost utility to them is the tax on wages. Part of the income tax in Germany now takes the form of a ten per cent tax on wages, which is deducted at the source by every employer every week, and as wages rise roughly in proportion to the depreciation of the mark, the yield of this tax keeps up pretty well, even in actual value. The best part of the return to direct taxation in Germany is really not income tax proper in our sense of the word, but it is this weekly tax on wages which is responding very well to the successive depreciations of the mark.

There is one other point of detail which illustrates the extraordinary anomaly of the situation. As I have just stated, many Germans and many German firms, partly out of prudence and partly out of a speculative spirit, own foreign assets. One would have supposed that if a man in Germany wanted to borrow marks the very best security that he could offer to his bank would be sterling in London—that he would offer to transfer sterling in London to his banker and borrow against it. That is precisely the form of borrowing which it is most difficult to do in Germany. Big firms will go to their bankers and ask for loans and will be quoted a most prohibitive rate, the reason for that being that the Reichsbank for two reasons discriminates against that class of operations. The Reichsbank has got it into its head, and it is half right, that if it allowed loans of that kind it would mean that there was absolutely no limit to the extent to which speculators could bear the mark because they would have, say £1,000 in sterling, and if they then borrowed marks against that sterling and then at once sold those marks they would then have some more sterling, and then again, no doubt, with appropriate margins, they could borrow some more on it, and the only way of stopping bear speculation in the mark is to have money tight. Therefore, if you take off the stopper at all and allow people to borrow against foreign assets and to speculate against the mark, you make it easier for that class of persons to borrow more money. Therefore you must not do it. You are driven to the absurd situation that you stifle industry, you prevent your factories from having enough money to carry on, for fear that if money could be procured your speculator would procure it and proceed at once to be a bear of the mark. That is, obviously, an absurd situation; but it is not quite easy to see what the cure for it is.

There is also a second reason which obviously ought to be cured. In the old days the Reichsbank had to keep, against its note issue, a reserve of one third in the form of gold. At the outbreak of the War a new decree was passed, making the Treasury bills of the Empire the equivalent of gold for the purposes of the note issue. That is the existing situation; so that the Reichsbank can, as you all know, issue notes to an unlimited extent on the security of Treasury bills. It cannot issue notes against any other sort of security. It is not permissible for the Reichsbank to issue notes against a bank balance in London. One would have supposed that the Reichsbank would have wished to have as many of its notes as possible represented by foreign balances of good currency, but that is precisely what is not permitted to it. The Reichsbank is not allowed to issue its notes except against worthless Treasury bills; so if the Reichsbank was to accept foreign balances as collateral they could not in any sense be made a legitimate, lawful backing for its notes.

One of the technical points that one would have to secure in any new system would, I am sure, be to facilitate the accumulation by the Reichsbank of foreign balances on gold exchange standard principles and the issue of notes against them. The Reichsbank is deterred from any change in the existing situation for the reasons I have just mentioned. At present with the existing lack of confidence they do not want to have loans against foreign assets because that might possibly facilitate bear speculation, although I am inclined myself to think that that is a short-sighted point of view.

One point in conclusion before I leave this section of my subject. I pointed out the total inadequacy of the amount of currency in circulation as compared with pre-war times, and I measured that by the figure of one-tenth. As a matter of fact, the scarcity is not quite so great as that in practice for a reason which I have not mentioned, namely, that that figure is arrived at by taking the gold value of the currency, whereas internal prices in Germany have not by any means adjusted themselves to the fall in the external value of the mark; so that money goes a great deal further in Germany in proportion to its gold value than it does here. I tried to obtain statistics, but matters were moving so fast that it was impossible to do so. Also commodities fall into three classes. Commodities which can be imported, which must be imported, respond very rapidly indeed to alterations in the gold value of the mark. Imported goods rise very nearly as fast as the exchange falls. Also, articles which can be exported, against which the export regulations are not severe, rise very quickly. In fact, small articles which tourists and persons of that kind can remove in their pockets or trunks have now risen to very great heights indeed. I should think that they are probably dearer than they are in London. I should anticipate that before long there will be a very brisk import trade into Germany of such things as watches, for example. Every foreigner who goes to Germany thinks that such a thing as a watch is going to be very cheap just in proportion to his lunch. He sees that his lunch costs him fourpence, and so he thinks that a watch will be extraordinarily cheap, and, as nobody knows what the right price of a watch is unless he is a watchmaker, he is apt to think that it is good business to buy two or three watches and put them in his waistcoat pocket and take them home. So articles of that kind rise in price very smartly indeed. I should think that they are above the world price, and you may anticipate a heavy import into Germany, just as, at an earlier date, there was a heavy import into Vienna of printed books and oriental carpets and other such bargains, which rose to such heights in Vienna that it paid to send them there from London. Those classes of goods rise rapidly. At the other end of the scale come a great many forms of services. There the rise is very much slower. Then there are also articles of food in regard to which there is a considerable amount of control and which are not allowed to be exported. They rise very much more slowly. There is an important class of articles in between which rise partly because they use raw material imported from abroad, but which do not rise to the full extent because they are still able to make use of cheap labour. I think that one's tendency from living in Berlin is to under-estimate the extent of the adjustment. I should have said, going about the streets, lunching in restaurants, taking taxis and so forth, that money went about five times as far in Berlin as in London; but I think that the adjustment is a great deal nearer than that. If you are doing that kind of thing, you are largely eating food and employing services. They are two of the things that have not risen proportionately. I should suppose that prices really are, perhaps, one third of what they ought to be if things were completely adjusted, whereas particular classes of things are not above one fifth. I was in Berlin immediately after a very big fall of the mark, and every week things were rising extremely fast. For the purpose of tips, for example, or anything of that kind, a penny went a very, very long way indeed. The cheapness of food at the present moment is very striking to any foreigner. That is one reason why the country is able to get along with one tenth of the gold value of the currency which was used before the War. It is, perhaps, really more like a third or a quarter, if you allow for the fact that prices are not completely adjusted. If prices were adjusted the people would require more currency even with their present habits of economising the mark.

That is enough for today. I propose to continue next week with various facts relating to the present situation in Germany, and then in later lectures I shall go on to other topics.

Lecture to the Institute of Bankers, 22 November 1922

MR KEYNES: Ladies and gentlemen, in the last lecture I was concerned with certain features of the situation in Germany today. I go on this time to an examination of the possible remedies that might be employed in Germany, and the conditions under which those remedies could be applied if people were willing to make those conditions exist.

In the minds of the German authorities two of the greatest obstacles to any plan of stabilisation are the budget and the balance of trade. At the present moment both of those are adverse. The budget is unbalanced and there is an adverse trade deficit. In many authoritative circles the view is held that there must be a more favourable situation in both those respects before it is any good to attempt to stabilise. It was held that, even if the Allies were to be accommodating about reparations and were to agree to a moratorium, it would be extremely rash for the Reichsbank to employ its gold in a scheme of stabilisation until the unfavourable symptoms of the unbalanced budget and of the adverse balance of trade showed signs of curing themselves or of being cured. Personally, I am not satisfied that that view is correct. It is certain that in the long run the mark could not be stabilised unless in the long run the budget was balanced and the balance of trade was not excessively adverse. That is perfectly true. You could not maintain stabilisation unless those conditions were fulfilled. Nevertheless, I think it can be argued that, speaking in order of time and thinking of provisional measures, stabilisation has to come first and that you will not balance either the budget or the trade account until you have, first of all, given things a chance of settling down by a measure of stabilisation. You must use your resources to stabilise for the moment and then, during the transitional period, you must try to get things straight, and then, if you do get things straight during that period, your stabilisation will be a lasting one. But to think that the budget or the balance of trade are going to put themselves right with the mark as it is at present is, I believe, much more optimistic than the alternative view which I have been advocating.

First of all, taking the budget in a little more detail, I think that I mentioned last week that in the case of the income tax you necessarily assess a man on his income at a date somewhat prior to the date of collection. The only exception to that is the tax on wages which can be collected weekly at source. The income tax on earnings of the type on which income tax falls in this country must be collected to a certain extent in arrear. The period on which you are assessing must be complete before you can hope to collect the money. If the unit of legal tender is depreciating as fast as is now the case in Germany, you are inevitably always collecting your tax in a worse currency than that in which you levied it and at which you have assessed, so that by no ingenuity that I can see can you hope to get a full return, the return which you ought to get, from direct taxation. You must first stabilise in order to be able to collect your revenue in the same unit as that in which you are assessing.

It is equally so in the case of state services. You cannot very well put up prices beforehand. The Government cannot presume that the mark is going to fall, and, therefore, inevitably all changes in postage, railway fares, and so forth are bound to be in arrear. I do not think that it need be as much in arrear as is, in fact, the case in Germany now. The costs of public services such as the Post Office, or railway travelling, or the telegraph are ludicrously low. When I was in Germany in August—I think that it might have been even cheaper when I was there in November—I sent a telegram of about twenty words inside Germany for a halfpenny. That was a degree of maladjustment that did not exist in prices outside Government control. Nevertheless, bureaucratic establishments cannot possibly keep pace with rapid fluctuations and, therefore, the revenue from state services will always tend to be inadequate. For these reasons, and also because of the general disturbance and destruction of real income which takes place with an unstabilised mark, it will, I think, be immensely easier for the budget to be balanced when you have stabilised than as a preliminary to stabilising. The German Treasury officials seem to think that, apart from the extraordinary charges under the Peace Treaty, there was no particular reason why they should not balance their budget with a stabilised mark, and, indeed, I cannot see any reason why they should not. It might mean that they must have public services on rather a niggardly scale; but the problem is a soluble one; whereas, when your money is falling all the time, it is very nearly an insoluble one.

There is one other illustration which I might have given a little earlier, but it left my mind for the moment. Germany has no longer a bread subsidy which she had for a considerable time after the Armistice; but she still imports wheat under the auspices of the state. There is still a department that imports wheat, and that department has lost money lately over its deals in wheat, so that indirectly there has been a subsidy, an unintentional subsidy, due to the fact that they were not raising

25

the price of their commodity in terms of marks as fast as the mark was falling. There is another illustration of the way in which you are almost bound to make losses on state trading in such conditions.

I say, therefore, that stabilisation must come first. If you wait until the budget is balanced you will have to wait for ever, unless in the meantime you have attempted stabilisation.

However, that point did not weigh so heavily with the authorities in Germany as did the other point, namely, the balance of trade. It is commonly believed that the balance of trade is heavily adverse, and the view is therefore held that if the Reichsbank was to use some of its gold—it need not use, perhaps, more than say half, which would be twenty-five millions sterling—such a sum would be engulfed in no time by the adverse balance of trade, and that it would be futile to throw in a part of the last reserve so long as the conditions continue to exist in which that could be absorbed in a very brief period.

I examined a great many figures in order to see what the adverse balance of trade was. Through no fault of the German Government, I think it is almost impossible at the present time to prepare reliable figures. The returns of imports and exports are made in terms of paper marks. Those paper marks have to be converted into gold marks at some rate of exchange. The method of the statistical office is certainly crude, because it was found half-way through my stay in Berlin that the rate of exchange as applied to exports was a month different in time from the rate of exchange as applied to imports. For example, for the October trade figure they had converted the exports at the figure—I forget which way round it was, but that does not matter—of the average rate of November, and they had converted the imports at the average rate of October and, as the mark had fluctuated one hundred per cent or two hundred per cent in the interval, it was clear that all the conclusions drawn were perfectly worthless. But even if they converted them both at the same month they were still nearly as worthless, first of

26

all because the fluctuations within the month were so big, and also because there was no sort of guarantee that the exchange would have been provided in the month and at the rate prevailing when the goods crossed the frontier. The actual marks may have been converted into foreign *valuta*, either at an earlier date or at a later date. In the ordinary way, of course, that does not involve a very big error if the fluctuations of the exchange over a period of three months are not portentous; but with the sort of fluctuations which have been going on in the last three months, when there have been periods when the mark has been one eighth of what it had been worth as short a time ago as three months previously, you can clearly get no clue worth anything at all as to what the real adverse balance is from the published trade figures. Further, owing to the numerous regulations that exist governing exports and also governing imports, one may be pretty sure that there will be a fair percentage of erroneous declarations and a fair percentage of complete evasions. A very considerable value of goods must be carried out of the country in tourists' luggage which probably escapes declaration almost wholly. Therefore, I am not prepared to believe, merely on the basis of the figures of the statistical office, that the adverse trade balance is as big as the German Government represented it to be.

According to their representations, there is an adverse trade balance at the present time of something between two and a half and four milliards of gold marks a year, say from one hundred and fifty millions sterling to two hundred millions sterling. They represented that they had an adverse balance of imports over exports to that extent.

Then, in addition to that, there are, of course, the payments under the Treaty and the coal deliveries, which amounted to a quite appreciable figure in the course of last year. Including payments under the Clearing, that is to say, pre-war debts, and the value of deliveries and the value of cash paid to the Reparations Commission, I think that probably something like sixty million sterling has been paid during the year. Then in addition, it is alleged—I do not know with what truth—that there has been some flight of capital from Germany, which, of course, throws a burden on the exchange. Personally, I doubt whether there has been any appreciable additional flight of capital during the past year. I think that some people have had to bring their capital back through lack of funds and other persons may have exported money; but I doubt whether German balances abroad have very much increased. However, the ordinary popular view is that they have increased. Therefore, on the debit side of her balance-sheet, Germany has had somehow or other to look after the adverse balance of exports and imports payments under the Treaty and the flight of capital. On that side of the account she has also had to meet a certain amount of interest on her foreign indebtedness. On the other side of the account there are the receipts from tourists, which, though not large, is not an entirely negligible item, and the purchase of marks and mark assets by foreigners. While at various dates in the past the purchase of marks and of mark assets by foreigners has, of course, reached a big figure, though not, I think, a figure so large as the figure generally mentioned, it is to me quite unthinkable that the purchase of marks and mark assets by foreigners during the past year can possibly have reached a total sufficient to balance the account on the hypothesis that the statistics given us were correct.

On the debit side, the net debit, on the hypothesis which I have stated, would amount to something like from two hundred millions to two hundred and fifty millions sterling. We will be modest and we will take the sum of two hundred millions sterling. I think that it cannot be argued seriously that, during the current year, foreigners have bought marks and mark assets to the extent of two hundred and fifty millions sterling. That would represent in terms of marks, at the rate of exchange which ruled during the past year, a quite impossible quantity of marks. One cannot do it exactly because the value of the mark has fluctuated so much that you would have to decide in exactly which month or even on which day the transactions had taken place; but if you take a rough shot at the thing I do not think that you would be far out in saying that if foreigners have really bought marks and mark assets to as large an amount as that, they would have had to buy practically all the ordinary shares quoted on the German stock exchanges, all the mark notes circulating in Germany and all the deposits in all the banks, which we know, in fact, is not the case. The actual additional sum purchased by foreigners must be a very much smaller sum than that. I, therefore, draw the conclusion that if Germany was relieved of the Peace Treaty payments, which, as I say, have come to something like sixty millions sterling during the past year, she should not be very far from balancing her accounts.

People will not understand that somehow or other trade balances every day, that for every buyer of exchange there must be a seller of exchange, that the total balance of payments is always level at every moment and, consequently, there never is in the strict sense of the words an uncovered balance. It may be that the balance has to be covered by a bank having an open position or by a speculator stepping in temporarily (that may be the case: it is the case from day to day), but the uncovered margin of that sort which the financial world is prepared to carry is not very large. It is much too risky for them. Therefore, you are thrown back for any important sum on the more long-period speculator, not merely on the person who carries over from day to day to deal with the adverse balance in the evening. If you get it firmly in your head that somehow or other the balance of payments is always covered every day, that it is as impossible for there to be an uncovered balance as it is for a man to pay out money that he has not got—if once you understand that, you will, I think, dismiss from your mind the idea which is popular in regard to a great many European countries that there is somehow a permanent adverse balance that is not covered at all in any way and that you have to get rid of that. The truth is that the exchange has to fall until somehow or other the thing is balanced, until the country in question has either cancelled certain purchases, or speculators or investors or somebody or other have been tempted by the rate of exchange which is quoted. Once having got that clear, I think you will cease to be as pessimistic as the Germans are themselves as to the possibility of their balancing the budget if they were granted a moratorium. If they were relieved of payments under the Peace Treaty they would be that much better off as compared with the past year, and that sum would be sufficient, I should have thought, to make the difference. I agree with the view that as long as they have to make important indeterminate reparation payments, payments under the Treaty and other payments of the kind, it may be right to argue that stabilisation is impossible and that any resources which might be used for that purpose will be poured unavailingly into the sea. But once there is a moratorium, and once Germany is relieved of those payments, then I see no impossibility in the case.

That is on the statistical side; but I rely even more on a more theoretical argument which it is very difficult to make appeal to the minds of practical people. That is that once you have a sound currency regulated on sound lines it cannot become depreciated by what is called the adverse balance of trade, and it acts as a corrective to the adverse balance of trade and prevents an unduly adverse balance of trade from existing. In pre-war days Turkey had practically no paper circulating. She had only gold and silver. Nobody could maintain that, because Turkey was an impoverished and ill-governed country and liable, therefore, to an adverse balance of trade, her money must therefore become depreciated. When Turkey was importing too much some of her gold and silver would flow out in payment therefore, and before more than a very small amount had flowed, various corrective forces would be brought into operation and the thing would tend to get straight. So, provided that the German Government was in the position to have a currency, the amount of which could not be increased at will, you might leave the balance of trade to look after itself. Once you have really established a situation in which, by having balanced your budget and having got a certain amount of reserve resources, you are confident that you will not have to increase the volume of your currency, you need not bother any more at all about the balance of trade. It will be impossible for you to make certain payments if more money is demanded of you than you have got; but there will not be some subtle trade influence which you cannot control making the adverse balance and depreciating your currency, because as soon as the thing begins to work, as soon as the imports are beyond what the country can afford, a corrective is brought into play, tending to bring you back into equilibrium. Whereas, under the present state of affairs that corrective is not brought about in the orthodox and correct way; it is brought about by the exchange falling to such a point that people cannot afford to buy at all.

If trade must balance every day there are two ways in which it could happen. You may have your population not having enough money to make the purchases, or you may have the money they have got falling in value to such an extent that it will not cover the purchases. In both cases the ultimate result is the same. When you have a depreciating currency a country is prevented automatically from importing more than it can pay for by the fact that the money it has got is falling in value all the time. If you have an orthodox currency of a proper limited kind which has a stable basis in terms of foreign *valuta*, then the country is prevented from importing too much by the fact that it has begun to buy more than it can afford. So the idea that when you have established sound arrangements they can be upset by the ordinary movements of trade as distinct from sudden demands on the Government by a foreign authority is really a bogey which plays a very large part in responsible German mentality at the present time—(certainly one of the things which fill them with timidity is the statistics which they

31

have collected)—that they have this enormous uncovered balance, and there is an inability to see the theoretical arguments why that is not so formidable as it looks. You find responsible bankers in Berlin at the present time solemnly assuring you that the situation in Germany is such that, even if she were let off reparations entirely and permanently, she would have to have a foreign loan each year in order to enable her to balance her accounts and that she must live at the expense of other people permanently. Of course, that is an absurdity. It is only seen to be an absurdity, I think, if you get firmly into your heads this point that I keep on repeating that, somehow or other, the balance of payments is equal every day, and that therefore she is somehow or other paying her way at this moment, and that if she gets an appreciable relief from her present situation she is to that extent definitely on the plus side.

So much for the two great obstacles. I am assuming, by the way—it is hardly worth mentioning—that a moratorium is required. As long as you demand from Germany resources which she does not possess and insist on her Government attempting to sell paper in order to fail in obtaining the resources, you can do nothing. That is obvious. Without the moratorium you have no basis for discussion of any kind, and I have not heard any rational argument to the contrary or any person whose opinion was worth anything asserting it with any backing to his assertion. But having put that out of the way, let me say that I do not agree with those who hold that the budget and the balance of trade remain insuperable obstacles. Having got to that point, that a stabilised mark is not necessarily impracticable once a moratorium is granted, what are the methods that you would employ?

For the transitional period you must plainly have some reserve resources. I have said that you must first stabilise and then trust to your budget and trade to get balanced, and then that will enable you to make your stabilisation permanent. But during the preliminary period you must be prepared to support

32

your scheme by paying out foreign reserves if required. You must, therefore, have some sort of original nest-egg. A great matter of controversy is how that nest-egg should be provided. For my part, I do not think that a very large nest-egg would be required if the scheme was properly managed. Owing to the extreme dearness and shortness of money which I mentioned in my last lecture, as soon as people believed that there was any chance of stabilisation holding good, money would tend to flow towards Germany rather than to flow out, and it is unlikely that she would have to find any large amounts of resources in the earlier period. The danger would be a considerable number of months later. I think that the first effect of a stabilisation scheme might actually be that the Reichsbank would gain gold rather than lose it. There are not enough people who have marks that they can spare, that they have not an immediate urgent demand for, for them to be able to throw them at you to any important extent. The gold in the Reichsbank now amounts to several times the value of the note issue, so at the present rate of exchange the Reichsbank could buy up all the notes there are and still have a large amount of gold left. There is not really, therefore, any danger of a very appreciable drain in the first instance. The risk would be nine months or a year later in the event of the attempts to balance the budget failing and inflation continuing so that you were always issuing more notes available for redemption. But I think that you would have to take the risk that in the period of a year's grace, say, you would manage to balance your budget. If by bad management or by misfortune it turned out to be impossible to balance in that period, then the drain on your resources might come nine months or a year later, or a little longer. You would not run a very big risk in the first nine months. I believe, therefore, that the technical position is such that you could do it with a comparatively small amount of gold, and I think that the Reichsbank's gold would be probably adequate for the purpose, even though there was no question of using anything like the whole of it. The Reichsbank

33

has fifty millions of gold sterling. If half of that was used as a pool, if that was combined with a prolonged moratorium and a firm policy, I believe it ought to be sufficient to put things straight, and I think that it would be reasonable, if Germany was granted a moratorium, to require of her that she should make a sincere effort to use her gold for that purpose. I should doubt if there is any case in history of a currency having gone to such a complete smash as the mark has while it had a gold reserve and while it was covered by gold at the prevailing rate of exchange to the extent of several times its value. It is a most extraordinary situation and one which can only exist on the hypothesis that the existing inflation will not merely persist but will increase a great deal. If there was a moratorium and if a good attempt was made to balance the budget there is no reason in the world why the assumption that a great deal more inflation will take place should be justified, and as soon as it ceases to be justified the gold reserve of the Reichsbank is fully adequate to sustain the value of the notes.

However, in Berlin a different view is widely held. The Reichsbank, like all Continental banks, believes that gold is not kept in reserve to be used on any occasion whatever. They are rather inclined to the view that the correct theory of a gold reserve is that you only make it available when you are absolutely certain that it will not be required. That view is not only held by the Reichsbank. It is traditionally held by all Continental state banks. The opposite view has been traditionally held for more than a hundred years past now in England. One of the great foundations, I believe, of our financial security has been this simple point of the correct theory about the gold reserve. We have very often had to use it, but not to a great extent; but the fact that we were prepared to use it has been of the utmost importance. There was one episode during the War which is not generally known and of which the details have never been published, in which, in my opinion, we only saved our position and enabled ourselves to keep our credit by the fact that we were prepared to throw in our gold [*JMK*, vol. XXII, pp. 10–11.] As it turned out, we did not have to use all of it, but there was a moment when we had to decide whether, if the pinch came, we were going to use our gold or were going to hang on to it. The fact that we were willing to use the gold carried us through. That doctrine is the traditional English doctrine established as a result of many arguments and much pamphleteering and so forth a hundred years ago. Although it has had its occasional opponents, it has sunk deep into the tradition of the City of London that there are circumstances, not ordinary circumstances, when you do bring your final reserves into play. But the tendency on the Continent is never to bring them into play, but when things have gone completely to smash perhaps to fritter them away under force of circumstances. The doctrine stands very much in the way of any stabilisation notions now.

There is also another reason. What corresponds to 'the City' in Berlin suffers from the illusion that even in present conditions they have a real prospect of getting a foreign loan. Their minds have been on that subject ever since the Armistice. I was the responsible official during the Armistice negotiations in reference to the question how the food which was going to Germany was to be paid for [*JMK*, vol. XVI, pp. 391–404.] It was then a question of their using part of their gold or part of their own resources. We spent all our time trying to persuade the Germans that in the months of January and February, 1919, it was not possible to raise a loan on their behalf either in the City of London or in New York. They were very reluctant to believe it. At every date since then they have had that same illusion, and they are extremely unwilling to use their own gold so long as they think that people here will put up money for them. It is not quite a certainty, and they would much rather have the funds supplied here. As I say, I think that that is a complete illusion. There, again, it is useless to suppose that you can borrow money before your credit is re-established; but when Germany, if she ever is, is stabilised and when her credit is restored to a certain extent, ordinary loan operations might possibly be feasible. The notion that the foreigner is going to lend to you before your stabilisation and that he is going to take the risk of your stabilisation breaking down seems to me to be quite preposterous and to be a piece of extremely bad psychology.

As you will have observed from the replies of the German Government to the Reparations Commission, they still make their plans contingent upon foreign assistance. If they put forward a good plan, they ought, I think, to have all the co-operation possible of international financiers. I think that moral aid ought to be given to them and convenient overdraft facilities against their own gold and so forth, and even, perhaps, small overdraft arrangements in addition. All that might be useful and might have a great effect on the psychology; but the notion that at this stage in the affair you are going to make your stabilisation scheme mainly dependent on foreign capital seems to me to be very wide of the mark. The worst of the present situation is that the talking of so much outrageous nonsense on our side has provoked a situation in which no sense is talked on either side. You find almost as much outrageous nonsense talked in Berlin in one direction as you hear in Paris and London in the other. Therefore, while I have been spending the last half-hour explaining why I think stabilisation to be technically a feasible proposition, and I see no reason except human wills why the thing should not be put straight, I do not have any very optimistic hopes because the psychological situation does not seem to be one which will enable the technical solution to be put into operation.

Assuming that point, I pass on to the next stage of my argument. Assuming that Germany was granted a moratorium, supposing that we were sensible on our side and supposing that she was prepared to use her own resources with what aid we could give her—because I hope that we should be able to give her some practical assistance if she was prepared to use her own resources in a genuine attempt to put things straight—what, in those conditions, would be the right technical plan? Two plans were discussed in Berlin, one of which was incorporated in the report of four of the foreigners called in, and the other of which is in the report of the other three. I do not think that the readers of the newspapers have got quite clear what the essential difference between the reports by the two bodies of experts really was.

The four experts held that the only chance of success was stabilisation: that is to say, that you should fix some rate as appropriate, the rate being selected with reference to the degree of adjustment in existence at the moment when the change was introduced—say, at the present moment, something like fifteen thousand marks to the pound sterling, though it may be quite a different rate months hence—and, having fixed it, to have some official body which was prepared to buy and sell foreign *valuta* at that rate. We held that you should abolish all exchange regulations whatsoever and that you should have absolutely free and unfettered dealings, and that there should be a buying and selling rate for foreign *valuta* which might be, say, one or two per cent apart, corresponding to the gold parity, as it were, but that at those fixed rates the official body would be prepared both to buy and sell unlimited quantities of marks. That would knock out any hopes from speculation, and therefore you would be back on the genuine demands of the country both ways, but you would be protected by the fact that there is at present a shortage of money in Germany so that you could not possibly have an undue amount of marks thrown at you. You would rather have people who would want to take advantage of the very high rate of interest prevailing in Germany to buy marks from you than to sell marks to you. We would combine that with a prolonged period of dear money in order that the present incentive to remit money to Germany rather than otherwise, apart from the fear of loss of money on the exchange, should continue to operate. We would have absolute fixity, we would have an absolute abolition of exchange regulations, and we would have dear money. We would also rather put away from our minds the idea of a subsequent improvement in the mark. I think that a long period of deflation would be a very disastrous thing and might bring German industry almost to a standstill. Possibly in the early part of the period for a short time your rate might be a little tentative; but the idea that some people have that you might start, say, at fifteen thousand marks to the pound sterling and then improve the rate by easy stages till it was ten times as valuable and had got down to fifteen hundred marks to the pound sterling seems to me to be a disastrous idea because, with the constantly falling prices in Germany, you would have constant struggles over wages, you would have the whole industry of the country thrown into disorder and you would have all the trouble that we have had during our industrial crises worse tenfold. No modern industrial community could stand the prospect of official recognition that the legal tender was going to appreciate in the course of the next few years by one thousand per cent, which is what that scheme would amount to.

One recognises, of course, that if the mark was raised in value it would be a pleasing thing to foreign speculators, and it would also restore persons inside Germany who had been cheated of their savings by what has happened; but it does not seem to me to be a practicable thing. It is not feasible that the holdings of foreign speculators should be appreciated in that way, and, as regards the people inside Germany who have suffered so much by that, that is a thing that is done and cannot at this date be remedied. The suggestion was a fixed rate, free dealing, and no intention of altering the rate except possibly that it might be a little tentative at the very beginning of the period.

We added one technical point, which is important, and to which I should like to call your attention; that is, that the official body which was in control of the exchange should not only deal spot but should also deal in forward exchange; that is to say, at appropriate rates it would always sell you marks spot and buy those marks back from you forward one month or three months.

That would mean that a German who had foreign assets which he would like to employ for the time being in Germany but did not dare remove altogether from the form of foreign assets because he was not certain that the stabilisation scheme would last, would be perfectly protected. He could then replenish his resources in Germany by handing over his foreign *valuta* spot against marks. He would receive marks in Germany, and he woud have a forward contract that three months later he could have the foreign *valuta* back again at an appropriate rate, and the difference between the spot and forward rates would have to be corresponding to the rate of discount inside Germany. In effect it would be a way by which the Reichsbank or the official body controlling the exchange could borrow foreign *valuta*. I believe they might receive a considerable amount in that way, which would have the effect of putting in the hands of the official exchange body the foreign floating resources of Germany. At present you may have Germans with foreign resources which they would like to use temporarily in Berlin, particularly when money is as tight there as it is now, and they simply dare not because they cannot. If they sell their foreign *valuta* spot they cannot at present buy it back again forward at any reasonable rate.

As I explained in my last lecture, the reason for that state of affairs is that the present position is said to be a check on speculation. Perhaps it is; but it has these various other bad consequences. Once you have stabilised things I can see no objection to developing a free foreign market in exchange. That would enable the Reichsbank to collect temporarily loans of foreign *valuta* which would not be drawn upon probably all at one time. That would concentrate Germany's resources and would enable additional currency that must be put into circulation to be put into circulation against the security of foreign currency instead of Treasury bills. That is a little extra to the scheme, so to speak, but it is not an unimportant part of it technically.

The other three experts took a different view. They held that at present, even in the event of a moratorium, the whole situation is too precarious for it to be safe for the Reichsbank or for the body controlling exchange to guarantee any fixed rate. Their notion was, therefore, that the Reichsbank would form a foreign reserve, partly by means of its own gold and partly by a loan from foreign capitalists, and that that reserve would be used for intervening on the exchange market whenever the mark looked particularly weak, and whenever you suspected that there was a bear campaign going on you would raid the bears by buying marks heavily and so give them a good fright. You would get a corresponding appreciation of the mark in the next day or two, and you would do that always trying to raise the mark to a higher level, gradually supporting it at a rather better level than you had supported it at the previous month. I think that is technically an entirely hopeless plan, if I may say so. It seems to me that if you do not fix the thing, you will preserve the whole of the existing state of uncertainty, and it is quite likely that you would dribble your resources away without having got anything like stabilisation because you would not have knocked out speculation. You would rather have encouraged it, although speculators would, no doubt, have to have in their minds the possibility of these counter raids by the Reichsbank. They would probably become quite as clever at it as the operators of the Reichsbank, and, I should think, would very likely so arrange their operations that the Reichsbank dealings would be in their favour rather than against them. Secondly, if there was the idea that the policy of the Reichsbank was steadily to raise the value of the mark over a period, for the reasons I have already given, you would tend to bring business to a standstill. If the scheme was unsuccessful you would dribble away your resources. If it was successful you would have all the evils of deflation in Germany on a pronounced scale, and you would very soon reach a point when your labour troubles became of an extraordinarily severe character. It seems to me that in the matter of stabilisation you have to go the whole way or not at all. It may be that the conditions for a courageous policy do not exist; but there is no middle course really between leaving things as they are and fixing them. Merely intervening irregularly and throwing some resources in, without any real fixed policy, is exactly what you are at and is the way to throw money away. I should have thought that the whole history of the spasmodic interventions of foreign bourses in support of particular exchanges showed that that policy never succeeded.

The persistence of these two schools of opinion shows the practical difficulties of the case. I believe that our plan is much the safer, that you would run far less risk if you fixed your rate and tried to make your rate believed in; but the other party hold that it is a much rasher policy and that theirs is a much safer one, because if at any moment you saw that your policy was being a failure and was not working, you would withdraw your support, you would keep the rest of your gold unused, and therefore you would not have committed yourselves to anything, and so you could draw back. But the very fact that you had not committed yourselves to anything would be what had ruined the scheme. It would be known that the support might be withdrawn at any moment, and if the Reichsbank was losing gold it would lose heart also and, almost directly, there would not be any real strength in the market at all. That half-hearted kind of policy is not the real one for such circumstances as these.

I have now given you two divergencies. One is whether the Reichsbank gold by itself would be sufficient or whether there must be a foreign loan. The next point is: Are you going to stabilise exchange or are you going to support it? There is a third policy which I think everybody will admit to be a *pis aller* (I do not myself fancy it), but which on theoretical grounds is not open to particular objection. That is the idea of having a parallel currency to the existing one; not of attempting to fix the existing mark at any particular level but of introducing a new unit, say a gold mark, and providing that the new currency issued should be the gold mark and that the gold mark should be redeemable for gold. By that means you would also make both the gold mark and the paper mark legal tender. You would allow people to fix their contracts in either and to pay in either at the official rate. So you would then have these two currencies, the gold currency and the paper currency, with a fluctuating rate between them. You would fix that rate from time to time by a legal notice in conformity more or less with the market rates prevailing at the time, and the official rate fixed would be one at which you could discharge in one currency obligations incurred in the other.

One can easily see that there are certain advantages in that scheme. To begin with, it would provide German merchants with one of their great *desiderata*—namely, a sound money of account. Everybody could keep their balance-sheets in terms of the gold mark. It would also provide Germans who must have money which would be of permanent value as reserves, with something other than foreign currency which they can use for that purpose. Such persons could acquire gold marks and the new gold marks—which would be a paper document, of course—would serve the purpose that foreign currency has to serve now; so that Germany could reduce her requirements of foreign currency. It would meet those two points: a good money of account, and a good store of value. But so long as the paper mark fluctuated in terms of the gold mark, one of the great problems would be left unsolved, namely, the existence of a stable unit in which taxation could be collected. People would still have their taxes fixed in paper marks or, at any rate, they might have their incomes in them, and unless the paper mark was a completely exploded thing, as long as it existed side by side with the gold mark, you would have instability in your budget, and I do not think that you would have gained by any means all the advantages, whereas it might be just as difficult to keep up the value of your new gold mark as it would be to keep up the value of the entire currency. Assuming that no more paper marks were issued, in the other things you would be able to be successful. The present gold value of the existing paper marks is not a thing that need alarm anybody. Therefore if you feel strong enough to lay it down that all future issues shall be of a gold mark which you will keep at a stable value, you may as well, I think, go the whole hog and not go in for this *pis aller* which solves part of the problem, but by no means the whole of it.

That is the essence of the case as it now stands. I explained to you the chief facts of the German situation in my first lecture and in this lecture I have tried to analyse the possible cures that have been put forward in different quarters, the arguments as they appear to me for and against, and the psychological atmosphere which, I fear, makes the carrying out of any of them a little improbable at the moment.

Lecture to the Institute of Bankers, 29 November 1922

MR J. M. KEYNES: Ladies and Gentlemen: I propose to give this lecture on the subject of devaluation. You probably all of you know what that means. It may possibly be safer if I were to repeat that it is concerned with stabilising the value of certain legal tender monies somewhere near their present value in terms of gold, in place of attempting to restore them to their pre-war value in terms of gold. That is to say, of accepting existing facts and fixing the level to which they are now adjusted permanently rather than attempting to go back.

For the purposes of the devaluation argument currencies fall into three groups. The first group are the very bad currencies such as the mark and others about which it is not really a matter of dispute. People may be in favour of raising them above their present level, but no-one proposes that those currencies can be restored to their pre-existing value.

Then there is another group of currencies of which our own is a leading example, which I will deal with towards the end of my lecture, in which the divergence from the pre-war parity is not very considerable, so that there can be very little doubt that they could be restored to par if it is thought wise and expedient to do so.

In between comes a very important class of which the franc and the lira are the most important examples, where the depreciation certainly exceeds 20 per cent and is very often a good deal bigger than that, but where it is not as fantastic to propose you should restore them to the pre-war level as in the case of the mark.

I shall devote the first part of my lecture to these intermediate currencies, and I shall return at the end of the lecture to the rather special case of sterling.

About eight months ago I published an article [*JMK*, vol. XVII, pp. 355–69] about devaluation in which I went so far as to propose some actual details of a scheme which at that time I thought could be put into operation. That was just before the Genoa Conference. This subject was considered very carefully by the Financial Commission at Genoa, and the Conference reported decidedly in favour of stabilisation at the existing level rather than at the pre-war level in the case of all currencies which were seriously depreciated. I do not think it is very easy to find any reasoned statement of the arguments on the other side. There is a good deal of dispute about currencies in the position of sterling, but amongst accredited authorities there is not very much divergence as regards the franc and lira. One might have supposed, therefore, that I was not wasting my time, though I might have been putting forward a bad scheme in principle, so to speak in proposing actual details. But what has happened since that time has convinced me that nevertheless I was, and that although the opponents of stabilising somewhere near the existing level are not free from that argument nevertheless the other side has by no means won over universal opinion, and that we still have to do a great deal of enunciating the fundamental facts of the case before it is worth while going into the details of an actual scheme.

I want therefore with your approval to run through the

fundamental simple facts of the situation, which I think ought to be universally recognised and ought to govern all discussions on the subject. Although the Genoa Conference declared in favour of devaluation unanimously I think the representatives of France, Italy and Belgium, in approving the principle, stated at the same time that they wholly repudiated it as regards its application to their own individual countries. Those gentlemen may have been guided by political rather than intellectual considerations, but that they should have thought it desirable to deny what their intellect had just approved is a measure of the difficulty which still exists in putting these things into force. Genoa approved it in principle, but all the countries most affected repudiated it in particular.

One argument which weighs so much with many people, which has to be dealt with first of all, is the argument of justice. It is thought that it would be a grave injustice not to put back these monies to their pre-war parity. Some injustice is always wrought by economic changes. That one has to admit. But to regard the weight of gold as the measure of justice rather than the purchasing power of the currencies is, I think, a very technical form of justice, and yet no-one suggests in the United States, for example, that it is an act of injustice not to restore the dollar to its pre-war purchasing power.

Quite apart from that, justice means presumably that you must put back people who have entered into contracts into the position which they had reason to anticipate they would be in when they entered into those contracts. If all contracts expressed in terms of money had been entered into prior to the War there might be a strong case on those lines, but the actual fact is that the vast majority of the contracts have been entered into much more recently. In particular war loans, which form a very important category, were contracted to a very great extent since the Armistice in terms of the depreciated money. So that you would be giving a large uncovenanted bonus to the lenders if you were to restore the value of the franc and lira to their pre-war value. In the case of the United States Irving Fisher has roughly calculated that contracts in terms of money are on the average about a year old, so that if you put the value of money back to a very different value from what it has now with reference to a period eight years ago you are almost certainly doing more injustice than you are doing justice if you are considering the relative position of creditors and debtors who are the parties to the money contracts now in existence. There might be a case on this head for a certain restoration, but the longer the depreciation lasts the weaker the case is. More and more contracts will have been entered into at the depreciated rate, and more and more of the holders even of those contracts which have a history back to pre-war times will have changed hands [*sic*] in the interval.

I think therefore there is a great deal of misapprehension first of all in making the criterion of justice a quantity of gold rather than a quantity of purchasing power, and secondly in supposing that the contracts which would be affected by any change mainly relate to a pre-war epoch. I therefore argue that that particular reason for making great sacrifices in order to get back, while it has some force has not so much force as some people think it has.

That is the argument of justice. The next argument is the argument of possibility. When the question of possibility is considered it is common to look to the existing rates of exchange and to the balance of trade, and to criteria of that kind. That is a mistake, I think, when one is considering a long period problem of this kind. From the long period point of view I say that a different criterion is the one that settles the matter. The long-period obstacle to any possible improvement, for example of the franc, is the burden of the internal debt. You can always restore the currency to any value you like if you want to, if you think it worth while and adopt a sufficiently stringent policy to do it, provided that it does not increase the claims of the bond-holders beyond what is tolerable. If it does, the Government is certain to be forced to inflate again, and the work will be undone.

In the case of France and Italy, I shall deal with France in detail as an illustration. The policy of internal finance which has been followed has brought up the burden of the internal debt to a point which already makes it nearly impossible for their budgets to balance. If you were to restore the franc and the lira to their pre-war parity you would make the problem quite hopeless. In the case of France you would rather more than double the present burden of the internal debt; in the case of Italy you would approximately multiply it by four.

Now what does this burden of the internal debt amount to? It is not a question of economy and extravagance. Questions of economy and extravagance can always be dealt with in the last resort. It is a question of the distribution of the national wealth between different classes. The burden of the national debt is the measure of what the active earning part of the community have to hand over to the *rentier* or bond-holding class. No community ancient or modern will tolerate more than a certain proportion. You will never induce the active earning taxpayer to surrender more than a certain proportion to the inactive bond-holding *rentier* class, and the general principles of contract have all through history had to moderate themselves and to yield to that grand principle of expediency that you cannot increase the claim of the bond-holder, of the inactive person, beyond a certain extent, and those persons who would press a contract to its extremity and say that justice in the matter of contract must be done at all costs are the people who are really the greatest enemies of the sanctity of contract, because policies of that kind are what bring the whole thing into complete disrepute and eventually bring down the entire structure. The whole thing if you are dealing, not with individuals, but with nations and with epochs, has to be handled with moderation and with reason, and it is utterly impossible to compel the active part of the community to hand over an undue proportion to the bond-holding class.

Therefore I say that the long-period criterion is this: Will the improvement in the value of the currency so much increase the burden of the internal debt as to make the proportion that is so to be handed over an intolerable one?

If it is intolerable there are only three solutions open. The first solution is repudiation, which as regards internal debt in Western Europe I think we can neglect at present. The second way out is a capital levy which, when the necessary circumstances arise, seems to be much the justest and wisest instrument, because you can make the burden fall in the right place. But the capital levy, as we have seen in the recent election, is a thing difficult to explain or to understand, and the terrifying ignorance of the real arguments on either side shown in the columns of the Press shows that it is an expedient which a modern community will very likely reject even when the conditions for applying it exist. I do not want to be taken to imply by this that I am in favour of a capital levy in this country at this moment. I am not. I think you ought to have a capital levy only when it is clear that the proportion of taxation which has to be handed over to the bond-holder is more than the country can support, and that premise has not yet been demonstrated beyond controversy in this country. But most of the arguments raised against a capital levy seem to me to be a little childish in character, and not to go at all to the root of the matter.

I throw that out rather in parenthesis, but the controversy with regard to the matter has I think brought home to everybody how very difficult it will be to bring in a capital levy even when it is the right thing. Therefore I strongly suspect that the continental countries, who indubitably ought to have a capital levy, will probably not do so but will follow the line of least resistance, and the line of least resistance is to let your money depreciate. You can always have a capital levy that way; you can always allow the unit in which your money debts are expressed to fall in value. In Austria, in Russia and in Germany they have already had a capital levy of 100 per cent. In France they have already had a capital levy of 50 per cent; and in Italy of about 75 per cent; and other countries in varying degrees. Experience

shows that the population will quietly accept enormous de-
predations by this instrument when they would throw out of
power any Government that attempted to take one tenth of the
amount from them by juster and more scientific methods.

The great objection to the method of depreciation as compared
with the capital levy is that it falls entirely upon persons whose
wealth is in the form of claims to legal tender, to money, who
are generally, amongst the capitalists, the poorer capitalists. It
is entirely ungraduated; it falls on small savings just as hardly
as on big ones; and incidentally it benefits the capitalist
entrepreneur class, because those persons who borrow money and
possess assets, which is the case with the *entrepreneur* capitalist
class, benefit by depreciation. So that by that means you make
a capital levy which falls mainly on small savings and on
moderate savings. At any rate it treats them just as hardly as
it treats the richer man, and it may actually enrich the ordinary
entrepreneur capitalist. The small savers who have most to lose
from depreciation are precisely the sort of conservative people
who would be most alarmed by the capital levy, so that they
would probably oppose it. On the other hand, the *entrepreneur*
capitalist class would obviously prefer depreciation which does
not hit them very much and may actually enrich them. The
combination of those two forces will generally bring it about that
a country will prefer the unjust, inequitable, disastrous method
of depreciation rather than the more scientific one of a capital
levy.

For those reasons I think that if the countries cannot balance
their budget at the present level they will probably have a bit
more depreciation until they can, rather than have a capital levy.
But anyhow, it is utterly impracticable for them to go back.

The advocate of stabilisation somewhere near the present
level takes a middle course. He says we accept the *fait accompli*.
It is quite out of the question for budgetary reasons to go back
on our steps, and also it would create a great deal of injustice
and a great deal of harm to trade. We must accept the

depreciation that exists, but let us at any rate make an effort to avoid further depreciation. That will be immensely facilitated by fixing it if we can somewhere near the present level. But he has to admit that those forces which make it impossible to go back may also make it inevitable that there shall be further depreciation.

Let me illustrate that by reference to the particular example of France. The internal debt of France amounts at the moment to about 250 milliards of paper francs. That is excluding all external debt including what she owes her allies. The further borrowing already definitely in sight and more or less provided for will, including reconstruction loans which the Government has guaranteed, bring the aggregate internal debt by the end of 1923 to somewhere about 300 milliards of francs. The service of that debt will be about 18 milliards of francs, that is to say at 6 per cent. That I think allows a certain amount for statutory sinking fund, for while the recent debt has been raised at 6 per cent, some part of the debt has been raised at lower rates. I am not quite sure how much that sinking fund allows for, but I think I am not far wrong in saying that including the statutory sinking fund the service of that debt will be somewhere about 18 milliards of francs. That figure happens to be the budget estimate of the ordinary revenue from all sources for the year 1923. So that by the end of 1923 the service of the internal debt will absorb 100 per cent of the revenue. That is rather optimistic, because it is assuming that all external debts are cancelled; and it is also assuming what certainly will not be the case, that after the end of 1923 France will be in a position to assume that the burden of the external budget, that is to say pensions and further expenditure for reconstruction will have vanished. But still, take it at that. Within a short period the service of the debt will absorb the whole of the revenue. As the necessary expenditure of the Government is probably 10 or 11 milliards at least, that means that even at the present level of the franc the Government will have to increase the yield of taxation by something like 60 per cent in order to make both ends meet, and if the franc was materially to improve in its value in terms of commodities the amount which the Government would have to take from the taxpayer in terms of commodities in order to satisfy the claims of the *rentiers* would become something fantastic, something quite beyond the taxpaying capacity of France.

Therefore I say in the long run that is the fundamental reason why the franc cannot possibly return to parity, and I go further and say that the difficulty of balancing the budget even now will prove a strong temptation to France to pursue a policy of further depreciation.

This figure I think is an interesting one. If the franc was to fall to 100 to the £ sterling it would be possible to balance the French budget by taking very little more in terms of commodities from the taxpayer than is taken now. The French will have to come to some compromise between increasing taxation and diminishing ordinary expenditure and reducing what they owe their *rentiers* by means of a further depreciation, and I have not the smallest doubt that the French Government will consider that course, as they have hitherto, as far more conservative, far more orthodox, far more in the interests of the class of small savers than they would a justly constructed capital levy.

Those figures I give in detail because they are particularly striking, but something very similar, or at any rate if not quite similar in degree the same in kind is also true of other countries. On the one hand, therefore, when M. Picard, speaking for the Government of France at Genoa, said it was the policy of the French Government to restore the franc to par he was talking rubbish.

The reasons I have given are reasons why the critics of devaluation from the point of view of improvement cannot maintain their case. But of course there is another class of critic who have much more reason on their side, who must be met, namely those who say that the chief European currencies are so very likely to go much worse that it would be a foolhardy thing to try and fix them at their present level, and that the time has not yet come at which there is any real hope of balancing. I think there is a great deal of force in that criticism. I think it is very likely that the governments are not strong enough to enforce a policy of stabilisation, but I think it ought to be possible, if the will is there and if the thing was understood, to stabilise at a rate not very much worse than the present. I think it is very unlikely that it will happen, but one has in these cases to preach an ideal policy rather than to dilate on what is going to happen, and if their affairs were conducted with wisdom I do not think it ought to be impossible to stabilise at some rate not very much worse than the existing levels of the exchange.

Why am I so anxious to stabilise? It is obvious that it would be foolish to try and improve the value of the currencies, but what is the overwhelming argument for fixing them? The argument that is much the most important in my mind is one which is fairly familiar, but I think it is under-emphasised. It is this. Even though a country may be in adjustment with other countries in respect of its balance of trade and so forth over a year as a whole, it does not follow that it is perfectly balanced every day. It is well known that industrial countries which buy large amounts of agricultural products find it convenient to make the bulk of their purchases, or at any rate a larger proportion than normal of their purchases, rather early in the crop year. That was very familiar in pre-war days. Even when the balance is level for the year as a whole, the industrial countries are in debt to the agricultural countries in the autumn and winter, and they get level with them again in the spring and summer. If you want to have just the quantity and just the quality of the leading crops you do well to buy them rather early in the year. That is an ordinary practice of trade which has not been abandoned even in post-war times. That was recognised in the pre-war financial world, and one of the most important functions of international banking used to be to adjust this temporary balance between two seasons of the year, and very admirable machinery has been devised by means of which that function was carried out at very small cost to trade. When the banker knew that there were gold points, so that his loss on the exchange was limited, he was willing to move floating balances between London and New York, for example, for a very moderate commission. A little higher rate of discount in the temporarily debtor country so that his money earned a little more there than it could in the other country, together with a slight exchange turn due to movement between the gold points, was enough to remunerate him. He was content with a normal banker's commission, the reason for that being that his losses were definitely limited, and his profit was more or less calculable beforehand. He did not have to be rewarded for taking a risk, because he was not taking an appreciable amount of risk.

That worked extremely well, but what happens now? The autumn pressure comes along just as usual, but now the banker is not content or able to move his balances for small turns, as he could formerly, because he now has no guarantee at all as to the rate at which he will be able to bring his money back again later in the year. He may have a very strong opinion as to the course of the exchange, but the transaction is no longer a calculable one. He is bearing a risk, and owing to what has happened in recent years he estimates the risk as a very big one. And even apart from the fact that he has to be remunerated for risk, it ceases to be quite a banker's business. A banker, even though he thinks the risk is actuarily rewarded by the prospective profit, cannot afford to run risks of that kind on a big scale. Consequently this business that used to be a proper banker's business for a small term has become a speculator's business. The balancing of the account in the autumn, quite apart from the account for the year as a whole, has to be looked after in part by the suppliers of speculative finance. In order to attract the suppliers of speculative finance there has to be a very large movement. They will not come in and support the market until the exchange has moved to a figure which in their judgment gives them good prospects of profit when the next easy season comes round. Moreover, as speculative finance of that kind is discouraged by other banking institutions, and by state banks and so forth, it is generally in short supply. The amount of speculative finance going is barely enough to look after the autumn trend in its pre-war dimensions. Where a banker would not at all mind in the old days remitting millions to and from New York, hundreds of thousands are now as much risk as even very big people care to look to. So that, partly from the shortage of people who are in a position to look after that kind of business, and partly because they, estimating the risk to be a large one, do not operate until they see a big profit, you may have a very large seasonal fluctuation of the exchange even though the thing is in perfect adjustment over the year as a whole. You will not get a steady exchange until you have a 'pegged' exchange, because, until you have that, every little up and down is bound to have a disproportionate effect on the exchange, because the adjustment has to be effected by persons who are speculating rather than by persons who are conducting banking.

It is no good therefore to think, as some people do, that you must first of all wait for the exchanges to be stable, and after you have seen them stable for a year or two you will then fix them. They never will be stable until you have fixed them; you have to act first. And it is extremely important to do so in the case of any country for which it is practicable, because this seasonal fluctuation and the big rewards which have to be paid to speculative finance are a very heavy burden on trade. It means partly that those merchants who make their purchases according to the pre-war rule in the autumn have to finance them at a very unfavourable rate of exchange as compared with the average exchange of the year, and also to a certain extent it means that merchants deterred by the bad exchange rates that are offered them in the autumn postpone a part of their purchases to a season of the year in which they hope the exchange will be better, but one which may be far less convenient and efficient from the point of view of the transaction of their business. Nothing but harm therefore results from these big seasonal swings.

That is known in a general way, but I wonder how many people realise the extent to which the fluctuations of sterling and of francs and lire during the last three years have been seasonal rather than progressive. In the year 1919 when the exchanges were unpegged because the inter-allied arrangement for finance came to an end, there was a very heavy fall in francs and lire and sterling of a non-seasonal kind. All through the early part and the middle of 1919 they were falling for that reason and for non-seasonal reasons. There has also been this year an improvement in sterling which is of a non-seasonal character, and it may be for the reasons that I have just given relating to the internal debt that at some future date there may be a non-seasonal decline of some of the continental exchanges. But although those facts are true—two of them are true, and one of them possible—nevertheless the bulk of the movements between the autumn of 1919 and the autumn of this year have been seasonal and not progressive.

I will put on the blackboard, if I may, a rather striking table. It is a table of percentage of dollar parity. The figures I shall put down represent the percent of dollar par that each currency reached at various dates, and I will give the lowest and higher for each season. For this purpose a season has to run from, say, August to August, rather than the calendar year, but I have not taken any exact period. Taking 1919–20, and beginning with sterling, the lowest percentage of dollar par that sterling touched was 69, and the highest was 82. In the following year 1920–21, the lowest percentage of dollar par reached by sterling was 69, and the highest was 82. In 1921–22, the lowest reached was 73, and the highest 93. In 1922–23, only half of which season is over, the £ sterling has fallen below 90.

Now here of course there is an improvement which is independent of seasons, but it is remarkable how steady the lowest figures are, and how steady the highest figures are, and how very big the fluctuations between the lowest and the highest are. It looks to me from that as though the fluctuations between the lowest and the highest were mainly seasonal, but you have to fall down to that point before the speculator would come in to look after the seasonal adverse balance. The difference between the two sets of figures is some measure of the enormous burden thrown on trade.

It looks from that table as though, supposing we had decided as long ago as 1919–20 that we would stabilise the £ sterling say at 75 per cent of its pre-war parity, we could probably have kept sterling pegged without any disturbance to trade through the whole of this period, and I believe it would have been a very much wiser policy to have done so.

Sterling is a fairly impressive case, but the franc and lira are in a way, I think, even more impressive. We realise that the movement of sterling has been mainly seasonal, but the extent to which it is true of the franc and lira is equally striking.

Let us take the franc. In 1919–20 the lowest point of the franc was 31, and the highest point was 44. In the next year the lowest was 30, and the highest 45. In the following year the lowest was 37, and the highest 47. This year so far the lowest has been 34.

I think that this is an extraordinarily striking table. There has not been any clear movement of the franc either up or down if you take the highest figures in each year, and the lowest figures in each year. But there is an enormous divergence between the highest and lowest figures. So that the man who imported his goods in the autumn and covered his exchange has had to pay a tremendous fine for the convenience of importing then rather than later in the year, and the people who have eventually accommodated him in the exchange have reaped an enormous profit. Surely it would have been much better all through this period to have stabilised the franc at some intermediate figure. Although for the reasons I have given I am not very optimistic for the future, I think it looks from this as though it would have been practicable for the Bank of France to have taken a figure such as 40 and to have kept the franc pegged at 40 all through that period. They would have lost reserves at certain seasons, but they would have gained them at others, and they would have added enormously to the prosperity of the country.

The lira, which is my last example, is almost the most striking of all. The lowest point reached by the lira in the first year was 22, and the highest was 32. In the next year the lowest was 18, and the highest 29. In the following year the lowest was 20, and the highest 27. And in this year the lowest has been 20 so far.

One sees from that [that] the lowest points of the lira in terms of the dollar have been 22, 18, 20 and 20, while the highest points have been 32, 29 and 27. But whereas the lowest points are steady, and whereas the highest points are steady, the fluctuation between the lowest and the highest has been as much as 50 per cent, and has never been less than 35 per cent. That shows that the violent movement of the lira has not been a progressive movement, but it has been a seasonal movement.

Therefore I argue that if you are thinking of the hindrances to trade, it is the seasonal point which one must largely attend to. And I also draw this conclusion: that so long as the exchanges are not stabilised by policy they will never come to an equilibrium of themselves. You may get smaller oscillations than these. Suppose this sort of thing went on year after year people would learn by experience, and no doubt the oscillations would not be nearly so large. Speculators would come in a little sooner, and importers would make even greater efforts to spread their importations more evenly over the year. But even so, I should think there would always be a very substantial difference between the busy season and the slack season so long as nobody knows at what level these currencies are going to settle down.

While people talk as they do at present there is, quite apart from underlying facts, an enormous risk in the matter. You have all the official authorities threatening to bring back the franc and the lira to par, so that any operations on the one side are very dangerous. On the other hand, you have the condition of internal finance which I have just been talking about, which indicates that they might possibly go a great deal worse. So that nobody knows with certainty, or even with probability, whether they are going to be a great deal better or very much worse. Therefore you must have a very wide fluctuation before people will come in purely from motives of self-interest to balance the day to day fluctuations and the month to month fluctuations as distinct from the annual fluctuations.

Signor Mussolini has lately threatened, I am told, to bring back the lira to 50. It is such an awful threat that I should think the Italians will do almost anything rather than accede to it. But would Signor Mussolini have said that if he had understood what he was saying? Suppose he put it like this: I propose to halve wages, double the burden of the national debt and reduce by 50 per cent the prices which Sicilians will obtain for the export of oranges and lemons. If he put his policy in that form, it would not have been as popular. But that is what his policy amounted to.

When you have those kinds of remarks being made on one side, and the hopeless state of the internal debt on the other side, naturally you have a complete uncertainty of mind which can only be cured by the government adopting a deliberate policy and saying we are going to do all in our power to prevent further depreciation, and we are not going to be so crazy as to try to perform an impossible task and restore our currency to par. When they do that you may be in sight of getting rid of this enormous hindrance and expense to trade by these vast seasonal fluctuations.

There has been one country—I should like to point the moral from this—which was unusually in a position to adopt a course of wisdom. That is Czecho-Slovakia. Early in this year Czecho-Slovakia found herself with a budget that was not very far from balancing, with, comparatively, a freedom from the internal debt that oppresses France and Italy and other countries. Her credit was good. She raised quite important loans in London and in New York. Nobody would have blamed her for fixing the Czech crown at the level which then prevailed. It had been ruined by no fault of her own, and was an inheritance from the Hapsburg Empire. At that time the Czech crown was worth about one twelfth of its pre-war parity. Czecho-Slovakia was in a splendid position for stabilising. She had the foreign resources to make a reserve fund, and there was no internal reason why the thing should not have been perfectly successful. In the light of what has actually happened it is clear she could have stabilised with complete success. What did she do? She has used the funds that she raised on the New York and London markets to buy Czech crowns over the exchange, and gradually to raise her exchange until the Czech crown is now worth double what it was in the spring. The consequence of that has been to throw out of gear the whole of her industries. She has had very severe unemployment, and a crisis through the greater part of her industries. She now finds herself a year later with her foreign resources partially depleted, with her crown worth one sixth of its pre-war parity instead of one twelfth, and still completely unstabilised, blown about by the breath of the seasons and the wind of politics. Could anything have been more foolish.

How long is it to go on? Is Czecho-Slovakia going to go on having industrial crises until she has raised her currency to six times its value? It is no easier for her to stabilise now than it was six months ago; indeed it is more difficult because her resources in foreign currency are no longer quite intact. What good has she done by deflating the value of legal tender? Apart from the satisfaction and pride in getting back to pre-war parity, it is very little better to have it at one sixth than to have it at one twelfth. The whole thing, as far as I can see, has been entirely purposeless, and it has been the result of deliberate policy. M. Alois Razin the Finance Minister, has dogmatic views on this subject. He is one of the leading bankers, and unfortunately he has had the opportunity of putting his tenets into practice. There has been a strong opposition, but he has overcome it. I should like to have it explained to me what good of any sort or kind he has done his country by this revolution in the value of legal tender money?

The modern capitalist world is even less suited in my opinion for violent fluctuations in the value of money upwards than it is for violent fluctuations in the value of money downwards. Either form of action is very ill advised, and ought never to be undertaken on purpose. I give that example partly as illustrating the disadvantages of following a false doctrine, but also as showing the state of opinion at the moment. When you do get a country which could stabilise, it immediately follows this vain and empty project of improving the value of its currency up to an undetermined point.

I have left over two questions which I must deal with. I should like to deal in a little more detail with the effect of a deflationary policy on industry, and I should also like to deal with the rather peculiar case of our own country and with the relation of sterling to the dollar. But if you will excuse me, I will not embark on that part of the argument today but will postpone it till next week, when the lecture, as Mr Steele [the chairman] has said, will be given on Tuesday instead of Wednesday.

Lecture to the Institute of Bankers, 5 December 1922

MR J. M. KEYNES: In my last lecture I discussed some of the general principles governing the proposals for devaluation, and I went into some particular details relating to France and to Czecho-Slovakia, but I made no comment as regards this country. In this lecture I propose to repair that omission. I have kept this country till the last because it raises rather separate questions from other countries, I think. To begin with, the problem of restoring sterling parity is a perfectly possible problem. There is no reason why we should not put sterling back to its pre-war parity if we wish to. So that one of the strongest arguments which I mentioned in the case of foreign countries, that any attempt was bound to be futile in the end, does not hold good in our case. There are also, owing to our past history, and owing to our position as an international financial centre, some rather specially strong, if sentimental reasons, if you like, for returning to the old parity. I recognise the force of those arguments. In the course of the wars of Napoleon, sterling suffered a depreciation just as it did in the course of the late war; but after many years, by a persistent effort, we succeeded in returning to par. It would naturally be a matter of great pride to this country if, after even the worst war of the twentieth century, we were again able to return to our previous undisturbed parity. These matters cannot be neglected in any monetary affairs where confidence, security, and all that, are of very real weight. So that not only is it possible for us to return to par, but there are special reasons both of self-interest and of pride why we should wish to do so. If it is our policy, and I believe it is, that we should return to par, then certainly it is to our interest that we should do so as rapidly as possible. The transitional period of uncertainty is undesirable, and if sterling is going to par with the dollar, the sooner it gets there, in my judgment, the better for all of us; and it looks now as if it were quite conceivable—whether it will stay there or not—that sterling may touch par at no very remote date. Nevertheless, while we have pursued this policy, and while it looks as though we shall pursue it with a considerable measure of success, I still think that the policy of restoring sterling to par was a mistake. In spite of the arguments which I have mentioned, and to which I give full weight, I think we should have been better advised if in the course of the last two years—perhaps two years ago—we had stabilised, say, somewhere between four dollars and four and a half dollars to the £ sterling. What I want to go into in detail are the reasons why it seems to me that we should have been more prudent to have adopted a policy of stabilisation which, at the level to which I think experience points, would have been possible at any time in the course of the last two years.

My first argument why that would have been a wise course brings me back to one argument I emphasised very much in my last lecture, namely, the burden of the national debt. In the case of France, as I pointed out, the burden of the internal debt is an overwhelming reason why the restoration of the franc to par is impossible; but it is also an argument which must not be neglected in the case of sterling. We are in danger of being the only country which will have a very heavy internal debt in relation to its resources. The countries of which the money has become depreciated have been relieved, as I explained in my last lecture, of a very large part of their burden. In the United States, while the nominal figure is considerable, in relation to the wealth of the country, it is no serious burden. We, however, will have to govern our tax system for a long time to come by reference to the tremendous burden of debt, and that, I think, may hinder the prosperity of our industry in relation to the prosperity of other countries which are not similarly burdened. I think the policy of bringing sterling to par renders it decidedly less likely that we shall be able to do without a capital levy. You will remember how in my last lecture I put the capital levy and currency devaluation as to a considerable extent alternatives. I think there is a slight prospect that we may be able to come to an equilibrium without a capital levy. But if sterling goes to its old par and is kept there, unless gold prices rise—of course, a fall in the value of gold might see us out—it will make very much more probable the necessity of a capital levy. I will illustrate that by some very rough figures. Suppose we put the burden of the debt, which is fixed in the terms of legal tender, at somewhere about £350,000,000 a year. I am not sure how exactly accurate that is, but it is a round figure. Suppose, after making what economies we can at the present level of prices, we are able to reduce the other expenditure to about £500,000,000, so that we are spending £850,000,000 altogether. Well, that will be an extremely heavy burden on the country. It is quite likely that we shall not be able to get below that at the present level of prices. If the value of gold falls and prices rise, the yield of taxation, generally speaking, will respond sooner or later. This part of the expenditure will also probably respond and increase proportionately sooner or later, but the other part will remain fixed; so that the real burden of the debt will be diminishing. The argument is equally true if you are comparing stabilisation, say, at four dollars to the £ sterling, with stabilisation at the old parity. If that is the situation with sterling at par, if we had stabilised at four dollars to the £ sterling, then you may suppose that that figure would have remained the same, that the expenditure would have risen, say, 20 per cent, to £600,000,000, and the revenue, which I am assuming just balances that, would also, without any increased real burden to the people, have risen 20 per cent to £1,025,000,000; so that we should have a surplus of £75,000,000 for the reduction of taxation. That margin of £75,000,000 is again the amount which you might hope to save by a moderate capital levy scheme. The schemes that I have seen drawn up which are not very oppressive, and which allow for hard cases, I think can be made to yield something of the order of an annual equivalent of £75,000,000 to £100,000,000 sterling. So that if a capital levy of that sort is brought in, it would make just about the same relief to the Budget in the long run as we should have obtained by fixing sterling at four instead of at the old par. Taken in conjunction with various other factors, I believe it would be a far less disturbing thing to have done to have a fixed sterling at four, rather than to have the burden of internal debt which is very near the limit. As I said in my last lecture, I do not know yet whether it is above what we can support without a capital levy or not—I think only time can show—but everybody will agree that it is very near the margin. I think those people suffer from a certain confusion of mind who simultaneously hold we must indubitably restore sterling to par, in all circumstances we must respect contract, and in no circumstances must we have a capital levy. If you lay down those things as *a priori* absolute principles, you will land yourselves, or you may land yourselves in an *impasse*—you will produce a situation which you cannot possibly solve on those principles, and you will have to give way to persons of other ideas who may solve them, on principles not moderately opposed to your own, but radically opposed to your own. The right way of preserving stability is not by *a priori* principles of that sort, but by considering the whole matter coolly and intellectually. That is my first reason for thinking it would be more prudent to have stabilised sterling at an early stage.

The next argument is of a more fleeting kind, and of the disadvantages of which we have already borne the greater part of the brunt. The depressing influence of a prospective fall of prices in relation to world prices on trade, hardly needs to be pointed out. Sterling is now about 7 per cent below its parity. Well, if it is going to its parity, that means that English prices, sterling prices, must drag 7 per cent behind American prices. If American prices remain steady then English prices must fall 7 per cent. If American prices rise a further 7 per cent, then English prices need not, in fact must not follow them. In the meantime, nobody quite knows what will happen, and you have a continuance of the depressing influence we have had in the last eighteen months, and a further prospective possible fall in prices. In the first place, that reacts on trade in many more ways than one easily realises at first sight. The Manchester merchants are complaining very much that the price of cotton goods is too dear. Well, in the terms of sterling, the prices of cotton goods are not very dear. They are a great deal cheaper than they have been for a good many years. The real trouble is that the silver exchange is so adverse to the silver-using countries. I take one instance in one particular kind of country. What makes Manchester goods dear in China is not their sterling price, but their sterling price taken in connection with the present value of silver. As silver has a world value, every time you raise the value of sterling, you put down the sterling price of silver. Every time that the sterling goes nearer to par, it makes it more difficult for China to buy our cotton goods, until China has shaken down to the new level of prices. All this has a fleeting influence. Once you have reached your equilibrium it is all over. But we have already had about eighteen months of it, and the prospect of another six months of it is, I think, a very serious damper on trade. My own view is that, apart from the depressing influence of the actual and prospective rise of sterling, and apart from the European situation, which I take very seriously, apart from those two influences, trade is straining at the leash, and will easily have a very fine revival. The European situation may develop at an early date, of course—I am not speaking of that today—but the other influence, the course of sterling, is one which has been under the control of our financiers, as European policy has not been; and I think the policy they have actually adopted, although I understand the honourable motives which have prompted it, has certainly prolonged the trade depression. It may have been worth it—I do not say it was not—but it is a very important argument on the other side if I am right in thinking that the slowness of the revival of trade in this country as compared with what is now going on in America, is due to an important extent to the course of the sterling exchange. The tremendous fillip that trade has had in America through the rise of prices has hardly been reflected here. The rise of prices in America has been counterbalanced here in the improvement in the rate of sterling, so that things are left here very nearly as they were. That is hindering our merchants, I think, partly because trade will never go ahead until people are certain they have touched bottom. They will never be certain that they have touched bottom until they see them going up a little; so that I am in favour of a moderate rise in prices as the only way of getting out of the present period of depression, and I think the improvement of sterling towards par is a hampering influence on that. Indeed, it is obvious it must be. In that connection, in connection with a rise of prices being necessary, the more I study statistics the more convinced I am that we shall not be in equilibrium until wholesale prices have risen from 15 to 20 per cent. The business of forcing down certain levels of wages, and so forth, into equilibrium is almost hopeless, or it will take a long time. The continuance of unemployment is to an important extent due to the fact that we have got the level of wages, particularly the level of wages of the unskilled, out of gear with everything else. The only way in which they will get into gear will be by an increase in the level of prices. Some figures have been lately published which are very striking in showing just how we are out of gear. At the moment you may say, broadly speaking, that food and the cost of living generally is somewhere about 60 per cent above pre-war. It is also interesting that this year we have been paying for our imports generally about 60 per cent above the pre-war price. On the other hand, the average level of wages is about 80 per cent above pre-war. That is the level of weekly wages. The level of unskilled labour is very materially more than that, the level of skilled labour rather less; and it averages out at 180. The skilled labourer is being paid by no means too much, rather to the contrary; but one of the things that has happened is that the old margin between skilled and unskilled labour has largely disappeared, and the unskilled labourer is now being overpaid in relation to the cost of living, and in relation to what the skilled labourer is getting. At any rate, the thing averages out at somewhere about 180, or more. I am putting it rather low at 180, because I think in that index number some of the more highly paid unskilled labourers have not been taken full account of. That is weekly earnings; but owing to the reduced hours of working, the wages that were paid per hour are probably double pre-war, that is to say, 200. 200 is the remuneration of labour compared with pre-war 100 per cent of work done; but food and raw materials are only 160. The effect of that 200 means that we are actually having to charge for our exports a materially higher price that we are having to pay for our imports. Our exports generally during this year have been sold at a price double the pre-war price exactly corresponding to the wages. High wages are compelling us to ask double for our exports when the world level of prices as measured by what we must pay for our imports, is only about 60 per cent up. It is clear that that is not a situation which can go on permanently. People will not pay us for our exports at so discrepant a price from what goods generally are worth in the world; and we see the fruits of high prices in the diminishing volume of our exports, and in our complete incapacity to employ the whole body of labour. I do not mean that that is the whole reason—I think there are many reasons why we are unable to employ all the available workmen—but I think one important reason is that we are attempting the impossible task of raising their remuneration something like 20 per cent more than is justified by the prices they have to pay for their food and living, and what we generally have to pay for our imports. I do not see much prospect of bringing that 200 up to 160, but I think there is a very real likelihood of the 160, that is to say, the general level of prices, rising to 200. Every hindrance in the way of that puts off the day when we shall be in equilibrium, and when we can employ our population.

The business of raising the value of sterling 20 per cent has put off the moment of equilibrium from anything from six months to two years, so we have had to pay a very high price for the sentimental satisfaction to our pride in the prolongation of the industrial depression, and in the immense volume of unemployment which we have had, and still have, and are likely to continue to have, I think, until the basic statistics of our economic life have got into some better equilibrium than they are at the present.

But there is also a third reason which ought not to be neglected, and that is this. Sterling still fluctuates, and even if sterling reaches par in the course of the next spring season, it is uncertain, to my mind, whether it can be kept there during the autumn pressure. We have already suffered for two or three years the immense expense of the autumn seasonal fluctuation which I expounded in my last lecture; and it is not at all unlikely that we may have to suffer that for at least one year more. Measured in money, I believe that the expense to trade and efficiency of the uncorrected seasonal swing is enormous; whereas though we could have probably stabilised with complete success at a lower value, it is uncertain how soon we shall be able to stabilise at par.

Even though the upward swing of this spring takes sterling to par without any difficulty or effort on our part, there is no guarantee that it will stay there. So that the present policy, apart from the first two arguments, puts off for an unduly long period the moment when we can get back to complete stability of the exchanges. One particular reason for doubting whether we can keep it there is the still unsolved question of the payment of the interest that we owe to America. I should like to say a few words about that, because it is quite impossible to come to a conclusion as to how easy it is to maintain sterling at par until one has thought a little about the payment of the interest to America which we have not yet discharged on the basis of a full year's payments. I confess that I am a little alarmed at the light-hearted way in which some authorities talk about the supposed ease with which we can discharge that liability. I quite agree that if we are called upon to pay it we must pay; but I think it is a great mistake to pretend that it would be an easy thing to pay, or that it will not create very great disturbance to all parties concerned. We have to think out a great deal more carefully than we have what the exact course of events is likely to be. If we are to pay the debt within the limits of the present Act of the American Congress, that is to say, interest plus sufficient sinking fund to discharge the debt in 25 years, that will cost something between sixty to seventy millions sterling annually, according to the rate of exchange. I think at the par exchange, it will be a little over sixty millions sterling, or at $4.40 it would be about seventy millions sterling. That is an enormous sum, 300,000,000 dollars, to be found over the exchange every year. When Mr McKenna was speaking in America he pointed out quite correctly that it must be within the capacity of this country to pay that sum, if it was already lending a more than equivalent sum to foreign borrowers. Our annual investments abroad, even now, on their diminished post-war scale, probably amount to not less than £70,000,000. That is a reason for supposing we can pay that sum of money. I quite agree with that; but we have to follow out the causal train a little more carefully. Supposing the American investor would step straight into our shoes, and would take over precisely the same loans that we otherwise would have taken over from the same borrowers on the same terms, then the payment of this £70,000,000 a year can be arranged with the least possible disturbance. There would be no particular reason why the dollar exchange should be affected, and no particular reason why the balance of exports and imports need be interfered with. They would merely hold in their safes documents from foreign debtors which otherwise we should hold in ours. But it will not happen automatically. When we announce that we are going to pay 300,000,000 dollars a year to America, nothing will automatically happen to make Americans step into our shoes as lenders. At present the foreign borrowers come to London because the terms they can get in London are more satisfactory to them in some cases—not always, and then they go to New York—than the terms they can get in New York. They do not come here for any other reason. At any rate, they would not go to New York instead of coming here until New York is offering them more attractive terms than London is offering them. Something will have to happen, therefore, which will make the New York market more attractive to borrowers than London to the extent of 300,000,000 dollars a year. If the American investor is very nearly primed for this class of investment, if he is only just hanging off because he would like another quarter per cent, or something of the kind; if he just cannot quite compete with the terms London can offer to India or to Australia, or whoever it is, if that is the case, then a comparatively small amount of pressure of dear money in London might make borrowers go to New York instead. But I am not sure that that is the case. One of the difficulties is not the rate of money, but the fact that New York is more inclined than we are to insist on tying up the loans with contracts. If the loan is tied up with conditions as to who gets the contracts, then the substitution of America as the lender will not help us to pay the debt, because other factors in the balance of trade will also be altered. It is only a loan on the same conditions as we make the loan which will help us to pay the debt. That is one reason. The other reason is that it is very doubtful whether the American investor for a very long time to come is going to take the attitude towards foreign investment that we in this country traditionally have taken. In the first place, in a great undeveloped country of that kind, there are immensely more opportunities for investment at home. Secondly, in a country like America, the average investor necessarily knows far less about the outside world from an investment point of view than a country like this, where such an enormous number of business men have direct connection with international trade, and are in a position to know of their own knowledge a good deal about the relative credit of foreign borrowers. Thirdly, there is another influence which I think is rather alarming. America has in fact lent on a very large scale during the last two or three years, and if you look through the list of what she has lent I think that any London issuing house would think she has lent a good deal rather injudiciously. The Americans have taken up a great many loans that the best issuing houses in London have been inclined to turn down. It is not at all outside possibility that a good many of those loans which America has made lately will not turn out very well for her. If that is the case, there will be a very considerable reaction against lending abroad. The combination of that with other factors I have mentioned may make a very great reaction against lending abroad, so that the American investor will only be willing to step into the shoes of the London investor on very different terms from those which the London investor has been prepared to take.

Suppose we start paying 300,000,000 dollars a year to America, as I say, nothing will automatically happen to stop the foreign borrower from coming to London, and send him to New York instead. In order to preserve our exchange under the burden of the payment of 300,000,000 dollars, we shall have to take steps to induce or to drive the foreign borrower to go to New York. There are various ways in which we could do that. The Bank of England might exert its influence and take a very stiff line against the admission of any foreign borrowers to London at all. It probably would be within the power of the Bank of England to exert very great influence in that direction. That is one way. But while we may prevent the foreign borrower from coming to London, we could not ensure that he would be entertained in New York, and if the class of foreign loans which we have been making are not made at all, that may have very serious reactions on foreign trade generally. That will not leave things exactly as they are. It will not mean that our exporting industries can go on exactly as they have done if the countries which are in the habit, for reasons of development, of being large borrowers, are cut off from the market altogether. If America steps into our shoes, well and good, but if they are merely cut off from London by the attempt of England to preserve the London market from a charge which is incompatible with our paying the American debt, then the situation is in all respects different.

Another method would be to keep money in London for a long period very dear—decidedly dearer than in New York. We might have a policy which we intended to maintain over years of keeping money, say, effectively two per cent higher in London than in New York, in order to make sure that the price which we should have to charge for loans for foreign borrowers would be very much higher than they could probably get accommodated with in New York. There would be a great objection to that on our part. People do not like very dear money going on for years. They would point out quite justly that, while it might be effective for the particular purpose, it would also hinder our own industry enormously that they should have to pay a rate for money which was not justified on its merits, but which was merely a deterrent rate to keep foreign borrowers away. If, on the other hand, you try to meet them by attempting, as was the case at one time during the War, to have a different rate for foreign money from what you have for home money, I think you are landed into all kinds of interference with the freedom of finance which is the essence of the success of London. During the War it was necessary to do it, and during the war there were so many interferences with freedom that one more did not very greatly matter; but a continuing policy of interference, not merely for months, but for years, I believe would be extraordinarily injurious to the position of London, and to its whole finances. For all these reasons, therefore, I think that the Bank of England, the Treasury, and the City generally, will have their work cut out to make sure that borrowers to the tune of 300,000,000 dollars per annum, who would naturally come to London, shall not come to London but shall visit New York instead, and be favourably entertained there. Unless that can be arranged, there will be enormous difficulties in our paying the interest on this loan. We could not do it merely by an alteration of exports and imports without undergoing a significant change in our level of life, and in fact no one really thinks we could do that. The source from which we are supposed to be going to pay it is the source which I am mentioning, namely, that fund which we are now investing abroad will be transferred to America instead of to the pockets of people who would otherwise borrow from us. Nobody looks to any other source. But the business of diverting that source from the channels into which it naturally flows into the channels into which it would have to flow in the future, is going to be extraordinarily difficult and anxious, and it is not likely that we shall discover quite the right way to do it possibly for a few years to come. We shall make experiments, but we shall have a new problem of extreme difficulty which our financial genius may enable us to solve sooner or later, but which will not be easy.

During the transitional period, before we have solved how to get that adjustment brought about, it will be very difficult to stabilise sterling for good at the old par—in fact, it will be difficult to stabilise it anywhere, and it will probably be more difficult to stabilise at a high level than at a lower level which gives us a certain margin in hand. Unless, therefore, there is a distinctly satisfactory solution in our favour of the American debt question, the whole future is very full of anxiety, and trade will be very liable to be burdened for a considerable time to come with the expense, inconvenience, and uncertainty of the big seasonal fluctuation, which, for the reasons I gave in my last lecture, is bound to take place till you have sterling pegged again. Unless you have sterling pegged, there is no possible way of avoiding the seasonal fluctuation, though as time goes on, it may keep within rather narrower limits than has been the case in the past.

All this I am saying tonight is a little complicated, and it is not very clear-cut; but it is these things which have to be in the mind of the banker when he is deciding what his policy is towards the levelling of sterling and all these linked-up questions of the repayment of the debt and so forth. I am not satisfied, from the discussions which I have heard, and from the discussions which I have seen in print, that all these considerations have been taken fully into account. The thing has been done a little blindly. People have said, 'Of course we must go back to par, and we can do it, and honour requires it', and so forth. But we have put a bandage round our eyes and just plunged blindly in that direction. If it was absolutely required by honour,

I agree we ought to do it; but for the reasons which I quoted from Professor Irving Fisher in an earlier lecture, that is not really the case—we are under no such obligation. In fact, in so far from injuring creditors by having sterling below par, we are helping foreign debtors. A great many countries owe us money in terms of sterling. The more we raise sterling in the terms of value, the more they owe us. That is one of the subtle advantages we get, but, so far as the outside world goes, they owe us much more sterling than we owe them. It is quite untrue, therefore, to suppose that we are cheating the rest of the world in any sense by fixing legal tender at a new value. Legal tender has constantly been fixed at new values in history. We have a long history, but even after the wars of Napoleon a change was made. Our standard is the only one which has existed for a hundred years. There is no other standard in Europe which has lasted for fifty years, and all the precedents are in favour of change. The worst of it is they generally take place, not judiciously, not moderately, but under the pressure of events, immoderately and injudiciously, and very often with a considerable flavour of dishonesty. It is worth mentioning again, if there is any question of justice, surely it is a stable purchasing power you have to give to people rather than a stable quantity of metal. However, I see the point of view of those who hold the opposite opinion, only I say those who hold the opposite opinion must not take it light-heartedly. Those who think that for reasons that they regard as overwhelming we must fix it at par must face, which I do not think they do, the cost of that. They must not do it without facing the cost. Just as I agree with those who say that we must pay America what they call upon us to pay, also we must not say that light-heartedly, or without thinking a very great deal about what the consequences are going to be. It is so easy to get a good reputation by saying, 'Of course we shall pay', without going into any detail about it. That is not, in fact, the way we shall pay. We shall only pay if we go into full details and arrange our policy in all particulars so as to bring about the result to which we have committed ourselves.

That completes what I have to say about devaluation in this country. I just have one word in conclusion on a small theoretical point which I think is a little interesting; that is the difference in the method of adjustment of a currency to the outside world when the exchanges are pegged and when they are unpegged. Under present conditions, as soon as we import too much or export too little, the exchanges move against us; and when the exchanges move very rapidly the price of every article is changed—the price of imports and exports is changed almost forthwith. In Germany now when the exchange falls, prices adjust themselves not completely, but very rapidly so that as soon as the country is buying too much, prices rise very rapidly, and the reaction sets in—it economises and it purchases less. So that the unpegged exchange has one curious advantage which people overlook—it puts the brake on very rapidly. If, on the other hand, you have a pegged exchange, then if you are purchasing more than you can afford, there is a tendency for gold to flow out in payment of the adverse balance. The effect of the outflow of gold is to make money dearer by slow stages which are familiar to people. That reacts on trade. It makes trade curtail itself rather, and gradually, by a very slow causal process, forces home prices down, until the home price is no longer attractive to the importer because it is falling below the outside price, and the country then economises in its consumption. But it is a very long and slow process. You do not get adjustment anything like as fast as you do with the unpegged exchange; consequently the pegged exchange is very hard to operate except in rather stable conditions, because the method by which correction comes into play is such a very slow one. That is one of the very deep reasons why in unstable conditions you almost invariably do have an unpegged exchange. The advantage of the pegged exchange is that as the method is a slow one a mere seasonal or temporary deficit does not produce an excessive result. If it is a seasonal or temporary deficit, the method of correcting this, long before parity, which operates under the pegged exchange, has had time to work itself out, so that things are left undisturbed; whereas, the unpegged exchange is sensitive, not only to influences to which it ought to be sensitive, namely, when the country has been buying too much, but it is sensitive to mere fleeting influences, mere news in the news-papers, or the mere season of the year, and so on; so that you have home prices bobbing about for reasons which are not permanent causes at all. The unpegged exchange is so sensitive that it is valuable for certain purposes, but it is far too sensitive for other purposes; yet one has to admit that the pegged exchange is so slow in its operation that it is dangerous for a country to adopt until it is sure that the basic conditions are fairly sound: then, as a correction to the seasonal movement, it is essential. That is an argument which is rather of the opposite tenor to most of what I have been saying in these lectures, but it is of sufficient interest and importance, and has enough relevance on the other side of the case for it to be right that I should mention it in conclusion.

Keynes sent a copy of the transcript of his lecture of 5 December to Stanley Baldwin, the Chancellor of the Exchequer.[4] He met Baldwin on 18 December.

During the remainder of 1922 and early 1923, Keynes returned to international matters. However, he also began work on what was to become *A Tract on Monetary Reform* (*JMK*, vol. IV). On 15 January 1923 he reported on his progress to his publisher.

To MAURICE MACMILLAN, *15 January 1923*

Dear Mr Macmillan,

I am preparing for early publication, I hope in March, a short volume entitled 'Essays on Money and the Exchanges'. I enclose a provisional Table of Contents.[5] I estimate that the length ought not to run to more than 40,000 to 50,000 words.

---

[4] See *JMK*, vol. XVIII, pp. 99, 101–2.
[5] This has not survived in Keynes's own papers.

I am proposing to make use in this volume of the material of articles which I have contributed during the past year to the *Manchester Guardian* Special Supplements on *Reconstruction in Europe*, of which I have been the Editor. But the volume will be a continuous one, by no means a mere reprint of articles. I am discarding a good deal of what I printed in the articles, on the other hand adding a good deal of new matter, and, generally speaking, modifying and re-arranging the whole so as to weld it into a continuous story.

I should be grateful if your firm would publish this volume on the same terms as you have agreed to for my other recent publications. I think the format might be the same as my last volume, *A Revision of the Treaty*, on which I estimate my matter would run from 160 to 200 pages. I am in a position to send more than half the copy to the printer forthwith, and as I should like him to get on with the proof sheets without delay, I should propose to send this to you for transmission to Messrs Clark (if they are to print the volume) as soon as I hear from you that you are willing to undertake publication.

The book will differ from my other recent volumes in that it will be suitable for use as a textbook in universities, and as it contains a considerable amount of new matter adapted either for advanced or relatively elementary work I think it might have a considerable vogue as time goes on for this purpose. This means that the sales are likely to be spread over a long period, and not so much concentrated as was the case with my pamphleteering works. I should also hope, however, for a considerable immediate circulation in financial circles, and should propose to print a first edition of 5,000 copies.

As regards the American rights, I am writing to Messrs Harcourt, Brace & Co., who have published my two volumes on the Peace Treaty.

Yours sincerely,
[copy initialled] J.M.K.

On 31 January, during his speech as Chairman of the National Mutual Life Assurance Society, Keynes returned to domestic affairs.

From a speech to the Annual Meeting of the National Mutual, 31 January 1923

My own view is that the strong tendency towards the revival of trade and confidence in this country, which has already begun, will need facts, and not merely fears, to hold it back. Many favourable conditions are now developing, and although the growth of confidence about the level of prices has been necessarily retarded here, as compared with the United States, so long as the rise of the sterling exchange has continued to depress sterling prices in relation to dollar prices, the end of this movement must come sooner or later. Whether political developments are good or bad, I expect a rise, rather than a fall, of prices, which, however, is not necessarily the same thing at all as general prosperity. The number of men in employment is now about the same as before the War, which is something to set against the depressing facts that no work is at present available for the substantial increase in the employable population since 1913, and that those who are employed are probably producing on the average about 10 per cent less than formerly for approximately the same real wage. Without great improvements in the technique and intelligence of trade and industry, it looks doubtful whether, on these terms, we shall be able to employ the whole employable population except at the very top of the periodic booms. The above estimate is in conformity with the indications of several other groups of statistics that the general turnover of trade is now on the average somewhere round about 10 per cent below the *pre-war level*.

Keynes's comment was picked up by several newspapers and by Ramsay MacDonald, the leader of the Opposition in the House of Commons, during the debate following the King's Speech; Keynes then clarified his views.

To the Editor of The Times, *14 February 1923*

Sir,

A statement which I made as chairman of the National Mutual Assurance Society about the capacity of this country to find work for the whole employable population has been so widely quoted in a form slightly but materially different from that in which I made it, notably by Mr Ramsay MacDonald in the course of the debate on the Address, that I beg leave to explain myself.

I estimated, speaking broadly, that the working classes were receiving approximately the same real wage as before the War for an output (largely due to a diminution of working hours), perhaps 10 per cent less, and then went on to say that I doubted 'whether *on these terms* we shall be able to employ the whole employable population except at the very top of the periodic booms *without great improvements in the technique and intelligence of trade and industry*'.

The words which I have italicised have been generally omitted by those who have quoted me. But they are important. I limited myself to doubting whether the present standards of working-class conditions of life were compatible with the provision of full and continuous employment, failing more economical production by some means or another.

Nevertheless, even though we may still hope to get relief from the progress of science, the accumulation of capital, and more good will and skill, in their respective functions, from workmen and from employers; yet, if the young men entering on their working life continue to exceed in number the old men completing theirs by 100,000 to 250,000 every year, sooner or later knowledge, saving, industry, and skill may be outpaced, and the standard of life decline. I meant to suggest, therefore, that the problem of unemployment is already, in part, a problem of population.

Your obedient servant,

J. M. KEYNES

Except for an article 'Some Aspects of Commodity Markets' (*JMK.*, vol. XII) and a reply to a criticism of the National Mutual's investment policy (*JMK.*, vol. XII), Keynes then remained out of public print until control of *The Nation and Athenaeum* passed in May to the group of Liberals of which he was chairman. Thereafter, he was a regular contributor to that journal, both in longer articles, initially dealing with international affairs, and in a weekly contribution under the general title 'Finance and Investment', often with a more informative sub-title.

From The Nation and Athenaeum, *5 May 1923*

THE RISE IN GILT-EDGED SECURITIES

The prolonged rise in long-dated Government stocks from their low point at the end of 1920 has profoundly modified the rate of interest obtainable. If we take Funding Loan as representing the general movement (Funding Loan, Conversion Loan, and Local Loans Stock all yield nearly the same rate of interest), the interest yield (allowing for redemption) has been as follows:—

	£	s.		£	s.
Jan. 1, 1920	5	8	Jan. 1, 1922	5	6
April 1	5	18	April 1	4	15
July 1	5	18	July 1	4	12
Oct. 1	6	0	Oct. 1	4	16
Jan. 1, 1921	6	2	Jan. 1, 1923	4	14
April 1	5	15	April 1	4	9
July 1	5	14	May 1	4	6
Oct. 1	5	12			

Deducting income tax at 4s. 6d. in the £, the net yield to the investor on these stocks has now fallen as low as £3 7s. per cent, which is within a few shillings of the corresponding net yield on Consols in 1914. That is to say, the return to new savings has practically gone back to its pre-war figure. This seems rather remarkable having regard to the vastly increased supply of Government securities, the shortage of available capital for (e.g.) housing and many other desirable enterprises, and (according to the general belief) the diminished volume of saving. Thus a question arises of the greatest possible interest and importance to every banker and insurance company, and even to most trustees and average investors: Is the movement of recent months an indication of permanent tendency and of a return under peace conditions to a low yield on new savings? Or is it, in part at any rate, merely a phase of the business depression out of which we are just emerging and a consequence of low Bank rate, which is certainly not going to last for ever.

It is very much the fashion just at present to give the first answer. The conventional advice to trustees and others is that the rate of interest may be expected to fall further and that they will do well, therefore, to get into long-dated securities. Yet we cannot help thinking that this may be just the contrary of what is wise. To begin with, the conventional advice is often wrong, because of the natural tendency, in the absence of a reasoned opinion, to believe that what has been happening lately is going on happening for the future; whereas, in truth, every rise in Conversion Loan makes a further rise not more, but less, likely. When, three years ago, long-dated securities were falling in price and beginning to look attractive, that was just the moment when the conventional advisers put it about that short war bonds were the only safe investment.

But there are deeper reasons than this for thinking that the present prices of long-dated securities may be connected with the present phase of the business cycle, and may weaken when, in due course, this phase gives place to the next. We have now had cheap money and low rates of interest on bank deposits for a long enough time to affect the slow-moving mind of the general public. Money rates fell by half during 1921, but bank deposits were undiminished. During 1922, while money became still cheaper, deposits began to diminish steadily. For nine months now, ever since last July, the banks have paid only 1 per cent upon deposits. And at last, this spring, bank deposits have experienced a really sharp fall—£100,000,000 in two months. Probably part of this money has been paid over to the Government in taxes and has enabled the Treasury to redeem debt, and part has flowed into the investment market. A movement on this scale cannot continue long, and, when Bank rate rises again, the deposit account may recover its popularity with the public and will certainly be needed by the banks to finance trade.

If and when trade and business activity revive (and they show many signs of recovery), a direct influence will be felt on the price of long-dated securities. At present stocks of goods of all kinds are low and average prices have not risen materially. Thus firms which are financially strong are not yet in need of all their resources and have temporarily invested many millions in the gilt-edged market. So far the reduction of bankers' deposits has been mainly met by a reduction of the banks' holdings of Treasury bills, which are now only half what they were at the beginning of 1922. Consequently, when their customers again require an expansion of advances, it may be necessary for the banks to sell investments to provide the funds.

To a material extent, therefore, the present strength of the gilt-edged market is due to the ease of the money market and the low Bank rate. Thus it depends for its continuance on a continuance of these conditions. Is such a continuance likely? When we look at what is happening in America it hardly seems so. Conditions in America have been of late about six months ahead of conditions here. Experience there is not encouraging to holders of long-dated securities. In New York gilt-edged securities touched their highest prices last September. Since then they have depreciated about 8 per cent. During the same period similar securities in London have appreciated 9 per cent. Thus within six months relative bond prices in the two centres have changed by 17 per cent. A big volume of buying of bonds by London in New York has been the inevitable result—a factor which may largely explain the fall of the dollar–sterling exchange so early in the year (from 4.72 touched in February to 4.63 this week).

The same situation is apparent in the bill market (sixty to ninety day bills). Last September the average New York rate for these maturities was 4 per cent and the London rate about $2\frac{1}{2}$ per cent—already a dangerous difference in favour of New York. At the present time the New York rate has risen to 5 per cent; that is to say, a difference of $1\frac{1}{2}$ per cent per annum has widened to 3 per cent within the last six months. New York is anxiously watching lest the intense business activity there should flare up into a boom, and the tendency of money with them is upwards rather than downwards. Thus the London position is highly unstable. The sterling exchange is already showing great sensitiveness, and it is unlikely that we can get through the usual autumn pressure with such a disparity of discount rates between London and New York.

The general upshot is that—at present prices, at the present season of the year, at the present phase in the credit cycle, with present conditions in New York—Conversion Loan, Funding Loan, and the like are a highly speculative proposition, unsuitable for timid investors, and especially unsuitable for businesses which will want their money liquid if trade and prices revive.

From The Nation and Athenaeum, *12 May 1923*

FURTHER REFLECTIONS ON GILT-EDGED SECURITIES

Several comments in the City columns of the Press on the contents of this page last week include, amongst much complete or partial agreement, some friendly criticisms. The City Editor of *The Times* points out that the reduction in the supply of Treasury bills may have played a considerable part by driving the banks into longer-dated securities. If this is the case, the effect has probably been produced rather by the banks' customers transferring deposits, against which the banks had held Treasury bills, into long–dated securities than by direct purchase of such securities on the part of the banks themselves. Between January, 1921, and the present time, the banks' deposits have fallen by about £200,000,000. During the same period the banks' advances fell by £100,000,000, and their discounts by £113,000,000. Thus the amount of the reduction of their bill-holdings was almost wholly required to meet the falling off in the excess of deposits over advances.

Moreover, the banks, so far from increasing their investments in recent months, have largely diminished them. Between August, 1921, and August, 1922, the banks' investments were rising, but since last August they have fallen by more than £60,000,000. The complete figures are worth giving in detail:—

Nine clearing banks (£000,000s)

	Deposits	Advances	Excess of deposits
Jan. 1921	1810	845	965
Jan. 1922	1826	752	1074
July 1922	1730	721	1009
October 1922	1686	724	962
Jan. 1923	1693	726	967
March 1923	1596	742	854
April 1923	1606	744	862

Thus the banks have for investment £212,000,000 less than at the beginning of 1922, the other side of which is shown by the following figures:—

	Discounts	Investments	Total
Jan. 1921	362	317	679
Jan. 1922	440	333	773
July 1922	335	386	721
Oct. 1922	309	370	679
Jan. 1923	320	358	678
March 1923	250	333	583
April 1923	249	327	576

Thus whilst since the beginning of the year the public have been taking their money off deposit for investment, the banks have been busy turning their investments out. The public have been buying what the banks have been selling.

In arguing along these lines, however, one is liable to overlook that the Government can only pay off Treasury bills out of the receipts of taxation or new bond issues. Thus the deposits lost by the banks, in excess of the amount used to pay off the banks' own advances and to buy investments which the banks are selling, must have been spent, directly or indirectly, either in paying taxes or in buying the new bond issues, leaving nothing over to compete for pre-existing bond issues. The word 'deflation' used in this connection is perplexingly ambiguous. If the gradual replacement of Treasury bills by Treasury bonds and other longer-dated Government issues is called deflation, Mr McKenna has constantly proclaimed, from his vantage post of knowledge, that this policy has actually retarded the rise in the gilt-edged market. On the other hand, one must accept the argument of *The Times* that the reduction in the supply of Treasury bills has been a factor in keeping money cheap, which in turn is largely responsible for the strength of the gilt-edged market.

Perhaps a complicated situation can be summed up like this: a relatively small excess of demand over supply for long-dated British Government securities, due to the lack of competing uses for money has been able with the assistance of favourable sentiment and the unattractive yields on short-dated securities, to drive up their price. But if this is right, the tendency may be rapidly reversed as soon as competing uses for money revive and the yield on short-dated securities improves. In short, we get back to the same conclusion as before, that the prices of long-dated securities will find it hard to stand up against a revival of enterprise and a higher Bank rate.

It must be admitted that this argument leaves open one contingency, in the event of which long-dated securities may continue to rise in price, namely, a prolonged period of stagnation and lack of confidence such as was experienced in the 1890s. If loans for foreign governments and home industrials are both distrusted, the rate of interest obtainable on British Government securities may remain artificially low.

These broad movements are hard to analyse correctly. More simple-minded correspondents ask—if they are not to buy Conversion Loan and the like, what *ought* they to buy? On the assumption that they are limited to trustee securities, there is really only one answer—5 per cent National War Bonds, due in 1927 and 1928. These investments, allowing for a small loss on redemption (they stand at about $106\frac{5}{8}$ and will be paid off at 105), yield a shade more than Conversion and Funding Loan, namely, about $4\frac{3}{8}$ per cent. They have only shared very slightly in the recent rise, and should not fall much even if the gilt-edged market has a set-back. Incidentally, they have the advantage of a continuing option of convertibility into 5 per cent War Loan (at the rate of £$105\frac{1}{4}$ War Loan for each £100 War Bond); an option which costs next to nothing at present prices, since with War Loan at 101, the amount of War Loan into which £100 War Bond is convertible is worth £$106\frac{3}{8}$. Thus in order to prefer Conversion Loan and the like to these War Bonds, it is necessary to be fairly confident that there will not be a revival of trade between now and 1927 sufficient to bring Conversion Loan *at any time* materially below its present level. Many authorities believe that Conversion Loan is on an uninterrupted progress to a 4 per cent basis, which would mean a price of $87\frac{1}{2}$ as compared with the present price of nearly 81. It would be rash to deny the possibility of this. But Conversion Loan will be poised between two opposing sets of influences, and might just as well fall by $6\frac{1}{2}$ points as rise by that amount.

Those investors for whom stability of money income over a large number of years to come is of paramount importance can properly ignore these arguments. But there are just as many for whom stability of capital value is important. Amongst these, firms holding more money than they can use in the business for the time being must certainly be included; and for them War Bonds seem clearly the right alternative.

All readers of *The Nation* who hold 5 per cent National War Bonds (3rd series) due September, 1923, ought to do something about it immediately. Owing to these bonds having an option of conversion into 5 per cent War Loan, they stand at present at an artificial price. This option, however, must be exercised at latest within a fortnight of June 1st next. Holders should, therefore, either sell and deliver their bonds before the option right expires, or exercise the option themselves. Otherwise they will incur a certain loss of about $4\frac{1}{2}$ per cent. The present price of the bonds is $106\frac{5}{8}$ *plus* accrued interest. On September 1st next they will be paid off at 102. It is an unusual pleasure to be able to give a piece of financial advice which will almost certainly benefit some reader of *The Nation* and will quite certainly be right!

From The Nation and Athenaeum, *19 May 1923*

THE FOREIGN EXCHANGES AND THE SEASONS

The dollar-sterling exchange merely compares the value of the dollar and of the pound. The value of the dollar is what it will buy in the United States. The value of the pound is what it will buy in England. Therefore the rate of exchange depends on the level of prices in America compared with the level of prices here. That, in a nutshell, is the modern theory of exchanges, which perplexes nine-tenths of the world under the honorific designation of purchasing-power-parity.

In theory and even in practice there are some refinements to mention. But if we are comparing one year with another they are comparatively unimportant. Ever since the Armistice the theory has *worked* on the whole amazingly. If you draw curves of the actual rates of exchange between the United States, England, France, and Italy, and then another set of curves showing the ratios of the price levels in these countries, you find that the two are seldom far apart and always tend together again after every divergence. For example, between the United States and England the actual rate of exchange and the ratio of the price levels in the two countries have been within 1 per cent of one another in September–November, 1919; March–April, 1920; April, 1921; September 1921; January–June, 1921; and February, 1923. If, however, we are comparing, not one year with another, but one week with another, or one month with another, there are two other influences which are very important.

The first is *speculation*. A country's exchange is more sensitive than its price level to what the world thinks is going to happen but has not happened yet. Speculators may sell or buy a country's money because they *anticipate* that it is going to fall or rise in value. But this influence obviously cannot last very long. Speculators can only cause the exchange to rise or fall at an earlier date than it would have done otherwise. For they have to reverse their transaction in due course, buying back or selling out as the case may be; so that, whether the thing which they anticipated has happened or not, their influence washes out sooner or later. Generally sooner rather than later, because the mass of speculators take short views and lose heart very quickly if there is any delay in what they anticipated. The various Reparation Conferences of recent years have caused the most ridiculous fluctuations in the franc exchange, but the lasting influence of the speculation to which they have given rise has been absolutely *nil*. Most people vastly exaggerate the effect of speculation on the course of exchange. Its momentary effect is often so sensational that we forget what a fleeting affair it is—worth three months hence about as much as a leader in today's *Daily Mail*. It is only really important on the very rare occasions on which it precipitates a panic—that is to say, imitative action on a large scale by numbers of people who are not speculators at all, but are just terror stricken.

The other is the *season* of the year. This influence is as much under-estimated by the public as that of speculation is exaggerated. Sensible speculators ought to observe a close season for shooting at the franc just as much as at other high-flying birds. Economical tourists will find it, as a quite general rule, decidedly cheaper to travel in France and Italy in the summer and autumn than in the spring—quite apart from the fact that these countries are always much colder at Easter than is generally supposed. If France had walked into the Ruhr in July instead of in January, the franc exchange might have told quite a different tale.

Why is this? It is mainly due to the revolution of the earth round the sun. Western Europe buys from the rest of the Northern Hemisphere the fruitful produce which the soil yields in the late summer and autumn. If her merchants are to get what they want on the best terms and of the right quality they must buy a considerable proportion just after harvest, when the agriculturalist is selling it. Somewhat earlier than this—some time between June and August—they begin to make their financial preparations. Simultaneously, America tends to call in her floating balances from abroad to help her in financing the crop movements. Thus in the summer and autumn Europe owes America money which she can only pay off gradually over the average of the year. This has always been so—before the War just as much as now. But when the exchanges were fixed within narrow limits, by virtue of the convertibility of the various national currencies into gold, international finance found on easy terms the credit required to tide over the seasonal difficulty. But now, when no one can say for certain what sterling, francs or lire are going to be worth in terms of dollars six months hence, it is not worth anyone's while to run the risk of supplying it except for an expectation of considerable profit; which expectation can only be provided by the European currencies, which are being pressed for sale, falling to a price decidedly below what, on balance is thought to be the probable price six months hence. Recently these expectations have been, on the whole, pretty well realised in practice, and international finance has pocketed its reward for the risk it has run. Perhaps this favourable experience may lead to its being prepared to do the business a bit cheaper this year, which would mean a less violent seasonal depression of the Western European exchanges. But the volume of risk-carrying required is so large, and the effect of affairs like the Ruhr is so upsetting and makes the calculation of risk so precarious, that we may possibly see this summer a fairly sharp movement of the usual kind. If the Ruhr business were to be settled, that, of course, might make a considerable difference; and short-range speculators may make themselves felt for a moment whenever the rumours in the newspaper suggest that something is in the air.

In 1919 the European exchanges fell heavily as a result of the Inter-Allied credits coming to an end. In 1922 there was a definite recovery of sterling, and this year there has been a definite deterioration of the franc for obvious reasons. But the following table shows how largely recurrent the movements have been:—

Percentage of dollar parity

	Sterling		Francs		Lire	
Aug.–July	Lowest	Highest	Lowest	Highest	Lowest	Highest
1919–20	69	88	31	66	22	56
1920–21	69	82	30	45	18	29
1921–22	73	92	37	48	20	28
1922–23*	90	97	29	41	20	27

* August–May.

During the past three years, francs and lire have been at their best in April and May, and at their worst between October and December. Sterling has not been quite so punctual in its movements, the best point of the year falling somewhere between March and June, and the worst between August and November. It will be seen that we are just approaching what has been hitherto the turning point of the year, and it will be interesting to watch what happens.

From The Nation and Athenaeum, *26 May 1923*

FINANCE AND INVESTMENT

Investors have short memories, and it is not easy to remember just what proportion the recent slight slump in industrial securities bears to the previous rise. For such a comparison the index number of twenty representative industrial ordinary stocks, published weekly by *The Economic Review*, is very useful. It tells the following story:—

1919	Jan. 1	148	1922	Oct. 14	114
	Nov. 1	173		Dec. 30	119
1920	Mar. 1	187	1923	Feb. 3	122
	July 1	149		Mar. 3	129
	Dec. 1	130		April 7	130
1921	Oct. 20	91		April 28	138
	Dec. 31	100		May 11	133
1922	April 1	103		May 18	132
	July 15	112			

In the past week there has been a further fall of about one point. Thus the reaction has merely obliterated the big improvement between April 7th and April 28th, and has lost very little of the progressive improvement of nearly 50 per cent since the low point of October, 1921. The latter also shows how very far off we still are from the boom conditions of 1920. We are not yet back at the level prevailing immediately after the Armistice.

The reaction in the United States began a little earlier,—in the middle of March; and has progressed rather further. Indeed, the downward movement on the London Stock Exchange has not been by any means an isolated phenomenon. Staple commodities, of which the price is sensitive,—copper, tin, rubber, cotton, jute and linseed, for example—have suffered at the same time quite a substantial fall. Memories of the slump are still so vivid that markets are unduly nervous, and everyone is on the look-out to avoid losses like those of 1920–21. The Ruhr situation is also extremely damaging to confidence. Nevertheless, the underlying conditions do not seem to be compatible with any serious set-back. Money is cheap and stocks of many commodities are in short supply. The business world is borrowing too little rather than too much. A renewal in due course of the upward movement is therefore the more probable alternative.

We are reaching the season of the year when the first forecasts of the harvest prospects begin to appear. In India a large crop has been just gathered. The Argentine crop harvested at the beginning of the year has also been large,—20 per cent better than last year. The Australian crop, however,—though this is not a big factor in the situation—was only moderate. The prospects in North America, to judge from the acreage and the condition of the winter-sown wheat, are fairly good, but are not unlikely to show some decrease on last year, when the Canadian crop realised a record figure. The most striking and fortunate feature is the unusually good promise of the European crops. In France the acreage has been increased by 10 per cent, and the condition is very good. In Italy the acreage is only slightly better, but the condition is brilliant. Throughout Germany, Austria, Hungary, and Jugo-Slavia the prospects are satisfactory to good. It is too early to say much about Russia. But there is more land under wheat than a year ago, and the outlook is promising. M. Krassin has published an article forecasting a considerable export surplus next autumn. The only important exception to these favourable conditions is in Roumania, where there is a serious reduction in acreage, mainly due to a huge falling off in Transylvania, and it does not appear at present as though there would be much surplus this year for export. Our own crops are rather backward. There was not enough frost in the winter and too much cold lately. But whilst British farmers can never be cheerful, they need never despair. Anything can happen.

From The Nation and Athenaeum, *2 June 1923*

TRUSTEE INVESTMENTS—HOME, COLONIAL, AND INDIAN

A note of caution was sounded in this column a few weeks ago [above, p. 86] about the merits of long-dated British Government stocks, such as Conversion Loan, as compared with short-dated stocks, such as National War Bonds. We pointed out that the latter offered less risk to any investor for whom stability of capital value was an important consideration. Nevertheless, if we are comparing not British Government stocks amongst themselves, but British Government stocks with other trustee investments, there are strong arguments for sticking to our own home securities. It is generally a good rule for an investor, having settled on the class of security he prefers—long-dated, or short-dated bonds, trustee investments or foreign government bonds, or bank shares, or oil shares, or investment trusts, or industrials, debentures, preference or ordinary, whatever it may be—to buy only the best within that category. The extra yield obtainable on the second-best seldom compensates adequately for the increased risk and diminished marketability. This is not less true in the gilt-edged than in other markets.

The extra yield obtainable just now on Indian and colonial stocks is too small to justify the investor in preferring them to home stocks. It is not prudent for those who take long views to overlook either the precarious element in the Indian situation or the great weight of foreign debt accumulating in Australia in proportion to population. The slump in India stocks some little time ago may have been overdone; but the subsequent recovery has left no adequate margin to cover contingencies. And on Australian and other colonial stocks the extra yield is so trifling as to do little more than compensate for their inferior marketability. The following comparisons exhibit the present situation, all the yields being calculated to allow approximately for accrued interest and for loss or profit on redemption:—

Long-dated stocks

	Price	Yield £ s. d.		
3½% Conversion Loan (after 1961)	80½	4	7	6
4% New South Wales (1942–62)	91	4	10	0
4% New Zealand (1943–63)	92½	4	8	0
4% Victoria (1940–60)	91¼	4	9	0
4% South Africa (1943–63)	91	4	9	0
3½% India Stock (after 1931)	71½	4	19	0

For the period between the dates given in brackets there is an *option* to the borrowing governments to redeem which they are free to exercise if it benefits themselves, and not to exercise if it would benefit the investor. Thus, in the case of the colonial stocks this option *against* the investor for a period of twenty years outweighs the advantage of definite redemption some forty years hence. Surely Conversion Loan is far preferable to any of these alternatives amongst long-dated stocks. Or if a somewhat higher yield is required, Bank of England stock yields, on the assumption of a continuance of half-yearly 6 per cent dividends, which the Governor's speech at the last Court seemed decidedly to encourage, about £4 15s. 6d. If a slight element of uncertainty is not disliked, is not Bank stock to be very much preferred to India Stock at the present level of prices?

Intermediate stocks

	Price	Yield £ s. d.		
5% War Loan (1929–47)	101⅛	4	15	6
5% Victoria (1932–42)	101½	4	17	6
5% New South Wales (1932–40)	102⅔	4	16	6
5% South Australia (1932–42)	102¾	4	16	0

Here again the British Government security seems the cheaper at the price, even allowing for the extra three years' run on the colonial stocks before the option to redeem operates. It is not worth while to leave the straightforward course of home Government stocks for a shilling or two per cent.

Stocks redeemable within ten years

	Price	Yield £ s. d.		
5% National War Bonds (1929)	106¼	4	10	6
5½% Treasury Bonds (1930)	105	4	13	0
4% New Zealand (1929)	95¼	4	16	0
5¾% New South Wales (1922–32)	101	5	15	0
5½% India (1932)	103½	5	5	6

For these maturities the extra yield on Indian and colonial stocks is much more adequate. For example, 15s. per cent extra is obtainable on the comparable Indian security, as against 10s. per cent extra on the long-dated stocks. Moreover, the risk attaching to India stocks is more likely to eventuate after 1932 than before that date; so that there are some attractions in a ten-year Indian security yielding five guineas per cent. Nevertheless, in this, as in the other categories, there is not really enough inducement to tempt the ordinary investor outside his home Government stocks.

The prices at which new colonial and Indian loans have been

floated during the past month indicate, however, that the ordinary investor *is* tempted. New Zealand has just borrowed £4,000,000 at £4 12s. 7d.; and India £20,000,000 at £5 4s. 4d. The New Zealand loan stands at a trifling discount, and the other at a premium. Part of the explanation is probably to be found in the preference of many investors for new issues which can be purchased by filling up a form cut out of the newspapers without the interposition of banks or brokers. Immense numbers of small investors have no regular broker, and do not know the address of one. This big gap in our investment system is difficult to fill, yet requires some remedy. The brokerless investor may be reminded, however, that for any family which has not yet acquired its full quota Savings Certificates are still by far the biggest bargains in the gilt-edged market.

The 6 per cent cumulative income stock of the New Town Trust, redeemable at 110 not before 1933 or after 1945, of which the prospectus has been published in *The Nation and Athenæum* (May 19th), and which is still open for subscription, makes it appeal not to the ordinary investor, but to those anxious to support Garden City developments. The company has been formed to work in association with Welwyn Garden City Ltd., which has already secured substantial success. The board of directors receive no remuneration. The Trust holds £20,000 shares and debentures of the Welwyn Garden City Company, and its purpose is the general development of the new Garden City, particularly in connection with the farming of the permanent rural belt through an agricultural guild. £34,082 of the income stock has been already issued, and also £12,771 of ordinary capital. This stock has speculative features without offering speculative rewards; but investment in it will assist an interesting social experiment.

Keynes used his 'Finance and Investment' columns of 9 and 16 June for comments on the situation in Germany and the League of Nations loan to

Austria.[6] He then took a break from *The Nation* to work on his *Tract on Monetary Reform* [*JMK*, vol. IV], only returning to its columns on 7 July.

From The Nation and Athenaeum, *7 July 1923*

IS CREDIT ABUNDANT?—THE GRAND TRUNK RAILWAY

In spite of a low Bank rate, it is doubtful whether credit is really abundant, or adequate to carry on the business that offers at the present level of prices. Indeed, there is some indication that a secret process of deflation—surely to be regretted with trade as discouraged and unemployment as high as they are now—still continues. The most fundamental figure of our banking system is that of the 'other deposits' at the Bank of England, because these furnish the basis upon which the other banks, by an almost unvarying rule, build up their advances and their deposits. The banks lend in the form of advances to their customers between 40 and 50 per cent of their deposits, and they keep a trifle over 11 per cent of their deposits in cash and at the Bank of England. Unless they are armed with deposits at the Bank of England, their hands are tied, however cheap money may look, and however eager borrowers may be. Now the outstanding fact is that the 'other deposits' at the Bank of England, which averaged £128,000,000 in the first quarter of last year, £118,000,000 in the second quarter, and £112,000,000 in the third and fourth quarters, have been steady for the past five months at an average of £108,000,000. £20,000,000 off the other deposits may not look big; but it means that the banks must bring down their deposits by £180,000,000 and their advances by £90,000,000. These reductions have been fully realised; although the banks have been able latterly to keep their advances about steady by severely reducing their investments and bill holdings. The figures show that it cannot be easy for the banks to find resources for additional loans. It is impossible to say precisely why the 'other deposits' of the Bank of England have fallen, because the

---

[6] See *JMK*, vol. XVIII, pp. 161–5, 176–9.

Bank works in secret and does not explain itself. But whether it is deliberate or accidental, this deflation of at least 10 per cent can have done no good, and must share with political developments in Europe the responsibility for the weakening of the trade revival and the severe continuing unemployment.

The settlement of the claims of the United States for the payment of the expenses of its army of occupation, amounting to about £50,000,000, has been scarcely noticed in the English Press. According to the *New Republic* the sum due is to be paid in twelve annual instalments;—for four years the United States is to receive a quarter of the cash paid by Germany after the costs of the Allied armies of occupation have been met, and after four years the American claim will be a first charge on the cash receipts. After the expiry of four years the arrears are to carry interest.

Only now is there a Bill before the German Reichstag releasing trustees from the obligation to invest in fixed-interest bearing securities. The result of this obligation, intended presumably to secure safety, has been the total loss of all trust funds. The result of compelling any class of persons to invest solely in titles to legal-tender money is, sooner or later, in almost any country—to judge from past history—to deprive that class of a large part of their fortunes. Indeed, modern legislation governing trustee investments could be regarded, if we take a long view, as a provision to secure the gradual disappearance of inheritances and to avoid the foundation of perpetual fortunes.

Not that other types of investment are immune from disaster. The history of the Grand Trunk of Canada is a lesson against investing in public utilities abroad. It is within the power of any government, by means of suitable legislation, to render valueless an investment in a public utility; and if the proprietors are absentee, the temptation to do so is considerable. In this particular case, however, the argument that the property is in fact altogether valueless has not completely convinced anyone outside Canada. There are two particular weaknesses in it which are worth pointing out. The incompetence of the late management is adduced as a reason for the worthlessness of the property. But this fact, precisely because it accounts for the absence of profits in the past, is, inasmuch as it is *remediable*, a bull point for the future. The worse the railway has been managed hitherto, the more hope for it in better hands. The other point is of a different kind. The arbitrators who judged the property to have no value seem to have believed that this result followed if, on the evidence, it was highly improbable that it would ever pay a dividend. This is not sound reasoning. Even if the odds were ten to one against a dividend being paid, still the property is not valueless; for a one-tenth chance of a dividend is worth something. No one could say, considering the future possibilities of increased population and prosperity in Canada, that the odds are more than a hundred to one against the first preference shares ever earning a dividend. But if not, then these shares have *some* value. The case of the Canadian Government must be based entirely on the argument that the liabilities of the Grand Trunk to the debenture holders of the Grand Trunk Pacific exceed the value of the Grand Trunk itself, and on the argument that it is within the power of the Canadian Government to render any railway valueless by its freight-rate legislation. It must not be forgotten, however, that the stockholders accepted arbitration, and naturally have no redress merely because the result of the arbitration is arguable. Apart from questions of equity, the attitude of Canada might be of doubtful prudence, —unless the country is prepared to be relatively independent in future of the type of foreign investor whose feelings and pockets are now suffering outrage,—if experience did not show abundantly how short memories are.

The path of the average investor is a miserable one. There is no financial reform more needed than a new and better organisation for taking reasonable care of ordinary savings.

On 5 July 1923, in the light of sterling's weakness on the foreign exchanges, the Bank of England raised Bank rate from 3 to 4 per cent. Keynes did not comment on the change at the first opportunity, *The Nation* for 7 July, but he turned to the issue the next week.

From The Nation and Athenaeum, *14 July 1923*

BANK RATE AT FOUR PER CENT

The raising of the Bank rate to 4 per cent is one of the most misguided movements of that indicator which have ever occurred. Trade is discouraged and declining; prices are falling slightly; employment is very bad; and the political situation is such as to damp down enterprise and hold everyone back from entering into new business. It is a moment when the business world requires every scrap of stimulus and encouragement which can be given it. There is *no necessary* reason why disturbances on the Continent need cause a million or two of Englishmen to stand idle. The present state of affairs is due quite as much, indeed much more, to depression in home trade than to loss of business with Europe. Our job is to do our best to free ourselves from the psychological reactions of foreign politics, which are found, in any case, to produce very considerable evils here also, and resolutely to keep our own business going as best we can. This is the moment which the Bank of England chooses deliberately to add one more discouragement, one more warning sign to anyone who contemplates new business that he had better wait a bit and keep his hands in his pockets, even if it means that his workmen must keep their hands in their pockets, too.

What is the explanation? It is not the practice of the Bank of England to give explanations. But there is not much doubt that the explanation is to be found in the fall of the dollar exchange (not at all unusual at this time of year) of about 2 per cent. That is to say, the Bank of England think it more important to raise the dollar exchange a few points than to encourage flagging trade. They do this under the influence of the Report of the Cunliffe Committee, a document written several months before the Armistice, necessarily without any knowledge of all the extraordinary post-war developments, and not containing a single reference to stability of prices and employment. The revision of this Report in the light of subsequent events is becoming a matter of first-rate political importance.

If the rise of the dollar were due to a rise in British prices, that is, to the depreciation of sterling, an increase in the Bank rate would be an appropriate remedy. But this is not the case. Many influences are at work,—a tendency of dollar prices to fall, the relative rates of interest here and in New York, the usual seasonal pressure, and political unrest. In so far as the fall of dollar prices is responsible, the dollar-sterling exchange *ought* to fall if, as Mr Baldwin said last week, we want to keep British prices stable. In so far as temporary transfers of funds are in question, by speculators on political prospects, or to meet seasonal requirements, the matter will cure itself sooner or later, and ought to be remedied, if the movement is severe enough to call for remedy, by the Bank's shipping gold or by the Treasury's postponing its purchases of dollars to meet interest on the debt. We are left, therefore, with the difference between the rates of interest in London and New York as the sole justification.

This difference is certainly *one* factor in the fall of the exchange. In this column, more than two months ago, [above, p. 83] we were amongst the first to point out the probable effect of the disparity on the dollar exchange. When the exchange is fixed within narrow limits, as it was before the War, relative interest rates are of paramount importance of determining the volume of short-period remittances,—a fact upon which the pre-war theory of Bank rate was largely based. When the exchange is not far off parity, as was the case earlier this year, this influence is still important. But with every movement of the exchange downwards its effect is diminished; and, as we have seen on several occasions in the recent past, a comparatively moderate fall in the exchange is sufficient to weaken the connection between the London and New York short-loan markets. That this must be so is made plain by straightforward arithmetic. If interest rates are raised 1 per cent per annum, the borrower for three months pays an additional $\frac{1}{4}$ per cent. At the present rate of exchange this is a little more than one American cent in the £ sterling; more exactly, the effect of the increased interest rate to the borrower would be counterbalanced by a movement of the exchange from $4\cdot57\frac{1}{4}$ to $4\cdot56$ between the date of borrowing and the date of repayment. A fluctuation of this amount is often experienced in a single day; a movement of ten times this amount has occurred in the past three months, and may very likely occur, one way or the other, in the next three months. Thus a trifling movement in the exchange would wipe out the advantage or disadvantage of paying 1 per cent per annum less or more for loans. The alleged American borrowing in London cannot be a pure interest transaction, but must be mainly an exchange speculation, either outright or in anticipation of the proceeds of sterling trade bills normally negotiated by American banks later in the year.

The effect on the exchange of raising the Bank rate at the present time is, in fact, limited to two influences. In so far as it is taken to indicate a determined policy on the part of the Bank of England to hold up the dollar exchange, it may have a temporary effect by inducing short-period speculators against sterling to close their positions. If such action is worth while—which is always doubtful, because the effect of such speculation cancels out over quite a short period—the same result can be achieved, without a bad effect on home trade, by shipping, or threatening to ship, gold, with the idea of buying it back again when the reaction comes.

The remaining influence, which is the only real and lasting one, brings us back to where we started. The paramount significance of an increase in the Bank rate must lie in its effect on sterling prices. Its real influence depends upon its leading to some curtailment of credit and some fall of sterling prices. It cannot be right to raise the Bank rate in present-day conditions,—which differ vitally from pre-war conditions, in that our currency is inconvertible,—*unless we deliberately desire to bring about a curtailment of credit, and to arrest a rising tendency or to produce a falling tendency in sterling prices.* This is not the case. The day before Bank rate was raised the Prime Minister and Chancellor of the Exchequer had rightly committed himself [*sic*] to the contrary. The Bank of England, acting under the influence of a narrow and obsolete doctrine, has made a grave mistake.

Keynes's article was the subject of extensive critical comment elsewhere in the Press. He dealt with his critics in the next issue of *The Nation*.

From The Nation and Athenaeum, *21 July 1923*

BANK RATE AND STABILITY OF PRICES— A REPLY TO CRITICS

The articles in *The Nation and Athenaeum* on this subject have been widely quoted and have succeeded in creating a lively and useful controversy. Even the *Daily Mail* has done us the honour of a leading article entitled 'The New Suicide Club', the main point of which is that the dollar exchange should be as high as possible, because in that case the burden of the American debt will be as low as possible—a point to which we will return in a later issue. The *Manchester Guardian* heads its comments 'An Inflationist View'—a charge which anti-inflationists can, I suppose hardly expect to escape. If a low Bank rate helps trade, why, the *Manchester Guardian* asks, should not the present writer 'go farther and advocate a 1 per cent Bank rate and Government inflation to assist in providing credit for industry? Where exactly does he propose to draw the line?' He draws it at inflation. Why not? Rising prices stimulate trade unhealthily; falling prices depress trade injuriously. If prices had continued to rise sharply, as was the tendency earlier in the year, an increase in the Bank rate would have been perfectly right. A policy of price stability is the very opposite of a policy of permanently cheap money. During the last boom the present writer preached vehemently in favour of very dear money, months before the Bank of England acted. But when employment is very bad, enterprise disheartened, and prices with a falling tendency, *that* is not the moment to raise the Bank rate.

Some of our gentler critics, notably *The Economist*, agree with us in our general contention, but point out that a 4 per cent Bank rate is really a very mild measure, since the rates at which most bank advances are made do not follow Bank rate downwards below 4 per cent, and are therefore unaffected by the recent increase (although they would feel the full effect of a further rise to 5 per cent). There is much force in this argument. In so far as raising the Bank rate has no consequences, it will do no harm. A four per cent Bank rate is not nearly so injurious as a five per cent rate. If the recent movement is not to be regarded as an indication of a policy which may soon require five per cent for its maintenance, but is, so to speak, a casual act, it need not, we agree, be taken too seriously. Nevertheless, even a four per cent rate does have consequences—psychological reactions which cause enterprise to hesitate, dearer rates for trade bills, and marked discouragement to new issues, all of which depress trade.

One apologist for the Bank—the City Editor of the *Morning Post*—has discovered a reason for its action which had not occurred to us, namely 'enormous speculative positions' in gilt-edged stocks.* The object of the Bank, according to this

---

* He did not support us, however, when, more than two months ago, we suggested in this column that long-dated Government securities might be standing rather too high.

authority, was to make these speculators unload, this step being required because they were absorbing funds 'required for trade purposes'. 'Enormous benefit,' the argument goes on, 'has accrued to speculators in gilt-edged stocks, who have been able to borrow money on such terms as to secure very large profits arising both out of appreciation in capital value and the difference between the interest payable on the stock purchased and the rate of interest paid to the bankers.' Earlier in the year, bull speculation in this market was certainly very profitable; but the argument overlooks the fact that for two months before the Bank rate was raised, these bulls, in so far as they exist, had been steadily losing money. Moreover, it is cruel for those who have been predicting week by week that Conversion Loan was going to rise many points further, to turn round in this way on those who have taken their advice. If the object of the Bank was really to bring about a slump in the gilt-edged market, it has scored a modest success. It is possible, however, to agree that there has been a great deal of unwise investment of temporary funds in long-dated securities, especially by the financially stronger of our industrial concerns, without thinking it worth while to raise the Bank rate merely to force these holders out.†

Many of our contemporaries, however, have shared our views in greater or less degree—*The Spectator*, *The Saturday Review*, *The Investors' Chronicle*, *The Economist* (on essentials), the *Westminster Gazette* (with an admirably clear argument), for example; the weight of opinion making it clear that, whilst a four per cent Bank rate may, by itself, have only limited consequences, the policy behind it will, if it is persisted in at the cost of a further rise, provoke a widespread hostile criticism. Indeed, so long as unemployment is a matter of general political importance, it is impossible that Bank rate should be regarded, as it used to be, as the secret *peculium* of the Pope and Cardinals of the City.

† *The Economist* goes further than the *Morning Post* and thinks that the object of the Bank was to bring about speculative liquidation of all types of securities, and to shake markets generally—rather a savage procedure in view of the fact that these markets had been drooping and shaky for some little time.

The criticism of *The Nation*'s articles set forth in the City columns of *The Times* was perhaps the most interesting of all, because of the divided mind between the old school and the new, very representative of the state of mind of the City generally, which these comments show. *The Times* begins by agreeing that the object of monetary policy is to keep the price level stable,— which is our main point. In the next paragraph it perceives that this might mean abandoning the gold standard, a step which would be 'too complicated and hazardous'. It continues that 'the official policy is to restore the old gold parity'; that 'the penal monetary measures' which such a policy might require are objectionable; and that 'that, at any rate, is no part of our present monetary policy,'—which finally boxes the compass. *The Times* account of the matter might seem comical, if it were not such an accurate reflection of the actual state of affairs. It used to be our policy to restore the gold standard. It has become our policy to keep prices stable. We have taken on the new doctrine, without, as yet, discarding the old, and when they are incompatible we are torn between the two. Fortunately, we cannot but feel, reading its comments carefully, that *The Times*, like *The Economist*, is really with us on the main issue. We attacked the grandmother of Threadneedle Street, which was very improper, and we must expect a slight peppering. But *The Times*, like nearly everyone else, shrinks from the practical measures which the old doctrine would require from true believers.

The next week saw him turn to another comment by the City Editor of *The Times*.

From The Nation and Athenaeum, *28 July 1923*

THE MEASURE OF DEFLATION—AN INQUIRY INTO INDEX NUMBERS

The City Editor of *The Times* writes:—' As prices have remained stable within the past eighteen months, it is difficult to appreciate the force of many arguments employed by those who are avowedly in favour of stabilisation.' This statement is nearly true if we take, for example, the Board of Trade index of wholesale prices as our measure of stability. But this is not the whole story. The following figures show that the raising of the Bank rate is only one more step in a policy of deflation which has been silently but steadily pursued for some time,—a policy which is partly responsible for the failure of trade and employment in this country to keep pace with the revival in the United States during the first half of this year. The following attempt at a rough statistical estimate indicates that the actual deflation of purchasing power during the past eighteen months has amounted to about 10 per cent.

	(1) Bank of England private deposits*	(2) Aggregate note issue*	(3) Average of (1) and (2)*	(4) Clearing bank deposits†
1922				
1st Quarter	100	100	100	100
2nd Quarter	92	99	96	97
3rd Quarter	88	98	93	94
4th Quarter	88	96	92	94
1923				
1st Quarter	91	93	92	92
2nd Quarter	84	95	90	90

* Average of middle of each month.
† Average of end of each month.

The Bank of England's private deposits and the note issue comprise between them the available 'cash', upon the basis of which credit can be created. The clearing banks' deposits are the measure of the credit actually created. There is, as there should be, a fairly close agreement between the two, justifying 10 per cent as the best available estimate of the amount by which purchasing power has been deflated.

What has been happening to prices in the meantime? The index numbers of wholesale prices have only fallen slightly. But, as stated above, these figures do not give a complete account of the situation. The cost of food (and the cost of living generally), and also the level of wages, both of which have an effect on the demand for purchasing power out of proportion to the weight given them in index numbers of wholesale prices, have fallen much more sharply:—

	Board of Trade wholesale prices	Food prices	Wages
1922			
1st Quarter	100	100	100
2nd Quarter	99	100	94
3rd Quarter	97	95	88
4th Quarter	96	92	83
1923			
1st Quarter	98	90	82
2nd Quarter	99	87	82

The cost-of-living index number has moved practically with food prices.

The effective demand for purchasing power depends partly on the volume of trade and partly on the level of prices and wages. The above figures indicate that the latter, so far from being stable, have fallen probably as much as 10 per cent— perhaps more. If this is correct the volume of trade must have increased somewhat,—a conclusion which is also in accordance with the direct evidence of the employment figures and other data. The volume of employment, for example, has risen nearly 5 per cent, whilst other tests, such as output of coal, iron and steel, shipbuilding commenced, and tonnage of goods entering and leaving British ports yield much higher figures of improvement. On the whole, if we are to risk a generalisation, it might be fairly accurate to say that during the past eighteen months, purchasing power has been deflated 10 per cent, the effective level of prices and wages has fallen 10 per cent, and the activity of trade and employment throughout the country has increased by 5 per cent or more.

This represents a gallant effort on the part of business, in face of a falling price level and curtailed credit. But it has seemed latterly, with the added discouragement of the European situation that the struggle is too severe. The above figures indicate that the Bank of England has succeeded in restricting credit to such an extent that no further increase of business activity is possible without a further fall in the level of prices and wages, —a process which necessarily discourages new business, so long as it is going on.

We have had, during the period under review, the rare combination of a falling price level and expanding business, —both of them are indicative that an expansion of credit is required. Nevertheless the Bank of England has been using its secret and enormous powers to *contract* credit by no less an amount than 10 per cent. No one, least of all the writer of this page, will deny the evil influence on trade of the Ruhr occupation. But this is an *extra* reason for not discouraging trade in other ways. If the Labour Party are interested in remediable causes of unemployment, they would do well to cast their eyes more frequently and searchingly than they have done hitherto in the direction of monetary policy.

We should like to support most strongly the recommendation of an admirable article by Dr E. C. Snow in *The Manchester Guardian Commercial* that there should be an authoritative inquiry into the methods of compilation of index numbers. Some of those which are most widely quoted are open to serious criticism, if not for all purposes, at least for many of those to which they are in fact applied. The method of compilation ought to depend upon the precise purpose for which the index number is to be used to an extent which is seldom understood. Two recent events reinforce his argument. The dockers' strike was partly due to lack of confidence in the official cost-of-living index number. The Board of Trade index number of the wholesale cost of food rose from 147 in May to 153 in June; whilst the *Statist* (Sauerbeck) index number, also of the wholesale cost of food, fell from 163 in May to 154 in June. If one of the two most familiar index numbers rises 9 points and the other falls 9 points during the same month for the same limited category of articles, what is one to say? In 1887 the British Association appointed a Committee of Inquiry into the subject, the report of which remained for many years the leading authority. Perhaps the subject is better suited for inquiry by learned bodies than by the Government. Should not the British Association, the Royal Statistical Society, and the Royal Economic Society be urged to appoint a Joint Committee of Investigation?

Keynes's comments of 28 July brought further comment from the City Editor of *The Times* to which Keynes felt bound to reply.

To the Editor of The Times, *1 August 1923*

Sir,

I thank you for the comments you make in your City Notes of today on some observations of mine in *The Nation and Athenaeum* about the course of prices and of deflation. We can agree without difficulty about two facts:—

(1) For the past three months prices have shown a marked tendency to fall. Your own index number of wholesale prices published today gives April 164·8, May 162·5, June 158·8, and July 155·6—a sharp and decided movement. If we consider a longer period—namely, eighteen months, and take account not only of wholesale prices, but also of cost of living and of wages,

which are of high importance in determining the effective demand for purchasing power, we find that a movement downwards rather than upwards (which I estimate at around 10 per cent) is characteristic of the whole period, in spite of the fact that wholesale prices of materials made a determined attempt to rise between September, 1922, and April, 1923—a spurt which they have been unable to maintain in the face of other conditions.

(2) The basis of credit, and the actual creation of credit have both been deflated about 10 per cent over the same period of eighteen months.

When we come to the connexion between these two facts and the question how far fact (2) is controllable, I admit that no one can dogmatise. Nevertheless, I am supported by expert opinion in the belief that over a period of months the connexion between the two facts is very close indeed, and also that it lies in the power of the Bank of England, and the Treasury, within wide limits, to determine in the long run how much credit is created. If the Bank of England had pursued a different policy, I believe that prices would stand at a different level. Indeed, this is a third fact about which the contending parties can agree; for the policy of the Cunliffe Committee assumes that the authorities have the power in the long run to fix the price level, just as much as the policy of price stabilisation assumes it.

There is also a fourth fact, equally undeniable, of great practical importance just at this moment—namely, that in recent weeks prices in the United States have been falling even more sharply than here. This fall is more significant than the index numbers indicate, since it has affected especially certain commodities—namely, wheat, cotton, sugar, and oil, of which the real importance is far greater than that assigned to them in most index numbers.

The reason why this last fact matters so much is that it brings to a head a divergence between two policies which was previously latent. So long as dollar prices were rising, the policy of improving the dollar–sterling exchange was compatible with the policy of keeping sterling prices reasonably steady. We have most of us been expecting that there would be a slight tendency towards inflation in the United States, which would help to lift the sterling exchange. This tendency may indeed reassert itself before long, if the sky clears, in which case, all will be well, but for the time being it is reversed.

The question which matters in this controversy, the answer to which we want to know and are surely entitled to know, is whether it is the policy of the Bank of England to protect the sterling exchange, even at the risk of causing sterling prices to fall. The oracles are dumb. When the Pythian Prophetess makes signs in terms of Bank rate, she allows her votaries to breathe ambiguous interpretations of her meaning. We may differ legitimately as to the right policy for this country in difficult and unprecedented circumstances. But we have a right to know what the official policy in fact is. The Federation of British Industries can fairly claim a clear answer to their question, presented to the Prime Minister in a moderate and cogently argued memorandum, whether or not the official policy of the Bank of England is the same as that lately acknowledged by the Prime Minister—namely, to promote confidence in the price level. For my part I believe that confidence in the price level is the biggest practical help which the official world can give to the business world; and that the lack of this confidence is a considerable cause, and probably the only remedial one, of present unemployment. If the Prime Minister were able to announce that he had consulted the Governor of the Bank of England and that the two of them were determined to do all in their power to promote and preserve confidence in the existing level of sterling prices (letting the dollar exchange go hang, if necessary), great good would result. Failing this, I hope that the Federation of British Industries will call to their assistance the Federation of Trade Unions and push the controversy home.

Yours, &c.,

J. M. KEYNES

After the issue of 28 July, Keynes's signed contributions to Finance and Investment ceased on a regular basis, although unsigned contributions appeared from time to time. Keynes continued to deal with the issues he had raised in these columns in other places.

On 8 August Keynes contributed a paper at the Cambridge meetings of the Liberal Summer School. It appeared in full in *The Nation* of 11 August.

From The Nation and Athenaeum, *11 August 1923*

CURRENCY POLICY AND UNEMPLOYMENT

It may be inevitable that the average real wages of labour cannot, with the resources of nature, of invention, and of industry at our command, be raised to so high a figure as we should like. But the absurdity of labour being from time to time totally unemployed, in spite of everyone wanting more goods, can only be due to a muddle, which should be remediable if we could think and act clearly.

The most serious charge which can be brought against the system of private enterprise in business and of capitalistic investment as it exists to-day, is that it has failed, so far, to deal with this muddle. As time goes on things seem to get worse rather than better.

Indeed, Socialists might, I think, have pushed home this charge more powerfully than they have, inasmuch as the main part of the explanation of this muddle is deeply rooted in the peculiarities of the *existing* economic organisation of society. I shall not attempt in this paper to cover the ground, and I must not be supposed to ignore other factors in the total situation, if, in what follows, I concentrate exclusively on one particular aspect of the problem.

With the development of international trade, involving great distances between the place of original production and the place of final consumption, with the increased complication of the technical processes of manufacture, and with the seasons governing the date of supply of farm products, there must be a considerable interval of time between the dates when effort is expended and the date when the commodity finally yields up its usefulness. During this interval the business world is entering into liabilities in terms of *money*—borrowing money and paying out in money for wages and other expenses of production—in the expectation of recouping this outlay by disposing of the product for *money* at a later date. That is to say, the business world as a whole must *always* be in a position where it stands to gain by a rise of price and to lose by a fall of price. Whether it likes it or not, the technique of production under a régime of money-contract forces the business world always to carry a big speculative position; and if they are reluctant to carry this position, the productive process must be brought to a standstill. The argument is not affected by the fact that there is some degree of specialisation of function within the business world, the professional speculator coming to the assistance of the producer proper by taking over from him a part of his risk.

Now it follows from this, not merely that price changes profit some people and injure others, but that a *general expectation* of falling prices may inhibit the productive process altogether. For if prices are expected to fall, not enough people can be found who are willing to carry a speculative 'bull' position, and this means that lengthy productive processes involving a money outlay cannot be undertaken,—whence unemployment.

If prices fluctuate in a manner which cannot be, or at least is not, foreseen, some groups in the community will lose and some will gain. This often occurred before the War, and it was bad enough, particularly because falls of price were often foreseen to a certain extent, such foresight bearing its inevitable fruits in unemployment.

A deliberate policy of deflation, however, greatly aggravates the situation. In so far as the business world believe that those responsible for currency policy really intend to carry out a declared policy of deflation, they are bound to feel some lack of confidence in the existing price level, in which case they will naturally draw in their horns to a certain extent with the result of diminishing employment. For this reason a modern industrial community organised on lines of individualistic capitalism simply cannot stand a declared policy of deflation. The business world, it is true, can save its pocket to a certain extent by refraining from new enterprises for the time being. But it can only do this at the expense of passing on to the rest of the community a heavy burden of unemployment and of unemployment doles.

I attribute the bad state of business and of employment more to a lack of confidence in the price level than to any other factor. This lack of confidence is certainly due, in its turn, to a number of different causes,—the political situation in Europe, recent memories of the slump of 1920–21, the fact that the price level is still much higher than it used to be in pre-war days, as well as to a policy of deflation. But none of these things *need* cause prices to fall, and the best way of remedying unemployment would be for those responsible to declare that they would do all they could by means of currency policy to avoid a fall of prices and to promote the confidence of the business world in the existing level of prices.

Let me amplify this point a little. At the present moment the situation in the Ruhr is rightly blamed for the falling off of trade as compared with the revival which was apparent in the spring. How does this happen? To a slight extent directly by cutting off Central European markets; but the purchasing power of Central Europe was very feeble even in the spring, and very feeble also during the boom of 1920–21. The main influence of the Ruhr is felt through its effect on *other* markets, which are induced to withhold their purchases because events in the Ruhr upset their confidence in the price level. Purchasers of tin-plates in Australia, of cotton goods in Asia, or jute products in South America, and so on, are afraid that, if they place their orders now, events in the Ruhr may lead to a fall in their price by the time they are delivered. If they felt confident that the price would not fall, they would not hesitate to buy. They put off their purchases, not because they lack purchasing power, but because their demand is capable of postponement and may, they think, be satisfied at a lower price later on. It is these postponements which are at the root of remediable unemployment.

Now there is no necessary reason in the world why political catastrophes should cause prices to fall. Indeed, in the long run, they generally tend to make prices to [sic] rise because of their inflationary effect on governmental finance. Why should the impoverishment of the world cause *more* goods to be obtainable for gold or for legal tender money? No reason at all. Sooner or later a rising tendency of prices will spring up again, Ruhr or no Ruhr, partly because postponed demands cannot go on being postponed indefinitely; partly because catastrophes tend to diminish the supply of goods and to increase, rather than to diminish, the supply of money. For this reason I am not so pessimistic as the President of the Board of Trade about the prospects of employment in the long run.

For the past eighteen months the authorities have been deflating; for the past six months political anxiety has been acute. Naturally, orders are postponed; inevitably there is unemployment. Some fanatics think that deflation is morally so admirable, that unemployment is a price worth paying for it. But to deny that deflation tends to increase unemployment is profoundly to misunderstand the working of our industrial system.

During recent months employment in a great part of the world has been moderate to good; in another part deplorable. The latter consists without exception of the countries in which deflation has been taking place, namely Great Britain, Sweden, Holland, and Czecho-Slovakia.

I argue, therefore, in the first place, that our existing industrial system is singularly ill-adapted to a policy of deliberate deflation, and that unemployment to-day is due to a very considerable extent not to the absence of markets or to the impoverishment of customers, but to a lack of confidence, arising out of many causes, in the existing level of prices.

I argue, further, that this lack of confidence is in some measure remediable by a resolute policy on the part of the Treasury and the Bank of England. At any rate these authorities can refrain from deliberately aggravating the situation, and should not continue to act, as they have been acting hitherto, on the deflationary recommendations of the Cunliffe Committee.

These observations have been directed, rather more than I intended when I began, to the immediate situation. But they illustrate a fundamental principle which I recommend to this assembly as likely to be of first-rate political importance in the near future. Modern individualistic society, organised on lines of capitalistic industry, cannot support a violently fluctuating standard of value, whether the movement is upwards or downwards. Its arrangements presume and absolutely require a reasonably stable standard. Unless we can give it such a standard, this society will be stricken with a mortal disease and will not survive. I have dwelt in this paper on the evils of deflation because these are with us now. But the evils of inflation, which were visited on us three years ago, although they are different in kind, are not less in degree. We can do with neither.

For these grave causes we must free ourselves from the deep distrust which exists against allowing the value of the currency to be the subject of *voluntary decision*. Only by wisely regulating the creation of currency and credit along new lines, can we protect society against the attacks and criticisms of Socialist and Communist innovators.

On the scientific side economists are as united about the theory of the matter as they are about free trade. The argument is not more intricate than that which underlies tariff controversies.

In reading a forecast of the autumn campaign of our leaders of which unemployment is to be the chief subject, I was disappointed to see no reference whatever to the regulation of credit, which, for good or for evil, must have a vast influence.

I hope that the forecast was incomplete. Nineteenth-century Liberalism was greatly concerned with the establishment of certain economic principles, which were, a hundred years ago, highly controversial, novel, and intellectually difficult. These found their chief embodiment in the doctrine of free trade. This battle has been nearly won, though vigilance is still required. I venture to propound this evening a newer doctrine of hardly less importance. I believe that the reform of the standard of value is, within the economic sphere, the question of greatest urgency now before us. It is a problem which Liberalism is by its traditions well adapted to attack. We cannot live for ever on fragments of our pre-war policies.

An editorial in *The Spectator* two months later under the title 'Deflation Means Unemployment' asked for Keynes's comments. A week later that newspaper printed his reply.

To the Editor of The Spectator, *22 October 1923*

Sir,

You ask me whether I am in agreement with your article 'Deflation Means Unemployment'. I agree most heartily, and I think that there are two steps, neither of them impracticable or dangerous, which ought to be pressed on the Government as immediately urgent: (1) The present Treasury Minute limiting the fiduciary issue of currency notes to the actual maximum of the preceding year should be amended before the end of this year. (2) A definite statement should be made, binding both the Treasury and the Bank of England, that these authorities attach more importance to the maintenance and stability of the price level than to the improvement of the dollar exchange, and that their policy will be deliberately directed to the former object rather than to the latter.

I am, sir, &c.,

J. M. KEYNES

Chapter 2

POPULATION, PROTECTION AND UNEMPLOYMENT

On 18 September 1923 at the meetings of the British Association for the Advancement of Science in Liverpool, Sir William Beveridge, the president of the Economics Section, delivered an address entitled 'Population and Unemployment'. In the course of his remarks he addressed himself to Keynes's *Economic Consequences of the Peace* (*JMK*, vol. II), especially his remarks on the terms of trade between bread and manufactures (pp. 5–6, 13–15, 161). On 22 September, under the title 'Malthusian Moonshine' the editor of *The New Statesman* welcomed Sir William's remarks. Keynes replied in the next issue.

To the Editor of The New Statesman, *25 September 1923*

Sir,

Since you refer to a criticism by Sir W. Beveridge, in his address to the British Association on 'Population and Unemployment', of a statement made by me some time ago relating to the course of the relative values of agricultural produce and manufactured articles between 1900 and 1910, may I say that Sir William's figures do not confute my statement, because they give little or no weight to the prices of manufactured articles? My rejoinder furnishing the evidence on which I was relying will be published in *The Economic Journal* for December next, together with the full text of Sir William's address.

Yours, etc.,

J. M. KEYNES

Keynes turned to another aspect of Beveridge's address in the columns of *The Nation*.

From The Nation and Athenaeum, *6 October 1923*

POPULATION AND UNEMPLOYMENT

Sir William Beveridge's interesting address, under this title, before the British Association has revived discussion on a matter which, whatever way it touches our hopes or our prejudices, must surely trouble the thoughts of anyone who concerns himself with political or social purpose. Sir William, in common with many other people, dislikes the idea of birth control; but, like the good economist he is, he remains on the broad issue a sound Malthusian. 'Nothing that I have said', he finally concludes, 'discredits the fundamental principle of Malthus, reinforced as it can be by the teachings of modern science.' His main themes were, first, that we must not be too ready to argue from unemployment to over-population, instancing the excellence of employment in Germany today, 'a nation which assuredly should be suffering from over-population if any nation is'; and, secondly, that an *obiter dictum* of mine in *The Economic Consequences of the Peace* about the state of affairs in 1900–1910 was unjustifiably pessimistic.

I will deal elsewhere with the criticism personal to myself. My main point in the brief passage taken by Sir W. Beveridge as his text was that the pre-war balance in Europe between population and the means of life was, for various reasons, already precarious; and from this I do not think that he seriously dissents. But I also threw out the suggestion that the turning-point in the strongly favourable developments of the latter half of the nineteenth century may have come about the year 1900. The suggestion is one which it is not easy either to refute or to establish, and the exact date is a matter of historical interest, and not one of decisive importance in relation to the present state of the world. But, in any case, Sir William Beveridge's statistics do not touch me, inasmuch as my suggestion related to the 'equation of exchange' between the manufactured products of the Old World and the raw produce of the New, an indication to which his particular figures, since they nearly all deal with raw produce, are not relevant. I shall discuss this statistical point, giving the evidence on which my statement was based, in the December issue of *The Economic Journal*, where those interested will also have the advantage of reading the full text of Sir William Beveridge's address.

Let us, however, turn to Sir William's first point, namely, the relation of unemployment to over-population. I agree with him that it would be rash to argue straight from one to the other. Unemployment is a phenomenon of maladjustment, and the maladjustment may be due to causes which have nothing to do with population;—as, for example, the maladjustment due to a transition, through deflation of purchasing power, from a higher to a lower price level, or that due to the necessity of changing over from supplying one type of outside market to supplying another because of a sudden change in the relative wealth and requirements of the rest of the world. Each of these influences is probably responsible for an important part of the existing unemployment in Great Britain.

But, on the other hand, unemployment may be a symptom of a maladjustment very closely connected with population— namely, that which results from an attempt on the part of organised labour, or of the community as a whole, to maintain real wages at a higher level than the underlying economic conditions are able to support. The most alarming aspect of the prolongation and the intensity of the existing unemployment is the possibility that transitory influences may not wholly explain it, and that deep causes may be operating which interfere with our continuing ability to maintain in these islands an expanding population at an improving standard of life. The doubt is a dreadful one. Our social aims and objects flow from the opposite assumption, and are rendered futile by its negation. What is the use or the purpose of all our strivings if they are to be neutralised or defeated by the mere growth of numbers? Malthus's Devil is a terrible devil because he undermines our faith in the real value of our social purposes, just as much now as when Malthus loosed him against the amiable dreams of Godwin. The *prima facie* case for doubting our ability to provide during the present generation for growing numbers at an improving standard, and for seeing some corroboration of this doubt in the present state of our labour market and of our staple industries, is so serious that it is frivolous to think we can dismiss it by mentioning that unemployment is not *necessarily* due to over-population and by pointing to the disastrous example of Germany, where the nation's submission, under the overwhelming pressure of events, to a drastic lowering of their standard of life and the impairment of their capital resources has put away this particular symptom for the time being.

No statistics can be decisive on such a matter unless they extend over a period long enough to eliminate other influences,— which means that their final answer may be too late to determine policy. But it is useful to keep ourselves reminded from time to time of one or two simple and well-known figures. In 1851 the population of Great Britain was about 21,000,000; in 1902, 37,000,000; and in 1921, 43,000,000. Thus, the population which is growing old is the remnant of a population not much more than half the size of the population which is growing up. Several conclusions follow from this.

(1) Although the birth rate is materially lower than it was half a century ago, nevertheless the absolute number of daily births in Great Britain today is nearly double the number of deaths.

(2) The fact that the average age of the population is less than it would be in a stationary population means that the proportion of old people of pensionable age, which the community will have to support as time goes on, will tend to increase to a figure not far short of double what it is at present.

(3) Most important of all, the supply of adult labourers will continue to increase sharply for a generation to come, irrespective

of the contemporary birth rate, because the number of boys now growing up to working age will greatly exceed year by year that of the old men dying or reaching pensionable age. In round numbers the male population between twenty and sixty-five years of age is now between 14,000,000 and 15,000,000. In the course of the next twenty years the boys (already born) entering these age limits will exceed by between 4,000,000 and 5,000,000 the old men passing out. That is to say, we shall have to find, within this short period, employment, equipment, and houses for 25–30 per cent more working-class families than at present; and the net productivity of these additional hands will have to support a larger proportion of old people, and, if the present birth rate continues, as large a proportion of children. Now that this surplus already exists, emigration may be a palliative. As a continuing policy, however, emigration is a ruinous expedient for an old country, as is obvious when one considers that, if the males are shipped abroad, a corresponding number of females must be sent also, and that the cost per head of rearing and educating a child up to working age is a heavy charge for which the country will get no return of productivity if the youth then emigrates.

(4) Very few of our staple export industries are operating above their pre-war level of ten years ago, and some of them, notably textiles, are seriously below it. Most of these industries are well satisfied if they see a prospect ahead even of their former level of activity in normal times. Their difficulties are increased in some cases by the fact that the American demand for certain essential raw materials has risen more than the total supply, and that America is able to pay a higher price than we can. We cannot rely, unless the material conditions of the rest of the world greatly improve, on finding markets for a much larger quantity of goods at as good a net return to ourselves. With Europe's present prospects, and with the growing tendency of the New World to keep its advantages to itself, we are not entitled to rely on so great an advance in our own opportunities.

These *prima facie* grounds, for fear and hesitation, and for straining our minds to find a way out, are not disposed of by the fact that many improvements are conceivable, other than restriction, which would postpone or alleviate the problem. Sir William Beveridge concluded his address, after admitting and emphasising the dangers of our economic situation, by urging that the cure was to be found not in birth control, but in peace and world trade resuming their sway. He might have mentioned many other desirable things which would put off the evil day,—a greater accumulation of capital, the swifter progress of science, a raising of the acquired and inborn endowments of the average man, more commonsense, intelligence and public spirit.

But it is not safe to leave the question of numbers unregulated, in the mere hope that we may be rescued by one of these conceivable, but as yet unrealised, improvements. And even if we do realise them, is it not discouraging that they should only operate to compensate an increase of numbers, when they might, if there had been no increase, have availed to improve the lot of the average man?

Is not a country over-populated when its standards are lower than they would be if its numbers were less? In that case the question of what numbers are desirable arises long before starvation sets in, and even before the level of life begins to fall. Perhaps we have already sacrificed too much to population. For is not the improvement in the average conditions of life during the past century very small in comparison with the extraordinary material progress of that period? Does it not seem that the greater part of man's achievements are already swallowed up in the support of mere numbers?

It is easy to understand the distaste provoked by particular methods, and the fear inspired by any proposal to modify the *laissez-faire* of nature, and to bring the workings of a fundamental instinct under social control. But it is strange to be untroubled or to deny the existence of the problem for our generation.

Keynes's final, published comment on Beveridge appeared in *The Economic Journal* immediately following the text of the latter's address.

From The Economic Journal, *December 1923*

A REPLY TO SIR WILLIAM BEVERIDGE

I

It is flattering but a little severe to be taken up through a Presidential address on the strength of an *obiter dictum* of a few sentences. (The subject is a large one and an author may have more to say in support of his general attitude to it than can be well expressed in a single page of a book on another topic.) But worse still when even that paragraph is mis-handled.

My main convictions relate to the present state of affairs— whether Great Britain and Europe can continue to support an increasing population on an improving standard of life now that the precarious equilibrium which existed before the War* has been fatally disturbed. Incidentally I expressed a doubt whether the state of affairs by which 'up to about 1900 a unit of labour applied to industry yielded year by year a purchasing power over an increasing quantity of food' may not perhaps have been already reversed about that date.

It is always difficult to trace, through the oscillations which obscure the long-period trend, the precise moment when a diminishing rate of improvement passes over into an actual loss of ground. But Sir W. Beveridge's paper makes me no clearer than I was as to whether I was rash to express the doubt in question; for the statistics which he quotes have no direct bearing on my remarks.

I was concerned with the ratio of real interchange between the manufactured products offered by the Old World, and the food and raw materials supplied by the New. I thought I saw a tendency of this ratio to alter, with the result that Europe was

---

* My phrases about this are those first quoted above by Sir W. Beveridge on p. 452.

having to offer more of her own goods in exchange for important agricultural produce. I made no fresh study of this question when I wrote *The Economic Consequences of the Peace*, but was merely repeating a view which I had expressed in *The Economic Journal* 1912 (vol. XXII, p. 630) [*JMK*, vol. XI], based on some figures given there and on the more comprehensive calculations set forth in Professor Bowley's well-known memorandum published in *The Economic Journal* in 1903 (vol. XIII, p. 628). It will be useful to repeat here the salient figures.

Professor Bowley's object was to make a table year by year, for the United Kingdom and for Germany, of 'the quantity of exports (the kind supposed unchanged) that were given for a uniform quantity of imports.' His results for the United Kingdom were as follows:

Volume of exports given for a uniform quantity of imports

1873	100	1883	118	1893	105		
1874	103	1884	115	1894	102		
1875	107	1885	114	1895	102		
1876	110	1886	113	1896	102		
1877	118	1887	111	1897	102		
1878	114	1888	113	1898	103		
1879	116	1889	112	1899	99		
1880	119	1890	104	1900	94		
1881	123	1891	105	1901	95		
1882	118	1892	106	1902	100		

This is *prima facie* evidence that our position, after deteriorating from 1873 to 1881, improved uninterruptedly from 1881 to 1900.

In my memorandum of 1912 (*loc. cit.*) I was reviewing the corresponding figures of the Board of Trade for the years 1900–1911 (Cd. 6314), which were as follows-*

1900	94	1906	99
1901	96	1907	98
1902	99	1908	98
1903	101	1909	103
1904	100	1910	104
1905	101	1911	101

* To render the series continuous with Professor Bowley's I have modified the base year.

This long series of figures seemed to indicate that a period of continuous improvement covering two decades had culminated about 1900 and had been brought to an end about that time.

The above figures compare all exports with all imports. For the full justification of my remark, however, it would be better to compare exported manufactures with imported foodstuffs. The result, the general character of which is much the same as before, is as follows:

Volume of manufactured exports given for a uniform quantity of food imports†

1881	132	1891	106	1901	95
1882	130	1892	112	1902	100
1883	128	1893	112	1903	100
1884	120	1894	107	1904	96
1885	114	1895	104	1905	99
1886	117	1896	106	1906	92
1887	116	1897	110	1907	92
1888	114	1898	111	1908	98
1889	116	1899	105	1909	104
1890	107	1900	93	1910	100

† Professor Bowley's tables for 1881 to 1902 distinguish 'Imported Food and Tobacco', 'Exported Textile Manufactures' and 'Exported Metal Products'. I take the first of these categories as representing imported food, and the mean of the other two as representing manufactured exports. The Board of Trade tables for 1900–1911 deal separately with their usual categories of 'Articles of Food, Drink and Tobacco', and 'Articles Wholly or Mainly Manufactured'.

Here also we have a progressive improvement culminating in 1900, with no further improvement after that date and some signs of deterioration. Incidentally it is interesting to notice how decidedly the boom of 1906–7 turned the ratio of real interchange in our favour, and how equally decidedly the depression of 1908–9 turned it against us. Since, however, we are concerned here with the long-period trend, the total result of the table can be best summarised as follows:

Volume of manufactured exports given for a uniform quantity of food imports

1881	132	1900	93
Decade ending 1890	119	Decade ending 1910	98
Decade ending 1900	107	1911	98

A table of this kind by itself cannot, of course, be regarded as conclusive. But some of the possible sources of error are not probable. For example, the prices of imported raw materials during the period under review suggest that, if these were eliminated from the prices of manufactures so as to give the net return to home manufacture, the force of the above table, whilst not much changed, would be increased rather than diminished.

Now from 1881 to 1900 there was certainly a great improvement in manufacturing technique. Thus not only did a unit of manufacture purchase more food, but it cost less labour. Not only so; as we shall see below, whilst we were producing at less real cost and selling at a better real price, we were also marketing a growing volume of goods. It was this fortunate combination of circumstances which made it possible for us to support a rapidly increasing number of workers at a somewhat improving standard of life. Between that time and the outbreak of war the situation may have been helped by some further improvement in manufacturing technique; and the volume of our trade was still increasing; but the other factor—the purchasing power of our manufactures—had ceased to help and seems from the above *data* to have begun to turn adverse. We were no longer able to sell more goods at a better price.

I claim, therefore, that the best evidence available supports the contention briefly stated by me in *The Economic Consequences of the Peace*. I was there speaking of the industrial countries of Western Europe, and suggested that, whereas 'up to 1900 a unit of labour applied to industry yielded year by year a purchasing power over an increasing quantity of food, it is possible that about the year 1900 this process began to reverse'.

What evidence does Sir W. Beveridge produce to confute this? His facts fall into two groups. The first show that Europe as a whole produced 3 per cent more wheat per head in 1910 than in 1900. His second show that the price of wheat rose less than that of other raw materials. Why he imagines that either of these facts confute my statement I cannot say. Let us consider them in turn.

Take his figures of wheat production. Two tables are given, one of which includes and the other excludes Russia and Poland. The first decade shows some increase in the production of food grains per head in the decade 1900–1910 and no figures available for 1910–20; the second shows a small decrease in the production of wheat and barley per head in the decade 1900–1910, compensated by an increase of rye and maize (which are not important articles of human food in this country) and a huge reduction all round in 1910–1920. I have the following observations to make:

(1) It is not obvious that his own table for 'Western and Central Europe', taken at its face value, namely:

	1880	1890	1900	1910	1920
Yield of wheat (bushels per head)	3·93	3·97	4·16	4·13	3·10

confutes my suggestion that the year 1900 marked a turning-point. Indeed it might be held by some to confirm it.

(2) He has, however, included in 'Western and Central Europe' the agricultural countries of South-Eastern Europe— Roumania, Hungary, Jugo-Slavia and Bulgaria. The inclusion of these countries vitiates an argument concerned with the situation of the industrial communities of Western Europe. 'More surprising still', Sir W. Beveridge concludes this passage, 'everyone but four (Belgium, France, Holland and the United Kingdom) shows an increase of wheat per head of total population in the decade (1900–1910).' But are not these four (together with Germany) precisely the countries we were talking about?

(3) Even if his facts were correct, they are not relevant to my contention about the ratio of real exchange between agriculture and industry; and, anyhow, it would be rash to treat them as an indication of progress without examining the attendant circumstances. If, for example, the wheat grown in Great Britain per head were at the present stage in our economic

development to show a considerable increase, it might well indicate a serious deterioration in our prosperity; for it might mean that as a result of hostile tariffs or other causes we were no longer able to obtain food on favourable terms in exchange for our manufactured exports and were being driven, as a last resort, to grow an increased quantity of food for ourselves.

Take next Sir W. Beveridge's tables of prices. Since these relate almost wholly to raw materials, and mainly to imported raw materials, I do not know what relevance he thinks that they possess to my statement about the relative values of imported food and exported manufactures. He seems half aware that they are irrelevant, and goes on to give other reasons for supposing *a priori* that, *if* his figures had related to exported manufactures, they would have supported his conclusion. But he seems to have clean forgotten the existence of the Board of Trade estimates, published year by year, of the very thing under discussion,—although the figures must, of course, be familiar to him in other connections.

II

Since Sir W. Beveridge's criticisms have caused me to recur to the subject of my inquiries of 1912, it may be of interest that I should now bring these inquiries up to date.

The Board of Trade continued to publish comparable figures for the years up to 1916 (though 1913 was the last year to be dealt with in a comprehensive white paper). For the years 1917 and 1918 the conditions under which our foreign trade was carried on rendered comparisons impossible, and no returns were compiled. Since 1919 the figures have been published quarterly in the *Board of Trade Journal*.* Reducing these official figures to the same form as in the table given above (p. 127), we have the following result:

* Up to and including 1922 the figures have been calculated in respect of 1913 as the base year. In 1923 the Board of Trade has returned to its pre-war (and preferable) technique of the 'chain-method' by which each year is calculated by reference to the immediately preceding year.

Volume of manufactured exports given for a uniform quantity of food imports

1912	102	1915	118	1918	—	1921	72
1913	97	1916	118	1919	91	1922	77
1914	105	1917	—	1920	82	1923	80
							(for 9 months)

It appears, therefore, that up to the outbreak of War, and also during the War years, the state of affairs, which dates from about 1900, was maintained, the table, repeated in terms of ten-year averages,* being as follows:

Volume of manufactured exports given for a uniform quantity of food imports

Decade ending	1890	119	Decade ending	1899	108	Decade ending	1908	97
	1891	117		1900	107		1909	97
	1892	115		1901	105		1910	98
	1893	113		1902	104		1911	98
	1894	112		1903	103		1912	98
	1895	111		1904	102		1913	98
	1896	110		1905	101		1914	99
	1897	109		1906	100		1915	100
	1898	109		1907	98		1916	101

This table shows that the uninterrupted improvement, which had been proceeding at a steady rate for a quarter of a century up to the decade (ending 1907–8) of which the middle year is 1903, came to an end at about that date.

In the light of this more extended table, my former generalisation should be modified by placing the turning-point at 1903 rather than at 1900 (the figures of the period 1899–1903 being much upset for purposes of comparison by the South African War and by the boom and the subsequent depression within that period), and by emphasising more decidedly the cessation of improvement and less decidedly the extent of the actual deterioration between that date and the outbreak of war.

* Ten-year averages are successful on the whole in eliminating the very disturbing influences on these tables of the periodic booms and depressions.

What is the situation as regards the post-war years? They show that my original generalisation was open to the criticism that by dealing solely with the *ratio* of real exchange without reference to the *volume* of trade it might be misleading. The figures quoted above for the pre-war years, taken by themselves, indicate, paradoxically, a vast improvement, even if we allow for a disturbance of the figures, as on previous occasions, by the boom of 1920* in proportion to the magnitude of the boom. A closer examination, however, shows that the improvement in real price has only been obtained at the expense of a disastrous falling off in volume. My generalisation would have been more accurately stated:—'We are no longer able to sell a growing volume of manufactured goods (or a volume increasing in proportion to population) at a better real price in terms of food.'

The figures of the volume of trade for earlier years can be found in Professor Bowley's memorandum (*loc. cit.*). Those for the years since 1900 (omitting the war years) are as follows in percentages of the volume in 1900:

	Total net imports	Food imports	Total British exports	Manufactured exports
1900	100·0	100·0	100·0	100·0
1901	102·1	102·4	101·0	100·8
1902	105·3	103·2	107·2	107·1
1903	106·2	106·9	110·1	109·8
1904	107·4	107·5	112·5	111·4
1905	108·4	104·3	123·6	123·6
1906	111·6	108·0	132·9	131·5
1907	113·1	107·5	143·6	140·9
1908	108·9	106·3	132·2	127·1
1909	111·9	105·2	137·8	131·7
1910	114·1	105·3	150·3	145·7
1911	117·6	108·7	155·7	150·8
1912	126·6	109·3	164·3	158·7
1913	131·2	115·6	170·8	164·6
1919	118·1	110·6	93·8	92·8
1920	115·5	99·8	121·1	125·9
1921	96·4	104·7	85·1	83·6
1922	113·5	114·6	117·7	109·5
1923	127·3	130·8	132·3	121·4
(9 months)				

* These tables show that with great regularity this country obtains a better *real* price than usual for its manufactured exports during a boom. To this extent the greater prosperity of industrial countries during a boom seems to be at the expense of the agricultural countries.

Broadly speaking, the volume of our manufactured exports has gone back to what it was about twenty years previously. Meanwhile the volume of our food imports has maintained a steady increase to a figure about 15 per cent above what it was twenty years ago, roughly corresponding to the increase of population.

Thus the improved prices of our manufactured exports, measured in terms of food imports, has compensated to a considerable extent, but by no means completely for the falling off in volume. Off-setting the one thing against the other, our manufactured exports are now buying *in the aggregate* about 12 per cent less foodstuffs than before the War.*

Looked at another way, since the War we have been asking for our exports (in round figures) a real price (i.e. in terms of food imports) 20 per cent higher than before the War and have been selling 30 per cent less in quantity. In the slump year 1921 we were asking a real price 35 per cent higher than in 1913 and were selling in volume 50 per cent less.

These figures suggest interesting reflections as to the elasticity of the world's demand for our manufactures in terms of foodstuffs. It looks on the face of it as though we are asking too much for our exports, and will have to ask less if we are to sell enough to pay for our necessary imports. But the post-war conditions of world markets are so materially different from pre-war conditions, that we cannot safely infer from the above figures by how much we shall have to lower our (real) prices for what we produce in order to find an outlet for a sufficient quantity of goods. We are bound to hope—and have reasonable grounds to hope—that the demand for our goods is elastic, i.e. that if we lower our (real) price the demand will increase *more* than in proportion. But I see no grounds for the expectation that

* Triennial averages (e.g. 1912 = averages of 1911, 1912, 1913) of amount of food imports purchased by the aggregate of our manufactured exports (1912 = 100):

Pre-war		Post-war	
1910	89	1920	77
1911	95	1921	86
1912	100	1922	85

we can obtain a (real) price a great deal higher (which we are asking at present) than the pre-war price for the pre-war volume of sales.

The following is an illustration of the way in which equilibrium might be restored. Food prices (in terms of money) might rise 20 per cent, money wages might rise 10 per cent, other manufacturing costs might be reduced (with a larger output and more efficiency) sufficiently to compensate the rise of money wages thus leaving the money-price of manufactures un-changed;* our real price for manufactured exports would then have returned to its pre-war level and this might encourage a sufficient increase in their volume to absorb an important proportion of our unemployed. But it must be observed that in this illustration the result would have been achieved at the cost of a reduction in real wages.

Arguments and figures such as I have been dealing with here can never do more than suggest conclusions,—they cannot prove them. But they do certainly suggest—in the absence of other indications to the contrary—that we could maintain a higher standard of life if we had fewer to employ and to feed, and that the more we have to force the volume of our trade (especially in existing conditions) the worse terms do we get. Numbers are already, if this is true, inimical to standards of life.

One more table of the ratio of real interchange, looked at this time from the standpoint of the New World, is worth giving. The Federal Reserve Board of the United States has published during the past year a monthly table of the price index of different classes of commodities as follows [see table, p. 135]:

This table shows that of the three classes of goods produced and consumed within the United States—raw materials, pro-ducers' goods and consumers' goods—the increase of price since

* I have neglected throughout the cost of the imported raw materials entering with our manufactured goods, because, so far as I can judge, their price has risen less than the price of the manufactured goods; so that if accurate account had been taken of this factor, my argument would not have been weakened. But this matter deserves a more exact examination than I have been able to give it in this article.

	Goods produced	Goods imported	Goods exported	Raw materials	Producers' goods	Consumers' goods	All commodities
			(1913 = 100)				
1922							
July	162	128	165	177	143	163	165
Oct.	161	135	163	179	150	156	165
1923							
Jan.	162	139	180	182	150	156	165
April	173	156	186	181	169	158	170
May	170	155	179	176	167	158	167
June	167	148	182	171	164	157	164
July	163	141	170	163	160	155	159
Aug.	163	137	166	162	158	157	159
Sept.	167	145	176	167	160	162	163

1913 has been greatest in raw materials, although the disparity has been diminishing lately. But the big divergence is between the price changes in imported goods and those in exported goods. In order to pay for a given volume of imports the United States does not have to export, it seems, more than 80–85 per cent of what it had to export before the War. In other words, the ratio of real interchange has moved some 15 per cent in favour of the United States and against the rest of the world.*

I do not wish at the present stage to draw any certain conclusions from the figures set forth in this section. But the indications are not optimistic. Sir W. Beveridge and I do not disagree about the disturbing possibilities of the present state of affairs.

III

Finally, I must emphasise strongly, what is perhaps obvious,— that conclusions as to the actual or impending over-population of the older countries do not stand or fall with the particular point of detail here discussed. This is only one item in a vast field of evidence and argument. I complain, therefore, that Sir

---

* If we compare goods imported with goods produced, the change amounts to 10 per cent, which might be the safer figure to take.

W. Beveridge should convey the impression that his criticisms, even if they were better founded than they are, would dispose of Malthus's Devil. Sir W. Beveridge seems to speak with two voices. It is on grounds which are flimsy and inadequate to the magnitude and significance of the subject (if he intends them to apply to the whole great issue) that he asserts: 'Mr Keynes's fears seem not merely unnecessary but baseless.' Yet the outside world has not heard with the same distinctness the other voice, which says later on: 'The last thing I wish is to over-emphasise points of disagreement with Mr Keynes...Nothing that I have said discredits the fundamental principle of Malthus, reinforced as it can be by the teachings of modern science.'

I offer Sir W. Beveridge the following few samples from the collections of the press-cutting agency, to show what the outside world thinks that he has said:

The Guardian. 'At the British Association Sir William Beveridge effectively laid the bogey and convinced most of us that there are no grounds for Malthusian pessimism.'

The Month. 'The bogey of an overcrowded earth, first raised by the short-sighted Malthus, and eagerly exploited by eugenists as a means of overcoming the abhorrence with which all decent people regard abuse of the marriage function, was effectively laid by the Director of the London School of Economics...We hope that our Government will follow, however belatedly, the example of France and America in making such publications (relating to contraceptives) a criminal offence.'

The New Age. 'No; we really shall not be able to take Malthus seriously until we see people starving with money in their pockets...There is only one famine to fear; and that is a money famine.'

Daily Mail. 'Sir William said there was no ground for Malthusian pessimism. Enormous areas of the world fit for cultivation were not yet cultivated, and in other areas only the surface has been scratched.'

Liverpool Post. 'It is surely obvious that the great and deplorable mass of unemployment in the country at present has no direct connection with the number of the inhabitants.'

Mr C. F. G. Masterman (in numerous organs of the provincial press): 'Sir William Beveridge, by the substitution of scientific investigation for theory, has blown into pieces the assertion that England is over-populated, or that Europe is over-populated, or that population is growing in excess of the development of food supply, or that the present unemployment in this country is in any way due to over-population.'

New Statesman. 'There is no evidence whatever of which we are aware, or which Mr Keynes or any other Malthusian has yet produced, to show that those limits (to the number of human beings who can find means of sustaining life) are being approached or are even likely to be approached for centuries to come...Economic and statistical science offer no ground whatever for what Sir William calls "Malthusian pessimism",...Sir William Beveridge's demonstration that the "over-population" bogey is moonshine is a most valuable and timely piece of work.'

Sir William Beveridge has given to ignorance and prejudice the shelter of his name. Can I not with these cuttings make him a little uneasy?

On reading Keynes's comments in the *Economic Journal*, Beveridge continued the discussion in correspondence.

From SIR WILLIAM BEVERIDGE, *1 January 1924*

My dear Keynes,

I have been looking at your reply and export and import prices and have got some rather remarkable results.

The first is that you only get your turning point about 1900 by switching (illegitimately) from Bowley's figures for textiles and metal products to the Board of Trade figures for exported manufactures as a whole. If you carried on with Bowley's figures and calculated in the way in which he has in fact calculated them, the uninterrupted decline would continue, the average for the decade 1913 being 93 as compared with the 98 with which you end.

The second result is that the uninterrupted decline itself from 1891 onwards is largely if not wholly bogus. It is there because Bowley in calculating the average price of exported metal products has (illegitimately) treated 'iron and steel manufactures' as a single group instead of breaking it up into its component parts (pig iron, hoops and sheets, wire, railway material, tinplates, etc.). These components vary very much in price and also in the proportion which they form of the whole. By breaking up this group one gets (on the basis of 1902 = 100) a price in 1881 for metal products of 105 instead of 90 as given by Bowley in the *Economic Journal*. And so one gets for the same year 124 instead of 132 as the quantity of textile and metal exports required to be given for a uniform quantity of food imports. The apparent improvement in our trading ratio is largely due to the increasing proportion of our iron and steel trade which consists of more finished instead of less finished products.

A third result is that the German figures for exported manufactures and imports of food show no trend at all.

I hope to send the draft of my next article to you but have been delayed by certain further discoveries. I think you will find that there is really nothing whatever to be made of import and export prices, and that my own address in the section on England gives you much better evidence for pessimism than anything else does.

Yours ever,
W. H. BEVERIDGE

The next month he sent Keynes a proof of a reply he proposed to make to Keynes in *Economica* for February 1924 under the title 'Mr Keynes' Evidence for Overpopulation'. He asked Keynes for any comments or criticisms he might wish to make. Keynes replied ten days later.

To SIR WILLIAM BEVERIDGE, *16 February 1924*

Dear Beveridge,

Many thanks for the proof. The discussion falls into two quite different sections: (1) the purely statistical question as to the right method of compiling a table of the relative cost of manufactured exports and imported food and the inferences which can justifiably be drawn from this table; and (2) the position of this particular piece of statistical evidence in my general argument about population.

As regards (1) there are several things that I could say. In particular, I am disappointed that you did not carry my figures for manufactured exports as a whole back to the earlier years instead of bringing Bowley's corrected figures forward. Since you do not criticise my post-1900 figures, that would have seemed the obvious thing to do. In this section of your paper, however, I have no complaint to make of any misrepresentation.

(2) On the other hand, as regards the general relation of all this to my main argument, let me summarise my objections as follows:—

(a) You imply in the third paragraph and elsewhere that I have set forth my case on this subject and pronounced definite conclusions in print. This is not so. I have never, so far as I can remember, printed in my a life a single word on the subject of population, with the exception of three pages in *The Economic Consequences of the Peace* and an introductory article of a few pages to other peoples' work, of a purely general character.* I have a definite opinion on these matters of course, and have expressed it in conversation; I also have, I believe, a body of arguments with which to support these conclusions. But you are mistaken in supposing that all these things are published to the world and open to criticism. Take, for instance, your reference to my advocacy of birth control. I rather doubt if I have ever used the word in print.† I have certainly never presented any arguments whatever in favour of it. It is flattering to be treated as the leading exponent of all these things on the strength of having written three sentences about them; but it inevitably leads to misrepresentation if these three sentences are treated as though they represented a three-volume exposition of all the author's arguments.

(b) The question whether what I wrote in *The Economic Consequences of the Peace* related to Europe as a whole or only to Western Europe seems to me, in your paper, a muddle. Some parts of the argument related to the one and some parts to the

---

* *Plus* what I have written since your B.A. address.
† I expect I have really, but I can't recall it.

other. Why not? In fact, one of the most definite statements in the book about population related to Russia. But when I was using the particular argument about manufactured exports buying less food it is obvious that this could only apply to the industrial countries, since for the agricultural countries it would work, if anything, the other way. Surely there is nothing illogical in maintaining both that Russia and that Great Britain were over-populated, but the precise statistical evidence of the statement in the one case would not be identical with the evidence of it in the other, the conditions of the two countries being quite different. There is no shift in my position on this matter.

(c) This is part of the general suggestion in the first part of your paper and elsewhere that the statistical point discussed under (1) is the whole or an essential part of my argument. For instance, the paragraph at the bottom of the fourth slip is, in my opinion, a serious misrepresentation. Take again the tenth paragraph on the first slip, where you say 'Had I realised that they were the basis of Mr Keynes's statements I should of course have discussed them'. The figures about export and import prices were not the whole basis of my statement about population. But they obviously were bound to be the basis of my statements about the relative values of exports and imports; and it still seems to be strange that you should not have realised that statements about the relative values of exports and imports would naturally be based upon statistics of export and import prices. Having now made this discovery you appear to rush to the conclusion that statistics of export and import prices are also the sole basis of everything I have to say about population in general.

(d) The point, however, where there seems to me to be the greatest misunderstanding of what I said in *The Economic Consequences of the Peace* can be illustrated by the first sentence of your second paragraph. I was not arguing in *The Economic Consequences of the Peace* that there had been an actual fall in the standard of life in Europe before the war.* Indeed this was notoriously not the case. Practically all your arguments, being directed to prove that there was no such fall in the standard of living, are therefore quite irrelevant to my position, since the point was never denied. The misunderstanding seems to arise in two ways. First, you seem to think that no country can be said to be over-populated until its standards of living are actually falling, from which, for example, it would follow that a country which was already at the lowest standard which could support life could never be over-populated. My definition of over-population would be totally different from this. The other source of misunderstanding seems to be that you do not remember that the gist of my argument in *The Economic Consequences of the Peace* related to the *precariousness* of the situation, that it was full of elements of instability, that many factors which had operated favourably in the preceding years could not, quite apart from the war, be relied upon to continue as favourable, etc., etc.† Thus you assume that my definition of over-population depends upon a lowering of the standards of life; you twist my statements as to the precariousness of the existing standards into a statement as to their absolute decline; and then, because no such absolute decline actually took place, which I was prepared to admit from the outset, you consider that you have disposed of my argument. If you will read again Chap. II of *The Economic Consequences*, you will find that it is quite different from the picture given in your latest article.

Well! I have set out fully, and not in the sort of way in which I should print anything, my reaction to your proof. But I do not know what to do about it. I could have wished you had confined your reply to the statistical question where, whatever differences of opinion or of inference there may be, there can be no question of misrepresentation. I feel that a continuance

---

* E.g. on p. 8 [*JMK*, vol. II, p. 5] the sentence immediately following the one which is the basis of your criticism runs as follows:—'But the tendency of cereals to rise in real cost was balanced by other improvements'.

† See, for example, my summary on p. 22 [*JMK*, vol. II, p. 16].

of this controversy on fierce lines tends to make the public and our pupils believe that we differ on the essential matters far more seriously that we really do?

Yours ever,
[copy not signed or initialled]

Beveridge replied almost a month later.

From SIR WILLIAM BEVERIDGE, *14 March 1924*

Dear Keynes,

I send you herewith a reprint of my *Economica* article. Your letter came when my final proof had already gone in, and I have since been too busy with University Grants Committee and other matters to go further into the question. Would you care, however, to develop your letter in a reply for the next number of *Economica*? We would be delighted, of course, to have it.

But I certainly contemplate myself abandoning the paths of historical controversy for consideration of the practical and present problem.

Yours sincerely,
W. H. BEVERIDGE

Keynes did not pursue the matter further.

One sidelight of Keynes's controversy with Beveridge was a letter from C. R. Fay, a contemporary of Keynes's at King's College, Cambridge who was then Professor of Economics at the University of Toronto.

From C. R. FAY, *27 March 1924*

Dear Malthus,

For more than a century you have been worrying about it and all the while the answer was in Shakespeare's *Tempest*, Act II, Sc. 1.

Gonzalo.	Had I plantation of this isle, my lord—
	. . .
	All things in common nature should produce
	Without sweat or endeavour...
	nature should bring forth
	Of its own kind, all foison, all abundance,
	To feed my innocent people.

142

Sebastian.   No marrying 'mong his subjects?
Antonio.   None, man; *all idle; whores and knaves.*

In other words leave the wheat crop alone. Concentrate on human beings. 10 years of Labour government will turn the unskilled labourers into idle knaves. 10 years of life in factories and on the street will turn the females into the social equivalent of whores, i.e. copulators without issue.

It was you and your school who from 1798 onwards exalted work and childbearing into virtues and so disturbed nature's balance.

But you will say, I have always opposed population. No, you have encouraged it. If men work, women will labour. If men are idle, women will be idle too. Paris knows this, Paris lives up to it. But Paris is frightened, because London and Berlin and the Pope will not follow suit. So [?] in your next Summer School, men & women in equal numbers: take as your subject all play and no work, & see that the women understand their part in it: and 'thus by contraries execute all things'.

No charge for this instruction.

Yrs
C. R. FAY

Meanwhile, on 25 October 1923, Stanley Baldwin, who had become Prime Minister when Bonar Law resigned owing to throat cancer the previous May, announced that he could only fight unemployment if he had a free hand to introduce protection. As Bonar Law had sworn off protection during the 1922 election, Baldwin's policy change involved another general election and he called one for 6 December. Keynes took some part in the campaign, speaking for the Liberals at Blackburn and Barrow on 4 and 5 December. He also contributed to the discussion of the election issues in *The Nation*, first of all with an unsigned leader on 17 November and then with a two-part article on free trade.

From The Nation and Athenaeum, *17 November 1923*

THE LIBERAL PARTY

The historic Liberal Party has been reunited this week, in the only conditions in which reunion can be sincere or desirable,— identical opinions and identical antagonisms on immediate issues of the first degree of importance.

The questions of to-day are not the same as those of a generation ago. It has taken a little time for the distinctions of temperament and ideal, corresponding to what we call 'party', deep, unchangeable and permanent though they are in the characters of Englishmen, to sort themselves out. Foreign policy and economic policy, each presenting in detail mainly new problems, are what matter now. Though the details are new, nevertheless the general lines, along which the Liberal and Conservative temperaments would try to solve them, have been predetermined. After a period of doubt, this is plain at last. For a short time it seemed as though the real differences between, for example, Mr Baldwin and Mr Asquith, were shadowy and indistinct. Party strife was half-hearted. The ideal of carrying on the King's Government by the best men, regardless of party, had a momentary plausibility. But the after-war twilight has suddenly cleared. We find ourselves, overnight, standing shoulder to shoulder in the old ranks.

Two pairs of speeches, lately delivered, illuminate the gulf. In the realm of foreign policy, Lord Birkenhead's Rectorial Address and General Smuts broadcasted oration disclose the opposite assumptions upon which the Tory and the Liberal Ministers of Foreign Affairs build their diplomacy,—the appeal to national force, which leads, the Liberal thinks, to universal suicide, and the organisation of international opinion, which leads, the Tory thinks, to the decay of national prestige. In the realm of economic policy, the speeches of Mr Baldwin at Manchester and of Mr Asquith at Dewsbury typify, on the one hand, the exaltation of a sort of mystical stupidity, with which the Tory, generally sentimentalising himself on these occasions as the 'plain, business man', likes to present his nostrums for the cure of economic facts; and, on the other, the intellectual answer, which the Liberal, whether he always succeeds or not, tries to give to an intellectual problem. Liberalism to-day must make us soft-hearted to foreign affairs and hard-headed to economic facts. Tories have shown themselves lately hard where we are soft, and soft where we are hard.

All Liberals of both wings must feel an exhilaration of spirit and a heightening of excitement. The party struggle is not an ignoble instrument for the advancement of human affairs. Old associates have joined their ranks again under their old leaders, by general admission the most famous and experienced body of statesmen in the world, with clear issues before them and with great hopes of winning much ground. Coalition has failed; and Toryism has failed. We too would like to try our hand at mitigating the moral and economic disorders of the stricken modern world.

We have not mentioned Labour. Does this invalidate our argument? We think not. An underlying current of weakness in the inner life of the Labour Party is obvious to any observer. It is possible that they may have some electoral success. But in power and in action, there is no likelihood of their accomplishing in the near future any part of their programme which is peculiar to themselves. Labour cannot accomplish anything at present which is not on Liberal rather than on Labour lines, and is not carried through with Liberal support,—not least because the best of their ability is drawn from good friends of our own who in the twilight temporarily strayed away. The Labour Party is no more a 'party', in the sense in which we have used this good old word, than super-taxpayers are. It includes every discrepancy of temperament from the highest Toryism to the wildest spirit of destruction, from the driest intellectualism to a degree of mystical stupidity which would satisfy the standards of Mr Baldwin. Let no man vote Tory to keep Labour out when his true preference is for the Liberal. In the short run it will be Liberal strength which will be most potent to check Labour excesses; and in the long run nothing but Liberal weakness can cause the eventual reaction from Toryism to play into the hands of extremists.

The precise form which Liberal reunion has taken is marked, in our opinion, by the wisdom which has characterised throughout Mr Asquith's handling of this problem. The two wings of the party retain their separate organisations, but they are to collaborate without reserve and without distinction of name. The joint action of the Conservative and the Liberal Unionist parties in old days, though in that case the separate designations were retained for many years, provides an instructive precedent. By this arrangement, the rank and file of Liberals in the constituencies can come together and fight for a common programme,—which has been the crying need; whilst the personal questions—which have been the difficulty—are left, deprived, for the moment, of their power to do harm, to the assuagements of time and the test of experience.

We predict that the coming election will be distinguished from the other elections since the war by a general return to political allegiances and a strict party vote. If it were not for the complications of three-cornered contests and the absence of an alternative vote, this election would probably indicate with considerable accuracy the relative strength to-day of the three great parties. For ten years before the War the Liberal vote dominated the country. Many, as yet incalculable, elements have been added since then. It is probable, nevertheless, that a return to 'party' will benefit Liberalism more than either of its rivals, and may achieve that moderate improvement of relative position which will be sufficient to make the Liberal Party a deciding power in the state. It is only necessary that Conservatives should lose forty seats on balance and that Liberals should win forty seats, for the Liberal Party to attain a relative strength in the new House of Commons, which, in combination with its middle position, would render it the only party capable—with support from the moderates of both the other parties—of carrying on the government of the country.

Liberal workers have, therefore, something to work for. Let them enter the brief fight with hope and with courage, determined if they can to restore Liberalism to its rightful task in this moderate and magnanimous country of finding a *via media* to peace abroad and contentment at home. It is on them that has now fallen the mantle of tranquility which won the last election.

From The Nation and Athenaeum, *24 November and 1 December 1923*

FREE TRADE

I

Before we examine Mr Baldwin's contention that new facts have changed the significance of old proposals, let us remind ourselves of some principles which have certainly not changed.

Free trade is based on two fundamental truths which, stated with their due qualifications, no one can dispute who is capable of understanding the meaning of the words:—

I. It is better to employ our capital and our labour in trades where we are relatively more efficient than other people are, and to exchange the products of these trades for goods in the production of which we are relatively less efficient.

Every sane man pursues this principle in his private life. He concentrates his energies on those employments where his efficiency is greatest in comparison with other people's; and leaves to others what they can do better than he can.

There are four, and only four, recognised types of exception to this principle, which apply equally to nations and to individuals:—

1. If, for non-economic reasons, a particular trade, or the conditions in which it is carried on, are degrading or unpleasant, or if, on the other hand, they are peculiarly desirable, we may recognise such facts by prohibitions and by encouragements. Such cases are certainly not to be found amongst manufactured imports or exports as a class. Many believe, however, that the encouragement of agriculture comes under this head.

2. If a particular article or service is of such a kind that it is not safe for nations or individuals to leave themselves entirely dependent on the services of outsiders, this is a reason for insisting that we should retain at least the capacity for providing it at home. This is the case of 'key industries'. It is already covered by existing legislation. The main objection to such

legislation is that, under cover of it, protectionists are apt to slip in articles which do not really satisfy the conditions.

3. Where relative inefficiency is due to a remediable lack of practice or of education on the part of our own industries, it may be worth while to spend something on gaining the necessary experience. This is the case of 'infant industries'. Here again the objection is that protectionists are apt to father on it elderly or unpromising 'infants'. It can hardly occur in an old industrial country, such as England, except in an industry based on a new invention. I do not know any important case of this, except possibly that of the motor industry,—which is already heavily protected.

4. Where, for special reasons, the cheapness of the imported goods does not look like being permanent, yet may bankrupt and destroy our own organisation so long as it lasts, temporary measures may be justified. This is the case of 'dumping' and of imports from countries of depreciating currency. Generally speaking, the occasions for action under this head are not so common as may appear at first. We have to weigh the direct benefit of getting the goods cheap against the indirect injury done to our organisation. It is not true, at present, that we are suffering seriously under this head; and in so far as it can be proved that we are suffering in particular cases, this is already provided for by existing legislation.

II. The second great principle is that there can be no disadvantage in receiving useful objects from abroad. If we have to pay at once, we can only pay with the export of goods and services, and the exchange would not take place (subject to the necessary exceptions just stated) unless there was an advantage in it. Every export, which is not paid for by an import, represents a decrease in the capital available within the country.

Thus an artificial interference with imports must *either* interfere with exports *or* involve an artificial stimulation to capital to leave the country. Now, if we are to interfere at all with the natural course of trade, surely it should be with the object of keeping capital at home, not of driving it abroad. With our shortage of housing and the need of factories and equipment to render efficient our growing supply of labour, we need to keep more capital at home, and so to arrange matters that our surplus resources are occupied in increasing our own equipment for future production and for the shelter of our own population. There is already, in my opinion, too much encouragement to the export of our capital. With our diminished savings and our increasing needs, we are not in the position in which we used to be for sending out goods to the rest of the world and getting back, for the time being, nothing whatever in return.

Our imports are our income. To put obstacles in their way is to be as crazy as a business man would be who tried to prevent his customers and his debtors from paying their bills.

Neither of these principles is in the least affected by whether or not foreign countries impose tariffs.

There is a third argument for free trade, but one far less absolute and more relative to changing circumstances than the first two,—namely, the principle of *laissez-faire*. This is never a final argument. The old view, that the self-interest of individuals, operating without interference, will always produce the best results, is not true. As knowledge increases and the arts of government improve, the public good requires many checks on the unregulated acts of individual traders. Nevertheless, in a case like this, where lobbying, expense, waste of time, and friction of all kinds will endlessly ensue, we require, to justify the change, not the momentary caprice of a minister who is short of material for a speech at a party gathering, but solid and certain advantages to the state, carefully thought out and clearly explained.

The above arguments are directed against import duties of which the object is to keep out foreign goods. This is Mr Baldwin's main object. It is these arguments, therefore, which are relevant to his proposals. Since, however, protectionists rapidly shift to other ground than that from which the argument is driving them, it will be safer to complete our rapid survey of the whole field.

There are three principal objects, other than the prevention of imports, for which import duties have been proposed at various times:—

1. The favouring of imports from some sources of supply rather than others, namely *preference*.

2. The annoyance of foreign countries, in the hope that they will offer you some concession to abate the nuisance, namely *retaliation*.

3. The exploitation of a position of monopoly or partial monopoly, in order, by restricting the volume of trade, to get a more favourable ratio of exchange, namely, *making the foreigner pay*.

In each of these cases it is a question of where the *balance* of advantage lies. There is nothing whatever new about them. They have been argued out, up and down the country, hundreds of times. I need only point out that the last of them is peculiarly inapplicable to our present circumstances. The imposition of an import or export duty with this object in view is equivalent to a combination of producers to extract from their customers a price higher than the competitive price. Such action is very imprudent unless those who take it feel confident as to the strength of their monopoly position and as to the inability of their customers to go elsewhere. It is not aimed at expanding the volume of trade; but the contrary. It is an attempt to get better terms from foreigners by contracting the volume of trade. Such an attempt would be exceptionally ill-advised at a time when we are already losing trade by charging too high.

The complication of the free trade issue has generally arisen in the past from the fact that, whilst protectionists have really wanted protection for its own fallacious sake, they have generally advanced under a thick smoke-screen of the exceptional cases,—agriculture and race-virility, key industries, infant industries, dumping, preference, retaliation, and making the foreigner pay. It is always more difficult to prove in a few words that certain possible advantages are unlikely or infrequent, than to meet the straight case—where there is and can be no advantage at all. This time, however, the air is clearer. There is no talk of food taxes. The only important industry—the motor industry—which could by the wildest stretch be called an infant, has a heavy duty already. Key industries and dumping are covered by the Safeguarding of Industries Act. Preference is already accorded almost to the full extent that is possible without food taxes. 'Making the foreigner pay' is a preposterous idea just now for the reasons given above. There remains retaliation available for an occasional mention. But the worst of this cry is its utter inconsistency with the main cry of providing permanent employment. For it is of the essence of retaliation that the duties are put on with the idea of taking them off again, soon and suddenly, when they have served their purpose. It is obvious that no expansion of home industry could be started under the precarious and deceptive shelter of retaliatory duties.

The truth is that since the war we have been experimenting (unwisely, in my opinion) with all the more plausible cases for protection, and already have quite a formidable array of trade obstacles. It has been reserved, therefore, for Mr Baldwin, the last and most foolish protagonist of this old play, to plunge headlong into pure error of the $2 + 2 = 5$ variety.

For if there is one thing that protection can *not* do, it is to cure unemployment. It is the central idea of protection *to contract trade*,—for the advancement of various ulterior objects which may or may not be wise. The characteristic of protection—admitted, I should have thought, by friend and foe alike—is that it is an attempt to trade on better terms or on nationally more advantageous lines at the expense of doing less business. The free trader has always been the expansionist,—the man who is accused of exchanging with the foreigner too cheap or sacrificing the character of the business, merely for the sake of carrying on a *large* trade. Whoever, before Mr Baldwin, dared to assert that putting obstacles in the way of trade would *increase its volume*?

There are some arguments for protection, based upon its securing possible but improbable advantages, to which there is no simple answer. But the claim to cure unemployment involves the protectionist fallacy in its grossest and crudest form.

Protection must mean—to this there is no exception—an attempt to limit the volume of trade; it must mean charging the foreigner more (more, measured in terms of goods demanded against goods supplied) at the expense of doing less trade with him. And in so far as the keeping out of an import does not involve a corresponding restriction of export, it must drive some capital out of the country.

Our problem is to find expanding markets and an increased capital equipment for a growing industrial population. A proposal to solve this by contracting markets and encouraging the export of capital is an imposition on the credulity of the country, which would be impossible if we had more than a fortnight to expose it.

II

What are Mr Baldwin's 'new facts' to justify his departure from old wisdom? It is difficult to extract anything clear from the nebulous orations of himself and his lieutenants. They have made no attempt to meet the *general* argument for free trade, the familiar outlines of which I repeated last week. But even if we abandon the processes of reason in favour of superficial appearances, the protectionists' campaign has been infertile. The cupboards of their minds are bare. The so-called 'new facts' boil down to one thing—the severity of the present unemployment.

One cannot attempt the cure of unemployment without first endeavouring to understand its causes. I should have thought that it was admittedly due to four main influences, and that the only matter of doubt was the relative importance of each of them.

We have serious unemployment to-day, first because we have had an unusually violent up-and-down of trade from the trough of which we are only just beginning to emerge. We suffered a violent inflation of credit followed by the inevitable reaction and aggravated in its later stages by an official policy of deflation. There are now many indications that we have seen the worst of this. Unemployment, though still very serious, is diminishing. The trade union unemployment figures are lower now than they have been for two and a half years. Organised short time in the cotton trade has been abandoned this week, and the prospective troubles of that industry are due to the shortage of the raw material rather than to a lack of demand for their goods. The iron and steel industries are definitely reviving, the output of steel being already a good deal larger than before the war. The production of coal is at a high level. Even shipbuilding—with the settlement of the boilermakers' dispute—is showing signs of life. I venture to predict that the unemployment due to the periodic trade depression will have largely disappeared before any protectionist measures can take effect. But apart from this, in what way could a tariff obviate the world-wide phenomenon of a trade depression? The United States suffered as severe a fluctuation of employment in spite of its tariff wall.

The second reason—who disputes it?—is the present state of Europe,—as much by its indirect as by its direct reactions. How will a tariff help this? Is a series of tariff wars going to help the world to settle down to stable economic conditions? It is not true that Europe is flooding us with goods. If we take France and Germany as typical of the two extremes in Europe to-day, the results are surprising. Allowing for the change in prices, the volume of our trade with these countries during the first six months of this year compared with the first six months of 1914 has been as follows:—

	Imports from France	Exports to France	Imports from Germany	Exports to Germany
1914	100	100	100	100
1923	74	130	25	65

The French tariff does not seem to have helped France much; nor the depreciated exchange, Germany. Free-trade England has been much more successful in selling her goods to these countries than they have been in selling to us.

The third reason is the high cost of our manufactures. Measured, not in money, but in terms of the amount of manufactured goods which we are offering in return for a unit of food imports, we are charging 20 per cent higher than before the war; and—not unnaturally perhaps—we are selling 30 per cent less in quantity. These high charges are due to a variety of causes. Some of them are being remedied,—this year is better than last year, and last year was better than the year before. But clearly a tariff must make matters worse; for it must, on the average, raise charges.

The fourth reason is the increase of population. We have more mouths to feed, and more hands to occupy in productive tasks. Readers of *The Nation and Athenæum* may know that I regard this with anxiety. But it is clear that this factor can be compensated in no other way than by expanding our international markets so as to sell more goods to pay for the needed imports. How can a tariff help this? By placing obstacles in the way of trade and increasing costs, it must hinder, not help, the expansion of our foreign markets.

Thus a tariff will not remedy any of the main causes of unemployment. Why does Mr Baldwin think that it will? I believe, as I wrote last week, that it is because he is a victim of the protectionist fallacy in its crudest form. If we keep out an imported article, he argues, which it is not impossible to make at home, some Englishman, now unemployed, will be employed on making it. *Voila tout*,—Mr Baldwin sees no further than that.

Does he suppose that we now get that import for nothing? If it has crossed his mind that we probably pay for it by an export, is it his idea that for the future we should make a present of that export to the foreigner? I have found no indication that Mr Baldwin and his friends* have advanced a step beyond this elementary folly when they prescribe a tariff to cure unemployment.

If protectionists merely mean that under their system men will have to sweat and labour more, I grant their case. By cutting off imports we might increase the aggregate of work; but we should be diminishing the aggregate of wages. The protectionist has to prove not merely that he has made work, but that he has increased the national income. Imports are receipts; and exports are payments. How, as a nation, can we expect to better ourselves by diminishing our receipts? Is there anything that a tariff could do, which an earthquake could not do better?

Let us pass from the general arguments to the immediate statistics. Our 'manufactured' imports, as classified by the Board of Trade, include many items, such as lead, copper, tin, oil, leather, &c., which for practical purposes are raw materials. Excluding these, we are importing manufactured goods to the value of about £130 millions a year,—a much smaller volume than before the War. Much of the value of these goods, however, comes from the raw materials which they contain and which we could not produce ourselves. For example, the largest single item is silk goods. Many other goods are specialities which we do not make here at all. Other important classes, e.g., motor-cars are taxed already. The industrial labour which would be required if we excluded all goods which we could make ourselves at a reasonable price would not be worth above £30 to £35 millions a year at the outside. Much of this labour would have to be highly skilled and highly specialised, and could not be

* See (e.g.) Mr Amery's 'reply' to Sir W. Beveridge in Wednesday's *Times*, where Mr Amery's argument clearly contemplates cutting down our imports by £100,000,000 and leaving our exports as they are. Mr Amery offers to the public in that letter, not new facts or plausible exceptional cases of a difficult balance of advantages, but just nonsense.

drawn from the ranks of the present unemployed. A more detailed analysis, showing that the vast bulk of our unemployed are in industries where there is no competition from manufactured imports, has been given in *The Times* (November 27th) in a most valuable communication from Sir William Beveridge. 'It is almost inconceivable', he concludes, 'that any committee of impartial and competent inquirers, who, as a preliminary to dealing with unemployment in this country to-day, looked at the facts of unemployment, would give a second thought to protection of the home market as a serious contribution to their task.'

But this is not the end. Mr Baldwin has made promises to agriculture, to Empire cotton-growing, and to consumers of tea and sugar, which will cost £25,000,000 to £30,000,000 to fulfil,—promises for which he proposes to pay out of duties on those manufactured goods which continue to come in. If the tariff is levied on classes of goods which we now import to the value of about £130 millions, the tariff would have to average 20 per cent all round to yield the required revenue, even if *no* goods whatever were kept out. Mr Baldwin has not given any indication how high a tariff he contemplates. Let us assume a tariff *averaging* 40 to 50 per cent *ad valorem* all round; he could then get the revenue he requires, if about half the goods were kept out. But obviously, taxation on this scale would change the direction of consumption; people would do without the taxed goods and buy more of the untaxed imports. Nor could our export industries be unaffected by the colossal rise which would ensue in the price of many goods. No one would believe in the permanence of a tariff on this scale, whilst a severe dislocation of industry must be the first result. The proposal to cure the present unemployment by a tariff on manufactured goods, which will also bring in a revenue of £25 millions, is a gigantic fraud, comparable in its intrinsic absurdity to the fraud of the 1918 Election about Germany paying for all.

The results of the election saw a decisive rejection of protection. The Conservatives, while still the largest party in the House of Commons with 258 members, lost their majority, while the Liberals elected 158 members and Labour 191. Baldwin did not resign until he met the new House and was defeated in the debate on the Speech from the Throne. Labour took office on 23 January 1924.

Chapter 3

MONETARY REFORM AND UNEMPLOYMENT

Keynes's *Tract on Monetary Reform* (*JMK*, vol. IV) was published on 11 December 1923. Keynes took advantage of its publication and a winter series of lectures at the National Liberal Club organised by the Liberal Summer School to discuss 'Currency Policy and Social Reform' on 13 December. He gave the same lecture in Edinburgh the next evening to the Young Scots Society.

Notes for a speech at the National Liberal Club, 13 December 1923

I have so big a subject today that I cannot hope to cover it. It falls naturally into two parts.

The importance of controlling currency and credit policy in the social interest.

The technical methods to be employed

I propose this evening to concentrate on the first of these topics.

I am not addressing an audience solely of experts.

Technical matters of some complexity are more easily apprehended in writing and [than?] by word of mouth. And I have the better excuse for adopting this course in that I have just published a book where my proposals are set forth in detail.

To begin with a few words about what should be the attitude of Liberalism towards social policy.

We are traditionally the party of *laissez-faire*.

But just as the economists led the party into this policy, so I hope they may lead them out again.

It is not true that individuals acting separately in their own economic interest always produce the best results.

It is obvious that an individualist society left to itself does not work well or even tolerably.

Here I agree with Labour.

I differ from them not in the desirability of state action in the common interest, but as to the forms which such interference should take. Their proposals are out of date and contrary to human nature.

But it is not safe or right just to leave things alone.

It is our duty to think out wise controls and workable interferences.

Now there is no part of our economic system which works so badly as our monetary and credit arrangements; none where the results of bad working are so disastrous socially; and none where it is easier to propose a scientific solution.

In the City of London there is a widespread belief that the pre-war system was as nearly perfect as the frailty of human nature permits, and that we need nothing but to return to it in every particle. This is a superstition which, if it did not exist, one would have deemed incredible.

Two kinds of changes in the value of money
(1) long period
(2) credit cycle

During 19th century gold moderately good in (1) but not very good,
necessarily a failure in (2)

In 20th century a failure in both.

In last ten years a dreadful and disastrous failure in both and for reasons I will give no grounds for expecting good behaviour in future.

Why do changes matter?

Under a regime of money-control
Expectations are based on stability

The investor lends in terms of money

The entrepreneur incurs liabilities in terms of money

If money fluctuates, expectations are upset and the harmony between individual interest and social interest is destroyed

If prices go up investment is discouraged
and enterprise discredited

If prices go down enterprise is brought to a standstill
(Example in full)

The triple evils of modern society
> Vast enrichment of individuals out of proportion to any services rendered
>
> Disappointment of expectation and difficulty of laying plans ahead—i.e. the precariousness of our economic system
>
> Unemployment   Strikes

All these mainly due to instability of standard of value.

The more troublous the times, the worse does a *laissez-faire* system work. I believe that the times are likely to remain troublous for a generation and that the magnification of the evils of monetary instability which we have suffered in the past 5 years are likely to continue unless we do something about it.

Arguments against gold standard
1st long period
> Accidents of 19th century won't be repeated
>
> No longer in circulation
>
> No longer in general use
>
> No longer a natural but already a managed standard
>
> Gold standard is now a dollar standard

Much as I admire the Americans, when *laissez-faire* takes the form of agreeing to do whatever the Americans do, I am a little terrified.

2nd short period
> Progress of scientific investigation since the War
>
> Hawtrey, Harvard Cambridge everywhere

One of the biggest jumps forward ever achieved in economic science

Although widely bruited, not yet taken in detail outside limited scientific circles.

Ups and downs of trade long existing back to 18th century

Various theories   Sun spots   Colds in the head

Now recognised as mainly monetary

The diagnosis almost complete

Now even if gold was stable over long periods, it cannot deal with short periods

For the cure for short period fluctuations depends on being able rapidly to expand or contract the volume of money.

The Bank of England since the war has always done exactly the opposite of what the latest science recommends. I conclude from this that their opposition comes, not from mere obstinacy or conservatism, but from their not yet understanding the point. I am, therefore, optimistic about the future.

What is the alternative to gold?

Our existing system but worked self-consciously and for a wise, deliberate purpose.

Here lies our golden opportunity,

Practically no legislation required

The object so to regulate the supply of Bradburies and of bank credit that their volume in terms of goods will be reasonably steady; i.e. that the index number of prices will never move far from a fixed point.

The methods essentially the same as with a gold standard. Under a gold standard we do not actually use gold as legal tender, but we try so to regulate the supply of legal tender that it has a fixed value in gold. Under my system our object is that it shall have a fixed value in goods.

A stable measuring rod

Contract requires it just as much as in weight

A sound money as great a step forward as when in the 32nd millennium B.C. Dungi conceived stability of weight

Since I am speaking under political auspices, I must mention the question often asked me

Can it be made a subject of platform controversy? I doubt it except in the most general terms if you mean platform meetings at a general election. But that is true of most serious, scientific reforms in our complicated economic life

Truth is complex.

But in study circles of serious Liberals such as this—certainly.

If I can persuade the younger generation of the City and the younger generations of Liberal politicians that what I am saying is wise and sensible, it will prevail.

The arguments are new and sufficiently complicated.

But I should like to warn the gentlemen of the City and of High Finance that if they do not listen in time to the voice of reason their days may be numbered. I speak to this great City as Jonah spoke to Nineveh that great city. I prophesy that unless they embrace Wisdom in good time, the system upon which they live will work so very ill that they will be overwhelmed by irresistible things which they hate much more than the mild and limited remedies offered them now.

The publication of the *Tract* brought several letters of comment. The first came from Cecil Lubbock, the Deputy Governor of the Bank of England.

From CECIL LUBBOCK, *12 December 1923*

Dear Keynes,

(I write to you this familiarly because we did meet the other day—at the Pol. Economy Club—and, chiefly, because we are both old K.S.'s,[1] though not of the same election.)

I am very grateful to you for sending me a copy of your book, which I began last night, and shall study carefully. Whatever my 'reaction' will be when I reach the end, I shall learn much from it.

We should all be grateful to you (1) for writing on economics in a style which 'an educated man' (as Broadbent would say) can read with pleasure and (2) for having your books printed in a type and got up in a style which makes them pleasant to deal with.

Believe me,

Sincerely yours
CECIL LUBBOCK

A week later, he heard from Alfred Marshall.

From ALFRED MARSHALL, *19 December 1923*

My dear Keynes,

Many thanks for your fascinating *Monetary Reform*. I have several times as much 'half-baked' work on hand, as I can hope to bring out of the oven: but I have been unable to keep my eyes off it. As years go on it seems to

---

[1] King's Scholars at Eton.

become even clearer that there ought to be an international currency; and that the—in itself foolish—superstition that gold is the 'natural' representation of value has done excellent service. I have appointed myself amateur currency-mediciner; but I cannot give myself even a tolerably good testimonial in that capacity. And I am soon to go away: but, if I have opportunity, I shall ask all new-comers to the celestial regions whether you have succeeded in finding a remedy for currency-maladies.

Yours ever,

A.M.

Another note came from Sir Charles Addis.

From SIR CHARLES ADDIS, *21 December 1923*

Dear Keynes,

I had ordered a copy of your book but am glad to have one from the author. Many thanks.

I find myself in agreement with nearly all of it, I think, except the conclusion. A managed currency may come some day, but I do not believe we are ripe for it yet. It would be ill to work except in an atmosphere of confidence and belief which at present is non-existent.

Believe me,
Yours sincerely
C. S. ADDIS

A final note came from Sir Basil Blackett, then Finance Member for the Viceroy's Council in India.

From SIR BASIL BLACKETT, *31 December 1923*

My dear Keynes,

I received yesterday from Montagu Norman a copy of your *Tract on Monetary Reform*, and read it through with immense interest. I think in chapter II you have brought out clearly for the first time what inflation is as a method of taxation. I at any rate feel I was much clearer about it than before after reading your book. In chapter V, though I agree with your self-criticism that you have compressed the argument unduly (p. 185) [*JMK*, vol. IV, p. 146], you have, I think, described the system actually in operation in England today very well. I do not think I agree with your proposals for the future. They seem to me to be further outside the realm of practical politics than I should have expected from you, though I am very likely wrong. I agree rather with Hawtrey. Indeed, I would go no further than Hawtrey in demanding a return to the gold standard as a preliminary to an attempt to stabilise the value of gold.

I send you another copy of a speech I made on December 4th; I believe I already sent you one. It is remarkable, I think, how closely our minds have been travelling in the same sort of direction. You will see that at the time you were writing your book I was anticipating your recommendation on page 156 [*JMK*, vol. IV, pp. 127–8] to defend the Government of India on the ground of the advantages of stable internal prices. I seem to have used almost your phrases on more than one occasion.

I have just completed a year here, and am starting again with a new Budget. But for the extraordinary uncertainty about the attitude of the Swarajists in the new Assembly, I should say that things are looking up financially for India. Something depends on what happens at home. I fear Baldwin seems to have made a bad mis-calculation.

With best wishes for 1924,

Yours sincerely,

BASIL P. BLACKETT

Keynes returned to the subject matter of the *Tract* in the new year with an article in *The Nation*.

From The Nation and Athenaeum, *2 February 1924*

GOLD IN 1923

Recent discussions about the future of gold lend special interest to Messrs Samuel Montagu & Co.'s annual bullion letter. Almost the whole of the world's output of gold is absorbed by India and the United States. 'In neither country', Messrs Montagu point out, 'is the gold put into circulation as currency. In the former it is regarded as a precious metal bearing a ratio towards rupees differing from that set up by the Imperial Government. In the latter, it is interned in the reserve of the Federal Banks, and its accumulation watched with anxious care, lest it should operate to the prejudice of prices and trade. In other words, the United States is suffering to some extent from the trouble that afflicted King Midas.'

The output of gold in the British Empire and the rest of the world respectively (taken at £4 4s. 11¾d. per fine oz.) has been distributed as follows:—

| | (000s omitted) | | | |
| | 1923 (est.) | 1922 | 1921 | 1920 |
	£	£	£	£
Transvaal	38,800	29,800	34,500	34,700
Canada	5,000	5,200	3,900	3,300
Australasia	3,300	3,700	4,200	4,700
Rhodesia	2,700	2,800	2,500	2,300
India	1,800	1,800	2,000	2,100
West Africa	900	900	900	1,000
British Empire total	52,500	44,200	48,000	48,100
Rest of the world	20,000	19,800	20,000	21,200
World's total	72,500	64,000	68,000	69,300

The stock of gold now held in the United Kingdom is:—

	£
Bank of England	126,000,000
Currency note reserve	27,000,000
Total	£153,000,000

The rest of the British Empire holds a visible stock of £105,000,000, distributed as follows:—

	£
Australia	24,800,000
New Zealand	7,900,000
Canada	38,200,000
South Africa	11,000,000
India	22,300,000
Straits Settlements	800,000
	£105,000,000

The United States, on the other hand, now holds more than three times as much gold as the whole of the British Empire, namely, £784,000,000, made up of:—

| U.S. Treasury | £145,500,000 |
| Federal Reserve Banks | £638,500,000 |

During 1923 gold imports into the U.S. have proceeded at a rate of some $25,000,000 (*net*) monthly. Not a dollar of this was wanted, and the gold reserves of the Federal Reserve System have now reached the unprecedented figure of 80 per cent of their note issue and deposits combined. Thus it has cost the United States during the past year about £100,000,000 to maintain gold at a purely artificial value (made up of about £30,000,000 interest on idle reserves and £70,000,000 for fresh redundant gold imported). Yet if the United States were to close their mints to the reception of further gold, everything would go on exactly as before, except that an additional £70,000,000 of capital reserves would become available during the year for use in other forms. It cannot be reasonable to suppose that this sort of thing will continue indefinitely. For example, it will take less than three years at the present rate—assuming that inflation is successfully avoided—for the gold of the Federal Reserve Banks to reach 100 per cent of their liabilities. What will they do then? They must close their mints to gold, or suffer an involuntary inflation.

If, under the pressure of such circumstances, the United States were to close their mints to the reception of imported gold—which could be done without upsetting any American interest and without interfering with the convertibility of American legal-tender money into gold—the producers of gold elsewhere would probably have to accept the Bank of England price for the bulk of their output. In this case sterling would immediately recover its full gold value whilst remaining at a discount on the dollar. And unless we were prepared to step into America's shoes and waste our money on bottling up gold (which we certainly could not afford), we also should be faced with the alternative of closing our mints to gold or suffering an involuntary inflation.

These ideas may be based on an extreme hypothesis. But they illustrate how precarious the future of gold now is, and what a cataract of superstition must cloud the eyes of those who think it reasonable to assume as a matter of course that the future value of gold in these altered conditions will be governed by just the same sort of considerations as before the War.

Some say that the large interest of the British Empire in gold-mining, as shown in the above figures, is a reason why we should strain ourselves to maintain the value of gold. If we are to abandon arguments about the general social advantages of a sound currency for calculations of this kind, it is worth pointing out that our debt to America is fixed in gold, that the annual burden of this is several times as large as our annual profits from gold-mining, and that every fall in the value of gold lightens this burden.

It would be rash to prophesy the future of an object to which the human race has been so anciently attached as gold. But the situation is peculiar. Only twice before have we had a state of affairs comparable with that produced by the dissipation, through the War, of the temple hoards (i.e., bank reserves) of Europe;—once when Alexander pillaged the bank reserves (i.e., temple hoards) of Persia, again when Spain pillaged those of Mexico and Peru. On each occasion there followed a catastrophic fall in the value of the sacred metal. If we are to judge the present situation by experience, we must cover a longer range of history than the City quotes; if we are to judge it by the light of reason, we must let our minds be bold.

Currency reform has two objects: to remedy the credit cycle and to mitigate unemployment and all the evils of uncertainty; and to link the monetary standard to what matters, namely, the value of staple articles of consumption, instead of to an object of oriental splendour, it is true, and one to which Egyptian and Chaldæan Bank Directors attributed magical properties, but not otherwise useful in itself and precarious in its future prospects. The time may come when currency reformers will appear plainly, not as suspects of inflation, but as the only safeguard against it.

The next week, acting under the guise of 'a French Correspondent'.[2] Keynes turned to another subject.

From The Nation and Athenaeum, *9 February 1924*

THE FRENCH PRESS AND RUSSIA

(*From a French Correspondent*)

L'Humanité, the chief organ of the French Socialist Party, has recently published, under the sweeping and sensational title of 'L'abominable vénalité de la Presse Française', a series of documents, which it states to be drawn from the secret archives of the Russian Government, demonstrating that from 1897 and particularly during the Russo-Japanese War (1904–5), right up to the Revolution of 1917, the Imperial Russian Government controlled a substantial number of the leading Paris newspapers, dictated their attitude on foreign policy, and supplied them with considerable sums. The fact that most of the papers attacked have taken so little action against the Socialist organ, seems to indicate that the documents published are authentic.

The Russian Minister of Finance had a representative in Paris, M. Raffalovich, with considerable sums at his disposal to use as he liked. It was he who handled the funds for the French press. He did not pay out anything himself, but only through the Syndicate of Bankers or through the Banque de Paris et des Pays-Bas, and on the advice of the head of the Stock Exchange, M. de Verneuil. Doubtless he feared to what dimensions its demands might reach, if the Press got wind officially of the fact that the Russian Government thought it important enough to vote it a large appropriation.

[2] Keynes had been in Monte Carlo for a holiday after Christmas.

Leaving aside the year 1897, when the first distributions were made, let us come at once to the years 1904–5, the time of the Russo-Japanese War and the Moscow riots. Raffalovich then forced the Parisian press to conceal the news of the Russian disasters in the field and the revolutionary troubles at home. On August 30th, 1904, he wrote to M. Kokovtzev, Minister of Finance, with the object of establishing his appropriation on the basis of the current year. 'For the first ten months,' he wrote, 'the abominable venality of the French press will have absorbed (over and above the advertising of the loan of 800 millions) a sum of 600 thousand francs, of which the banks have put up half... This payment is made to maintain Russian prestige, and to soften the systematic attacks made upon the Russian Government in general, though it cannot prevent them. If, in course of time, we wanted to get anything into the papers, we should have to take advantage of circumstances which had given us some influence over them.'

On March 1st, 1905, he further outlined his plan. 'It is necessary, according to Verneuil, that we should put great pressure on the political section of the newspapers to publish, along with the telegrams, editorial notes calculated to reassure the public about the solvency of Russia and the improbability of revolutionary success. He reckons the expense at between two and three millions for the year. It seems a lot; in February, 1904, it took 1,200,000 francs.'

This programme was carried out. One can guess to what extent the French public was kept informed about the real position of affairs in the country of her ally. M. Raffalovich effected these payments either in the form of financial advertisements, or bogus subscriptions, or even by private cheques slipped from hand to hand.

It would be tedious to set out here the names of all the papers which, according to the published documents, were effectively subsidised by the Russian Government, and the amount of the sums which they received. But among the papers with large circulations, Raffalovich shows that *Le Petit Parisien*, *Le Petit Journal*, *La Liberté*, *Le Figaro*, and *Le Temps*, cashed the largest subsidies. *Le Matin* also figures on the list with considerable sums. But it claims to be able to justify the sums it has received by authentic advertisements, not that that signifies that its attitude was uninfluenced by such lucrative contracts.

It may be interesting by way of example to read the following lines from Raffalovich's pen. They show how cleverly the representative of the Russian Finance Minister checked the attacks on his own Government, and indicate the degree to which the news in the most serious and representative organs was independent. The *Temps*, in spite of the 100,000 francs it had received in 1905 from the Banking Syndicate, had published a gloomy report upon the state of Russian finance, at the time of the issue of the loan. Raffalovich writes, on March 9th, 1905, that he has sent 1,000 francs 'to Hebrard, the editor of the *Temps*, to influence him'. On July 2nd of the same year he is more precise: 'Having found it essential to put an end to the veiled attacks of the *Temps*, I have given orders to bring about an arrangement, which has been carried out, in return for another 3,000 francs.'

The *Temps* went on receiving money from Russia for a long time. In the middle of the War, when the Empire was tottering, it undertook to publish special numbers on Russia. A contract on this subject was agreed upon in Petersburg in January, 1916, between the Imperial Minister of Finance and M. Charles Rivet, the Russian correspondent of the *Temps*.

The following are its two essential clauses:—

'The Russian Minister of Finance has complete liberty to settle the text of the Russian numbers, which will be published under his sole control. He can therefore dispose as he likes of the whole or part of the 5,000 lines or the equivalent space in each number.'

'...The Finance Minister gives M. Charles Rivet an annual subsidy of 150,000 francs.'

That is only one example. The list of cheques sent by Raffalovich to be distributed to the French press, which M. Souvarine publishes, is a long one. It amounts to several millions. Even so, these sums did not suffice to attach the press securely. As soon as the distributions ceased the papers started on new campaigns, doubtless to induce renewed outpourings. From 1906 to 1912 the subsidies decreased. M. Iswolski was able to write to M. Sazonov, Foreign Minister, on October 10th, 1912:—

'From then (1906) until now there has not been one copeck spent on the French press, and that has undoubtedly resulted in the press campaigns against us of 1908 and 1910.'

In 1912 the largesse was resumed.

What aggravates these acts of corruption—if the documents are authentic—is that the French Government knew about them, encouraged them, and on occasion directed them. In 1905 Rouvier consulted Raffalovich. In 1912, in the letter which we have already quoted, Iswolski was able to write: 'From my conversation with M. Poincaré I feel sure that he is ready to give his co-operation in this matter, and to show us the most suitable lines along which to spread out the subsidies.'

On February 14th, 1913, he added, still writing to M. Sazonov:—

'In my letter of October 10th/23rd last I told you the cogent reasons in favour of our financial deal with the French press. In the course of my conversation with the ex-President of the Council, M. Poincaré, now President of the Republic, I was convinced that he shares my opinion on this matter. Furthermore, M. Poincaré has expressed a wish that nothing should be done unknown to him, and that the distribution of the sums should be effected in co-operation with the French Government and through M. Lenoir.'

On June 4th, 1914, M. Kokovtzev, instructed by Raffalovich, wrote to M. Sazonov the following lines, which indicate the attitude of the Government of the Republic:—

'M. Klotz [he was then Minister for the Interior] insists upon the necessity now of disbursing large amounts to the Press because of the possibility of a campaign against the new military law, and also because of the general embarrassment of the French Government.'

One hesitates to speak of the action of a Minister who relies on the funds of a foreign Government to 'influence' the press of his own country in favour of the Government to which he himself belongs. Neither M. Poincaré nor M. Klotz has given an explanation in Parliament of the value, authenticity, and bearing of these documents

Thus, with the consent and support of the French Government, a foreign power was able by the vilest methods to suborn the greater part of the Paris press. The enslaved papers— assuming the correctness of the revelations in *L'Humanité*— encouraged the French public to subscribe to Russian loans which were often described as *formidable escroquerie*. They hid from France the advancing decay of the Empire to which she had bound her fate. They defended, for purely selfish interests, a policy which, by its ambitious designs, often inspired solely by dynastic sentiment, helped to create the atmosphere of trouble and ill-will which rendered the conflagration of 1914 inevitable. But this corruption, injected by a foreign Government, did not prevent the so-called patriotic newspapers from denouncing as traitors, as 'in the foreigner's pay', those statesmen and politicians who dared to face the danger and tell the truth at the peril of their lives.

A nation pays dear for such things. Who knows what part such systematic poison, extending over many years, may have played in preparing the way for the War? However this may be, the unhappy French investors who were deceived by these methods have totally lost a sum approaching one thousand million pounds sterling—probably more than one-half of the total savings of the country during the period in question.

A week later, however, he was back on the subject of gold.

From The Nation and Athenaeum, *16 February 1924*

THE PROSPECTS OF GOLD

In an interesting letter, which was published in *The Nation and Athenaeum* last week, commenting on my article 'Gold in 1923', Sir Henry Strakosch [a South African banker and member of the Financial Committee of the League of Nations] writes as follows:—

'America has so far refused—for reasons of her own—to accept from her foreign debtors payment either in goods, services, or securities. She has accepted gold from them, and in doing so has secured a free option to acquire goods, services, and securities in exchange for the gold whenever it happens to suit her.'

This passage, which is representative of a widely held opinion, can serve as my text in a further attempt to make clear why I differ from it.

I hold that gold flows to America because America offers in return for it a greater value in commodities than the gold is worth to the rest of the world. As none know better than Sir Henry Strakosch, gold is freely offered for sale in London every week; America is open to buy unlimited quantities of it at an almost fixed price in terms of goods (since, as Sir Henry points out, her price level has remained admirably stable for two and a half years); whilst the amount which the rest of the world wants on these terms falls far short of the current output. So long as these conditions continue, nothing on earth can prevent gold from flowing to the United States. She does not refuse to accept payment in other forms. She merely rates this particular form of payment at a higher value than the rest of the world does, with the result that it is profitable for the rest of the world to pay in this form rather than in any other.

It is not true, therefore, that she 'has secured a free option to acquire goods, services, and securities in exchange for the gold whenever it happens to suit her', if this means 'getting as much goods for the gold as she originally gave for it'. She can only get rid of the gold by selling it at a sacrifice,—that is to say by lowering its price in terms of goods.

This she can do in two ways only:—

1. By inflation, thus raising the dollar prices of goods and, which is the same thing, lowering the commodity price of gold in the United States; or

2. By closing her mints to the reception of further gold, thus allowing a fall in the value of gold without involving a corresponding fall in the value of the dollar.

As regards the first way, one trembles to think how much inflation would be required to enable her to get rid of an important proportion of her gold;—something so terrific, I should say, that this expedient may be ruled out of practical politics. Quite likely she will inflate; but not enough, I should anticipate, to lose any large quantity of her gold. Probably, therefore, she is stuck for all eternity with what she has already got, unless she is prepared to clear it at a great sacrifice. Thus her choice really lies between a continuance of the present state of affairs with gold steadily flowing in, more in some years, less in others, and occasionally perhaps a small outflow, and closing her mints as above. I suggested in my original article that in course of time the United States might tire of carrying the ever-growing weight of the golden calf, with its vast and vain expense.*

A third way out could only come through the rest of the world *raising* its relative valuation of gold. Some people think that a general restoration of the gold standard might bring this about. I agree that such might be the case to a certain extent. But even in this event the rest of the world would not want much more

* Sir H. Strakosch ignores, in his calculation of the cost to America, the burden of accepting additional gold. His figures represent, not what the gold standard costs America now, but what it would cost them if they were to take my advice and close their mints to new gold.

gold than it has already, or relieve the United States more than slightly. The more solvent countries of Europe, e.g., Great Britain, France, Sweden, Spain, and Holland, already have enough gold to run a gold standard, if the other conditions were present necessary for the restoration of such a standard; whilst the less solvent, e.g., Germany, Russia, Hungary, could not afford for many years to accumulate large stocks of barren metal.

It is commonly believed that the United States could relieve herself of her redundant gold if her investors would become more willing to lend abroad and to purchase foreign investments. This is a delusion,—unless the new foreign loans were of a purely inflationary character. If Americans were to invest their savings abroad instead of at home, there is no reason why this should cause any drain of gold out of America, any more than in the case of other countries which have invested abroad. If foreign investment always involved a drain of gold, it would have to be confined to gold-producing countries. A drain of gold would only follow if America's foreign loans did not represent real savings and involved an internal inflation; which brings us back to where we started, namely, that America can only get rid of this gold by depreciating the dollar through inflation.

The United States have, in fact, embarked on a vast valorisation scheme for the commodity gold, just like other valorisation schemes, e.g., that of Brazil for the commodity coffee;—but with much less prospect of the world demand overtaking the world supply. The value of gold depends upon the United States being willing to continue this valorisation scheme year after year, regardless of cost. It is for this reason, amongst others, that I declare the future prospects of gold to be precarious; particularly the prospects of gold mined outside the United States. The United States has no sufficient interest in spending £50,000,000 or more each year to absorb the redundant world supplies of a commodity she does not want. For a time she may continue,—partly because 'metallist' superstitions cloud men's eyes where the sacred metal is concerned, partly from the argument of 'protecting' the value of the existing stock, the usual argument when top-heavy valorisation schemes are getting too expensive; but, surely, not for ever.

There is a further question, just touched on in my previous article, which Sir Henry Strakosch and also Mr Coutts raised last week in their letters to the Editor,—namely, the effect of a fall in the commodity value of gold on the position of creditor countries. I do not think that currency policy ought to be determined, one way or the other, by such considerations; for the point arises with every change in the price level, whatever the cause or the direction of the change may be. But I agree with these correspondents that, when the calculation is made, there are several items to be reckoned on both sides of the account. Nevertheless, this question does not arise, except where foreign loans have been expressly contracted in terms of gold. The United States, it is true, both owes and is owed certain sums in gold. It is not the case with Great Britain. Our loans are in terms of sterling, not of gold; and during the ten years which have elapsed since we were on a gold standard, no suggestion to the contrary has ever arisen. If, indeed, we were proposing to raise the commodity value of sterling, our creditors might have a grievance in equity; but this is not the intention. If the commodity value of sterling were to be stabilised near the present level, our debtors would still be repaying us in a currency much less valuable than that in which the debt was originally contracted; and since they pay us in goods and services, this is what matters to them. If, however, it were thought necessary, for this or any other reason, to protect the value of gold by artificial means, it would be much cheaper to buy up the South African mines in order to close them down, rather than to buy their output year by year in order to bury it. The United States could buy all the mines in Africa and cement them down securely for about twice the sum which they now expend in a single year in purchasing and burying their output. I recommend this programme to the devotees of the gold standard.

On 23 February Keynes began what was to become his series of comments on the annual speeches of the chairmen of the London clearing banks.[3] Three weeks later, he turned his attention to the French financial situation.

From The Nation and Athenaeum, *15 March 1924*

THE FRANC

The expected has occurred; and it has occurred so precisely as it was expected that we are almost surprised. The watched pot has boiled. We can, after all, repeat:—

> *Raro antecedentum scelestum*
> *Deseruit pede Pœna claudo.*

But what, everyone now asks, will happen next? In a confused situation one must cling to first principles. The value of the franc will be determined, first, by the quantity, present and prospective, of the francs in circulation; and, second, by the amount of purchasing power which it suits the public to hold in that shape. The former of these two elements depends on the loan and budgetary policies of the French Treasury; the latter (in present conditions) mainly on the trust or distrust which the public feel in the prospects of the value of the franc.

With the franc between 100 and 120 to the £ sterling, the control of the former does not appear to the outside observer to be unduly difficult. When the internal price level has adjusted itself to this figure, the yield of many of the existing taxes in terms of paper francs will naturally be increased. On the other hand, the biggest item of expenditure, namely, the service of the internal debt, will remain the same as before. Thus, even apart from additional taxation, the mere movement of the exchange has in itself a tendency to restore the budget towards equilibrium, provided always that public faith is maintained in the prospects of the national currency. It is in this second factor, therefore, that the crux of the situation lies,—namely the attitude of the

[3]   It appears in *JMK*, vol. IX, pp. 188–92.

French public towards their own currency. I emphasise the fact that the matter lies in the hands of Frenchmen themselves, not in those of any foreign persons. For the amount of francs owned by foreigners is probably not very great,—not much more than what is still left in their hands as the remnant of disappointed 'bull' operations; whilst the obstacles are insuperable to 'bear' sales by foreigners of francs, which they do not possess, on a really large scale. On the other hand, the volume of franc notes and franc bills and other short-dated investments held in France itself is enormous,—far beyond the minimum required for the convenient transaction of business. If Frenchmen get it into their heads (as, each in their turn, Russians, Austrians, and Germans have done) that their national legal-tender money and titles to legal tender represent a depreciating asset, then there is no limit to the fall in the value of the franc. For, in this event, they will diminish their holdings of such assets; they will keep fewer Bank of France notes in their pocket-books and in their safes, will liquidate their *Bons de Trésor* and will sell their *Rentes*. No law or regulation will avail to restrain them. Moreover, the process will be cumulative; for each successive liquidation of franc assets and their transference into 'real values', by provoking a further fall, will seem to justify the prescience of those who fled first from the franc, and will thus prepare the way for a second outbreak of distrust.

In this case the fall of the franc will not be prevented even by a reformed budget or a favourable surplus of trade. For it would be necessary for the Government to absorb the redundant bank notes and franc bonds and bills, which the public no longer cared to hold,—a task unavoidably beyond the Government's power. We have the experience of many countries to demonstrate that unbalanced budgets are the initial cause of a collapse, but that the real *dégringolade* only comes when the confidence of the general public is so far undermined that they begin to contract their holdings of the legal-tender money.

The central task of the French Government at this moment

is, therefore, to preserve confidence in the franc in the minds of the widest circles of the French public. For it is the failure of this internal confidence, not speculation by foreigners (though foreigners and Frenchmen too may take advantage of a collapsing currency to win great gains), which would prove their undoing.

Now, if they go the right way about it, there is nothing impossible in the task of restoring and maintaining confidence. The examples of Russia, Austria, and Germany are not a just parallel. Those who foresee the future of the franc in the light of such previous experiences may make a big mistake. For in those countries the problem of balancing the budget was, during the earlier phases, a virtual impossibility. The initial impulse towards collapse was, therefore, also a continuing impulse. This is not so in France. There is no impossibility in achieving a fiscal equilibrium, provided that reconstruction expenditure is reasonably postponed. I applaud the efforts of M. Poincaré and the French Treasury in this direction. But this is not enough by itself. It is also necessary to restore public confidence; and in this sphere of action every step taken by M. de Lasteyrie has been away from wisdom.

For upon what foundations does the credit of a currency rest? They are much the same as with a bank. A bank can only attract and retain the deposits of its clients so long as these clients possess a complete confidence in their freedom to withdraw their deposits for exchange into other assets, if they have a mind to do so. As long as this liberty is beyond doubt, it will not be exercised;—the deposits will rest and grow. But if it is once called in question, they shrink and disappear. So is it with a currency. Men hold a part of their resources in money, because they believe it to be more readily and freely interchangeable, than any alternative hoard, into whatsoever object of value they may select hereafter. If this belief proves false, they will not hold money and nothing can make them do so.

Now the prime object of most of M. de Lasteyrie's regulations is to restrict the liberty of holders of francs to exchange them at their discretion into other forms of value. So far, therefore, from protecting the franc and restoring its credit, they are directly calculated to shatter confidence and to destroy its credit. A sufficient number of regulations would destroy the value, precisely because they would destroy the utility, of any currency in the world. As soon as there is a doubt as to whether francs (or *Bons de Trésor*) are a truly liquid asset, these instruments cease to serve the purpose for which they are held, and holders hasten to dispose of them before the doubt is resolved into a certainty and yet further obstacles can have been placed in the way. Just as a man draws out his deposits at the bank, whether he needs the money or not, as soon as he has reason to believe that he may not be free to do so later on; so the general public and the financial world alike withdraw their resources from a currency, if they fear a limitation on their subsequent freedom of withdrawal.

What course then should the French Treasury now take in face of the dangers surrounding them? It is soon said. First, the Government must so strengthen its fiscal position that its power to control the volume of the currency is beyond doubt,—the necessity of which is at last accepted. Secondly—and especially during the interval which must needs elapse before the first category of measures can be brought into full operation—the Government must restore such complete confidence in the liberty of the franc that no one will think it worth while to enter by way of precaution into sales of francs not immediately urgent,—the equal necessity of which seems to be overlooked.

To achieve this latter object nothing more is required than a reversal of the recent policy of restrictions on dealing, of the useless hoarding of gold, of a relatively low bank rate, and of secrecy about the actual position of the Treasury and the Bank of France. The chief measures which are necessary can be summarised under three heads:—

(1) All limitations on the use of francs to purchase foreign currencies, foreign bonds, or goods, whether for immediate or for deferred delivery, should be wholly repealed.

(2) The discount rate of the Bank of France should be raised to a high figure, probably not less than 10 per cent in present circumstances (though it might not be necessary to maintain such a high rate for any length of time), so as to counteract anticipations, well or ill founded, as to the possible depreciation of the franc. In view of the high rate of interest now obtainable on French Government securities (let alone the rates on forward exchange) the present rate of discount does not correspond to the facts of the situation and is calculated to stimulate over-borrowing. Possibly some increase of the Bank of France's rate may have been effected by the time these lines are in print.

(3) A considerable sum, drawn from the still ample gold reserve of the Bank of France, should be made the basis of a foreign credit, either by outright sale or by borrowing against it, to be available for use without stint in supporting the exchange near the present level and restoring confidence during the interval before fiscal reforms can produce their full effect. An advance of a hundred million dollars from Messrs J. P. Morgan has actually been arranged on these lines since the above was written.

I warrant that these simple well-tried measures, in combination with political moderation and with the drastic economies and taxes without which no other measures can finally avail, would have a marvellous efficacy. After a few weeks of this medicine and with a benevolent reception by M. Poincaré (or his successor) of the forthcoming Experts' Reports,[4] the franc might be as steady as a rock. But if, on the other hand, distrust in the franc is countered by the methods of the Holy Inquisition, if Frenchmen prefer the concealed capital levy of inflation to other forms of taxation, if France remains the trouble-peace of Europe—then the franc may follow the course of other once-noble tokens.

---

[4] In December 1923 two committees of experts were appointed under the auspices of the Reparations Commission to enquire into the possibilities of (1) the restoration of Germany's financial stability, and (2) the expropriation of German capital abroad. For Keynes's view of the work of these committees, which reported on 19 April, see *JMK*, vol. XVIII, pp. 235–46.

From 25 to 27 March the League of Nations Union held a conference in London on Unemployment in its National and International Aspects. Amongst those who took part were Edwin Cannan, T. E. Gregory, H. D. Henderson, Keynes and Barbara Wootton. Keynes addressed the conference on the first day as part of a panel dealing with financial factors.

From Unemployment in its National and International Aspects[5]

MR J. M. KEYNES'S SPEECH

Mr J. M. Keynes, C.B. (author of *The Economic Consequences of the Peace*, etc.) said:

I think it may assist clearness in this discussion if we try to disentangle several distinct issues that have arisen out of the speeches of the two preceding speakers. There is, first of all, the question: Is the financial factor a big one in causing unemployment? The second question (assuming that the first is answered in the affirmative) is: Are our bankers of such feeble intellect that they are incapable of applying up-to-date remedies, with the result that up-to-date remedies are not worth discussing? The third question is: Are the up-to-date remedies really efficacious? Professor Cannan, I think, denied all those three things in part. I should like to take them in order.

First of all, is the financial factor an important one in causing unemployment? It was not quite clear what Professor Cannan's answer to that was. He told us that the financial factor was not the sole factor. That is agreed. But I did not hear any other argument as to its not being an important factor.

According to Professor Cannan, there were two other very significant factors at the present time: first, that owing to the interruption of the war labour was often in the wrong place, that labour was arranged to produce a different category of articles from that which was required. That is certainly so. If, for example, in England now there were 50,000 fewer men in the

---

[5] International Labour Office, *Studies and Reports*, series C (Unemployment), no. 9 (Geneva, 1924).

engineering, iron and steel industries and 50,000 more men in the building industries there would probably be less unemployment. The second cause he gave was that with better unemployed pay there is not quite the same pressure that there used to be on the individual unemployed man to secure employment. Well, the point may be approaching when those two causes are beginning to be responsible for a large part of the residuum. The unemployment figures which, a little time back, were of the order of 12 per cent have now fallen, I think, to 7 or 8 per cent, and may easily fall in the near future towards 5 per cent; and when we reach 5 per cent it may be correct to argue that the other causes to which Professor Cannan called attention are largely responsible.

I would add a third possible cause, and that is that wages may be maintained by the power of trade unions at a higher level than the export trades can support, with the result that at that level of wages all the men cannot be employed. Those three causes: the fact that in some industries wages may be too high, that in other industries there may be more labour than can be absorbed and the labour ought to go to other industries where they are short of labour, and the fact of better unemployed pay compared with old days—those causes may be the predominant ones when we have got unemployment down to 4 or 5 per cent, and in that case they may be a very significant factor now.

But Professor Cannan has not only to maintain that; he has to maintain that they were a very predominant factor a year ago or more when our unemployment figures were 12 per cent. The worst of the slump, in my opinion, is nearly over. The great damage done on this particular occasion by the financial factor is working towards its conclusion, as is always the case. When you are near the end of a slump, when you are even perhaps at the beginning of the new boom, the financial factor has ceased to be an important one for unemployment. I should think that it still plays a part, though a very much less important part, than it did when the unemployment figures were 12 per cent.

I do not believe that it is possible to make a plausible case for supposing that when unemployment was 12 per cent, such factors as were mentioned by Professor Cannan were predominant ones, and it is quite sufficient for the purposes of this discussion that at certain phases of the credit cycle the unemployment should be largely caused by the monetary factor, because what we want to deal with is the cause of unemployment which makes these very bad unemployment figures. When we have got unemployment down to 4 or 5 per cent, then there are other causes which also have to be tackled by other methods, but, if you have the financial factor responsible for the difference (say) between 5 and 12 per cent, then it is an enormous cause of immense poverty, immense suffering, and it is a matter which it is well worth bending our energies to get rid of.

I daresay that Professor Cannan would not deny that, when unemployment was 12 per cent, the financial factor was important; and if he agrees that the financial factor was important at that point, or that it was important in the depressions following pre-war times, then we agree that the consideration of the means of curing the financial factor is one of the chief things to which those people interested in getting rid of unemployment have to pay attention.

Operation of the financial factor

The precise way in which the financial factor operates is, of course, a big question which one cannot deal with fully in the course of a single afternoon's discussion. Mr Henderson dwelt on a great many sides of it. I should like just to mention in passing one aspect which perhaps he did not stress so much as I should. That is, quite apart from the positive action of the banks, the effect on the business world of an *anticipation* that prices are going to go up or down.

The business world has to provide for the considerable period which elapses between beginning the process of production and the consumer getting the goods and paying for them. In different industries that interval of time varies, but in many industries it is not less than six months from the beginning to the end of the process, and, where long distances are concerned, it is very often a great deal more. All through that time the entrepreneur is engaged in paying out money for wages, and in other ways, which he will recoup when, at the end of the process, he sells his article for money. All his normal calculations as to rate of profit and correct level of wages and so forth are based on the assumption that money is going to be worth more or less the same at the end of the period that it is at the beginning. If it is worth a very different amount, then such sound calculations are thrown out. If it is worth a great deal less—that is to say, if prices have risen—the entrepreneur receives a very large unexpected, uncalculated bonus; if, on the other hand, money has risen in value and prices have fallen, he suffers a very large loss. It therefore is an important part of his business to try to predict which of these two things is going to happen, and if he anticipates that prices are going to fall it is very often (not always, but very often) the case that the only way in which he can protect himself from this very large loss, for which he cannot make any adequate provision in his normal profits, is by reducing his scale of operations and more or less going out of business.

Thus you get a situation in which the individual employer has an interest in acting in a way opposite to the public interest. So far as the community as a whole is concerned, the thing is as broad as it is long. If the article in question is worth a given amount of effort to produce to the community, if the amount of effort that it is worth to the community is the same at the beginning of the process as at the end, it is in the interest of the community that it should be made; but it does not follow that it is in the interest of the employer, because of this calculation of money which comes in. It is only worth his while if the calculations that he makes about the value of money are borne out.

Therefore I should say that one of the principal ways in which the financial factor operates is to cause, rightly or wrongly, an expectation in the minds of individual persons that prices are going to move in a certain direction; and if the business world as a whole is widely of the opinion that prices are going to fall, then there will be numerous individuals who can only protect themselves from loss by throwing their employees out of work, although the things those employees would make if they were in work are necessary and useful and desirable, at that cost of effort, to the community as a whole.

So the method of curing that would be to prevent, so far as one could, that there should be any reason why business men should expect that prices are going to fall. If you have a paper deflation, if the government announces that prices are going to fall, then, of course, the thing being almost a certainty, you have unemployment at its worst; but without that being the case circumstances may arise—often have arisen in the past—in which the business world has valid reasons for expecting a fall of prices, and the way of handling that must be to have a new method of regulation so that it would be a very rare thing—if possible, a thing that never happened—that there would be any valid reasons why the business world as a whole should entertain the expectation of falling prices.

Mental capacity of bankers

That is all I am going to say about the question whether the financial factor causes unemployment. I think myself that it is a thing absolutely outside argument: it is certain that it does. The next question is: Are our bankers intellectually so feeble that they are incapable of applying the up-to-date remedies? Dr Cannan expressed the opinion that they were. I do not agree with him. I think that those bankers who would be responsible for this class of control are perfectly capable of carrying it out.

But let us consider the alternative. Let us imagine Professor

Cannan's answer to the people of this country. Suppose it is true that the financial factor is the cause of unemployment, suppose it is true that there is an up-to-date remedy which, if intelligently applied, would cure that unemployment. Professor Cannan is going to the people of this country and he is going to say: 'You have those unemployed, and the reason why is because bankers are intellectually feeble, and as it is necessary that bankers should be intellectually feeble you will always have unemployed and there is no more to be said about it.' That does not seem to me a situation in which the public are likely to acquiesce. If it is true that the bankers are incapable of exercising this kind of control, obviously they must be replaced by other persons and there can be no question that that is the attitude which the community would rapidly take.

But I think there is one great mistake about this. There are two kinds of banking: there is the kind of banking undertaken by the ordinary banker as the public thinks of him, who deals with his customers, whose main business is to see that his customers are solvent and suitable to lend money to, and who directs the deposits of the community into the most advantageous channels. That is a business in itself, a business which bankers, I think, carry on in this country with great efficiency. But there is also this totally different problem of national policy in the matter of the aggregate of credit as a whole, as distinct from the particular individuals who obtain it.

A wholly different question requires different training and different gifts, and that the bankers who are largely occupied in the first task should not always be the most suitable persons for carrying out the second is no more surprising than that stockbrokers should not be the most suitable for insurance brokers. It is not more surprising and not more discreditable to them than that the persons who canvass for the Prudential should not be the right persons for managing the investment policy of the Prudential Insurance Company. But as a matter of fact it is of no great importance, because no one would propose to hand over this sort of control to the particular individuals who are mainly engaged in that kind of banking.

As Mr Henderson pointed out, this is a matter which should be in the hands of the Bank of England and of the central authorities generally. Exactly what division of functions there would be between the Bank of England and the Treasury, one could talk about for a long time. The matter would be in the hands of the central authorities, and they would have totally different tasks in front of them from those the ordinary individual banker has had. For a very long time past the kind of tasks that the Governors of the Bank of England have had to carry out have required gifts of quite a different kind from those which were needed from the ordinary joint-stock banker, and I do not think there is the slightest reason for supposing that the talent of the country available for work of that kind is in any way short of what it ought to be. I think that the intellectual ability which has controlled the policy of the Bank of England over past years has been extraordinary. New ideas have lately grown up as to what the aim of their policy ought to be. That is one thing. But the success with which they have in the past carried out the daily technique of quite as difficult a problem namely, the maintenance of the gold standard in conditions where gold is not the primary medium of circulation, is quite enough encouragement. At any rate, I do not think that we could seriously be stopped from using this particular cure for unemployment for such reasons as Professor Cannan suggested under that heading.

Dual method of credit control

I come to the third heading, which is much the most difficult and most important. Are these new-fangled remedies adequate to solve the problem? That seems to me the real serious subject of discussion. It is extraordinarily difficult to demonstrate that any new remedy which has never been tried on an important scale will be effective. One will never have a final answer to this question until one has tried. In the case of any new proposal all one can do is to show that there are some theoretical reasons for thinking it might be effective, and then, if the importance of the occasion justifies it (which it would in this case), to make the experiment and see how successfully it can be carried out.

I think that Professor Cannan expressed scepticism on this head, partly because he has not appreciated—or, at any rate, did not mention—the nature of the method that we propose to employ. He seemed to think that the sole method of effecting this would be by movements of the Bank rate very much as they used to move prior to the War, and to argue quite plausibly that the extra expense of paying a high rate for money for a short period would not be a very important element entering into the calculations of business men.

But why does he suppose that that is the only method which would be employed? It is one of the methods, but I personally have come more and more to the view that the more powerful method—certainly the weapon upon which one would have to depend in the last resort—would be variations in the volume of deposits in the Bank of England available to joint-stock banks as the basis of their working credit. For all practical purposes joint-stock banks leave their cash in the strict sense and their deposits at the Bank of England. They then use those almost in accordance with rules of thumb for building up a superstructure.

Now, there are two ways in which the amount of credit they offer can be reduced, partly by raising the price—that is the method of the Bank rate—and partly by diminishing the supply or increasing it, as the case may be; that is to say, by varying the amount of the deposits of the bankers at the Bank of England. That is a matter which is just as much under the control of the Bank of England as the Bank rate is, because by buying or selling Conversion Loan or any other security they can reduce the bankers' balances or increase them within considerable limits at will, and I believe the limits are quite big enough to produce a drastic effect, so that the actual technique of the business would be by expanding and curtailing the basis of credit quite as much as by raising or lowering the price of credit.

The psychological factor

But I should depend almost more upon the third factor, namely, the psychological factor. Suppose the business world believed that this policy was going to be put through with determination, so that when there was a tendency for prices to rise all the forces of the financial world would be brought to bear to prevent them rising further, then the kind of expectation of which I have spoken would never arise strongly enough to make them go out of business and reduce the extent of employment to the degree they do now.

It is not the actual rise or fall or prices that causes unemployment, although the actual rise and fall of prices causes profits and losses to business men. What chiefly causes unemployment is the anticipation of falling prices. If, therefore, this policy can be put strongly into force, so that the business world knows that when prices have risen more than a certain amount every possible measure will be taken to prevent them rising further, that will very much diminish the expectation of falling prices which they would otherwise entertain. It may not abolish it altogether. In the early days they will not feel as much confidence as they will later on, so in the early days you may have to allow yourself a little more oscillation than you have to have later on, and have to act rather more ruthlessly than you would wish to as a permanency. But if you can by success on some critical occasion convince the business world as to the efficacy of your weapons, if you use them to the full, the psychological effect will be that on future occasions it will probably be quite unnecessary to use anything like such drastic methods as you had to use on the first occasion or two.

If both those weapons were used, I must say I cannot understand a doubt as to their producing some effect. Again, one is up against the kind of argument which Mr Henderson foreshadowed. Of course, the thing will not be absolutely successful; therefore it is no use at all. That is the kind of argument one is constantly having to deal with. It will be quite sufficient to justify the attempt at the experiment if it would produce some results, if action of this kind would diminish the expectation of falling prices and damp down the extent of the oscillation. Enthusiastic individuals, or those who have more faith in these theories, may entertain exaggerated hopes, may think they will cure it entirely; but it is not necessary for the general public to go all the way with you to agree that the experiment is well worth trying. Though very partially success-ful, it would still have done a great deal of good and no harm whatever.

A case for experiment

If one is making only that limited claim for it, I find it very difficult to doubt the efficacy of the weapon in the hands of the Bank of England. Of course, those persons who dispute altogether the relation between the volume of purchasing power and the level of prices will be impressed no more by this argument than by any other rational argument on the subject of money. But those who agree on the fundamentals of monetary theory with Professor Cannan and myself—I do not think we differ in the slightest on that—can hardly doubt, I should have thought, that contracting and expanding the ultimate volume of purchasing power on which credit is based must have its effect on prices and on the expectation of rising and falling prices; and, if that is the case, you have a sufficient *prima facie* argument for trying this great experiment.

It happens that, at the moment, we can try it without jeopardising anything else. We are not on a gold standard basis;

we are not likely to be in the very near future. The policy of deflation has been abandoned, and we therefore have an extraordinary opportunity of trying the experiment of the new policy without doing any harm to anyone.

I would like to say, in conclusion, that I think the situation may arise in which possibly Professor Cannan and I will be happily agreed once more as to practical politics. There is an extraordinary tendency in the world to think that if you are in favour of dear money at one time you must always be in favour of it, and if you are in favour of cheap money at one time you must always be in favour of cheap money. Many people are congenital deflationists and many others congenital inflationists. In many circles it is considered almost as indecent to be sometimes in favour of a high Bank rate and sometimes a low Bank rate as to be sometimes a Conservative and sometimes a Liberal. Just as every little boy and girl is supposed to be born into the world either Liberal or Conservative, there are supposed to be born dear-money children and cheap-money children, and any oscillation between those two tendencies is very incorrect.

That is all rubbish. Any sensible person is in favour of dear money in certain circumstances and cheap money in other circumstances. When one is in favour of dear money one is considered highly respectable amongst the congenital deflationists and a great obstructionist of the progress of industry amongst the congenital inflationists; and the other way round when one is in favour of cheap money one becomes highly disreputable in the minds of the congenital deflationists and one gets a lot of unmerited sympathy from the congenital inflationists.

I was in favour of dear money before the break of the boom in 1920, and got into a good deal of trouble for wanting a 7 per cent Bank rate at what was called an inappropriate date. When the whole thing had broken and we had the depression, cheap money seemed to me to be an absolute *desideratum*. I then became a disreputable person in the eyes of Professor Cannan and his friends. I believe that not many months will elapse before I shall be in favour of dear money again. In the ordinary course the present slump will come to its final conclusion, and, just as on previous occasions, a boom will begin; so that we may be able to make our first experiment with the new policy, not in checking the slump, which will bring one to discredit with Professor Cannan, but in checking the boom, which will bring one to credit with him.

If, therefore, by the date at which one could hope that some of these ideas may be beginning to fructify, the slump is thoroughly over and the boom beginning, we shall make our first experiment in the form of putting on dear money at a very early date compared with previous occasions and avoiding the impending boom of 1925 or 1926; and that may, at any rate for the moment, unite with the reformers that respectable body of persons who think that what one really requires is always falling prices rather than stable prices.

So I look forward to an opportunity in the near future of making a little test as to the efficacy of the new ideas. I stress the fact that they are new ideas because I think very few economists held quite the view on this subject ten years ago that they hold now. An enormous amount of work has been done, an enormous amount of thinking and investigation of details. I believe that a great leap forward has been made, economists have really discovered something thoroughly useful for once, and if they have the chance of experimenting with these ideas in circumstances in which, even in the eyes of Professor Cannan, they can do no harm, we may make a great step forward in the solution of the problem which this Conference is to discuss.

On 5 April Keynes returned to the columns of *The Nation* to provide an anonymous leader on recent financial dealings in the newspaper world.

From The Nation and Athenaeum, *5 April 1924*

NEWSPAPER FINANCE

We had occasion six months ago to comment on the finance of the Rothermere Newspaper Trust. This week the Messrs Berry (whose principal newspaper properties are *The Financial Times*, *The Graphic*, and *The Sunday Times*) have gone one better. Last Monday's issue of £4,750,000 8 per cent preference shares of the Allied Newspapers Ltd. has carried to its extreme point the policy of utilising a boom period and the powers of giant advertising to unload on the public the financial risk and burden of one of the most speculative of industries, whilst retaining for the inner ring the surplus profits, if any, together with complete control of the newspapers, in return for next to nothing.

Let us start with the bare facts. Last autumn the Daily Mail Trust purchased the Hulton Press at a net cost of £4,750,000 (after allowing for the proceeds of certain portions of it which were disposed of immediately). These same properties, *minus* the valuable London properties *The Daily Sketch* and *The Illustrated Sunday Herald*, are now sold by them for £5,500,000 in cash and debentures. Thus the Daily Mail Trust has secured an immediate profit of £750,000 *plus The Daily Sketch* and *The Illustrated Sunday Herald* for nothing. The subscribers to the Daily Mail Trust debentures do not touch much of this, although it was they who found the money for the original deal; nevertheless they are to have half their holdings repaid at 10 per cent premium, so that they have no reason to complain that another party has been found to carry the baby.

Unless Sir Edward Hulton, who may be presumed to have understood his own papers, sold outrageously too low, it appears on the face of it that the new purchasers have bought outrageously too high. But this is not the end of the deal. The new purchasers are in the first instance the Sunday Times Ltd, but this company immediately resells to a new company, the Allied Newspapers

Ltd, which has been floated for the purpose, the above properties *plus The Sunday Times* at a price equal to that paid to the Daily Mail Trust *plus* £400,000 in cash and £2,000,000 in ordinary shares. Since the Sunday Times Ltd distributes £510,000 of these ordinary shares to the underwriters of the new issue, the sale price of *The Sunday Times* appears to be £400,000 in cash and £1,490,000 in ordinary shares. The present capital of the Sunday Times Ltd is £67,257 in ordinary shares, all owned by the Messrs Berry, and £30,000 in preference shares. Thus the Messrs Berry obtain in cash what looks like a full price for *The Sunday Times*, and get in addition ordinary shares in the new company, which may be worth much or nothing, but give them in either case effective control of the newspapers. (The preference shareholders do not vote, in normal circumstances, unless their dividends are in arrear, and even then will have to organise themselves energetically to outvote the holders of the ordinary shares. The principal officials have five-year contracts.) The public are asked to put up a sum which a reasonable person might estimate to be not less than the full value of the properties, whilst surrendering to the promoters the right to surplus profits and the control of the papers.

What security have the public for the due payment of their dividends? We notice at the outset that, whereas the Daily Mail Trust offered 7 per cent *debentures*, the new Company offers 8 per cent *preference* shares, with £1,500,000 debentures in front of them, and ordinary shares, which are wholly water, behind them. Next, the published figures disclose the fact that in no year prior to 1922 were the profits of the joint concerns sufficient to pay the preference dividend in full. In 1920 there was a net loss, explained by the high price of paper. On the average of the four years 1918–1921 the surplus profits, after meeting debenture charges, were equivalent to an average of less than $3\frac{1}{2}$ per cent on the preference shares now issued. The capitalisation is entirely based, therefore, on the results of the two years 1922 and 1923, on the basis of which the preference dividend is covered rather less than twice. The interest is cumulative, but

195

there appears to be no provision for building up a fund for the equalisation of dividends in poor years. If the present boom in the profits of big newspaper syndicates continues two or three years longer, the large temporary surplus can be drained away out of the business into the pockets of the ordinary shareholders.

How is the public induced to swallow this prodigious proposition? The answer to this question is not the least interesting part of the business. There have been several recent issues, of which the expenses have been out of all reason. But here again the Messrs Berry go one better. The expenses of the issue are estimated at £150,000 for preliminary expenses, of which stamp duty presumably accounts for £82,500, *plus* £354,000 in cash and £510,000 in ordinary shares as underwriting commission and expenses of the offer for sale. Thus the mere flotation, exclusive of stamp duty, and apart from promotion profits, costs more than £400,000 in cash and £500,000 in shares. This must constitute a record! Evidently the risk that the public would not bite was reckoned high. But enormous commissions to the financial world and enormous advertising expenditure in the newspaper world can go a long way towards silencing criticism. The fear, lest the hand might this time have been overplayed, proved baseless. The public oversubscribed the issue within a few hours. As *The Financial Times* put it next morning, 'investment was not deterred by slightly prattling criticism'. Apart from *The Daily Mirror*'s headline *Lists Open for Golden Chance*, most of the daily papers refrained from good words and quoted the prospectus without comment, the City Editor of *The Times* and *The Daily Herald* being almost alone, amongst the leading organs, in outspoken criticism. The names of the Westminster Bank, Lloyd's Bank, and Barclay's Bank appear on the prospectus, and not all of the public are aware that the name of a bank on a prospectus means nothing as to the merits of the issue.

The episode is now over. The money of the public is engaged, and we must hope for the best. But we can draw the moral from this and other recent experiences that the power of large-scale advertising in securing the savings of the public is altogether excessive. It means, first of all, that very large issues of capital have an undue advantage over moderate issues which cannot support the expense of an intensive campaign in newspapers and through outside brokers. It means also that a company which squanders a fifth or a tenth of its capital in getting floated is more likely to secure capital than one which does not, yet is, by precisely that amount, a worse investment. The source of the trouble probably lies in the fact that savings, very substantial in the aggregate, accumulate in the hands of investors who are not in touch with regular stockbrokers, and find it much easier to invest in response to appeals advertised in the press than in any other way. It is impossible to prevent offers for sale at an unduly high price. But an addition to our company law, prohibiting expenditure on underwriting and issue expenses in excess of a prescribed percentage of the capital on offer, might check a growing abuse. We cannot afford to allow the direction of the savings of the public by advertisement into inferior channels.

No one in the City seems to think it his duty to protect the public, when these episodes occur. Yet it is low standards in such matters, not Socialism or Bolshevism, which are the real enemy of the system for which the City stands.

Also on 5 April, Keynes resumed his contributions to the *Nation*'s Finance and Investment column, this time anonymously. His columns echoed many of his current and forthcoming concerns.

From The Nation and Athenaeum, *5 April 1924*

TRUSTEE SECURITIES—WAR LOAN CONVERSION— FOREIGN ISSUES

The *Investors' Chronicle and Money Market Review* published last week the following useful table showing the yields at current prices on Home Railway prior charges, as well as the surplus profits in excess of the amount required to meet each of these charges:—

	Price	Yield £ s. d.	Annual interest require- ments £	Surplus over interest 1923 £
Great Western				
2½% debentures	52	4 17 3 ⎫		
4% debentures	83	4 17 0 ⎪		
4¼% debentures	88½	4 16 9 ⎬	1,463,931	6,207,324
4½% debentures	92½	4 19 9 ⎪		
5% debentures	103½	4 17 0 ⎭		
5% rent charge stock (cum.)	101½	4 19 0	385,412	5,821,912
5% cons. gtd. stock (cum.)	99½	5 0 6	1,190,827	4,631,085
5% cons. preference	98½	5 1 6	1,387,738	3,243,347
London and North-Eastern				
3% debentures	61	4 19 3 ⎫	3,608,798	9,427,206
4% debentures	81	4 19 9 ⎭		
4% first guaranteed (cum.)	79	5 1 3	1,244,469	8,182,737
4% second guaranteed (cum.)	78	5 2 6	1,107,777	7,074,960
4% first preference (non-cum.)	77xd.	5 4 0	1,928,752	5,146,208
4% second pref. (non-cum.)	76xd.	5 5 3	2,641,306	2,504,902
5% preferred ord. (non-cum.)	82xd.	6 2 0	2,117,673	384,510
London, Midland and Scottish				
4% debentures	82	4 18 0	4,071,643	14,557,379
4% guaranteed stock (cum.)	80	5 0 0	1,627,716	12,929,663
4% preference	78	5 2 6	4,858,850	8,070,813
4% 1923 preference	77	5 4 0	1,605,359	6,465,454
Southern				
4% debentures	81	4 19 6	1,520,701	4,516,100
5% guaranteed pref. (cum.)	98½xd.	5 1 6	254,328	4,261,772
5% preference (non-cum.)	97½xd.	5 3 0	2,080,660	2,181,112
5% preferred ord.	82xd.	6 2 0	1,376,554	804,558

With the exception of the two preferred ordinary stocks given in this table, all the above have the status of trustee securities.

In view of the provisions of the Railways Act, 1921, any of these is a very well-secured investment. The debentures and guaranteed stocks, in any case, are beyond criticism, yet yield a better income (particularly the guaranteed stocks) than long-dated British Government securities. A minor consideration to be borne in mind is the fact that a transfer duty of 1 per cent is payable by the purchaser, a burden from which Government securities are exempt. Nevertheless, several of these stocks seem decidedly superior to Funding Loan or Conversion Loan or Local Loans for the trustee investor who attaches primary importance to the permanent yield; whilst for those who are prepared to be a little less secure in order to get a little more income, the preferred ordinary stocks offer an admirable 6 per cent investment.

Next week we hope, in response to numerous requests, to offer in this column some general advice to investors in trustee securities. Will readers who are interested kindly keep the above table at hand for purposes of reference and comparison?

The Treasury have offered to exchange £103 of 4½ per cent [Conversion] Loan (1940–44) for £100 of 5 per cent War Loan (1929–47) up to an aggregate of £200,000,000, which is about one-tenth of the outstanding War Loan. The proposal is a curious one, and seems scarcely worth while, because it does not seem to offer any palpable advantage to either party. The investor accepts a reduction of income from £5 to £4 12s. 8d. (or £4 14. 8d. allowing for the £3 profit on ultimate redemption), in return for a moderate extension of time before the Government has an option to redeem the Loan. The Treasury saves £730,000 in annual interest, or about £600,000 after allowing for income tax; pays the Stock Exchange up to £500,000 in brokerage if they persuade their clients to make the exchange; and adds £6,000,000 to the capital of the national debt. They also surrender their option to redeem between 1929 and 1940; while the date when they are *bound* to redeem is brought nearer by three years. It is not clear how the transaction helps the Treasury, or why any investor should make the exchange. Probably the Treasury consider that it is worth making sure of even a slight reduction in the effective interest on part of the War Loan, as what remains is more than it would be easy to convert, should the rate of interest fall substantially between 1929 and 1940. Perhaps it is the first of a series of transactions.

We welcome the outspoken disapproval by the City Editor of *The Times* of the flotation in London of the City of Amsterdam sterling loan for £2½ millions. The interest is 5½ per cent, and the issue price 96½; so that the return is about £5 14s. per £100 subscribed. The credit of the City of Amsterdam stands high; and *The Times* does not criticise the loan from the standpoint of the individual investor, though it may perhaps be questioned whether, in view of the kaleidoscopic changes which history shows can take place in fifty years, the credit of any foreign municipality can be good enough to justify such a low rate for a loan which is not repayable till 1974. But how does the matter stand from the national standpoint? The object of the issue is to 'consolidate expenditure' already incurred in acquiring and preparing land for building purposes. It stands, therefore, as *The Times* points out, on a different footing from 'loans for sound, reproductive enterprises, the spending of which will directly and immediately assist British trade'. It is true that in the long run any foreign investment must be translated into exports; but this may take a very long time to happen; and the channel through which it happens, it is well to observe, is the depression of the British exchange. When, a few months ago, the prospect of a Labour Government terrified a foolish section of the British public into putting their money into foreign securities, the City rang with denunciations of such unpatriotic behaviour. But it makes not the slightest difference to the effects whether a man purchases an existing foreign security out of panic or subscribes with a feeling of virtue to a new issue like the City of Amsterdam loan.

Sir James Wilson has recently prepared an interesting table showing the gold value of various national currencies in March of each of the last three years:—

Gold value of paper currency as a percentage of the corresponding gold coin

Country	In March 1922	In March 1923	On 17 March 1924
United States	100	100	100
Sweden	97·5	99·3	98·4
Canada	97·0	98·0	96·8
Holland	94·3	98·2	92·0
Switzerland	100·9	96·3	89·6
Great Britain	90·0	96·5	88·0
Japan	95·5	97·2	86·0
Argentine	88·8	87·6	80·0
Spain	94·2	80·2	65·2
Denmark	78·7	71·6	57·6
Norway	65·7	67·8	50·4
France	46·7	32·7	25·6
Italy	26·6	25·2	22·1
Belgium	43·8	28·4	21·1
Austria	0·075	0·007	0·007

This table must be a signal disappointment to those who have taken the view that the world is steadily returning towards the restoration of its former gold parities. It will be seen that practically every country in the world is further away from its nominal gold parity this year than it was at the same date last year; and further that most of them are also further away than they were two years ago. Great Britain in particular has made no progress on balance towards a return to the old pre-war parity during the past two years.

A welcome feature of the Annual Report of the Prudential Assurance Company is the further decrease which they record in the expense ratio in their industrial branch. The expenses have fallen steadily from just over 40 per cent of the total premiums in 1920 to just under 30 per cent in 1923; and the Prudential have accordingly been able to issue a new prospectus offering higher benefits to the assured.

Keynes's comments in the Finance and Investment column on the City of Amsterdam issue brought criticism from *The Economist*. To this Keynes replied.

To the Editor of The Economist, *14 April 1924*

Sir,

May I ask a question about your article, 'Discrimination in Lending'? You seem to suggest that the consequences of the flotation in London of a loan like the recent Amsterdam loan are in some way different from the nervous movement of British investors into American securities alleged to have occurred last autumn. Do I misunderstand you? If not, what is the difference?

Did you welcome the so-called 'flight from the pound' last autumn on the ground that it would stimulate our export trade? If not, should you not have done so on the principles you now enunciate?

Personally, I think that there is a good deal of muddle in circulation about the supposed advantages of the prevalent type of foreign investment, and I believe that the City Editor of *The Times* was more nearly right than you allow.

Yours faithfully,
J. M. KEYNES

In the next issue of the *Nation*, Keynes provided more advice to investors.

From The Nation and Athenaeum, *12 April 1924*

ADVICE TO TRUSTEE INVESTORS

Every man must choose for himself the *class* of investment that he wants. And, having settled that matter, he will do well always to buy what appears the *best* of that class, even at the cost of some diminution of income. Advice comes in most usefully in helping him to judge which is the best in the class he has decided to favour. We will endeavour this week to give our readers some assistance of this kind in the field of gilt-edged investments.

There is, first of all, the choice between long-dated securities, where the investor is certain of the *same* money income for many years; short-dated securities, where the investor is certain of the return of his capital in full at an early date; and optionally redeemable securities, where the investor is liable to be paid off either soon or late at the option of the borrower. The following are typical long-dated securities. For the sake of clear summary the interest yields (which allow for accrued interest included in the price and for loss or profit on redemption) are given in groups, which are accurate for the individual securities within 1s. Detailed particulars of the railway securities were given in last week's *Nation and Athenaeum*:—

| | Net interest yield | | |
	£	s.	d.
Funding Loan Conversion Loan Local Loans	4	10	0
L.C.C. 2½%, 3%, and 3½% stocks	4	13	0
South Africa 4% (1943–63)	4	13	6
Nigeria 4% (1963)	4	15	6
Bank of England stock	4	17	0
G.W.R. L. and N.E.R. L.M. and S. Southern Railway — Debentures	4	16	0
Ditto Guaranteed stocks	4	18	0
Ditto First Preference stocks (non. cum.)	5	0	0
India 3% and 3½% stocks	5	7	0

We think that the investor in this class would do best to take the middle of the list and to leave both extremities alone. In the case of the railway preference stocks and the Government of India stocks, the investor is giving away too much in respect of absolute security for the sake of the extra yield. On the other hand, Bank stock and the railway debenture and guaranteed stocks are as good as any man can ask for security, and it scarcely seems worth while to sacrifice $\frac{1}{4}$ to $\frac{3}{8}$ per cent per annum in income for the sake of the extra gilt of British Government and London County Council stocks. The colonial stocks mentioned above appear to be preposterously over-valued. South Africa 4 per cent stands at nearly the same price as Funding Loan 4 per cent. Nigeria stock (which has no British Government guarantee) yields about the same as London and North-Eastern Railway debentures. It seems strange that there should be investors who prefer the former.

The typical short-dated securities are:—

| | Net interest yield | | |
	£	s.	d.
5% National War Bonds due 1927	4	6	0
5% National War Bonds due 1928	4	8	0
5% National War Bonds due 1929	4	8	0
War Loan 3½% due 1928	4	10	0
Exchequer Bonds due 1930	4	11	0
Metropolitan 3½% due 1929	4	13	0
India 5½% due 1932	5	8	6
Queensland 5½% (1926–1929)	5	11	6

It may be presumed that the investor in this class *either* attaches importance to being able to realise his holding without material risk of capital depreciation within the next three or four years, *or* believes (as well he may) that the combined effects of trade revival, housing schemes and the like, high income tax, and diminished savings are likely to raise the rate of interest (and, which is the same thing, diminish the price of long-dated securities) in the near future, thus giving him better opportunities than exist now of exchanging into a permement investment. Such an investor had better avoid half measures, and plump for National War Bonds due 1927; for a small difference in interest yield is of far less importance in a short-dated than in a long-dated security, and should not divert him from his main purpose. Next after this, the 3½ per cent War Loan (1928) and the 3½ per cent

Metropolitan stock (1929) have substantial attractions. For those who are not afraid of possible developments in India, the $5\frac{1}{2}$ percent 1932 stock is much preferable to the long-dated Government of India securities.

The intermediate securities, where the borrowing authority has a considerable latitude as to the exact date of redemption, are as follows. The pair of dates, given in brackets after each security, indicate the period within which the borrower can exercise his option to redeem,—he can redeem at any time after the first date, but not later than the last date. The net interest yields are worked out on the hypothesis least favourable to the investor.

	Net interest yield		
	£	s.	d.
5% War Loan (1929–47)	4	16	0
5% South Africa (1933–43)	4	18	6
5% Australia (1935–45)	4	19	0
5% Victoria (1932–42)	5	0	0
5% Southern Rhodesia (1934–49)	5	0	0

In this class there can be little doubt as to which is to be preferred. Our own War Loan is surely better than any of the Colonial stocks. The additional income obtainable from the latter is negligible, and the additional period before the right to redeem comes into force is very short. It is remarkable that Southern Rhodesia—a place in the middle of Africa with a few thousand white inhabitants and less than a million black ones— can place an unguaranteed loan on terms not very different from those of our own War Loan. One of the surest pieces of advice which can be given to trustees at the present time is to avoid colonial stocks, the prices of which are far nearer to those of our own Government and other home gilt-edged securities than the permanent facts of the situation are likely to warrant.

The exchange from 5 per cent War Loan into the new $4\frac{1}{2}$ per cent stock (1940–1944), which has just been offered by the

Treasury, supplies a stock which is neither long nor short, giving a net interest yield (at present prices) of about £4 13s. We dealt with this offer in last week's *Nation and Athenaeum*. Compared with other stocks, it does not seem to offer to the investor any particular attractions, and we prefer the 5 per cent War Loan.

There remains one other British Government security, not yet mentioned, which is the best of all for those investors who have not already secured their quota,—namely, National Savings Certificates. A certificate (of the third issue, which is now current) costs 16s. At the end of the first year 3d. interest is added, and thereafter interest is added at the rate of 3d. for each complete period of four months up to the end of the tenth year, when a bonus of 1s. is given, making a total of 20s. after six years, and 24s. after ten years. The interest and bonus are free of income tax, and no mention of these certificates need be made in any income tax return. No individual may hold (in general) more than 500 certificates; but, since the certificates can be registered in the names of children, a family man can secure altogether a substantial holding. The rate of interest works out, if the bonds are held for the full ten years, at nearly £4 3s. per cent free of tax, equivalent to about £5 7s. per cent subject to deduction of tax.

On 14 April 1924 the Royal Economic Society held its annual meeting. After concluding its business meeting, the Society held a discussion on monetary reform with Sir Charles Addis, Edwin Cannan, R. G. Hawtrey and Keynes as speakers. Keynes's comments ran as follows.

From The Economic Journal, *June 1924*

Mr Hawtrey has defined for us very clearly the issues to be discussed. First of all there is the problem whether we want monetary reform at all or whether we want to get back to something as near as possible to the pre-war system. Secondly, there is the question what precise device we should adopt, if we want reform, in order to bring it into operation. I will begin with the first problem.

Mr Hawtrey has emphasised what is perhaps the main difference between the attitude of a good many economists now and their pre-war attitude, namely, their greater confidence as to the connection between monetary causes, the credit cycle, and unemployment. Mr Hawtrey himself has been a great pioneer in the exploration of that subject. I myself believe that there is no longer any reason to doubt the connection. Professor Cannan referred to an equation which I published recently in the form $n = pk$, where n is the volume of money, p the level of prices and k the quantity of goods for which it suits the public to have purchasing power in the form of money. The view used to be that k was not subject to rapid fluctuations. It would move up and down over long periods, but over short periods it did not change very much. Therefore if you kept the quantity of currency stable you probably kept prices reasonably stable. It was argued from this, that, as you would not have in any one year any very big change in the volume of money, therefore you could not have in any one year any big change in prices, so that though gold might move up or down slowly over a long period of years, a fair measure of stability would be secured over short periods. It is true that this was not in fact borne out, because booms and depressions occurred in pre-war days just as much as since; but the tendency was to explain these by particular causes. Many economists now take a different view from that. They think that k, and accordingly the quantity of real purchasing power required, is itself capable of sharp fluctuations, and in fact that it is the leading characteristic of booms and depressions that there should be a variation in the magnitude of k, so that it is this variation which makes those price fluctuations that occur even when there is no marked change in the total volume of money. That being so, attention is naturally transferred to a certain extent from the mere volume of money to this other element. We no longer believe that prices can be kept as steady as they might be simply by securing a constant volume of money, and we hold, rather, that we can only keep prices steady by varying the quantity of money to balance changes in k. If the public, for some one or another cause, decide on the average to keep more purchasing power than before, prices must fall to counterbalance this, and the tendency of prices to fall may produce a situation likely to provoke unemployment. That theory in a clear form is essentially new; and if it is correct it opens up enormous opportunities for far-reaching social reforms.

If we really have the power to control in some measure credit cycles which cause unemployment and other social disturbances experienced in the past, surely it is our duty to follow up this line of thought to the utmost, to make experiments and to see whether by a control of the monetary machine we cannot cure one of the greatest and most dangerous social evils of the economic system. We feel that those who oppose monetary reform ought to make it clear how far they agree with us on that diagnosis. If we have even a half-chance of getting rid by monetary reform of the evils of the credit cycle, I should have thought most people would have agreed that it was worth while, and that it is no good for Professor Cannan to talk about a barbarous age if his object in speaking thus is to keep it barbarous. We certainly live in a barbarous age, but our object should be to emerge from it, and if there is a new weapon forged for that purpose we have no right to overlook it. It is not so much a change in the whole theory of our view of the credit cycle, as the increased clearness with which we now see the various steps, that is the reason why the minds of some of us have changed since pre-war days.

But there is another reason also for change which has arisen out of events connected with the War. Can we rely on gold to give in future even that amount of stability that it has given in the past? Formerly there was a great deal of gold in circulation in people's pockets. Many countries were rich enough and sufficiently inclined to hoard resources to keep a considerable amount in gold in banks and elsewhere. Any given country might suffer sudden changes in that respect, but it was not likely that in a short period of time there would be a simultaneous change of any magnitude in a number of different countries. As a result of the War, however, there is now extremely little gold in circulation in the world; in most countries none whatever. It is unlikely that gold will return into circulation both because of the expense and because of the change of habits. It is also much more difficult than it used to be for some countries to hold large amounts of gold in banks or to increase their holdings. A great stimulus has been given to all those methods of economising the use of gold, which have been gradually developing as a result of the growth of the credit system. We may even tend now to be up against the ultimate truth that a perfectly conducted gold standard does not require any gold at all, or practically none. Suppose those who manage the credit policies of banks were to acquire sufficient skill in the management of international adjustments, no actual gold would be required at all; and while we are still very far from that position, we are probably already in the position in which the necessary quantity of gold for the maintenance of the existing price level is far [and] away less than the volume of gold in the world, and the difference between the two is getting larger every day. This redundance of gold pressing upon the world is a phenomenon which someone has to look after, and the problem of preventing that redundance from causing sudden changes in its value is much more acute than it was.

Those of us who are in favour of monetary reform support it, therefore, for two main reasons: first, because we believe that we ought to do all we can in any reasonable way in the direction of the social aims already referred to; secondly, for fear that gold left to itself may prove a much less safe standard of value than in former times. I do not believe that there is sufficient weight on the other side to outweigh those two considerations. There are, of course, two sides to every argument, and it is generally a question of weighing advantages. It is not that there are no advantages on the other side, but rather that a return to our pre-war system does not offer sufficient advantage to outweigh the factors I have emphasised.

We come next to a further most interesting question. Assuming that we want to reform our currency, what is the right way to do it? There is a certain difference of opinion between Mr Hawtrey and myself, though I should be perfectly ready to accept his system it it turned out to be practicable. Mr Hawtrey wants to placate a good deal of feeling that exists in the world by pretending that he keeps [a] gold standard, whereas in fact he establishes a commodity standard. He proposes to erect a façade of gold and then to regulate its value on the same principles as would be adopted by those who aim at the stabilisation of general prices. In monetary affairs there is a great deal to be said in favour of placating prejudice. I do not underate any of those advantages. And Mr Hawtrey may be right, that this is the best way to do it. But I should like to point out two important disadvantages in his plan. First of all, there is the question who is going to bear the expense of maintaining the value of gold. On his system there would still be mined, I suppose, about as much gold as is mined now. There is also the problem of existing stocks. At present the United States is bearing the expense of that, both in maintaining stocks and in absorbing new supplies. Mr Hawtrey's system would mean a very difficult debate on the question how expenses should be shared in the future, and presumably we in this country would have to bear some reasonable proportion of them. We should have to consider, therefore, how many millions a year it was worth wasting in order to maintain this façade. We should also be embarking on a system which would become more and more artificial and indefensible as time went on, and would, therefore, be inevitably unstable in the long run. It would be too absurd to go on indefinitely mining gold out of the earth with great labour, in order that certain countries should bury it again after having met the expenses of mining. Sooner or later the world would see that no sufficient advantages accrued from it, and everyone would seek to escape from the burden of spending a certain number of millions a year in maintaining the value of gold.

It is, perhaps, a more fundamental objection against this proposal that it involves very far-reaching agreements between a number of central banks. Mr Hawtrey and I have both had a certain experience of international conferences, but they seem to have left him more optimistic than they have left me. My feeling is that for some years to come we shall never secure a binding agreement of that kind. Putting all other countries on one side, I think it would not be easy even for the Bank of England and the Federal Reserve Board of the United States to arrive at any binding agreement. It would be very difficult to decide how, when there was a difference of opinion, the matter was to be settled. Moreover, I believe that any such agreement would weaken the hands of the Federal Reserve Board in the United States. There is difficulty enough in any case in pursuing a sound policy, and if the Board was open to the suggestion that they were not acting solely in American interests but at the dictation of the Bank of England, they would be in a much weaker position than they are in now, when no one can possibly accuse them of being governed by any other motive than American interests. I should prefer, therefore, that we should enter into no binding agreement as to the relation between the British standard of value and the American standard of value, but rather than each country separately should aim at stability, and in addition co-operate by the exchange of information and in all other possible ways. If this co-operation were to be successful, then we should also have a policy of a stable dollar exchange, and we and the United States between us could probably manage the rest of the world. It would require no international conference or binding agreement of any kind, and we could gradually improve our methods as experience showed us the way. The only disadvantage it could have might be, that, since we should not accept gold into our mints here unless we wanted it, America herself would probably get tired of the burden of absorbing the world's gold, and that she too would close her mints to gold, with the result that the value of gold itself would fall. Nevertheless it would be better, I think, to face the opposition of the gold-mining interests rather than to embark upon the very costly and difficult path of trying to stabilise the value of gold itself by means of a binding agreement between ourselves and the United States.

In conclusion, let me turn to the matter of immediate policy which Mr Hawtrey also dealt with. What ought we to do at once? I suggest, as he also suggested, there is room at the moment for a considerable measure of agreement even if we differ for the future. I am afraid there is no room for agreement between us and Sir Charles Addis, if Sir Charles insists on immediate deflation. On that matter the Government, I think, are in a contradictory position, both this and the previous Governments, when they state that their object is to get back to a gold standard as soon as possible, yet also at times admit in public, as Mr Baldwin did, that the policy of deflation has been definitely reversed. The Government think it wise to placate Sir Charles Addis by stating that their intention is to return to the gold standard. But fortunately they are not so foolish as to take any active steps in that direction. They have, in fact, no clear policy, but so far as they have one at all they seem to aim at some measure of stability for the present and, as Mr Hawtrey suggested, have postponed making up their minds any further, until they see what happens to exchange [rates], hoping that the natural course of events will bring sterling to its parity with gold without any degree of deflation. I agree that this expectation may very well be realised, that a further fall of prices in America is not very likely, being indeed wholly unnecessary from any point of view, and that sooner or later the Federal Reserve Board is likely to be overwhelmed by the incoming tides of gold, with the result that a sufficient depreciation of the dollar will take place to bring our own exchange to par—though that this may require a depreciation in the value of the dollar amounting to more than 10 per cent is also likely, since prices here, in the event of this policy being adopted, would follow dollar prices to a certain extent. Thus it is certainly quite possible that we shall return to our former parity of exchange without resorting to deflation. I should like to point out, however, that the policy of waiting for that to happen and thereafter depending on the Federal Reserve Board to prevent any further depreciation of the dollar seems to assume that the Federal Reserve Board is going to be overwhelmed to precisely that degree which it pleases us should occur, and that when that has happened they are not going to be overwhelmed a scrap further, but are going to retain their price level at just that figure which happens to suit us at the present time. A nice balance is assumed between skill and want of skill on the part of the Federal Reserve Board. This policy requires that the Federal Reserve Board should lose control of their own situation and should then begin again to exercise skill just at the time that *our* policy requires that they should. I am not confident that this is a coincidence we can rely upon.

At any rate, let us suppose that this is the position, that the Government is disinclined to take any further steps towards deflation, and also that the underlying facts of the situation may quite likely bring sterling back to par. What is our right course? Well, we have a golden opportunity for making on an adequate scale precisely the experiment that I want. Why should we not aim for the present at keeping our own price level steady and, in order to please other parties, postpone any final decision until our exchange has reached parity. The arguments of all the speakers seem to me really to imply that at one stage or another the price level *is* under our control. No one wants to diminish the value of our money. If, then, we do not want to increase the value of our money, which would mean deflation, why should we not spend the next few years in keeping prices steady, and seeing if we can do it, meanwhile learning, perhaps, how to do it without exciting prejudice? If after having done this successfully for a few years we reached our old parity, I myself would have a great deal of confidence that the success of the method would justify its continuance, that after having kept prices steady without the use of gold for some appreciable time, we should be rather loth to abandon it and to follow a tide of involuntary inflation by linking ourselves once more to gold, which by hypothesis would have just been depreciating substantially. I believe that currency reformers will experience much less prejudice and hostility when it is a question of letting sterling go above its old gold value rather than of keeping sterling below it. I believe many people in the City of London have much more feeling about the return to parity than they have about sticking there, when it is once attained and not going above it. For instance, Sweden, it has been reported, in the last week or two has decided upon a new policy of convertibility by which the krone will not be allowed to fall below the old gold parity, but with no provision, however, to prevent its rising above it. This is a return to the gold standard in its most harmless form. To undertake that the value of the currency shall not fall below its old parity, whilst allowing the value of the currency to rise above it, is quite possibly the most practicable solution. It would be sound policy in the United States at this moment to maintain convertibility, but at the same time to close the mints to further foreign gold. A plan of maintaining convertibility into gold at a fixed ratio, but of not accepting further gold into the mints when gold is redundant and depreciating, may prove the right compromise between old and new wisdom. If we return to the old gold parity, I would prefer that compromise to the plan which Mr Hawtrey suggests. I do not suggest that his would not be an improvement, if it came into operation, on what we have had in the past. But the practical difficulties operating against it are far greater than those operating against the alternatives which I myself prefer.

Keynes also continued to make anonymous contributions to 'Finance and Investment'.

From The Nation and Athenaeum, *3 May 1924*

THE BUDGET—THE DISTRIBUTION OF THE NATIONAL DEBT

'I am not appalled by the total figures,' said Mr Philip Snowden in 1910, discussing a budget which threatened to approach what was then widely regarded as the appalling figure of £200 millions. 'I hope to live to see the time when the Chancellor of the Exchequer will stand at that box and propose a budget of 300 or 400 millions.' Fate, as the fable tells us, takes a grim pleasure in fulfilling our wishes in an unexpected way. Mr Snowden has lived to 'stand at that box' himself, and propose a budget which for the first time in the last ten years falls just short of 800 millions. He comes not to increase but to remit taxation—to remit, indeed, a sum which would have sufficed to abolish the income tax three times over in Mr Gladstone's day. The audacious critic of orthodox financial traditions, who saw no advantage in reducing debt, now devotes long passages to emphasising its 'vital and first-class importance'. The chief bogey-man of the City has succeeded in delighting it more than any other Chancellor in recent years. In this there is some change in Mr Snowden himself; there is still more in the financial situation.

The chief doubt raised by the Budget is whether Mr Snowden is justified, from the standpoint of sound finance, in remitting so much taxation. He estimates his surplus, on the basis of existing taxes, at £38 millions, while he puts the revenue he will lose from the tax reductions at £34 millions, and at £48 millions when they have produced their full effect. Thus in the present year he keeps only £4 millions in hand to meet the further expenditure which Parliament is almost certain to sanction. The removal of the Old Age Pensions thrift disqualification, which the Government have undertaken to deal with, would alone (in a full year) swallow up this sum several times over. Mr Snowden, indeed, does not profess to hope that his £4 millions will be enough; he relies on further administrative savings to avert a deficit in the present year. But all the administrative economies which it is reasonable to expect will be required in subsequent years to meet the additional £14 millions loss from the tax reductions. On the other hand, it is of the essence of housing schemes, of a reversal of educational engines, and the like that they entail an expenditure which is modest at first but grows rapidly. Thus Mr Snowden is confronting himself or his successor next year with the strong probability of a heavy deficit. This probability is not likely to be confuted this time by an unexpected buoyancy in the revenue returns; for Mr Snowden has made a sanguine (though we do not think too sanguine) allowance for this factor in the estimates.

The Economist published recently a very interesting calcula-tion of the distribution of the National Debt among the various categories of holders. The calculation may be roughly sum-marised as follows:—

	£ millions
External debt to U.S. and other Governments	1,100
Held by banks (including Bank of England and savings banks)	1,140
Held by insurance companies	350
Held by railway companies	80
Treasury bills held by bill-brokers and others not included above	300
Held by other companies, colleges, hospitals, trade unions, trusts &c., and by persons abroad	1,550
Held by savings bank depositors	240
Held by other private persons	2,350
Held by the Government itself (Treasury note reserve. &c.)	310

Some of these estimates relate to market values, and would need to be increased to represent the nominal value of the debt so held. Perhaps the most striking feature of the calculation is the comparatively small proportion of the debt held by private persons. This suggests strongly that the idea that a capital levy designed to raise £3,000 millions, and confined, of course, to private individuals, could be paid mainly by handing over Government securities, is a delusion.

The preference shares of the Allied Newspapers Ltd, upon the terms of offer of which we have already commented, now stand at a discount of about 1s. per £1 share. It is stated that there were over 30,000 applications, which were met in full up to seventy-five shares, so that nearly half the issue was spread in this way over a vast number of small holders. Since the Daily Mail Trust shareholders received 80 per cent of their application and most other applicants 60 per cent, it is clear that the *average* amount of the subscriptions was not much more than £200. It is the small and ignorant investor who has been reached by giant advertisement.

The German Government have lately prepared some striking figures of the reduction of domestic consumption in 1922–23 as compared with 1913:—

	Date	Amounts (kg per head)	Date	Amounts (kg per head)	Decrease per cent
Wheat and spelt	1913–14	95·8	1922–23	47·6	50·3
Rye	1913–14	153·1	1922–23	91·9	40·0
Potatoes	1913–14	700·2	1922–23	573·2	18·1
Meat	1913	40·26	1922	24·98	38·0
Coffee	1913	2·44	1922–23	0·59	75·8
Rice	1913	7·23	1922–23	4·25	41·2
Cotton	1913	2·49	1922–23	1·64	34·1

The enormous percentage reduction of the consumption of staple articles of food per head is a striking and irrefutable testimony to the reduction in the standard of life of the great bulk of the population. Few countries have exhibited such contrasting extremes as Germany at the present day. The effect of the inflation of the currency has been to transfer millions of pounds' worth of wealth from the many to the few, with the result that whilst the country as a whole and the vast majority of individuals have been frightfully impoverished, there is at the same time a large class of those who have been newly enriched on a prodigious scale and are in a position to live in as much luxury as the wealthy classes of any part of Europe.

The new edition of the *Stock Exchange Official Intelligence* has been reduced in price from £4 to £3, although, as usual, the size has been somewhat increased, and now runs to about 2,000 pages quarto. At this price it is a very good investment for anyone who takes an active interest in his Stock Exchange securities. The special chapters for the year deal with municipal, Indian, and colonial finance, with company law in 1923 and with the Railways Act, 1921. But the real value of the volume lies, of course, in its exhaustive précis of every single Stock Exchange security, all the essential facts about the board, accounts, dividends, capital, recent prices, &c., being given in the most convenient possible form. Many more private investors ought to have this volume than has been the case hitherto, and the reduction in price shows that the Committee of the Stock Exchange, under whose authority the volume is issued, want to encourage such purchases.

On 12 April, in the columns of *The Nation*, Lloyd George stated that he viewed Britain's immediate economic future with grave misgivings and suggested that the most urgent task facing her industrial and political leaders was improving production. During the weeks that followed discussion continued in the columns of the *Nation*, with contributors such as Sir William Beveridge, A. L. Bowley, Norman Angell, Walter Layton and Lord Wier, before Keynes added his views.

From The Nation and Athenaeum, *24 May 1924*

DOES EMPLOYMENT NEED A DRASTIC REMEDY?

The discussion on this subject in the columns of *The Nation* has not lacked a few optimists. Nevertheless most of those who have taken part share in some degree the misgivings which Mr Lloyd George voiced in opening the debate. If a country, with no new advantages of raw materials or competitive power, with a larger population, produces less and lives better, it seems probable that its poise may be unstable, and that something more drastic is needed than merely hoping for the best. But what? It is in the lameness of the answers to this question—we must all admit—that *The Nation* discussion has proved weak.

What is the magnitude of the problem? The number of unemployed adult males is now about 770,000, after having been 1,200,000 at the beginning of 1923, and 1,450,000 at the beginning of 1922. If the figures be analysed we find a great concentration of unemployment in the shipbuilding and engineering industries (i.e., nearly four times the percentage elsewhere). Outside these industries, unemployment amongst adult males does not now much exceed 4 per cent of the employable population. The following is a rash guess at the composition of the total:—

1. Normal unemployed (i.e., brief intervals of unemployment between jobs, &c.) — 200,000
2. Unemployables from age, disablement, temperament, &c. — 100,000
3. Excess of labour supply in engineering and associated industries — 150,000
4. Excess of labour supply in other industries — 320,000

770,000

It seems very optimistic to assume, with Mr Layton, that the figures in the third and fourth groups will cure themselves if we merely sit by smiling and avoid gross errors of policy. No one has a firmer belief than I in the relation between unemployment and monetary policy, and when, two years ago, the figures were nearly double what they are now, this disastrous situation was, I am sure, largely attributable to the slump provoked by a misguided inflation and prolonged by a misguided deflation. But the evil effects of these policies have been working themselves out. Perhaps this cause is not yet eliminated entirely,—but a monetary policy which aimed at reducing the unemployed by more than (say) a further 100,000, would run dangerously near another inflation. On the other hand, the settlement of Europe, if it takes place, and the resuscitation of German export trade will not be an unmixed blessing to our own export industries. To what favourable influences, then, do the optimists look? I do not know.

I agree, therefore, with Mr Lloyd George, Mr Baldwin, and Mr Sidney Webb, that there is no place or time here for *laissez-faire*. Furthermore, we must look for succour to the principle that *prosperity is cumulative*. We have stuck in a rut. We need an impulse, a jolt, an acceleration.

Unluckily this good principle has often got into bad hands. It is the grain of truth behind the false promises and hopes of protectionists and inflationists alike. They see the initial impact of their policies on the lumbering car of state, and assess justly the social value of an impulse, yet slip backwards through overlooking remoter adjustments and indirect results.

But this is not a good reason for doing nothing. There may be stimulating medicines which are wholesome. There are many examples of cumulative prosperity, both in recent and in earlier experience. British prosperity in the nineteenth century owed very much to the railway boom in its first half, beginning at home and extending abroad, and to the immense building activity of its latter half. In the past five years the rebuilding of the devastated areas has, independently of its inflationary features, given a stimulus to French enterprise which has much enriched the nation. The boom in motors and in building, combined, no doubt, with many favourable attendant circumstances, has carried the United States to an unprecedented standard of high living. Is there no tonic draught for us to give us courage and confidence to be active?

Business is weighed down by timidity. It lacks conviction that anything good will continue for long. It watches anxiously for the signs of retrogression; and, as soon as the army wavers, individuals bolt. No one is ready to plant seeds which only a long summer can bring to fruit.

Yet some of the causes of our unemployment are of such a kind that this halting, wavering mood is fatal. Part of it is due to the immobility of labour as between industries; part to the fault of trade unions; and part to a disparity of wages between what are called the sheltered and the unsheltered industries. But we cannot cure these ills by forcing labour into new directions by the pressure of starvation, or by breaking the power for evil, and perhaps for good also, of the trade unions, or by reducing wages in the sheltered industries to the level of the unsheltered. From these thoughts the mind must be averted, for from such directions help will not come. Rather we must seek to submerge the rocks in a rising sea,—not forcing labour out of what is depressed, but attracting it into what is prosperous; not crushing the blind strength of organised labour, but relieving its fears; not abating wages where they are high, but raising them where they are low. And there is no way in the world of achieving these better alternatives but by confidence and courage in those who set enterprise in motion.

Is there not a chance that we can best achieve this by recreating the mood and the conditions in which great works of construction, requiring large capital outlays, can again be set on foot? Current savings are already available on a sufficient scale—savings which from lack of an outlet at home, are now drifting abroad to destinations from which we as a society shall gain the least possible advantage. Private enterprise unaided cannot stop this flow. The policy of preventing public utilities from yielding more than a modest private profit has gone so far that it is no longer worth the while of private enterprise to run a risk in a field where the gain is limited and the loss unlimited. We are in danger, therefore, of interfering with private initiative, yet substituting nothing for it. The advances under the Trade Facilities Act, begun for a temporary emergency and on a small scale, point the way, perhaps, to a new method of administering an important part of the savings of the public. The next developments of politico-economic evolution may be found in co-operation between private initiative and the public exchequer. The true socialism of the future will emerge, I think, from an endless variety of experiments directed towards discovering the respective appropriate spheres of the individual and of the social, and the terms of fruitful alliance between these sister instincts.

In the light of such reflections, we can indicate the next steps. The Chancellor of the Exchequer should devote his sinking fund and his surplus resources, not to redeeming old debt with the result of driving the national savings to find a foreign outlet, but to replacing unproductive debt by productive debt. The Treasury should not shrink from promoting expenditure up to (say) £100,000,000 a year on the construction of capital works at home, enlisting in various ways the aid of private genius, temperament, and skill.

It is for the technicians of building, engineering, and transport to tell us in what directions the most fruitful new improvements are awaiting us. But three fields of construction are already known to everyone in a general way. It should not be beyond the technical accomplishments of our engineers to devise a national scheme for the mass production of houses which would supplement the normal activities of the building industry and make up in five or ten years the deficiency with which the latter has proved unable to deal. The adaptation of road-building to the needs of motor transport must plainly be undertaken some day, whether in detail Sir W. Acworth or Lord Montagu is in the right. The development of economical means for the transmission of electrical power is in its infancy in this country. Unaided private enterprise is not capable of dealing with any of these projects, even when their technical soundness is beyond doubt.

I look, then, for the ultimate cure of unemployment, and for the stimulus which shall initiate a cumulative prosperity, to monetary reform—which will remove fear—and to the diversion of national savings from relatively barren foreign investment into state-encouraged constructive enterprises at home—which will inspire confidence. That part of our recent unemployment, which is not attributable to an ill-controlled credit cycle, has been largely due to the slump in our constructional industries. By conducting the national wealth into capital developments at home, we may restore the balance of our economy. Let us experiment with boldness on such lines,—even though some of the schemes may turn out to be failures, which is very likely.

Keynes's article brought a comment from the City Editor of *The Times* on 26 May which doubted whether there would be anything to gain by adopting Keynes's suggestions which, he suggested, relied on raiding the sinking fund and other surplus resources of the Treasury.

To the Editor of The Times, *28 May 1924*

Sir,

I thank you for your comments on my article in last Saturday's *Nation*, with much of which I agree, but must ask leave to correct a misunderstanding about my attitude towards the sinking fund. The sinking fund consists in raising by taxation a substantial surplus over current expenditure and applying this surplus to the reduction of the War debt. I agree with yourself in strongly supporting this policy. It would be disastrous to abandon it. I regret that the wording of my article should have left this open to doubt. My concern was with a different matter—namely, with the investment of the liquid capital accruing from this policy. Perhaps I can make my point clear in five sentences:—

1. The application of £50,000,000 to £100,000,000 a year to the redemption of War debt throws this amount of funds on the market seeking investment in a similar type of security.

2. Private enterprise at home is not providing an outlet for these amounts *plus* new savings on anywhere near adequate scale.

3. Consequently they find an outlet in foreign and colonial government loans, most of which do little directly to stimulate British industry and can only operate by depreciating our exchanges: I cannot agree with you that 'we have very few loans of this type'.

4. Rent Restriction Acts, the control of profits and charges of public utility undertakings, and the fear of further developments in the same direction have deprived private enterprise of sufficient incentive to embark on new schemes of construction involving great expenditures. If steam locomotion were to be discovered today I much doubt if unaided private enterprise would build railways in England.

5. The Trade Facilities Act, as administered hitherto, having been a comparative failure, we must make new experiments to stimulate capital investment at home.

I am strongly opposed to encouraging non-economic projects, by subsidies or otherwise. But, for good or for evil, in present-day conditions *laissez-faire* can no longer be relied on to furnish economic projects with the capital they need. We are drifting into financing port improvements, housing, electrical developments, &c., abroad at low rates of interest, while forgetting similar projects at home. Yet it is not true that there is nothing at home which wants doing.

The only reasonable object of a sinking fund is to reduce the dead-weight debt. This can be achieved just as effectively by converting it into productive capital at home as by paying it off and offering no alternative investment.

Yours, &c.,

J. M. KEYNES

On 7 June, Keynes returned to the columns of *The Nation* to answer other critics.

From The Nation and Athenaeum, *7 June 1924*

A DRASTIC REMEDY FOR UNEMPLOYMENT: REPLY TO CRITICS

The main purpose of my article in *The Nation* of May 24th was to ask whether it might not be in the national interest that the State should intervene to direct a larger part of our savings into capital enterprises at home. In the course of it I rashly mentioned the sinking fund, and thereby pressed with careless finger one of those irrelevant buttons which stud the public brain, and released the reaction—'We should regard it as a retrograde step if the Chancellor were to raid the sinking funds.' Half the comment which the article evoked has been directed against my supposed impiety in this matter. I apologise for misleading many readers, and will try again to make my argument clear.

The maintenance of a sinking fund means raising a surplus on revenue account and devoting this surplus to the reduction of the dead-weight debt. With a heavy public debt and reduced private savings, I agree unreservedly that a substantial sinking fund is a cardinal point of policy. My heresy consists in proposing not to abolish (or raid) the sinking fund, but to use it. The sinking fund releases liquid resources for capital purposes,—that is its whole object. Do my critics want to apply these resources to consumptive expenditure? No! Then they want to apply them to productive, capital expenditure? Yes!

Then let them join with me to discuss how we can do this to the greatest social advantage.

The problem on a big scale is new. Before the War the proceeds of the sinking fund were a trifling proportion of the national savings. Recently, ranging from £40,000,000 to £100,000,000 a year, they have dominated the investment market. We have extracted these sums from the taxpayers, and using them to pay off debt, we have thrown an equal amount on the capital market seeking an outlet of a similar kind. It is dangerous to do this on so great a scale without giving a thought to the supply of alternative investments.

At first Local Loans, home municipals, and industrial debentures partly filled the bill. But with the advent of deflation, the Geddes Axe, and industrial depression, the supply has dried up.* The lack of supply of home investments involving new capital expenditure has now been acute for at least two years. During the past six months it has almost reached vanishing point. I estimate that, omitting issues which are merely conversions, or re-sales of existing enterprises, the total investments offered to the public to provide for new capital expenditure at home during the whole of the last half-year (which covers the busiest season) is in the neighbourhood of no more than £10,000,000. This includes issues under the Trade Facilities Act. Taken together with the acute depression in the engineering and metallurgical industries, such facts deserve consideration as a contributory cause of unemployment.

Meanwhile, the long rate of interest has fallen by about 1 per cent—to the delight of the Treasury (who, let me add in parenthesis, are in danger of desiring to keep the country depressed until 1929 in order to have the rate of interest low for their conversions). The rate of interest on foreign bonds is established $\frac{3}{4}$ to 1 per cent below the rate in New York for similar bonds. London has become—to the pride of many—the

* In 1921–22 Local Loans advances amounted to £50,500,000; in 1923–24 to £6,500,000. (See interesting figures relating to this and connected matters in *The Times*, June 2nd.)

principal, indeed almost the exclusive, international loan market, ready to lend to approved borrowers much cheaper than anyone else will lend. No other country in the world pursues this policy. So far from the United States exporting capital, the official figures for 1923 show that in that year, as the net result of all items on capital account, they actually imported capital.

In my opinion there are many reasons for thinking that our present rate of foreign investment is excessive and undesirable. We are lending too cheaply resources we can ill spare. Our traditional, conventional attitude towards foreign investment demands reconsideration;—it is high time to give it a bad name and call it 'the flight of capital'. But I must limit myself here to the single aspect which is relevant to the special problem of unemployment.

Some foreign investments lead directly to the placing of orders in this country which would not be so placed otherwise. Whether or not they are desirable on general grounds, such investments do no harm to employment. As a rule, however, this is not the case. A foreign loan does not, any more than a demand for reparations, automatically create a corresponding flow of exports. Let us take a particular example. Last week New South Wales borrowed in the London market £5,500,000 new money 'for railways, tramways, harbours, rivers and bridges, water supply, irrigation, sewerage, and other purposes'. A part of this may pay for orders placed here arising out of these undertakings. Probably the greater portion will not be used thus, but in paying labour on the spot, and importing supplies from elsewhere; that is to say, the resources will be transferred to Australia in roundabout ways. Sooner or later, the matter must be adjusted by increased British exports or diminished British imports. But this can only come about through the medium of a depreciation of the sterling exchange. Our exchanges have to depreciate so as to stimulate our export industries at the expense of our 'sheltered' non-export industries, and so redress the balance between the two. If the world demand for our exports at the present price level is inelastic, a considerable depreciation may be necessary to do the trick. Moreover, there may be violent resistances to the process of adjustment. The fall of the exchange tends to raise the 'cost of living', and the 'sheltered' industries may struggle to avoid the reduction of real wages which this entails. Our economic structure is far from elastic, and much time may elapse and indirect loss result from the strains set up and the breakages incurred. Meanwhile, resources may lie idle and labour be out of employment.

The old principle of *laissez-faire* was to ignore these strains and to assume that capital and labour were fluid; it also assumed that, if investors choose to send their money abroad at 5 per cent, this must mean that there is nothing at home worth doing at 5 per cent. Fifty years ago this may have been a closer approximation to the truth than it is now. With the existing rigidity of the trade-union organisation of labour, with the undue preference which the City organisation of new issues and the Trustee Acts afford to overseas investment, and with the caution which for many reasons, some good and some bad, now oppresses the undertaking of new capital investment at home, it does not work.

Can I now carry my critics with me this far,—that, if in the last six months, instead of £10,000,000 capital issues for new home developments and £50,000,000 for new developments abroad, the figures had been the other way round, this would have been a change for the better, and favourable to employment? Surely they cannot maintain that England is a finished job, and that there is nothing in it worth doing on a 5 per cent basis. Then let them agree with me in wishing, if we could manage it, to stimulate investment at home.

In considering how to do this, we are brought to my heresy—if it is a heresy. I bring in the State; I abandon *laissez-faire*,—not enthusiastically, not from contempt of that good old doctrine, but because, whether we like it or not, the conditions for its success have disappeared. It was a double doctrine,—it entrusted the public weal to private enterprise *unchecked* and *unaided*. Private enterprise is no longer unchecked,—it is checked and threatened in many different ways. There is no going back on this. The forces which press us may be blind, but they exist and are strong. And if private enterprise is not unchecked, we cannot leave it unaided.

For these reasons I claim to be nearer than Mr Brand to the realities and possibilities of the modern world in repeating that the next developments of politico-economic evolution will emerge from new experiments directed towards determining the appropriate spheres of individual and of governmental action. And proceeding to particulars, I suggest that the state encouragement of new capital undertakings, by employing the best technical advice to lay the foundations of great schemes, and by lending the credit and the guarantee of the Treasury to finance them more boldly than hitherto, is becoming an inevitable policy. There is no sphere where private initiative is so lacking—for quite intelligible reasons—as in the conception and execution of very costly projects which may be expected to yield from 5 to 6 per cent. The Trade Facilities Act continues to depend on private initiative, and only such projects are helped by it as private enterprise is already inclined to plan and to back. Mr Brand, the City Editor of *The Times*, and many others point to the unused balance of credit under this Act as convincing proof that there is nothing more to be done. I do not agree, because big new projects of a public character are not the kind of thing for which the Act is devised. Let us set against this the very recent report of the Chamber of Shipping Committee, which points out, the urgent need of expensive developments in many of our great ports, as one proof amongst many that the equipment of this country is not complete and up-to-date in all respects. Indeed, it is a bold and hazardous saying of my critics that our savings must drift abroad at 5 per cent because there is simply nothing worth doing in England at that price.

The Editor of *The Manchester Guardian Commercial* (May

29th) has written:—'Mr Keynes surely implies that there are opportunities for remunerative investment which the investing public have not the foresight to grasp, and which they will never grasp without the intervention of the Government. It is an argument which the Manchester Ship Canal, to take only one instance, effectively answers.' Certainly, this is what I imply, though perhaps I should substitute 'opportunity' for 'foresight'. Let me ask him to consider—for he is a very reasonable man—exactly whom he has in mind when he speaks of the 'foresight of the investing public'. Does he mean the average investor in trustee securities? Does he mean the great issue houses? (What pays them is to take a safe underwriting commission from a colonial government.) Is it worth the while, or within the power, of anyone to organise a new project costing £20,000,000 with the expectation of a return of 5 per cent? These persons 'exercising foresight' about new, costly, moderately remunerative projects do not exist. If there was no Manchester Ship Canal, does he suppose that a syndicate of private persons woud spring up today to construct it?

Mr Kiddy complains in *The Spectator* (May 31st) that 'the most extraordinary remedies' of my *Nation* article 'add to the complexities and dangers of the situation'. I am sorry. I respect Mr Kiddy's staunch principles. But vainly are his eyes cast backwards. Vainly does he treasure his copy-book maxims. (Condemn one, and he boils against you. Repeat one, and you are restored to his esteem.) The following extracts from his article afford a short but sufficient summary:—'The City views with profound concern...The City fails to comprehend...It is one thing to be entirely sympathetic with the deserving unemployed...Nor must there be lack of courage in expressing home truths to labour...It is felt in the City that there is all the more need for facing stern economic facts.' How remote one knows oneself to be from any kind of reality when one hears those dreary words,—milestones towards empty space!

A drastic reduction of wages in certain industries, and a

successful stand-up fight with the more powerful trade unions might reduce unemployment in the long run. If any party stands for this solution, let them say so. I believe that such a policy is not practical. Assuming, then, that the problem will not solve itself (which some maintain—I not amongst them), what more promising programme based on clear first principles, has anyone to suggest, than monetary reform coupled with an intensive encouragement of capital investment at home?

Keynes's reply to his critics naturally raised more comment, both in *The Nation* and elsewhere, and led to two more letters from Keynes, one to *The Nation* and one to *The Manchester Guardian*.

To the Editor of The Nation and Athenaeum, *21 June 1924*

Sir,

In reply to Mr Brand's letter in yesterday's *Nation*, I *do* agree with him 'that great difficulties face the application of Government aid to ordinary private *competitive* industry'. I have had in mind, in my contributions, to your columns, the development of what, in a broad sense, can be described as 'public utility' undertakings—though I should, for example, include in this description the mass-production of working-class houses. I join with Mr Brand in deprecating a policy of Government help to 'one shipbuilder against another or one steel manufacturer against another'. But this is just what the existing Trade Facilities Act does in certain cases. Perhaps you will allow me to take this opportunity of re-stating my reasons why the comparative failure of this Act is no argument at all against the policy which I have been advocating.

The Trade Facilities Act does not relieve those assisted of any portion of the risk of the enterprise—the Government guarantee stands behind, not in front of, the personal guarantee of the borrower. Thus the assistance given is limited to helping the borrower to borrow more cheaply than he would otherwise—say, at 5 per cent, instead of at 6 or $6\frac{1}{2}$ per cent. This is all there is in it. It is a modest subsidy. It is not a risk-sharing or risk-shouldering scheme. It helps private enterprise to carry through projects of the kind which private enterprise undertakes unaided, but which are just at the margin of profit.

My point is that private organisation, for promoting public utility enterprises of large cost and moderate prospective profit and for carrying the risk of such enterprises, is simply non-existent. The Trade Facilities Act does not touch this complaint, which requires initiative on the part of the Government or other public bodies. The odd thing is that the present Labour Government is so bent on satisfying the highest conventional standards and on avoiding the least suggestion of socialistic tendencies, that they are proving themselves more tenacious of *laissez-faire* in this and some other matters than (say) Mr Baldwin or Mr Brand himself.

Yours, &c.,

J. M. KEYNES

To the Editor of The Manchester Guardian, *9 June 1924*

Sir,

Your City editor has given in today's *Manchester Guardian* what purports to be a lengthy paraphrase of my article in this week's *Nation*. But all my arguments have suffered a slight sea-change, with the result that it is not nearly so persuasive as my original version! I feel myself, in reading it, in the presence of the pantomime constable under warning that 'everything you say will be taken down, altered, and used in evidence against you'. So, as I can't expect you to reproduce my article *in extenso*, I must ask any of your readers who are seriously interested in the matter to refer to the original if they want to know what I said.

Yours, &c.,

J. M. KEYNES

As well, on 7 June Keynes contributed another anonymous 'Finance and Investment' column.

From The Nation and Athenaeum, *7 June 1924*

THE FALL OF THE FRANC—BANK RATE, STERLING, AND FOREIGN INVESTMENT

Considerable mystery surrounds the policy of the French authorities with regard to the support of the franc; and the mystery is deepened if anything by the official communiqué issued this week. We are told, and can well believe, that all the dollars sold to support the exchange during March had been bought in again by the end of the month, and that from then on to May 7th the Bank of France and the Treasury were able to lay in a store of foreign currency on top of the replenished credits. After May 7th, to counteract the renewed fall of the franc, the Bank of France began to utilise these credits once more, 'in particular on May 12th and 13th', and it has since followed the same policy, 'taking action, as far as possible, and as opportunity occurred, to correct the too sudden jumps of the exchanges'. Most Frenchmen, we imagine, will regard a fall from 67 to 89 to the £ within a month as belonging to the category of 'too sudden jumps'; and so heavy a fall could hardly have taken place if the Bank of France had made sustained and determined efforts to prevent it. The references to 'in particular on May 12th and 13th', and 'as far as possible', show that its efforts have been neither sustained nor determined. Doubtless it has doled out small quantities of dollars or sterling from time to time, but not such as to make any appreciable hole in the credits that were intact at the beginning of the month. Essentially it has held its hand. Why?

There are various possible explanations. Some hint at a malevolent desire to discredit the parties of the Left, by emphasising the exchange sequel to their victory at the polls.

Central banks, at their worst, are not likely to subordinate to such motives all considerations of public policy. Have the French authorities at last grasped the fact that it is impossible to maintain permanently a rate of exchange as high as 70 to the £, and that their best policy is to save their resources until a figure is reached at which enduring stability is feasible? We believe that we shall be nearer to the mark if we assume a calculation bearing some resemblance to this, yet shorn of all its wisdom. The French authorities will have seen clearly enough that they would merely dissipate their resources by supporting the exchange in the neighbourhood of 70. But we suspect that they are waiting not so much for the moment when stability is possible as for the moment when they may hope to repeat their silly triumph of last March. Let the exchange continue to fall until a heavy bear position is again disclosed. Then they can intervene with decisive effect; send the franc bounding up once more, plunge the bears into confusion and loss, replenish their foreign credits on the upward swing, and emerge from the operation with a handsome profit. That certainly is the way to make profits from an exchange speculation. It is not the way to promote the stability of the franc or the welfare of France.

'Lombard Street,' declared the Financial Editor of *The Observer* last Sunday, 'is gravely discussing the possibility of a rise in the Bank rate. It is admitted that internal trade and monetary conditions do not warrant such a move, but rather the exchange position... Such a measure would, of course, raise an outcry.' It would, indeed; and we sincerely hope that these views are not strongly represented in the Bank Parlour. It is really an outrageous suggestion that, at a time when the Government is striving desperately under pressure from every quarter to find something which will give a stimulus to trade, the Bank of England should take a step directly calculated to depress it. For let there be no doubt about it; the only channel through which an increase in Bank rate can exert any lasting influence on the exchange is that of a depression of trade and prices here. It is, therefore, idle for the Financial Editor of *The Observer* to argue that, 'in actual fact bank charges are but an infinitesimal portion of the burdens borne by business'. If the effect on trade were negligible, the effect on the exchange would be negligible also. In present conditions, the effect would certainly not be negligible. The raising of Bank rate is important, not so much in itself as in indicating that the volume of credit, which is what really matters, is about to be curtailed. It is thus a recognised warning signal, which reacts directly on business confidence, and business confidence is not so strong at the moment that we can lightly cast an additional strain upon it.

The chain of causation between Bank rate and the exchanges was set out with admirable lucidity in the Cunliffe Report[6] itself, in the section describing the pre-war system.

The raising of the Bank's discount rate and the steps taken to make it effective in the market necessarily led to a general rise of interest rates and a restriction of credit. New enterprises were therefore postponed, and the demand for constructional materials and other capital goods was lessened. The consequent slackening of employment also diminished the demand for consumable goods, while holders of stocks of commodities carried largely with borrowed money, being confronted with an increase of interest charges, if not with actual difficulty in renewing loans, and with the prospect of falling prices, tended to press their goods on a weak market. The result was a decline in general prices in the home markets, which, by checking imports and stimulating exports, corrected the adverse trade balance, which was the primary cause of the difficulty.

Hardly anyone, we imagine, would seriously maintain that we should today deliberately create the conditions thus portrayed

[6] The reference is to the *First Interim Report* of the Committee on Currency and Foreign Exchanges after the war (November 1918, Cd. 9182), known by its chairman Lord Cunliffe, formerly Governor of the Bank of England.

for the sake of giving 'a tonic to sterling'; but there are many advocates of the Cunliffe policy who hug the illusion that we can adopt the means, achieve the end, and somehow dodge the *modus operandi*.

As regards the exchange problem itself, the position is materially different from what it was a year ago. The pound was then round about $4.70, and we took the view that this rate was well above the true economic level and was a material factor in the depression of our export industries. We saw no reason, therefore, to deplore the fall which occurred last autumn; indeed, a considerable part of the subsequent recovery in our trade is, we believe, attributable to it. But the exchange is certainly down to its true economic level now; and, though a further fall might force out further exports, the stimulus of an over-depreciated exchange is at least as unhealthy as the deterrent of an over-appreciated one, though in a different way. The weakness of sterling during the past week is clearly associated with the collapse of the franc, and need not be regarded seriously. But the prolonged weakness over the past half-year is a more ominous sign, for the powerful seasonal influences have been in favour of sterling, and will shortly turn against it.

To what is this weakness due? To the speech of Sir Montague Barlow[7], answers *The Observer*. We prefer the answer of *The Times*, to the abnormal volume of external loans which have lately been floated in London. It is, indeed, difficult to see how we can hope both to pay our debt to America, and to lend abroad on the scale on which we have recently been lending, without unsatisfactory exchange reactions. It is common to regard the dollar–sterling exchange as the barometer of our national prosperity. It is really the barometer of our foreign investments,

---

[7] On 9 October 1923, Sir Montague Barlow, the Minister of Labour, in a speech on remedies for unemployment, suggested that the Government was considering currency and credit inflation as a possible policy.

more than of anything else, a fall of the barometer indicating that these investments are becoming excessive. To welcome and encourage every new foreign issue floated in the London market, and to seek to correct the inevitable exchange results by raising Bank rate is an almost imbecile policy. Surely the right course is to leave our trade unhampered, and to safeguard the exchange by diverting our flow of capital into home investment.

Chapter 4

THE RETURN TO GOLD AND FOREIGN LENDING

On 18 February 1924 the Prime Minister reassured the House of Commons that the Government was still guided as to future currency policy by the recommendations of the Cunliffe Committee, which included an eventual return to the gold standard at the pre-1914 parity. A fortnight later the Chancellor of the Exchequer, Philip Snowden, told the House that he appreciated the advantages of amalgamating the Treasury's wartime issue of currency notes with the Bank of England's note issue. As a result of these statements, after consultations within the Bank of England, Governor Norman suggested to the Chancellor that the Treasury set up a Committee to consider the amalgamation of the note issues and proceeded to suggest possible members. The Chancellor agreed and on 10 June the Treasury set up the Committee on the Currency and Bank of England Note Issues, 'to consider whether the time has now come to amalgamate the Treasury Note Issue with the Bank of England Note Issue, and, if so, on what terms and conditions the amalgamation should be carried out'. The Committee's members were Sir Austen Chamberlain, a former Chancellor; Sir John Bradbury, formerly Permanent Secretary to the Treasury; Sir Otto Niemeyer, then in charge of the finance side of the Treasury; Gaspard Farrer, a banker; and Professor A. C. Pigou. At the time the Bank of England, the Treasury and members of the Committee all accepted that these terms of reference would allow a review of the problem of restoring the gold standard—especially as the Cunliffe Committee had recommended in 1918 that amalgamation of the note issues should follow a return to gold.

On 4 July the Committee's secretary approached Keynes.

From N. E. YOUNG, *4 July 1924*

Dear Mr Keynes,

The Chancellor of the Exchequer has appointed a Committee, of which Mr Austen Chamberlain is Chairman, to advise him privately whether the time has now come to amalgamate the Treasury Note Issue with the Bank of England Note Issue, and, if so, on what terms and conditions the amalgamation should be carried out.

Mr Chamberlain asks whether you would be willing to attend a meeting of this Committee at 10.30 a.m. on Friday next, 11 July, in the Conference Room at the Treasury. He suggests that, if so, it would be convenient if you would be prepared to make a general statement on the subject, on which you would then allow the Committee to ask questions.

I enclose a copy of the Interim Report of the Cunliffe Committee, which has been out of print until recently.

Yours very truly,

N. E. YOUNG

When Keynes appeared before the Committee on 11 July, all of its members were present except Professor Pigou. The Treasury transcript of the proceedings ran as follows.

From Committee on the Currency and Bank of England Note Issues, Minutes, 11 July 1924

COMMITTEE ON THE CURRENCY AND BANK OF ENGLAND NOTE ISSUES

Meeting held in the Treasury on
Friday 11 July 1924 at
10.30 a.m.
Present:
The Rt Hon. J. Austen Chamberlain, M.P. (*Chairman*)
Sir John Bradbury, G.C.B.
Mr Gaspard Farrer
Sir Otto Niemeyer, K.C.B.
Mr N. E. Young (*Secretary*)

Mr Keynes, called and examined

(CHAIRMAN) *I think our Secretary has communicated with you as to the terms of our reference, and asked you to be prepared to make a statement to us.* (MR KEYNES) Yes.

Would you begin by making a statement? The present plan of £1 Currency Notes and £5 Bank of England Notes side by side is anomalous in appearance, but it has no practical disadvantages of which I am aware. I do not attach much importance one way or the other to the proposal for amalgamation, as such, but it would be slightly troublesome to effect amalgamation, particularly at a time when the ultimate currency policy is unsettled. Therefore amalgamation would not be worth doing for its own sake unless it facilitated some other advantageous change.

The only important question to my mind is that of the rules controlling the aggregate volume of the two note issues. The present system is superficially like the pre-war system, that is to say there is a fixed maximum fiduciary issue of the two note issues together, just as there was a fixed fiduciary issue of the Bank of England note issue before the war. But in spite of the superficial resemblance, the present system is different from the pre-war system in two very important respects. The first one is the very familiar one that the maximum is liable to vary downwards from one year to another, and never liable to vary upwards. That is familiar. The other point I do not think is quite so familiar, although it is really obvious. It is that under the present system there is no means of increasing the non-fiduciary portion, so that, whereas under the pre-war system we had a fixed fiduciary issue and a fluctuating non-fiduciary issue varying with imports of gold, what we have in effect now is a fixed total issue. There can be no question either of the import or of the export of gold in the ordinary course in present circumstances. When the market was short of funds and the Bank reserve went down and so forth, in the pre-war system that automatically led to a replenishment of the basis of the currency. At present that cannot happen, and a system where the note issue is rigidly fixed in total is quite a different system from one where the fiduciary issue is fixed, but where it requires no great disturbance of the existing adjustments to enlarge the non-fiduciary portion.

(SIR JOHN BRADBURY) *To clear our minds on this point, you are really directing your observations to the position which exists so long as the exchange is below parity?* My remarks apply to the two issues taken in the aggregate, in a situation like the present in which the value of gold is in excess of the value of sterling. These provisions were of no great practical importance—in fact, were inoperative—until this year. Thus it is only quite lately that it has been worth while thinking about such points as what happens under the existing system when the actual note issue is quite close up to the permitted maximum.

I think that these are fatal defects—that although the actual note issue is very nearly equal to the permitted issue, that permitted issue should be liable to fall and not to rise, and that there should be no means of increasing it so long as sterling is depreciated. Therefore I do think it is important to modify the existing rules.

Nevertheless the question of modification seems to me to have little or nothing to do with the question of amalgamating the two issues which raises a different sort of problem. The existing rule is a relic of the time when it was the policy of the Government to carry out a progressive deflation, and this progressive reduction of the fiduciary limit was intended to enforce that progressive deflation. That policy, after falling gradually into desuetude, was expressly abandoned by the Government of the day just over a year ago when Mr Baldwin made his famous non-flationist speech. Unless, therefore, that policy is reversed, it would be foolish to maintain a rule the object of which is to enforce a policy contrary to what is the latest declaration of the policy of the Government in the matter. But even if that was reversed, even if we returned to a deflation policy on the lines of the Cunliffe Report, I still think that this rule would be a very inexpedient one, because we should surely carry out a deflation policy by curtailing credit, with the result that the demand for currency would contract automatically; and we should not think of tackling it by letting the currency limit become operative. The most that the currency limit could do would be to terrify us into doing what we intended to do anyhow, and, since there might have been some slight miscalculation in fixing the limit it might prove purely embarrassing. I cannot see how it could be useful.

(CHAIRMAN) *It would act as a signal, would it not?* It would act too late. If we waited until we were practically up to the currency limit it might be that nothing that we could do, short of inflicting general bankruptcy on the commercial public, would enable us to keep to the limit. We should have to act some appreciable time in advance, and in acting what we should look at would not really be this limit but the dollar exchange, the level of prices, the general state of credit, and all the reactions which we should have to bring about if we wanted to put a drastic deflation policy into operation. It seems to me that rigid limitation is unworkable. This view is not dependent on particular views on deflation or stability, and it is a mistake, for the reason I elaborated a few minutes ago, to think that this system of rigid limitation is the pre-war system. It is much more dangerous than the pre-war system, because the pre-war system was always capable of expansion without any very violent re-adjustment of the situation.

If the old rule is to be changed, the question arises what criterion can be put in its place. So long as the gold standard is inoperative, with the result that there is no question either of importing or of exporting gold, it seems to me clear that the criterion cannot for the time being relate to gold; it would be without serious significance to relate it to gold. If the criterion is not gold, I do not know of any alternative criterion which has been seriously put forward except the level of prices. But the difficulty of that is that we cannot easily—in fact, we cannot at all—apply that criterion, the criterion of prices, until we have decided whether our policy is to raise prices or to lower them or to keep them steady in the transitional period. I exclude the policy of any material rise in prices because I do not think anyone defends it.

(SIR JOHN BRADBURY) *You say 'transitional period'. Transitional to what?* Until there has been some final declaration as to what our ultimate currency policy is to be. I call it transitional because many people are in favour of a policy of stability of prices at present who are not in favour of stability of prices as a permanent policy. I did not want to raise that issue more than I need. Everyone who is not in favour of a very rapid deflation admits the existence of a transitional period. For many reasons, which I have printed in a book with which this Committee probably does not want to be troubled, I believe that deflation in the sense of lowering the price level—of course it is an ambiguous term—is contrary to the public interest, and I go further than that and I say that even if it were desirable, deflation at a rapid rate would probably prove socially and politically impossible in present conditions. If that view is accepted, we are left with a criterion which was explicitly adopted by Mr Baldwin, on behalf of the Government of the day, a year ago, of maintaining the price level steady. But whatever answer we give to the question I have just raised, whether our object is deflation or stability, the method of the Treasury and the Bank of England would be found in credit control rather than in currency control;—if only because currency control operates too late in the day to be effective. And therefore I think the function of any rule of currency limitation should be limited to the purpose of operating as a warning signal in the contingency, which one hopes will not arise, of credit control breaking down for any reason. So long as credit control is successfully conducted, the limitation on the volume of currency ought never to be operative; and if you have a limit at all it is only as a second line of defence and as a thing which might possibly strengthen the hands of the central authorities in the event of a serious collapse of their deliberate credit policy. If you use the currency limitation in that way, there should clearly be a reasonable margin between the permitted maximum volume of the note issue and the anticipated actual volume of the note issue, assuming for the moment that the criterion of price stability has been adopted. You do not want the warning signal to come into effective operation except for a fairly grave cause. The unforeseeable moderate fluctuations of the market you would not want to be complicated by this violent danger signal,—these you would deal with by the ordinary methods of the Bank rate and credit control.

I should like to say, at this point, that I do not myself attach importance to having any maximum at all, because if credit control does break down badly the damage is already done and it can only be undone by regaining control of credit. I do not think, for example, that the United States at the present moment suffers any danger or any inconvenience through having no operative limit to its note issue. There is, if course, a legal limit, but it is so very far from the actual issue that they are in just the same position as we were in a year or two years ago under the Cunliffe Committee, namely that the legal limitation is not a thing which enters into the calculations of the central authorities at all.

On the other hand, I do not see any very great objection to a maximum. It is a rule to which conventional opinion is accustomed, and I see that in certain circumstances it might act as a useful strengthener to the central authorities in endeavouring to do their duty. It is a thing intelligible to the public, to which the central authorities could refer when the reasons which actually govern them are more difficult to explain. I do not think it is of serious importance to the governing authorities themselves. I say that I see no objection to a maximum provided there is a margin sufficient to ensure that the limit will not be in fact operative unless credit control has really broken down, and also provided that the limit can be revised from time to time. I attach importance to this margin and to this power of revision, not only for the reasons I have given, but also because there is no constant mathematical relation between the level of prices and the demand for currency. The demand for currency depends on several things beside the level of prices; it depends, as has been long known, on the season of the year and on the briskness of trade, and it also depends, to an extent which has only been fully appreciated lately, on the point reached in the credit cycle and the general anticipations of the business world about the future course of prices. As an illustration of the extreme variability of the volume of the note issue in relation to the level of prices, in the two years between October 1920 and October 1922 prices fell by 30 per cent and the aggregate note issue fell by 14 per cent It might be, therefore, that in a certain condition of business psychology, a certain point in the credit cycle, the existing note issue would support a very much higher level of prices than we have now. For those reasons it is extremely difficult to achieve any result, whether with a gold standard or price stability, by fixing the level of your note issue;—if the maximum limit is to be operative you have to change it constantly at each season in the year and at each phase in the credit cycle, and if you knew enough to change the limit of the note issue accurately you would know more than enough to regulate the currency in other ways. It is the most difficult conceivable way to attain any result, to try to do it by regulating the note issue, because you are acting on almost the *last* event in the causal train. When a tendency is set up to cause rising or falling prices, the very last thing which happens is the movement of the note issue. It is like conducting a *post mortem*, like postponing all diagnosis until the *post mortem* and prescribing that steps should be taken to look after the patient as soon as it is ascertained for certain that he is dead. Of course, also, the appropriate volume of the note issue varies with the growth of wealth and population, and it also varies—a thing which may happen quickly or slowly—with changes in the banking habits of the community. If, for example, the Treasury were to take off the stamp duty on cheques, that might very appreciably alter the volume of note issue that was required to support a given level of prices.

(CHAIRMAN) *Do you really think that is so?* Of course, it is an estimate. But suppose cheques were more freely used for small payments—if you had not got to pay 2d. it might make a great difference.

In so far as notes are used in place of cheques, is it not because there are now small notes, and for that reason only, not on account of the extra penny duty? Before, you had to have either a cheque or a postal order for which you had to pay. Now you can put your hand into your pocket and pull out your ten shillings. Yes. I think that is why notes are used more now in that way, but my point is that if you take the stamp duty off cheques would be used.

I wonder. That does not matter. My point is that you may have changes of that kind in the facilities granted by banks or in the charges for them, which would make really a great variation in quite a short period in the extent to which people use currency notes for making payments. All this leads to the conclusion that if you insist on a fixed maximum for your note issue, this maximum should be appreciably higher—I should say by not less than 15 per cent; and I think even that is running it rather close—than you anticipated actual note issue. You ought not to aim at having the compulsory powers any nearer actuality than 15 per cent. There is a good deal to be said in favour of a margin of 20 per cent. A limitation of that kind would stand in the way of any serious inflation, such as has happened in many countries lately, or even such as happened in this country immediately after the War. It would stand in the way of any serious inflation without operating accidentally and without purpose in interfering with the considered credit policy of the authorities.

I have spoken so far as if the method of regulating our note issue would be in any case the method of a fixed fiduciary maximum. I agree with the Cunliffe Committee in thinking that a fixed maximum fiduciary issue is preferable to any of the other formulas in vogue in other countries. If the Committee is interested in any of the other formulas which have been suggested, I should be glad to discuss them, but the traditional English view seems to me to have everything to be said for it.

My practical conclusions, then, are that I see no particular object in combining the currency note and Bank note issues. On the other hand, unless there was some special purpose to be served, amalgamation would involve a troublesome bargain between the Treasury and the Bank of England, and there is also one incidental point I should like to mention—Sir Otto Niemeyer will be able to say whether it has any importance or not. I think it is an advantage of the present system that the Treasury has control over the securities of the Currency Note Redemption Account. In these days when the Treasury has big conversions and redemptions to be carried through, and is concerned in big market operations, the fact that a considerable volume of Government securities of one kind or another are held by what is technically known as 'Other Government Departments', of which the Currency Note Redemption Account is one of the largest, and that the type of security held in those funds can be varied quite privately, that facility is really of great importance to the Treasury in its operations. If you regard the Bank of England and the Treasury as virtually the same concern from this point of view, the change would not matter much, of course; but then I think you must make proposals of this kind on the assumption that these bodies are not necessarily the same thing. If they are the same thing, the whole discussion is of no importance whatever, but if this would mean that the Treasury would part with the control of the securities in the Currency Note Redemption Account to the Bank of England, I think it would be a retrograde movement. In the old days, when the amount of such securities was relatively small and when these operations were not being carried out except very infrequently, the matter was of no significance, but with their present magnitude and the operations the Treasury has in view in the next seven years, I attach a certain amount of importance to this point, because in practice that is the chief result which would flow from the amalgamation of the two note issues as such. I cannot see that amalgamation would make much difference, except that you would be handing over the control of this great body of securities out of the hands of the Treasury into the hands of the Bank of England. That is my first practical conclusion that amalgamation, as such, is not important, but there is more to be said against it than for it.

My second conclusion is that it is important to revise the present rule governing the volume of currency notes.

My third conclusion is that if you wish to keep the general principle of a fixed maximum, that maximum at the present moment ought to be about mid-way between the maxima that were established for the years 1922 and 1923, that is to say about 290 millions for the fiduciary issue of the Currency Note Account. I think that would be for the present a good practical compromise between various theoretical policies. As I have said, I should prefer no maximum; I should depend for price stability or deflation on the efficiency of credit control. There is another incidental point of Treasury interest I should like to bring up at this juncture. Suppose you had no maximum for the currency notes in ordinary circumstances, this would have no importance unless there is a complete breakdown of the central authorities over the control of credit; but it might be a very important point to the Treasury to be able to issue an unlimited volume of currency notes when dealing with its redemptions and conversions. It seems to me that suppose you have some big conversion scheme for the big 5% War Loan, and there was a certain percentage of holders who would not accept the general terms, it is important that the Treasury should be able to pay them off in currency notes and beat them down to accepting the Government terms, because there is nothing they could do with the currency notes. If the permitted maximum was intended to be a serious maximum there would be no margin for the Treasury to do that. It seems to me that the Treasury should be able to threaten to pay off a remnant of 25 or 50 millions in currency notes, as otherwise you might have a single big holder, or a very small group of big holders, or just a collection of people in the country, who could blackmail the Treasury in the most tiresome manner and possibly require special legislation. The loan is due on a particular date; these holders of 50 millions of the security would say, 'We do not accept your conversion terms; pay us off according to our bond', and there would be absolutely no way whatever by which the Treasury could legally pay them off. I think the inconvenience of that, particularly the inconvenience of the Treasury not having this weapon in reserve so that people could not even begin to talk in that way, is more important than the safeguard against the improbable contingency of the credit control breaking down,—particularly because my own belief is that if your first line of defence breaks down your second line of defence will break down simultaneously. It has nearly always happened in recent experience that the trouble has come through the first line of defence breaking down, through the authorities losing control of credit by reason of their excessive Government borrowings or in some other way, and I am not aware of a single example in which the first line of defence, that is to say credit control, has broken down in a modern community, where the situation has been saved in the slightest degree by having this second line of defence, a currency limitation. The rule of currency limitation is immediately waived. There are so many examples of that, and such recent ones, that it is hardly worth quoting particular cases.

In giving my practical conclusions, I should like to end up with one further point, namely, what my ideal system would be. My ideal system would be to hand over the country's reserves held to meet a foreign drain, whether those reserves consisted of gold or foreign balances or whatever they consisted of, to the authority controlling credit, i.e. to the Bank of England,

and I should place on the Bank of England the entire responsibility of controlling credit and maintaining their reserves at such a level as to maintain the parity of the standard, whether that parity was in terms of gold, dollars or commodities; and I would measure the failure of the Bank of England not by some arithmetical relation between the reserves and the note issue—which is a meaningless and quite illogical relation, since under modern conditions when the standard of value does not itself circulate, there is no reason why the one should bear any particular proportion to the other, but by any tendency of the standard to depart from its parity by more than the legal margin. That is the real fact of the situation for decades past. The relation of the amount of reserves to the amount of note issue is a fabrication. It relates to a system that existed a hundred years or more ago. It is kept up as a pure figment and no one ever works on these lines. The actual reserves you require are those necessary to meet unexpected fluctuations in your international position. There is no precise relation between the amount you require for that purpose and the amount of your note issue. The classical case in which this was argued out was the case of India, with which you are very familiar. It was not thought that the amount of the gold standard reserve ought to bear any particular relation to the note issue of India or the circulation of rupees. Sir Lionel Abrahams used to work out memoranda showing what on balance was the maximum net payment India might have to make abroad in a given period of time, and that was the only logical way of arriving at the reserve. That is the only way of arriving at the amount of reserve that the Bank of England ought to hold. I think it is a pure confusion to link that up with the amount of the note issue, and a confusion that may divert the authorities from their true purposes and may prove practically inconvenient. My system would be to link up the amount of reserve with the credit controlling authority and to put the responsibility on them to keep sufficient reserves to maintain the parity of the standard.

Having done that, I would issue without any arbitrary fixed limit such volume of notes as the state of credit required. Such issue would be automatic, and I would place it in the hands of the Treasury. I would place it in the hands of the Treasury because the profit belongs to the Treasury and you would therefore avoid awkward questions and difficult bargains, and secondly because it is helpful to the Treasury in their national debt operations to have under their control the great volume of securities held against the fiduciary issue.

There are three points I would like to repeat. One is what I mentioned at the beginning, that the fixed upper limit to the note issue is much more dangerous in present conditions than in pre-war conditions, since a fixed fiduciary issue is now in practice the same as a fixed total issue,—a thing which we never knew before the war; secondly, that in modern conditions currency control is a relatively unimportant second line of defence, the main line of defence being credit control—most of the conventional maxims about note issues have relation to the conditions of a hundred years ago and are empty words in relation to modern conditions. And thirdly, I would emphasise that most of what I have said this morning would be the same even if I were in favour of a hasty return to the gold standard. I do not think the subject matter of this Committee's discussions is very much connected with the question of stability of prices and the gold standard, because the only method of carrying out any policy is by credit control and not by currency control. It could only be a crazy person who would employ currency control for the purpose of achieving a gold standard, because a refusal to issue a volume of currency rendered necessary by the existing volume of credit would merely be general bankruptcy, and the first and biggest bankrupt would be the Treasury.

(CHAIRMAN) *Much of your argument has turned upon the present conditions under which gold cannot flow in as it used to do in old times. Would you agree that what prevents gold flowing in is the fact that if it flows in you cannot get it out again?* I should say that what prevents gold flowing in is that there is no purchaser in England who offers so high a price as purchasers in the United States.

At present there is an embargo on the export of gold? Yes. I do not think that embargo is the cause of the lower price offered for gold here than in America.

What would be the effect of lifting the embargo on the movement of gold? Would you mean by 'lifting the embargo', lifting the embargo as regards gold held in private hands, or permitting holders of Bank notes to take gold out of the Bank of England for export?

Taking gold out for export. I put aside gold for internal currency, which might or might not be included, but restoring the free market in gold for export. The first effect would be that a considerable amount of gold would flow, and the exchange would be immediately restored to parity. That would have many other consequences.

As the effect would be in a very short time to send the exchange to parity, do you think there really would be a great drain of gold? It does not follow that it would stay there. The immediate demand for gold would be limited to the extent to which the market was prepared to speculate on future requirements, and the extent to which the market would be prepared to speculate on future requirements would be smaller than what those future requirements would turn out to be. The market would never speculate to 100 per cent, partly because it would not be worth its while, and partly because it would never have confidence enough to do that. Therefore, as time went on various unforeseen requirements for dollars would be set up by this greater cheapness of them, and if no other steps were taken simultaneously, besides the removal of the embargo, to modify credit conditions and so forth, I should say that certainly after a time all the gold would have left the Bank of England and there would still be unsatisfied demands. If you were to offer more gold for sterling and make no other change, the demands for gold at this reduced price for export to America would be bound in the end to swamp you. Therefore that policy would have to be combined with a drastic credit restriction. You would therefore have to face the consequences of that. One of the first consequences of the restoration of sterling to par without any other change taking place simultaneously—I am assuming your instantaneous action—would be that all our exports would cost 12 per cent more in the world market than they cost now. That would mean in a great many cases that our export trade would be absolutely cut from under our feet for the time being.

On the other hand, there would be a correlative lowering of import prices of raw material and food? We should also tend to buy more, and the extent to which we should do that would depend on the confidence in this policy being permanently successful.

If your raw material and food prices fell, would not that tend to prevent the rise in prices of exports which you fear? Not at once, because you would not have wages falling automatically 12 per cent. Take the coal or iron and steel industries, where the imported goods they employ are insignificant. Even in the case of cotton goods the cost of the imported raw material in many cases is not more than about 30 per cent or something of that kind. So that a fall of 10 per cent in the raw material would only mean a fall of about 3 per cent in the finished product.

I put the question to you as if it were to be done with a stroke of the pen tomorrow; but now may I go to what is more practical? The embargo expires on the 31st December 1925. What would you do under those circumstances? This leads into rather big questions.

We are unable to keep them out. I hold very strongly that the Treasury or the Bank of England—whichever you like—must, I should say in perpetuity, keep a hold over both the import and export of gold. I should favour a permanent system of allowing both export and import of gold only by license of the Treasury or the Bank of England. That would mean that the rates at which gold was flowing in or out, and the level of prices and so forth, would be under their control. It might happen that for long periods together the licences would be granted to all comers without question, freely. You then have the advantages of the supposed free gold market. I have never heard what the advantages were, but they are often referred to. You would, at the same time, have no safeguard against being swamped with gold, which, I think, is the more likely contingency, or against suffering a sudden depletion of gold contrary to your policy. I see no reason whatever why the existing method of controlling gold imports and exports should not be made a permanent policy. I think there is a great deal to be said for it.

If you announced now, or between now and next December, that you proposed to introduce legislation to prolong, or to make permanent, the existing control over the export of gold, do you think that would have any effect on the position of our national credit? I think it would be unwise to say you would make it permanent unless you were at the same time announcing a permanent monetary policy in other respects. It would make people ask questions, and you would not know the answer to the questions. If you were merely to say that the existing arrangements are going to be continued for the present pending a final settlement of the currency policy, I think the effect would be nil. The number of people who are aware that this expires on a certain date is almost limited to the people in this room.

Do not you think that a great many people on becoming aware that it is necessary to prolong it would treat that as rather a serious declaration, rightly or wrongly? Would not they regard it as a confession on the part of the British Government of economic weakness? It would be a confession that it was not absolutely certain that we could return to the gold standard by the 1st January 1926. The opinion that we shall return to a gold standard on the 1st January 1925* is hardly held by anyone. That being so there is no reason to say anything particular just at present.

It would have to be said next year? This seems to me a question consequential upon other policies. I should pursue whatever was my exchange and currency policy, and should take this embargo off at the date when all my other policies had led to the result that the embargo was of no importance. Personally I should prefer to keep the embargo on even though it was not operative, as a safeguard.

It is an essential part of your views that we ought not to attempt to restore the old parity of the sovereign? No, that is not an essential part of my views. My own belief is that the policy I advocate—price stability—would almost certainly lead to a restoration of the parity of the sovereign, because I find it very hard to believe that American prices will not rise in time, unless they do improbable things. I am really at one with almost everybody on that point. I am against hurrying the day, but I regard it as probable that if we concentrate on a price stability policy we shall probably find ourselves at no very distant date at par. The peculiarity of my policy is limited to this, that

* This is what I said. There was a confusion about dates.

having got back to par I should like to accept the import of gold only by licence of the Treasury. That is to say, suppose there is a big wave of inflation in America which carries us back to par, I do not want to be carried on by that inflation. The advocates of the gold standard think it is very important that we should share in any inflation going on in the world generally. I want to stop at that point, and I think it is extraordinarily easy to stop at that point because the only way in which we have to alter our pre-war or present currency system is by saying—it is not a question of the import of gold—that the Bank of England should be the only party authorised to deliver gold at the Mints.

You would relieve the Mint of all obligation to coin at a fixed price? For all comers.

(SIR OTTO NIEMEYER) *And relieve the Bank of the obligation?* And I should also relieve the Bank of the obligation to buy gold at a fixed price. I should leave the Bank free to raise or lower its price. We should then be our own masters. If we did not want to share in the inflation that is hypothetically going on in the rest of world we should keep our prices stable.

(CHAIRMAN) *May I put a question in what I hope is a practical form? Do I understand that, from your point of view, we derived, as a nation, no advantage before the War from having an absolutely free gold market as contrasted with, say, the nominally free gold market of Germany which, in fact, was a controlled market?* The advantage we gained—you may call it consequential on that—was that our effective gold points were narrower than those of certain other countries such as France and Germany, and that made short-term loans and lendings on the London market by and to foreigners an operation more susceptible to small changes in the rate of discount than it could be if the gold points were rather wider; but it resulted not from the free gold market as such but from the narrowness of the gold points, and my policy would be that the Bank of England should announce limits corresponding to gold points for periods from time to time covering short loans. I think you can get the advantages of security in the minds of international borrowers and lenders if they have confidence in the rate at which they can get their money backwards and forwards by other methods than by the reception of gold in unlimited amounts. I think that the advantage of London was the certainty, over a period of three or six months, of the rate at which you could get your money in and out of England. That policy was contingent on the fact that almost the whole world was on a gold standard. If only a small part of the world was on a gold standard, that remains an advantage but a less extensive advantage. I think at present, under post-war conditions, which are different in very many respects from pre-war conditions, the danger of the pre-war system would be that New York, at certain times when money was very redundant as it may easily be under their present Federal Reserve System, would dump a lot of short money on London, relying on this way of getting it out again, so that any tendency towards inflation in America resulting from unduly cheap money would be at once reflected here in a way that we might not like at all. It would not always be an advantage to be a dumping ground for 2 per cent American money with an absolute guarantee that they could take it away at any moment. We should not know what to do with it. It would force our domestic rates down equally low. I think the absolute linking up of the London and New York money markets, while that has great advantages, is not such a safe thing as it used to be. In the old days the amount of floating funds in New York as compared with the size of the London market was not so menacing, as it would be now. One of the points of my policy is that, whilst I think there are other devices that the Bank of England can introduce for giving certainty to the market, the particular methods that secured certainty before the War are now dangerous.

(SIR JOHN BRADBURY) *Mr Keynes, do you, under present conditions, attach any importance at all to the fluctuation in the amount of the reserve in the Banking Department of the Bank of England?* You mean consequential on more Bank notes going into circulation?

The traditional pre-war policy of the Bank of England was to determine the credit policy of the Bank with regard to the movements in the reserve in the Banking Department. Under modern post-war conditions, do you attach any importance at all to those fluctuations as an indication for the purposes of determining the credit policy? At the moment when gold cannot flow in and out, none whatever. If gold flowed in or out, while I should attach some importance to the state of the reserve as one of the indications, I should not make it the sole criterion as under pre-war conditions.

One of the arguments for amalgamating the two issues is that the fluctuations in the volume of currency notes as well as the fluctuation in the Bank notes would be reflected in the movements of the reserve of the Bank of England? They are published every week now, and anyone who wants to know can make the calculation. That seems to imply that the Bank is so unacquainted with arithmetic that it is incapable of adding the two together.

I think you misunderstood the purpose of my question. No doubt the necessary calculations can be made; but the Bank of England, like other institutions, is susceptible to public opinion. If a variation of the Bank rate has to be justified to the public, to public opinion, the only justification before the War was that the increase had to be effected to protect the reserve of the Banking Department. My question rather is this: do you think in public opinion the old idea of the fluctuation of the reserve being an important barometer is a matter of any importance? Of very little importance. In so far as it is a barometer, I think it acts too late. If the Bank waits to put up its Bank rate, until it can have this justification for the public it will always put it up too late.

My point is this. So to speak we have now two barometers—the Treasury returns of the currency note issue and the ordinary Bank of England return. The skilled meteorologist has to compare the two and make the calculation from them. Would not there be some advantage, so to speak, in having only the one barometer by amalgamating the two, when the currency note return would be in the Bank of England return? I agree that to anyone at all skilled the business of adding the two together does not represent any difficulty. There are various financial weeklies which do the sum for the public every week. If the object is to make the public attach greater importance to it, I think it is obviously dangerous. I think it is dangerous for the public to say to the Bank of England, when the Bank wants to raise its rate, 'Why are you hampering trade when your reserve does not show any fluctuations'. I think it would be better that they should act in good time, and therefore to concentrate public opinion on the indication, which is a late-in-the-day indication, will weaken the Bank's position.

Is not it true that for the determination of credit the consideration of the Bank of England return, taken alone, is entirely useless? Taken alone, useless.

For the purpose of facilitating the consideration of these problems, could there not be something to be said for having, so to speak, an amalgamated return of the two? I think it would be just as useless.

(CHAIRMAN) *May I ask Mr Keynes this question? What are the indications upon which, in your opinion, the Bank ought to act? Set aside for the moment whether the relation of the reserve to the note issue is of any importance from the point of view of helping the public. What are the actual indications, arising long before that comes into operation as I understand, upon which you think the Bank ought to act?* May I illustrate that by what I should say about the Bank rate at this moment, which is very much under discussion. At this moment I should pay great attention to the ease with which the Treasury was able to get its dollars over the exchange. I should watch the level of prices in America. I should watch changes in the form of the assets of the 'Big Five' [clearing banks] as between advances, investments and discounts. I should watch the open market rate of discount. I should watch the new issues market, particularly the foreign new issues. Suppose that now or in the next three months I found that the Treasury was finding it difficult to get dollars, if I was told by bankers that cotton and wheat bills were coming on the exchange in heavy volume, if I saw American prices on the upward move rather than otherwise, I should be strongly inclined to put the Bank rate up. I should take into account the relative money rates here and in America, but I should take into account not less the money rates in Germany and France.

Supposing that the Dawes Report was to go through, so that confidence was increased, I should pay then more attention to high rates on the Continent, because I should think the political risks being reduced the English market would be more ready to take advantage of the high rates for money obtainable on the Continent. If all those indications, or a great many of them, were adverse, I should anticipate a combination of sterling exchange falling and American prices rising, and that combination would be almost certain to engineer a rise of prices here, which—possibly months later—would show itself in an additional issue of currency notes. But if I waited until the currency notes were pouring out as the final result of all this and let my exchange go against me in the meantime, and let the new issues market go on lending to New South Wales, and the private loan market go on lending to Austria and Germany, I should be in the soup. My only way out would be to try and bankrupt a lot of people.

(SIR JOHN BRADBURY) *I want to put this question to Mr Keynes on the credit policy. I take it you hold the view that the purchasing power, the unit of value, in this country ought to be determined entirely by whatever public authority controlled the issue of credit.* Yes.

Correct me if I misinterpret you. You do not under present conditions regard any kind of link with the commodity value of gold as a practical method for controlling prices, or any kind of link with exchanges? Well, I do not go as far as that. There are various compromises that are possible. One of the great objections to the gold standard is that I think that as time goes on, with methods of economising, gold will tend to be redundant, and one of the things I want to be protected against is inflation due to the depreciation of gold. If my opinion as to the relative abundance of gold is correct, a system of free convertibility into gold would be harmless. What we should require would be a system of licensing the import of gold for currency, so that when gold had depreciated in value we could lower the price of gold in terms of sterling, and we should then obtain for one pound sterling more gold than its equivalent on the pre-war basis of £3.17.10 per oz.

Would it be correct to say then that you think that the unit of value in this country should be maintained by credit control, plus the taking into account of various economic causes and tendencies, of which no doubt gold value should be one, but possibly not the most important? That is correct.

Of course that credit control becomes a very delicate operation? I do not think this difficulty is affected by what standard we adopt. I hold that the methods of credit control employed would be identical under my suggested scheme and under a gold system. When you have the credit system and no gold circulating I think the methods employed do not depend upon the aim, but are substantially the same whatever your aim.

May I put the point I want to get at in this way. The pre-war practice I

254

take it regarding this very delicate operation of credit control, which you say must take place at a very much earlier time, before the currency limits come into operation, was left primarily to the Bank of England. On the other hand, the Bank of England was operating in the exercise of its credit control with that rigid currency system of the country, in the background if you like, as a menace in regard to which their policy must be developed. Now, the question I want to put to you is this. Supposing we got rid of that menace, the ultima ratio *of the currency control, or made it more remote, would you think that the duty of credit control could properly be left entirely to the Bank of England, in consultation, of course, with the Treasury and other people?* I should reform the constitution of the Bank of England in certain ways. I think I should develop the power of the Bank's Committee of Treasury. [One] might make the representation of the Treasury rather more formal than it is at present. There has been a great change since the war in the relations between the Bank of England and the Treasury. I should leave it ostensibly to the Bank of England and should develop the power of the Committee of Treasury.

You would leave the Bank formally a private institution, and allow it to exercise its control without any external control? I do not regard it as a private institution. I regard it as one of our Heaven-sent institutions by which through anomalistic methods we get the advantages both of a private and of a public institution.

I said 'formally' I think I would meet criticism by making a little clearer the relations between the Treasury and the Bank of England.

(CHAIRMAN) *Would you advise any Chancellor of the Exchequer to accept for himself and his successors the responsibility for the alteration of the Bank rate?* No. I think that the function of the Government and of the Treasury is to determine the policy, whether it is to be a gold standard or whatever it is to be, but the the technical means of achieving that ought to be left to a body in the position of the Bank of England.

(SIR JOHN BRADBURY) *There is one point on which I want to put a question to you. One of your arguments in favour of the policy for a fixed maximum for the fiduciary issue was that if the Treasury had power to issue Treasury notes in any volume it might facilitate operations in connection with the conversion of the public debt. Do you regard it as entirely consistent with the contract between the bondholder and public creditors of this country generally that that kind of pressure should be brought on the bondholder, i.e., that emergency currency should be made for the purpose of giving advantages to one party to the contract—the Government—as against the other party?* I should regard it as perfectly proper, provided that the Treasury were offering a fair bargain. I think it would be iniquitous to use this weapon to enforce on the bondholder a manifestly unfair bargain. I am considering a case where the great mass of the bondholders have agreed that the offer is a fair one. It is to protect the

Treasury from the blackmailing power of persons who demand that they shall be paid back.

(SIR OTTO NIEMEYER) *Is not that a part of their rights under the contract?* I think the propriety of using this weapon would depend upon the actual bargain you made.

(CHAIRMAN) *It would be a tremendous power to put in the hands of the Chancellor of the Exchequer or the Government for the time being.* It was a threat that Goschen used, and there were some people who were inclined to think he was driving a hard bargain.

(SIR JOHN BRADBURY) *What he threatened was to pay them in gold?* It is the same thing.

(CHAIRMAN) *Is it the same thing as paying them in currency notes?* So long as you maintain the value of your currency notes.

If they could issue 20 millions of currency notes for the purpose of paying off, would the value be retained? You offer them as good a bargain as they can get from anyone else. Supposing you were offering a conversion loan at 2 per cent and there were plenty of good securities at 5 per cent, of course, then they will defeat you. If you offered them a fair market price they would have to come to your terms. It would not suit them to buy goods. I do not think the threat would be used. I think the reserve power of using it might be of some importance.

(SIR OTTO NIEMEYER) *On this last point, if you assume a case where, say, a third of the bondholders had to be paid off by notes in the way you suggest, would not the effect be to penalise the other two-thirds who accepted your terms? I am assuming that you had to put this into force?* Yes, but I think that really assumes it is an unfair bargain. I think if you had one-third of the bondholders of a big issue demanding payment, I think that would be a proof that the bargain offered was an unfair one.

I am putting it as an extreme case, but pro tanto *if one had to issue further notes, the effect would be, to that extent whatever it may be, to depreciate the value of the securities which you are giving to the two-thirds who had accepted.* Let me put a case the other way. Supposing you had a single big insurance company or a big bank which held 25 millions of a loan which is falling due, and you offered them in exchange securities which were the equivalent of the market rates at the moment. If they said 'Unless you offer us $\frac{1}{2}$ per cent better we shall want payment in cash' you would have no means of paying them off. If this company were prepared to take payment in bank credits, cash at the Bank of England, there would be no difficulty, but suppose they were blackmailing and insisted upon payment in cash which they are entitled to, then you could not get that cash.

You suggest this power should be kept as a weapon for dealing with debt. You would limit it to that purpose. Would you be able to do so? I do not think there would ever be a question of it in any other circumstances, unless you lost control of credit. It would operate exactly in ordinary circumstances as a limit which was comfortably above your note issue. It is a very secondary point.

My point is rather different. In the case you are putting the state has a large debt to pay which she cannot raise money to pay, and this is the means of escape. Supposing the state wanted large sums of money for other purposes, would you get the same principle applying? I should call that a complete breakdown of credit control.

You think you could distinguish between the two cases. You think you could confine the use of the power to the case of debt repayment? I do not think there would be any difficulty in saying which was one case or the other.

(CHAIRMAN) *Do you think you can trust the Chancellor of the Exchequer not to fill his Budget deficit or for the purpose of his favourite scheme to use this if he has it?* I do not think there are any means of strapping down a really wicked Chancellor of the Exchequer.

Well, you would try to stop him as much as possible? No. I should try to throw him out of office. On your assumption that there might be a Chancellor of the Exchequer who was borrowing by inflationary means, he would not do it by actually paying out currency notes. He would borrow on terms that led to inflation of credit and did not represent real savings, and would be exactly similar to any other inflationary movement. My opinion is that if you had a Chancellor of the Exchequer with these wishes, the operation of the limitation of the currency note issue probably would not come into effect in his time anyhow. To depend on that for checking your Chancellor of the Exchequer would be depending on a remedy that comes much too late.

(SIR OTTO NIEMEYER) *Don't you think you perhaps put the point about the issue of currency notes a little high?* I did not mean to put this secondary point at all high; if I did, I withdraw it.

I wanted to be clear. Let me put my question in this way. As you know, the main assets of the Currency Notes Account are not convertible loans; the main assets are short-term securities such as Treasury bills. No doubt that could be altered, and of course there is a certain convenience in having this power for the purpose of conversion, though the Government controls very considerable other funds, as you know such as savings bank deposits. Still as you said, in so far as the Currency Note Account is concerned the power is useful. And yet, if they were held on Bank of England account they could be used by agreement with the Bank. I do not know how high you put this. Well, I do not think my opinion is worth very much, because I do not know how this thing works out in practice, but it seems to me, for example, that the Treasury should have large resources for paying off issues at maturity and in advance of their maturity.

There are the powers they have under the National Debt Acts and the deposits in the Post Office Savings Bank. I have no information as to the relative importance. If it is rather small, the importance is less, but the aggregate of the assets in the Currency Note Account are so large that I should have thought they would be of very great help in certain circumstances. The really difficult moment has not arrived yet.

The assets are roughly the same as the Savings Bank Account? I should think they are important. Hitherto you have been dealing with rather small conversions, but in the future, between now and 1931, you have some enormous transactions to carry through, and I should suppose that it would be technically helpful in spreading your operations over a long period to have all these reserves.

You would agree that the issue having been transferred to the Bank, you would get very much the same result in practice? I said that if the Bank could be considered as the same thing, the whole of this discussion is not of very much importance. It is merely a change of name.

You said you were in favour of strengthening the connection between the Treasury and the Bank. Would you go on to say there ought to be a Treasury representative on the Bank Court, as there is in many other foreign banks? I think that the Financial Controller of the Treasury ought to be in very close touch with the Committee of Treasury at the Bank without having any power of veto. Whether that is best achieved by making him an ex-officio member or more informally, I think those in closer touch could decide better than I.

You do not suggest that the Treasury or their representative should have the power of veto? No. I think the Treasury should only come in, in deciding what should be the parity of the standard. I do not think the Treasury ought to have a final voice in the method of obtaining parity.

I think you also said that one of the difficulties of amalgamation would be the precise bargain with the Bank of England. You remember that in the Cunliffe Report it is suggested that the Bank of England should surrender all their profits on the note issue. Assuming one was working on that basis, do you think there would be any great difficulty in negotiating with the Bank of England? It is not always easy to say what the profits of the Bank of England are.

The profits on the issue? Even that. The assets of this very large fiduciary issue would necessitate an amount of shifting of the particular assets between this fund and the total assets of the Bank of England. If you try and draw up a formal contract in these matters, which you are quite sure cannot operate disadvantageously to the public interest, you will find it very difficult. The Bank of England often for other reasons has to hold a certain amount of assets that are not very lucrative.

But it would not hold such assets as against the note issue. Why not?

Well, I am assuming that against the note issue they would have to hold Government securities. What kind of Government securities?

You would hesitate to leave to them the choice? Take the simple point that the Bank of England should have a mixed bag of securities—some short-dated, some long-dated, and some intermediate-dated. They do not all bear the same rate of interest. I should also think it is desirable that the Bank should have the power of moving securities backwards and forwards between its various accounts, so that the particular yield of the securities it holds against the notes is not necessarily an accurate measure of the advantages which the Bank of England gets from this. Again I do not attach great importance to this, unless there is something to be gained by it. I think these bargains are difficult to achieve. After all, the Treasury has had experience of bargains with the Bank of England and it is not easy to know exactly what the profit is.

You said there was no means of reducing the fiduciary issue? Of the aggregate.

The two put together? Yes.

Theoretically, you can increase the issue by buying gold? You could not in practice.

It would be too expensive you mean? Yes.

It could be done at a price, but the price would be unreasonable? Yes. It would be a silly thing to do.

I am not questioning that. It could be done.

(MR FARRER) *You made a great point about price stability, i.e., price stability measured in sterling?* Yes; measured in sterling.

If there is a great movement of prices outside this country, I suppose that you would say that is all regulated then by the course of exchange. Yes.

So that if you insisted upon maintaining price stability in this country, you might have a considerable variation in exchange and price movements outside? If there are considerable price movements outside. Supposing America was to indulge in a really big inflation and we did not, sterling would rise quite high above parity.

You would put price stability in this country as more important than exchange stability? Certainly. I think it would be better, both from the point of view of immediate internal conditions and our ultimate credit, that we should not follow America in any inflation that she indulges in.

Of course, it might be with other countries? There would only be a fluctuation in the exchange if the other countries had lost control of credit. I think it is disadvantageous to engage ourselves beforehand to share in any debauch that the rest of the world might be involved in.

That would involve possibly very big fluctuations in the exchange? Only if you were avoiding very big dangers of inflation.

Coming back to the rather practical point of this credit control, you gave Mr Chamberlain a great many reasons which ought to influence the Bank of England Directors in making these changes. Do you think from past experience, looking over the last forty years, that we have had a breed of people who are capable of taking all those considerations and acting upon them, or do you think we shall have to breed a superman to do it? My memory of events does not go back forty years, but I do not foresee any particular difficulty with it. I should not entrust this to the whole body of the Court.

You do not think you are anticipating Paradise in your suggestion. No. I am not changing the methods. If the Directors of the Bank of England are as stupid as some people think they are, our currency will break down in any case. I do not regard my system as intrinsically more difficult. What is more difficult is to manage a credit regime under which gold plays no part in circulation as compared with the medieval system when it was otherwise. That is where the difficulties come. This change, which I propose, I do not think complicates the task, and I should not have the smallest hesitation in thinking that there would be always half a dozen persons in the City well competent to look after it. Once they had started it, they would not find any particular trouble.

Of course, you have to educate your public as well as your City men. You have got to have the great mass of the people all through the country more or less understanding what their policy is. I think the policy is very easy to understand whether it is the gold standard or price stability. The difficulty is to understand the technical means of achieving it, and that has never been understood by the general public. There are two types of banking ability, the type of ability of understanding customers and not lending more than one ought to particular individuals, and on the other hand the central banking mind. You have the type of people who have risen in the world because of their capacity in the first direction, and then later in life they are put into this entirely different sphere of central banking. I should have said that at all dates there have been a considerable number of first-class men of the skilled central banking type of mind. It is on them I think that you would have to draw. If one reads the literature on the bimetallic and other past controversies, I think it is remarkable what an immense amount of ability of this type always has existed.

I suppose you would agree that both as regards credit and currency, the ultimate basis of everything is production. Unless we go on producing and selling at a profit we shall break down? That is the basis of wealth which is the ultimate thing. It is not the basis of [the] price level. You can have a high or low price level with any conditions of wealth.

(CHAIRMAN) *Following on the question Mr Farrer put as to the amount of ability required in the Bank of England for this, you would agree that the ordinary manufacturer, the merchant, even the ordinary exporter, is not a great student of these problems?* Yes.

Certainly the producer very often has very little knowledge at all, if any, of the method by which his accounts are really settled for sales or purchases effected? Very often not.

Do you not think he will be much more puzzled with a stable price and a fluctuating exchange than he would be with a stable exchange and a fluctuating price level? No, I do not think so.

May I say why? The price level will be for him the level of the goods in which he is dealing. It is true that his knowledge is centred on what he knows most about. The exchange, on the other hand, is a thing that he knows less of. He, therefore, wants to eliminate the possibility of what he intends to be a sale becoming a gamble in exchange. At present the price level of his particular commodity is made up of the movements of that commodity relative to other things, in regard to which he may be assumed to be an expert, and movements of the general price level of which he knows nothing. Many of the disasters of recent years have been due to the fact that the particular dealer in a commodity was at fault in the second, while being quite right in the first. With regard to exchange fluctuation, that only influences him in certain portions of his dealings, and by dealing in the forward exchange market he can hedge against it. You have the forward exchange market, through which he can insure against movements of the exchanges, but a forward market in commodities by means of which traders can insure against the risk of movements of prices is limited to two or three of the very biggest trades. Why I want price stability is that it will minimise disastrous losses to traders through no fault of their own, through events which were quite beyond their cognisance.

(CHAIRMAN) *Thank you very much.*

The witness withdrew.

After Keynes gave his evidence to the Committee and presumably in response to the trend of the questioning, as well as in response to recent speeches and articles by Sir Charles Addis, Sir Robert Kindersley and Walter Leaf, he took to the columns of *The Nation*.

From The Nation and Athenaeum, *19 July 1924*

THE POLICY OF THE BANK OF ENGLAND

I. *The new threat of deflation*

In recent weeks two influential directors of the Bank of England, Sir Charles Addis and Sir Robert Kindersley, and the chairman of the Westminster Bank, Dr Leaf, have advocated an immediate policy of deflation with the object of restoring sterling rapidly to its pre-war parity with gold,—thus reversing the policy of Mr Baldwin's 'non-flationist' speech of just a year ago, in which he declared that the right policy was to do all in our power to keep prices steady and on a level.

Of these three authorities only Dr Leaf explained details. His ideas of financial strategy are on the same general lines as M. Poincaré's and would prove about as successful. He believes that the problem of the exchanges can be solved by a temporary, violent agitation of the speculators. M. Poincaré's remedy for the franc was to cause the bears to rush for cover; Dr Leaf's remedy for sterling is to excite the bulls to rush into the open. He thinks that to attract floating funds to London and to cause a belief that sterling is going to appreciate will do the trick, without, apparently, other fundamental adjustments. It was alarming to discover the Poincarist mentality in high quarters here, but reassuring to find a little later that Dr Leaf's light-headedness was not widely shared in the City.

For a few days Dr Leaf enjoyed a *quasi*-success in the daily newspapers. Mr Snowden, indeed, still sits on the fence, remarking that he must not 'rush in where angels fear to tread', telling a story that 'only two men understand the foreign exchanges, of whom one is dead and the other in a lunatic asylum', and declining to be drawn into a discussion; disappointing confessions from a Labour Chancellor of the Exchequer concerning an issue which almost all authorities from the Cunliffe Committee onwards are agreed in regarding as vitally relevant to employment. But in other quarters clear and decided voices were quickly raised in opposition. The Federation of British Industries petitioned the Bank of England to hear the views of industry before acting. The 'Big Five', led by the Midland Bank, are believed to have urged caution. The weekly press (for the division of opinion nowadays on really important issues is often not between parties, but between the daily press and the weekly press)—*The Nation, The Spectator, The New Leader,* and *The New Statesman*—weighed in with unanimous protests.

It is probable that for the time being the deflationist movement is scotched. To embark, indeed at this time of year and with the present tendencies of employment and sterling prices, on a campaign of rapid deflation to the extent of 10 or 12 per cent would be a crazy policy. In the early stages the excitement of the bulls might provoke a rapid upward movement. But before the final goal was reached, many other difficult and injurious things would have to come about. Let us consider—for the fortification of our position—four of the broad consequences of raising, deliberately and rapidly, the real value of our monetary standard by 10 per cent.

1. The real burden of the national debt would be raised 10 per cent,—equivalent to nearly £40,000,000 on to the Budget; for the payment of the fixed money interest on the debt would mean a greater real sacrifice by the taxpayer. This would come about by the revenue falling along with prices, whilst expenditure for interest charges would be unaltered.

2. Money wages throughout industry would have to be forced down by 10 per cent. This would not mean any reduction in real wages. Nevertheless the disturbance to industrial peace can be easily imagined.

3. If the improvement in the exchange value of sterling were to precede, and move faster than, the adjustment of internal prices, the cost to foreign purchasers of our staple exports, coal textiles, and goods of iron and steel, would have to be enforced by depression and increased unemployment in our export industries.

4. All producers of goods would receive warning that their commodities would (on the average) depreciate in price during the period of production, so that they would be better advised to cease or curtail output for the time being. All prospective purchasers of goods would be told that they would buy cheaper

by waiting and withholding their orders. All persons and companies contemplating new capital developments would put off their projects. For the fear of falling prices is bad enough;—the certainty *must* aggravate unemployment and retard productive activity.

A cheerful programme! Is it appropriate to the aspirations of a Labour Government? Would its execution enhance the prestige and the authority of the City? Would the public fall down and worship the gold standard with gratitude and awe?

These results would not follow from a rise of the sterling exchange in itself, if this were brought about slowly by the depreciation of gold, that is by rising prices in America. But they are the admitted results of a declared programme of forced deflation.

A new theory can never win its way in the field of practical affairs unless it is illuminated by vivid facts and supported by events. Those who subscribe to price stability as a deliberate policy are still in a minority; but recent weeks have shown what a weight of popular opinion, when it comes to practice, is thrown on their side.

II. *The Bank rate*

The policy of monetary control will be done an ill service if we allow the instrument of Bank rate to become associated in the public mind with the hated policy of deflation. Sooner or later—and perhaps fairly soon—a higher Bank rate may be required in order to preserve our position. When that time comes, the Governor of the Bank of England will need all the support he can get. There are always strong natural forces tending towards inflation. On this occasion monetary reformers have had to throw their influence against the fanatics of deflation, who would like to cut us with knives; next time it may be on the other side—against those who would intoxicate us with inflation. One has only to look back on Bank rate policy since the War to see that most harm has been done by not putting up the Bank rate soon enough.

It would be a serious blunder to raise the Bank rate now,—and a disastrous one if it was to be interpreted as a first move towards deflation. But I appreciate the underlying trend of events which is causing responsible authorities to be watching for the time when dearer money will be necessary. I think that they are right to be anxious, and that they should be helped to act promptly when the time comes.

The chief criterion for raising Bank rate in present circumstances can be explained quite briefly. Internal conditions at the moment—employment, the state of credit, the trend of prices—all favour cheap money. It is not likely in the near future that conditions will develop at home which call for measures of restriction. The danger signals on this occasion must be looked for abroad. If Bank rate has to be raised, it will be because our financial and economic relations with foreign countries are developing in such a way as to cause later, if they are not checked, a depreciation of the sterling standard.

The extreme cheapness of money in New York is a valuable assistance to us and may save the situation for a time by diverting funds from New York to London. This fact and the great importance of cheap money to the internal situation are powerful reasons for not acting prematurely.

But there are also strong influences working the other way. In spite of abundant funds, New York lends abroad very little, and London remains the chief centre from which the borrowers of the whole world endeavour to draw. Money may be abnormally cheap in New York, but it is abnormally dear in many parts of Europe; and European borrowers are more ready to borrow in sterling than American lenders are to lend in sterling. The Treasury has to purchase large amounts of dollars to meet the American debt, and it is doubtful whether we have yet adjusted our situation to this new burden. We are also reaching a season of the year when the financing of our imports, particularly cotton, is always heavy.

As a result of these influences the sterling–dollar exchange, left to itself, may—probably, not certainly—tend to depreciate. If this movement merely reflected falling dollar prices in America—as in the recent past—there would be no need to complain. But if an adverse movement of the exchanges were to be combined with a tendency of dollar prices to rise, some protective action on our part would be required. Such a contingency is not improbable. It is hard to believe that a few months of very cheap money in the United States will not initiate an upward movement of dollar prices.

The criterion for restrictive action, therefore, is to be looked for in simultaneous tendencies of the sterling exchange to fall and of dollar prices to rise. If this does not happen—and perhaps it won't—no action is needed. If it does happen, the particular method of correction to be employed should be worked out in such a way as to choke off credit to foreign borrowers as much as possible and to trade borrowers at home as little as possible. A situation, in which the external situation points to dear money and the internal situation to cheap money, is inevitably tiresome and difficult to handle. It is a problem of curing a maladjustment of the direction, rather than the amount, of credit, whilst doing as little indirect harm as possible during the process of regaining equilibrium.

From every point of view the only sensible policy, in the interests of the country, is to continue for the present Mr Baldwin's 'non-flationist' policy. This will not prejudge the gold standard question one way or the other. Indeed, a continuance of this policy will probably—by reason of the depreciation of the dollar—bring sterling back to its old parity in due course. It is only then that the controversy between the various monetary schools will really commence as a practical issue. In the meantime the mass of reasonable opinion would like to give trade and industry a chance to prosper, freed alike from the starvation policy of doctrinaire deflationists and from the intoxication policy of short-sighted inflationists.

Keynes sent early copies of his article to several people including Sir Austen Chamberlain, Reginald McKenna, Stanley Baldwin and Sir Charles Addis. Their comments are of interest.

From SIR AUSTEN CHAMBERLAIN, *18 July 1924*

Dear Keynes,

Many thanks for sending me your article. I am just off to the country, but I shall take it with me. I am afraid that on this occasion you have not made a convert of me.

> Yours sincerely,
> AUSTEN CHAMBERLAIN

From REGINALD MCKENNA, *19 July 1924*

Dear Maynard,

Many thanks for your article on the policy of the Bank of England. It is as good as only J.M.K. could make it. You are quite right in thinking that common-sense has been victorious for the time being. It is interesting for me to see that I took exactly the line you have taken in the last three paragraphs of your article.

> Yours ever,
> R. MCKENNA

From STANLEY BALDWIN, *22 July 1924*

Dear Keynes,

I always read the articles you are good enough to send me with interest.

I had meant to make a few observations on the 3rd reading of the Finance Bill, but in my position[1] I think I must wait till Chamberlain's Committee (the existence of which is unknown to the general public) has reported.

I want a holiday!

> Yours sincerely,
> STANLEY BALDWIN

[1] As Leader of the Opposition.

From SIR CHARLES ADDIS, *21 July 1924*

Dear Keynes,

You are a most courteous opponent. I wonder sometimes if we are as far apart as we seem.

Had I a magician's wand I should cause a definite statement to be made, probably in reply to a question in the House of Commons, that H.M. Government has no present intention of interfering with the ordinary course of events by which on the expiry of the Prohibition Act the free export of gold would be resumed on the 1st January 1926.

Second, that as soon as possible thereafter the two issues would be amalgamated by the emission of Bank notes for £1 and 10/- in substitution for the existing currency issue; the limit of the fiduciary issue to be fixed later.

Third, that the Bank would convene at an early date the convention of central banks to concert measures for preventing undue fluctuations in the price of gold.

The effect of such an announcement, if people really believed it, would tend to raise the sterling exchange, probably sharply at first and later more gradually; but, of course, the effect of the announcement would not be permanent unless it were followed up by the appropriate action of the Bank. We must be prepared to use the Bank rate boldly if necessary. I do not think it will be necessary to raise it at present and it might not be necessary at all. It would depend on the relative mutation of prices here and in the U.S.

The way to resume specie payments is to resume. The fear of being denuded of gold in 1821 in England and in 1879 in America proved to be groundless. What happened was that nothing happened. It is not without the bounds of probability that before free exports were resumed, gold might be flowing *in* to this country.

Eighteen months is long enough as a warning to merchants to put their houses in order and adjust their forward contracts. Stocks are low which would mitigate the absolute amount of loss by depreciation. A fall in prices would raise real wages until nominal wages re-acted; they might not re-act at all if, in the interval, trade improved. The export trade might be expected to gain as much by a reduction in production costs as it would lose by a rise in exchange. The burden of debt would be increased, but this is not very serious so long as the payments are internal. The burden of the external debt would depend upon whether the increased gold value of sterling was due to rising dollar prices or falling sterling prices.

Why not wait! Well I would if I thought there was a better chance of getting back to gold later on. Last year it would have been easier to get back to gold than it is now. Is there any reason to believe it will be easier in 1927 or 1928? I do not think so. It seems to me we are drifting in a state of uncertainty which is not good for trade. I think we shall have to depend more and more in this country upon our specialised manufactures, such as shipbuilding and the finer kinds of textiles, but also in our ability to supply the world with cheap freights, banking and insurance. In my own bank, the Hongkong Bank, we are financing through US credit about fifty million gold dollars a month of Eastern products to the States which were formerly almost entirely financed by sterling credits. I do not mean to say that the volume of trade is affected by this tendency but it does affect our commission industries where custom counts for so much. The tendency to fly from sterling, not only on the Continent but also in Egypt and Siam, has been more marked of late. We cannot expect to retain foreign balances here, note reserves &c. in fluctuating sterling. There are also the Dominions, who have a special interest in the matter, to be considered.

I regard, therefore, the case for a return to gold as urgent. I quite agree we should act prudently and with due regard to the circumstances. I do not agree with Leaf in his single proposal to raise the Bank rate to 5%, or with Schuster in his proposal to amalgamate the note issues before we have got back to gold. The policy must be judged as a whole and can only be successfully carried out by a series of interdependent acts. As a Director of the Bank of England, I am precluded from doing anything more than dealing in generalities. I cannot, at any rate at the present stage, advocate in public any particular plan of resumption. However much I might safeguard it by asserting that it was merely an expression of my personal opinion, there would be the usual insinuations that I was speaking for the Court; but I am under no restrictions in the freedom of private intercourse and I think you will admit that my plan offers the advantage of as little disturbance as possible. There is nothing to be done but to allow the Prohibition of Export of Gold Act quietly to expire when it comes to an end on the 31st December, 1925, and not to renew it. No legislation is required, except an Act to authorise the issue of £1 notes by the Bank of England; the Genoa Conference has already provided for the convention of central banks. The whole thing is largely psychological. If we say that we are going to resume the free export of gold and say it in such a way that people will believe it, you can take it as good as done. I think I ought to have your sympathy in the attempt to get back to gold since, as you justly observe, it is only after that that the real monetary controversy will begin!

Forgive this prolixity and believe me sincerely and always gratefully yours.

C. L. ADDIS

To SIR CHARLES ADDIS, *25 July 1924*

Dear Addis,

Very many thinks for your letter of July 21st. I am extremely glad to have a pretty full statement of your present point of view, and am relieved to find that you are not in sympathy with what I have described as 'Leaf's Light-headedness'.

All the same, the proposals you outline do terrify me very considerably. I quite agree that if we think it worth while to make the necessary sacrifices there will be no insuperable difficulty in our returning to the former parity with the dollar within the next 18 months. I also think it not at all unlikely that this result will come about without any particular sacrifice on our part, merely by the depreciation of the dollar. Nevertheless, I do think it most unwise to anticipate events which cannot be foreseen with certainty. It seems to me that the relaxation of the embargo on the free export of gold ought to follow events and not precede them. To commit ourselves to such a thing in advance without knowing whether events would favour such a course or not, or whether we should be able in fact to carry such a thing through, strikes me as imprudent. But apart from the question of imprudence, the notion of what you describe as an 18 months' warning to merchants to put their houses in order strikes me as a ruinous proposal. Either the Government's announcement is believed and the future is discounted immediately in the rate of exchange, in which case we suffer all the torments of a violent and sudden deflation; or else the Government's announcement is disbelieved, or only half believed, in which case we have a slow movement with the expectation of a further movement in the same direction, the effect of which on trade and employment hardly bears thinking about. It is not simply a question of merchants and forward contracts and the like. As soon as the business world has good reason to believe that prices are likely to fall, no course is open to it except to contract its engagements, draw in its horns and

270

go out of business as far as may be until the funest process is over.

To risk all these misfortunes merely for the sake of linking up the London and New York money markets, and so facilitating the work of international financiers—for this in my judgment is all it comes to—is going to lay the City and the Bank of England open to popular attacks the violence of which might be very great. It seems to me most unwise to act in such a way at the present juncture as to suggest that the interests of industry are being subordinated to those of international finance. I think this, although I agree with you that our profits from international finance are very great,—though I am not at all sure that we do not make more money out of the Americans and others in fluctuating conditions than in stable conditions, since they are generally wrong and we are generally right as to the prospective course of events. (This is not an argument I should use, but it is relevant when the question of the profitableness of international business is used as an argument.)

One further point. Are you quite sure that the rigid linking up of the London and New York money markets is all honey? The magnitude of the New York money market is quite different in relation to ours to what it was in pre-war days and in pre-Federal Reserve Bank days. The chances of redundancy of credit there on a great scale are also increased. Are you sure that you want London to be at any time the dumping ground of unlimited cheap American money liable to be withdrawn at a day's notice? It means that we should become without any power of helping ourselves, the victim of every inflationary boom that America may indulge in,—and that she will indulge in such from time to time is surely a probability.

However, all this is much too big a matter to discuss in a letter. The more I spend my thoughts on these matters, the more alarmed do I become at seeing you and the others in authority attacking the problems of the changed post-war world with—I know you will excuse my saying so—unmodified pre-war views and ideas. To close the mind to the idea of revolutionary improvements in our control of money and credit is to sow the seeds of the downfall of individualistic capitalism. Do not be the Louis XVI of the monetary revolution. For surely it is certain that enormous changes will come in the next twenty years, and they will be bad changes, unwisely and even disastrously carried out, if those of us who are at least agreed in our ultimate objects and are aiming at the stability of society cannot agree in putting forward safe and sound reforms.

I am now told by a good many friends that I have become a sort of disreputable figure in some quarters because I do not agree with the maxims of City pundits. But you know I ought not to be so considered really! I seek to improve the machinery of society not overturn it.

Ever yours sincerely,
[copy initialled] J.M.K.

In the next week's *Nation* a correspondent, who signed himself Monetary Reformer, took one statement from Keynes's article, that suggested that a policy of price stability would probably bring sterling to par with the dollar, at which time the controversy over monetary standards would really become a serious practical issue (above p. 266). He then went on to remark that if Keynes had said this in his *Tract* he would now have more influence in the City. Keynes replied immediately below the letter.

From The Nation and Athenaeum, *26 July 1924*

I fear that I must disappoint your amiable correspondent. My *Nation* article represented no change of view. If Mr Baldwin's 'non-flationist' policy, i.e., policy of price stability, is continued by general consent, those who favour this policy have no practical grievance. It is only if and when this course results in a return to parity with the dollar that, on the one hand, the removal of the embargo on the export of gold becomes feasible, and, on the other, the obligation of our Mint to receive unlimited quantities of gold becomes dangerous. That is what

I had in mind in writing the sentence which your correspondent italicises. I am aware how dreadfully easy it would be to recover what your correspondent calls 'influence in the City';—he must not tempt me to burn incense in that neighbourhood!

The same week, he contributed an unsigned leader on wheat.

From The Nation and Athenaeum, *26 July 1924*

WHEAT

Perhaps the most important events in recent weeks, transcending Dawes Reports, Housing Bills, Revolutions in Brazil, and Presidential Elections, has been the world-wide rise in the price of wheat.

In this country the price of flour has risen from 38s. a sack last March to 46s. 6d. today, or about 22 per cent. So far British wheat has not shared fully in the increase of price in the exporting countries. At a price of about 51s. per quarter, it is 3s. above the price of a month ago and 3s. 6d. above last year's price. It is also approaching its right figure in relation to other commodities, judged on the pre-war basis. Abroad, however, the rise has been much more sensational. Northern Manitoba wheat is now 10s. 6d. a quarter above its price of a year ago. The rise in Argentine wheat has been about equivalent. The dollar price of wheat in Chicago is now 30 per cent above its price at this time last year, at nearly 128 cents a bushel as compared with 97 cents a year ago and 84 cents in 1913.

All through the past year the supplies of wheat available in the world have been ample, and the rise in price is entirely due to a prospective reduction of supplies rather than to any shortage at the moment. Indeed, the carry-over at the date of the beginning of the current harvest will be bigger than for many years past. The anticipations of the market are mainly due to two causes. In Canada the crop, whilst by no means bad compared with the average of previous years, will not reach the remarkable bumper figures of the past two years;—the latest estimate is for 319,000,000 bushels as compared with 474,000,000 last year. Elsewhere, and particularly in the United States, the fact that the price of wheat recently has been unremunerative to the farmers has led to a general curtailment of the production of this particular commodity, not anywhere on a sensational scale but appreciable in the aggregate.

It is too early as yet to say whether the final outcome of the harvest will be such as to justify the current predictions of the market or whether the high prices lately established will be sustained through the heavy selling period of the autumn months. But it is quite possible that we are on the eve of the fundamental adjustment which many authorities have been anticipating for the past two or three years.

It is clear that compared with the years before the War the price of wheat, and to a lesser extent of some other agricultural products, has tended to be too low as compared with the prices of manufactured articles, with the result that the agricultural sections of the international market have been considerably impoverished. Some part of the so-called lack of purchasing power overseas has been attributable to this fact. It has been difficult for the farmers to know how to readjust their relative economic situation, and the process has not been rapid. But the readjustment, if it has now arrived, will be an economic event of the first magnitude.

As regards Great Britain, the effects are likely to be of opposed kinds. On the one hand, the cost of our imported supplies will be immensely enhanced, as can be easily calculated from the figure of 29 million quarters as the approximate total of our necessary imports. On the other hand, the transfer of purchasing power into the hands of the farming communities of the world may have far-reaching effects in the stimulation of markets for certain types of goods. The change, moreover, opens

274

out for British agriculture a prospect of relief from the depression which has long lain over it. Last September we ventured to predict, in the face of momentarily adverse tendencies, that our agriculture would obtain relief in this way before very long, pointing out that 'with the staple products of the world's harvests...it is often but a short step from a condition of apparently overwhelming abundance to one of dangerous scarcity'.

We draw the attention of our readers to a matter rather outside our usual field, because the readjustment between the interests of agriculture and industry throughout the world is the kind of event which often receives from the public much less attention than it deserves until the movement is almost over and is passing into history.

On 2 August 1924, at a session of the Liberal Summer School in Oxford, Keynes raised another issue which he had touched on earlier in the columns of *The Nation*, foreign lending. His remarks appeared in full a week later.

From The Nation and Athenaeum, *9 August 1924*

FOREIGN INVESTMENT AND NATIONAL ADVANTAGE

The established system, which we take as a matter of course, of being just about as willing to invest our savings abroad as at home, is not very ancient and is practised nowhere else. (France followed the same system for twenty years before the war; today Great Britain is in this habit unique in the whole world.) The belief that existing practice in this matter must coincide with the national advantage, which is a part of the orthodoxy of the day, certainly has historical roots. Whether it has also intellectual roots is the subject of my discourse today.

The hazarding of capital resources in foreign parts for trading, mining, and exploitation is an immemorial practice, which has generally proved of immense financial benefit to nations with the courage, the temperament, and the wealth to follow it. For the English and the Scotch it has been, beyond doubt, the foundation of their national fortunes. The risks are recognised to be great, but the profits are proportionate. Nor are the total sums, which it is necessary to embark in such enterprises, a burdensome proportion of the public wealth. Nothing that I say here must be interpreted as casting a doubt upon the national advantage of investments of this kind.

The next development of foreign investment virtually began with the railway age,—that is to say, the use of British capital to build public-utility works abroad. The railways of the New World and even of parts of Europe could not have been built when they were, except with the aid of the mid-nineteenth-century savings of the British middle classes. These investments, too, probably, in their day, redounded to the national advantage. We did not, as a rule, lend the money to foreign corporations or governments. We built the railways ourselves with British engineering skill, with our own iron and steel, and rolling stock from our own workshops. We opened up lands and territories from which, indirectly by subsidiary enterprises, we drew additional wealth, and we made possible for ourselves the supply of cheap food from overseas. But already before the War such investments, which had extended beyond railways to harbours, tramways, waterworks, gasworks, and power stations, were becoming precarious. The practice was beginning of controlling the rates charged by such undertakings, and hence the profits earned, thus depriving the investor of the possibility of large profits to balance the never-absent risk of loss. But, further, a jealousy of the foreign investor was growing up, and a tendency to treat him with less than fairness. I believe that there are now very few countries in the world in which a public utility undertaking mainly owned by foreigners is secure of fair treatment. The cases of ruinously unfair treatment are so numerous that any typical pre-war investor in such things has suffered heavy losses.

The third leading type of foreign investment consists of loans to governments and local authorities abroad. These loans have a fairly ancient history, but on a great scale they also are quite modern. They reached their utmost limit of magnitude and of imprudence in France in the twenty years preceding the War. No investments have ever been made so foolish and so disastrous as the loans of France to Russia, and on a lesser scale, to the Balkans, Austria, Mexico, and Brazil, between 1900 and 1914. They represented a great proportion of the national savings of the country, and nearly all has been lost.

Indeed, it is probable that loans to foreign governments have turned out badly on balance—especially at the low rates of interest current before the War. The investor has no remedy—none whatever—against default. There is, on the part of most foreign countries, a strong tendency to default on the occasion of wars and revolutions and whenever the expectation of further loans no longer exceeds in amount the interest payable on the old ones. Defaults, in fact, are world-wide and frequent. The Southern States of U.S.A., Mexico, all Central America, most of South America, China, Turkey, Egypt, Greece, the whole of the Balkans, Russia, Austria, Hungary, Spain, and Portugal have all defaulted in whole or in part at one time or another.

Who can maintain that the indirect national advantages of such loans are great, many of which have been employed to wage wars and without which the wars could not have been carried on? There is much good sense in the attitude of American investors, who expect from 8 to 12 per cent interest on such loans, and do not like them even then.

Let me give one instance for which I happen to have the aggregate figures. British investors have advanced to the governments, local authorities, and public enterprises of Brazil about £250,000,000. This yields at present a precarious rate of interest of barely 4 per cent, and, allowing for the fall in the value of money since the investment was made, about $2\frac{1}{2}$ per cent.

Thus it is doubtful whether in the past loans to foreign

governments and public utility undertakings have been really advantageous. Yet in the future the motives tending towards repudiation, partial or complete, may become much stronger. At present many of our debtors, especially in the Dominions, borrow afresh each year more than the interest on previous loans. So long as this is the case, the motive to repudiation is clearly non-existent. But in the long run, partly from the mere operation of compound interest, partly perhaps from our not having so large a surplus to lend abroad, this will cease. Our difficulties on a grand scale will then begin. The representatives of the Soviet Government, lately in London, have expounded with their accustomed frankness the connection between the acknowledgment of old loans and the receipt of new ones. But it is only in their greater frankness (this, indeed, is the head and front of their offence) that they differ from many other governments.

In short, the nineteenth century, as in so many other respects, came to look on an arrangement as normal which was really most abnormal. To lend vast sums abroad for long periods of time without any possibility of legal redress if things go wrong, is a crazy construction; especially in return for a trifling extra interest.

What is the old-fashioned answer to this?—That the investor is capable of looking after himself; that present arrangements allow him to place his resources where they will bring him the greatest net return; that in this way the national income will become greatest.

Why do I question this answer?—Because I doubt (1) whether the investor is capable of looking after himself and whether the present organisation of investment is such as to protect the individual investor's self-interest; and (2) whether, even in so far as the individual gains, it follows that the national income as a whole is thereby maximised.

My remarks so far have been chiefly directed to the question of what advantages have actually been gained, in the light of experience, by foreign investment in its latest phases. No one who has examined typical lists of investments made by middle-class investors in pre-war days would lightly maintain that, in practice, the investor has proved capable of looking after himself. Large resources, painfully gained and saved, have been spilt on the ground. But there is also something to be said about the bias in favour of investment in particular directions caused by existing laws and practices.

I call attention in particular to the present operation of the Trustee Acts. These Acts in their present form provide an artificial stimulus on a great scale to foreign investment within the Empire. The phenomenon is a fairly recent one; imperial piety has silenced tongues and criticism; and its results do not receive enough attention.

Before 1889 Consols was the only security in which trustees could invest, failing special powers. The present state of affairs dates from the Colonial Stock Act of 1900, which, in effect, brought almost all the loans of colonial governments within the field of authorised trustee investments. Some further change, beyond the extensions allowed in 1889, was evidently required to compensate [for] the gradually diminishing volume of Consols and the steadily increasing volume of trustee funds. But since the War this ground holds good no longer, and it is only now, twenty-four years later, that we feel the consequences of the change.

Loans to colonial governments now amount to about £670,000,000 and to the Government of India £260,000,000—say £900,000,000 altogether. This amount is being added to at a great rate,—since the beginning of 1922 £60–70 millions a year, net addition. Thus we are not only reinvesting the whole of the interest due to us on existing loans (say, £35–40 millions), but adding to it nearly as much again.

It is not true that these great sums flow abroad as the result of a free and enlightened calculation of self-interest. They flow as the result of a particular social organisation which—for the most part unintentionally—gives a bias in this direction.

A considerable proportion of the growing wealth of the

community accrues in the hands of individuals or of corporations which by law or by strong custom and convention are compelled to invest the whole or the bulk of it in the trustee group of securities. They are limited in their choice to what securities are available within this group. It follows that, if, in any year, there is no net increase in the amount of home trustee stocks, the *whole* of the annual increased savings available for investment in this form is *compelled* to go abroad. If, by reason of the repayment of Government debt, there is actually a decrease in the available home securities, the compulsion to invest abroad is even more stringent.

Incidentally, it is worth noting that to pay off our own Government debt out of the proceeds of taxation, without at the same time providing a supply of home trustee investments to take its place, involves taking money by taxation out of the hands of persons who might invest in home enterprises of a non-trustee type and transferring it to another type of person who cannot help investing the proceeds in trustee investments abroad.

It follows from this that large sums may flow abroad without there having been a vestige of deliberate calculation on the part of anybody that this is the best way of employing the resources in the national interest.

There is a further reason why the Colonial Stock Act of 1900 favours unduly the exportation of capital. Some colonial governments undertake as a government service many public-utility enterprises, such as harbours, which are not so undertaken in Great Britain. It follows that money for such undertakings abroad can be raised more easily and cheaply in London than for similar and equally profitable undertakings at home. For example, loans for harbour works in New South Wales can be borrowed more cheaply in London than loans for the Port of London itself, merely because the former, being undertaken by the Government of New South Wales, represent a trustee investment, whereas the loans of the Port of London Authority, although a public body, do not fall within the trustee category.

In general, any service in the colonies which is socialised can be financed more cheaply by means of British savings than any service at home which is not socialised. Yet who would maintain that it is always in our national interest to finance the former rather than the latter?

Merely on the financial side, the Trustee Acts, by creating a monopoly with a bias against new home investments, are probably worth not less than £20,000,000 a year to the Dominions and India.

These are my most fundamental criticisms against such foreign investments as are made, not on their merits, but as a result of the Trustee Acts. But there is also another objection. The Trustee Acts lull trustees and others into a false sense of security. It is felt that all such investments are, in a sense beyond criticism. Yet it is really very doubtful whether, in the long run, they are as safe as is supposed.

In some cases these loans are becoming dangerously large in relation to the population and the wealth of the borrowing communities. So long as we renew maturing loans when they fall due, and lend in addition twice the amount required to meet the interest on previous loans, the capacity and integrity of the borrowers to meet their liabilities is obviously altogether untested. But this cannot go on for ever. Can we feel perfectly confident in every case that the obligations will be met in their entirety? I will not raise heat and controversy by instancing the name of any colony. But is it right to leave trustees to suppose that the long-dated securities of the Government of India are wholly free from risk,—that these are better investments, where safety is the first consideration, than (for example) the debentures, or even the first preference stocks, of English industrial enterprises whose names are household words?

Perhaps the limit of the absurdity, to which the Trustee Acts can lead, was reached early this year when £2,000,000 was borrowed by Southern Rhodesia on about the same terms as a large English borough would have to pay, more cheaply than the Port of London, and much more cheaply than most of our great industrial and commercial undertakings at home. Southern Rhodesia is a place somewhere in the middle of Africa with a handful of white inhabitants and not even so many, I believe, as one million savage black ones. The security has no British Government guarantee behind it; yet unless such is implied the terms of the loan were farcical.

Thus the effect of the Trustee Acts is to starve home developments by diverting savings abroad and, consequently, to burden home borrowers with a higher rate of interest than they would need to pay otherwise.

A practical remedy is not far to seek. I would repeal the existing Trustee Acts and provide that no new issues, not carrying a British Government guarantee, should be added to the list except by special licence of the Treasury in each case. The Treasury should then use its power of licence to widen the list of admissible home investments and strictly to ration overseas borrowers. (Incidentally this would greatly assist the Treasury in protecting the gilt-edged market for its heavy impending conversions.) Further, the Treasury should be careful not to redeem debt, except when there is a need of new loans for home developments of a type suitable for inclusion in the list of trustee investments. This should be the criterion for the rate of reduction of the dead-weight debt. When there is no need of further liquid resources for investment in this particular sort of way, the money should be left in the hands of the taxpayer to find an outlet in other types of expenditure and investment.

I am afraid that I have not succeeded in separating so clearly as I had intended those of my arguments which relate to the private interest of the investor from those which relate to the public interest. But I will conclude with two of the latter type.

Consider two investments, the one at home and the other abroad, with equal risks of repudiation or confiscation or legislation restricting profit. It is a matter of indifference to the individual investor which he selects. But the nation as a whole retains in the one case the object of the investment and the fruits of it; whilst in the other case both are lost. If a loan to improve a South American capital is repudiated, we have nothing. If a Poplar housing loan is repudiated, we as a nation, still have the houses. If the Grand Trunk Railway of Canada fails its shareholders by reason of legal restriction of the rates chargeable or for any other cause, we have nothing. If the underground system of London fails its shareholders, Londoners still have their underground system.

With home investment, even if it be ill-advised or extravagantly carried out, at least the country has the improvement for what it is worth. The worst conceived and most extravagant housing scheme imaginable leaves us with some houses. A bad foreign investment is wholly engulfed.

My last argument relates to the reaction of foreign investment on our exports. It is often said to be the primary and sufficient justification of such investment that it stimulates our exports. This is quite true. But I see no special virtue in exports for their own sake, which are not required to pay for desired imports. The notion that the great thing is to get rid of goods out of the country is not sensible. Investment abroad stimulates employment by expanding exports. Certainly. But it does not stimulate employment a scrap more than would an equal investment at home.

Not only is there no special virtue in stimulating export for its own sake;—there is vice in it. For foreign investment does not automatically expand our exports by a corresponding amount. It so affects the foreign exchanges that we are *compelled* to export more in order to maintain our solvency. It may be the case—I fancy that it now is the case—that we can only do this by lowering the price of our products in terms of the products of other nations, that is by allowing the ratio of real interchange to move to our disadvantage. The more we have to force the volume of our exports, the lower the price which we have to accept for them.

A state of affairs, arising out of the arrangements of the

investment market and disconnected from the equilibria of trade and industry, which causes a bias in favour of, and may overstimulate, foreign investment, is capable of doing us a great deal of injury in the terms on which we conduct our international trade. It may be that we should do much better to be content with a volume of exports sufficient to pay for our imports, and to divert our surplus resources of capital and labour into the manifold improvements at home waiting to be carried out.

Our present system dates from a time when we had a surplus of savings which we could invest *much* more profitably abroad than at home and when the demand for our exports was highly elastic. The convention has continued, and its effects have been aggravated by the operation of the Trustee Acts, into a period when the benefit of such investment measured in rates of interest is greatly diminished, when the amount of our available surplus is diminished, and when the demand for our exports is weakened.

Last year we invested abroad about two-thirds of what passed through the investment markets, and probably between half and a third of our total savings. I believe that most of this could have been usefully employed at home, and indeed must be so employed in future, if our national equipment is to grow as fast as our population and our theoretical standards of life.

The issue of *The Nation* for 9 August also contained a letter from a Mr W. H. J. Woodward asking for an explanation for the rise in the Bank of England's gold stock since 1914, since when the commodity price of gold had been above the Bank's statutory buying price. Using a pseudonym he was to use in future, Keynes replied.

From The Nation and Athenaeum, *16 August 1924*

Sir,

Your correspondent Mr Woodward inquires where the Bank of England's new accessions of gold come from. I hazard two suggestions. Old ladies still fish golden sovereigns out of their stockings sometimes. Divers, each season, fish up quite a quantity of them out of the wreck of the 'Laurentic' off the coast of Ireland. Formerly the old ladies, latterly the 'Laurentic', have been the chief suppliers.

Yours &c.,
SIELA

At the suggestion of the editor of *The Manchester Guardian Commercial* and in response to some comments by 'A Stockbroker' in that newspaper, Keynes elaborated on his Oxford speech.

From The Manchester Guardian Commercial, *21 August 1924*

HOME VERSUS FOREIGN INVESTMENT

Further suggestions for revision of trustee list

In my address to the Liberal Summer School at Oxford I dealt briefly with several connected, but partly distinct, questions relating to our British policy of foreign investment. The interesting comments by A Stockbroker, in the *M.G. Commercial* for August 14, on what I had to say about the Trustee Acts encourage me to develop a little further this section of my paper.

My complaints against the present arrangements were, first, that they provide an artificial stimulus to overseas investment on a greater scale than is truly in the national interest, and, second, that they sometimes lull trustees into a false sense of security and are made an excuse for a lack of discrimination between one investment and another within the privileged list. I do not propose to repeat or develop here my reasons for these and other conclusions in my original paper, but, assuming that there is some substance in them, to consider what practical steps are desirable.

I suggested at Oxford that no new securities should be admitted to the trustee list unless either they carried a British

Government guarantee or they had obtained a special licence from the Treasury. I suggested, further, that the licence system should be used in practice to ration overseas borrowers and to widen the categories of admissible home securities. A Stockbroker, whilst sympathetic to some of my ideas, criticises very keenly any system of special Treasury licences as something which would never be tolerated in this country after our war experience of Treasury control of new issues. For this reason he would go farther than I did, and allow no additions to the list except where there is a British Government guarantee.

I admit that there is a great deal in what he says. A licence system would be troublesome to work in practice, and might be open to pressure on political grounds or to charges of partiality. I suggested it partly as a compromise, but partly because I attached importance to increasing the number of eligible home securities, yet feared that it might be difficult to define in advance precisely what categories should be included. On reconsideration, I think that my main object might be attained without introducing the objectionable system of licences.

I suggest, therefore, that the list of eligible trustee investments should be constituted in future on the following principles:—

(1) All existing trustee stocks would, of course, remain; but I would differ from A Stockbroker in also allowing replacement loans. I think that it would be anomalous to have a colonial government issuing two identical loans, one of which was non-trustee, yet the other a trustee investment for purely historical reasons quite unrelated to the security obtained by the investor. It would be better to let the old system gradually work itself out.

(2) All securities carrying a British Government guarantee would be in this list, but I should certainly include also British corporation and county stocks, subject to the same conditions as at present. (Perhaps A Stockbroker did not really mean to exclude the latter.)

(3) I attach great importance to giving the status of trustee

investment to the prior securities of the great public utility undertakings of the future. The danger of such enterprises being starved in favour of socialised public works in the colonies is one of my chief grounds of complaint against the present system. Just as in the past we have included the prior securities of British railways in the list, in spite of their being privately owned, so I should like to aid the flow of capital in the future into British ports, harbours, canals, motor roads, gasworks, waterworks, electric power stations, and the like, even though private initiative and methods of management continue to take some part in them. The prior securities of the Port of London, which I instanced, and of the Manchester Ship Canal, which A Stockbroker instances, are glaring cases. Centralised electric power stations, serving large areas within which they exercise exclusive rights, are likely to furnish in the near future important examples of what I have in mind. What will be the best way of dealing with these?

One way would be to include in the trustee list all bonds of public-utility undertakings of specified types which can be certified by the appropriate Government department as satisfying certain specified conditions. This might, in practice, get very near to the licence system which I suggested at first.

A second way might be found on the lines of the Trade Facilities Act, by which an actual British Government guarantee might be accorded in approved cases. A variant of the last, which is worth considering, might consist in charging the enterprise $\frac{1}{4}$ per cent per annum in return for a British Government guarantee, which would be paid into a reserve fund against which would be charged any outgoings in cases where the guarantee might become operative.

At any rate, the privilege of inclusion in the trustee list should be confined henceforward to home securities, since it is no longer in the least necessary to go outside these in order to obtain an adequate supply; nor should it be given in any case in which the security to the investor is not absolutely gilt-edged. If, on grounds of public advantage, it is thought desirable to give special encouragement to a capital investment, at home or abroad, which involves some risk, the trustee investor shall not be expected to assist without the security of a British Government guarantee.

The Governments of India and of the Dominions would, of course, be free to borrow, like anyone else, on the open market on such terms as their credit might be deemed to justify.

During the summer of 1924 the Commission of Gold and Silver Inquiry of the United States Senate asked Keynes for a memorandum on currency policy. After some discussion with John Parke Young of the Commission, Keynes finally replied.

To JOHN PARKE YOUNG, *15 September 1924*

Dear Mr Young

I have your letter of August 26th and enclose a brief memorandum for your Report. I have been in two minds whether to write anything, because it is so difficult to put one's views clearly in a short space. You will see that I have limited myself practically to one point. My feeling is that the United States will probably require a fairly severe dose of facts before they will have a ready ear for theories. If facts go in the opposite direction from what I anticipate, the situation will of course be changed. But if they go as I think they will, then will be the time for pointing out again the possibility of something a trifle more sensible than the existing state of affairs.

Yours very truly,
[copy initialled] J.M.K.

THE UNITED STATES AND GOLD[2]

The problem of the gold standard and of price stabilisation covers so wide a field, that one must either deal with it at considerable length, or select one or two points for special comment. Since I have written recently a book (*A Tract on Monetary Reform*) which gives my views on some parts of the subject, and since I hope in the course of the next year to write a further book which will develop these views more fully, I hope I may be excused if in this memorandum I limit myself to certain particular points, without arguing the general question.

The United States is admittedly accepting into her mints gold which she does not require. She is admittedly sterilising this gold from producing its full effect on the creation of credit and of prices. The results of this are: (1) to involve her in expense through the purchase of the gold and (2) to maintain the commodity value of gold at a higher level than it would otherwise have.

I think that this situation can be correctly described by saying that the United States is undertaking a valorisation scheme for gold, analogous to similar schemes which have been undertaken in the past for other commodities; that is to say, she maintains the commodity value of gold by taking off the market at a certain price such quantities of it as cannot find another buyer at that price. The scheme is unique in one respect, in that the bulk of the gold in the world is mined outside the United States, so that the valorisation scheme is mainly in the interests of foreign producers.

This policy on the part of the United States has not, however, been undertaken deliberately or explicitly, and it may be abandoned or it may break down at any time through the weight of gold influencing, after all, the creation of credit and the level of prices.

---

[2] Eventually published by the Commission in 1925 in a collection entitled *European Currency and Finance*. See below p. 370.

The reasons for this policy may be presumed to be: (1) that the United States, as a large holder of stocks of gold, is interested in protecting the value of these stocks; (2) that there is no alternative to the present policy, except to allow a serious inflation of credit to take place, or to make a new departure which might provoke criticism from conservative opinion; (3) because it is thought to be in the interests of the world that the gold standard should be restored, and that America's action is in the interests of herself and of other countries in that it prevents an obvious breakdown of the gold system during the transitional period; (4) because American opinion believes that the necessity of the valorisation scheme is likely to be temporary, and will come to an end shortly.

May I direct one or two comments to the two last of these reasons? As regards the third, if the United States is prepared to undertake the expense of providing the world with a stable gold currency, she would be performing a considerable service. I doubt, however, whether she would be prepared to do so if it would probably involve her in a permanent expense, one year with another, of perhaps as much as 200 million dollars per annum. Moreover, if the purchase of redundant gold has to be continued year in, year out, it will become more and more obviously absurd that the United States should pay this large sum in order to remunerate gold miners, mainly in South Africa, for laboriously extracting from the earth metal that is not wanted at the price.

It is doubtful therefore whether the third motive would operate unless the fourth motive operated also. At present this is the case, since, so far as one can judge, almost everyone in America believes that the present situation is temporary and will cease to exist as soon as an event known as 'the restoration of the gold standard' has taken place. This popular belief assumes that, if the currencies of other countries in the world were to be maintained at a gold parity, this would greatly increase the demand of those countries on the stock of the world's gold. I believe this to be a misapprehension. It is not lack of gold, but the absence of other internal adjustments, which prevents the leading European countries from returning to a pre-war gold standard. Most of them have plenty of gold for the purpose as soon as the other conditions favourable to the restoration of a gold standard have returned.

The following figures illustrate this point. The Cunliffe Committee fixed on the figure of £150,000,000 in the Bank of England and currency note reserves together as representing a sufficient figure for the maintenance of the gold standard in Great Britain. The actual gold reserve at present is £155,000,000. France has about the same amount of gold as before the War. Italy and Belgium have rather more than they had before the War. The Scandinavian countries and Holland have three times as much gold as in 1914; Switzerland two and a half times as much; and Spain five times as much. The Bank of Japan (in foreign balances and bullion together) has nearly five times as much. I do not think it can be argued that a single one of these countries requires a larger gold reserve than they now have in order to maintain a gold standard, even after allowing for the fact that gold has depreciated in value by 33 per cent. In the case of Russia, Germany, Austria and Hungary the gold reserves have been greatly depleted, but it is not likely that these countries would be able to afford, or even that they would think it worth while to afford, large purchases of gold in the near future; though they may absorb a certain amount gradually— particularly Russia. Moreover, the spread of the practice of keeping reserves in the form of interest-bearing balances in foreign centres, in place of barren gold, further diminishes the need of actual holdings of bullion on the part of progressive countries.

If none of the above countries absorbs large quantities of gold, where is the relief to the United States going to come from? In particular, Great Britain will always be in a position to avoid being forced to accept large quantities of unwanted gold, even in the event of the restoration of the gold standard, by anticipating debt repayments to the United States.

In short, I see no way of absorbing large quantities of gold unless either gold is again used in active circulation, which is not probable anywhere outside the U.S., or prices rise materially.

No doubt the actual amount of importations of gold into the United States will fluctuate from year to year and will be greater in some years than in others. But it seems to me that under the existing system, and unless she allows the redundant gold to take effect on her price level, the United States must look foward more or less permanently to receiving additional gold at the rate of between, say, 150 million and 300 million dollars per annum on the average.

If this view, or anything like it, is correct, I suggest that the United States will become discontented with the position sooner or later. When such discontent comes to a head there is an obvious remedy, namely to close her mints to the unlimited admission of gold and to constitute the American Treasury the only body which has the right to mint gold. This would not interfere with maintaining the full and free convertibility of existing and future United States currency into gold; nor would it prevent additions being made to the stock of gold if circumstances made this seem desirable. It would also be possible to make a concession in favour of American-mined gold if this was politically desirable, without incurring, in view of the relatively small amount of such gold, an undue expense.

In deciding not to keep her mints open to the unlimited reception of gold, regardless of whether or not the gold was required, the United States would, in my judgment, be protecting all her own interests; and I cannot but think it probable that this is the solution on which she will fall back sooner or later. The only reasonable alternative would be to continue the present valorisation scheme but to share the expense of it with other countries. If this could be arranged, which would be difficult, it might work for a time. But, even so, sooner or later it would be seen to be absurd to encourage in this way the mining of useless gold, and that too much was being spent for the mere purpose of keeping up appearances.

J.M.K.

15.9.24

On 27 September Siela made a second appearance in *The Nation*.

Sir,

'A. G. G.' has said in your last issue all that needs to be said on the personal side of the recent affair of the Prime Minister's motor-car. But does not this episode bring to a head the question of the emoluments of the Premiership as an issue of pressing practical importance?

In the eighteenth century the emoluments of office, direct and indirect, were so great that a political career might lead to great wealth. This undesirable state of affairs no longer existed in the nineteenth century, but the salaries were fixed at what, in terms of purchasing power, was a very comfortable figure. No compensation having been given in respect of income tax and super tax, or of the diminished value of money, what is still called £5,000 is worth less than half what it used to be worth; and this has come to pass just at a time when high office is being attained at least as often as not by men without private means; whilst after the War the Prime Minister was deprived even of his official right to a motor-car, merely because similar rights on the part of every jackanapes in the War Office had become a gross abuse.

Is it not essential in the public interest that the Prime Minister should be freed from pecuniary cares whilst in office and enabled to maintain a state of reasonable dignity and comfort? And is it not also essential that he should not be driven to cheap journalism, or the like, to maintain himself when out of office? It is not desirable that an ex-Prime Minister, who will almost certainly continue to perform public duties of high importance, should be compelled at the same time to earn his daily bread as best he can.

A suggestion in last week's *Spectator* that some private person should step forward to endow the Prime Minister is most unsuitable and contrary to the dignity of the state. If the office ought to be endowed, it is Parliament, and Parliament alone, that has the right and the duty to do it. I suggest:—

(1) that the Prime Minister's salary should be £5,000 free of income tax and super tax;

(2) that he should receive a house allowance sufficient to defray the expenses of running No. 10, Downing Street, including a motor-car;

(3) that every ex-Prime Minister who has held office for six months or more should receive, as of right and without question, a pension of £2,000 a year for life.

The abuses arising out of the absence of such provision are far greater than can possibly arise out of making it. Cannot the Liberal Party take steps in the coming sessions to push the matter forward?

Yours, &c.,

SIELA

In the autumn of 1924 Keynes faced another official committee. Late in July he was approached by the Assistant Secretary to the Committee on National Debt and Taxation. This Committee, under the chairmanship of Lord Colwyn, had been set up 'to consider and report on the National Debt and on the incidence of existing taxation, with special reference to their effect on trade, industry, employment and national credit'. After some correspondence with both the Assistant Secretary and the Secretary, during which the Committee received copies of 'Foreign Investment and National Advantage', Keynes appeared before it on 1 October.

THE RETURN TO GOLD AND FOREIGN LENDING

From the Committee on National Debt and Taxation, Minutes of Evidence,
1 October 1924

COMMITTEE ON NATIONAL DEBT AND TAXATION

ELEVENTH DAY

Wednesday 1 October 1924

Present: The Rt. Hon. Lord Colwyn (*Chairman*)

Sir Charles Addis, K.C.M.G.	Mr H. B. Lees-Smith
Sir Alan G. Anderson, K.B.E.	Sir William McLintock, K.B.E.,
Sir Arthur Balfour, K.B.E.	C.V.O.
Mr Henry Bell	Sir Josiah Stamp, G.B.E.
Mr J. W. Bowen	Mrs Barbara Wootton
Mr Fred Bramley	Mr R. G. Hamilton, *Secretary*
Professor Fred Hall	Mr G. Ismay, *Assistant Secretary*
Mr W. L. Hichens	

Mr J. M. Keynes, C.B., called and examined

Evidence-in-chief handed in by Mr Keynes

1. Income tax is especially deterrent to saving in so far as it falls on funds which naturally accumulate at compound interest and where no question of personal expenditure can enter in, e.g., the funds of insurance companies and the reserves retained by joint stock companies to provide further capital against an increase of their business. The latter in particular is increasingly the way by which industry secures additional funds. Since income tax is a tax on income as it accrues, whether in the hands of a corporation or of an individual, whereas super-tax is a personal tax falling upon individuals alone, a redistribution of the burden of taxation, by lowering the standard rate of income tax, bringing the super-tax limit lower, and increasing the super-tax rate, would be the most convenient way of exempting some forms of savings from taxation if it is thought to be in the interests of the community to do that. An expenditure tax, though perhaps theoretically sound is practically impossible. But our British distinction between income tax and super-tax might be so handled as to achieve to some extent the same object.

2. The criterion as to the amount of debt to be held in a short-dated form should, I think, be given by the appetite of the investment market for that type of security. The Government can borrow most cheaply by offering various types of bonds in such proportions as each is required by the

295

investment market and the money market. A large sum, probably a very large sum, can be borrowed more cheaply in the form of short-term debt periodically renewed, than in the form of long-term debt. It would be a sound policy to maintain the short-dated debt permanently at a high figure if that high figure could be kept afloat at a rate of interest lower (on the average) than the rate on long-term debt. In the case of short-term debt the capital value is guaranteed and the interest is fluctuating; in the case of long-term debt the income is fixed but the capital value is fluctuating. Abstractly there is nothing to be said in favour of the one rather than of the other. The idea that there is something unsafe in maintaining the short-term debt permanently at a high figure is based for the most part on false analogy. I may add that it would probably assist the steadiness of credit if the volume of the short-term debt were to be somewhat reduced in good times and somewhat increased in bad times.

3. Since it is sound policy always to have a certain margin in budgeting, it is right that a certain amount of debt should, if possible, be repaid every year. But it is not advisable to attempt blindly to repay large sums merely on the ground that the debt is something to be got rid of. The idea again is based on false analogy. Repayment of debt out of taxation is partly at the expense of other forms of saving. The higher the taxation becomes the larger is the proportion which is at the expense of saving. But even that part which is at the expense of expenditure is not necessarily in the public interest. If we confine our attention to that part which is at the expense of saving, the effect of the repayment of debt is to drive the savings into a particular channel instead of letting them find their own outlet. When holders of debt are repaid they will probably prefer to re-invest the money in bonds of the gilt-edged type. If, on the other hand, the savings are left in the pockets of the taxpayer there is no such presumption, and they may find their outlet either in industry or in any other way. In present conditions, therefore, a rapid repayment of debt affords an artificial stimulus to savings to flow into the channel of gilt-edged investments. At a time when there is a very heavy demand for this particular type of investment this may be sound policy. For example, if the Local Loans Authorities, or Borough and County Authorities, are involved in heavy expenditure for housing or public works, which they can only cover by borrowing in the gilt-edged market, then a simultaneous repayment of national debt by the Treasury may be just the right thing to do. But it is not necessarily right in all circumstances. If the supply of new gilt-edged securities is limited, thus indicating that the demand for capital by borrowers of that type is not extensive then repayment of national debt on a large scale may be very harmful. This sort of consideration should weigh more than the mere idea that blind repayment of debt must be good for its

own sake. To take money from industry and from individuals by taxation and give it back to the gilt-edged section of the Stock Exchange, regardless of whether there is a ready outlet for it there, is injudicious.

4. In an address which I delivered recently, and copies of which have, I understand, been circulated to members of the Committee, I gave reasons for thinking that the present Trustee Acts should be considerably modified. Some of the considerations which I urged may not be particularly germane to the inquiry of this Committee. But in so far as they are concerned with the renewal of the abnormally large amount of debt which falls due between now and 1929, the desirability of the Treasury exercising a more effective control over rival trustee issues, than it has at present, is worth emphasising. Both in the interests of the investors themselves and of the community as a whole and of the Treasury, I think it would be better to allow no securities in the future to enjoy the benefit of the Trustee Acts except home securities of certain specified types.

My anxieties under this heading are connected with those under paragraph 3. If our own national debt is repaid on a large scale, and if the bulk of the new issues of trustee securities consist of colonial obligations, the effect of these two things together, namely repayment of debt and the Trustee Acts, is to afford an artificial stimulation to foreign investment which may be exceedingly contrary to the public interest. Repayment of debt takes forcibly resources from the community at large and compels their utilisation in securities of the trustee type; and it may then happen that the bulk of the net additions to the list of trustee securities are overseas investments.

5. I have mentioned above that the Government will borrow most cheaply by supplying such types of bonds as the different sections of the investing public find suitable to their requirements. I suggest that there is one further type of bond not yet in issue which might prove popular with particular individuals and so enable the state to raise funds a little more cheaply. I suggest that there should be issued bonds of which the capital and the interest would be paid not in a fixed amount of sterling, but in such amount of sterling as has a fixed commodity value as indicated by an index number. I think that an official index number should be established for such purposes on the lines of the optional tabular standard recommended long ago by Dr Marshall, and that it should be open to anyone, including particularly the Treasury, to offer loans, the payment of the interest on which and the repayment of the capital of which would be governed by movements of the index number. I can say from knowledge that there are many investors, who wishing to take no risks would naturally confine themselves to trustee stocks, yet feel a natural anxiety in being compelled to invest their whole resources in terms of legal tender money, the relation of which to real value has been

shown by experience to be variable. Throughout almost the whole of Europe investors of the trustee type have been deprived in the past ten years of the greater part of the value of their property. Even here in England all such investors have suffered a very large real loss. We may hope that great instability in the value of the currency may not be one of the things which the future has in store for us. But it is natural that some people should be anxious about it. Unless, therefore, the Treasury hopes to make a profit through the depreciation of legal tender, it would lose nothing, and might gain something in terms of interest, by issuing such bonds as I have indicated.

3880 (CHAIRMAN) *Will you first of all amplify the points in your paper?* I should like, if I may, in dealing with the first heading of my evidence, to put the matter a little differently from the way in which I have put it in my written summary. In England historically the income tax has been, not a personal tax, but a tax on income as it accrued, in whatsoever hands it was. That is a point which is not always well understood, but it has been a very vital feature of our income tax system. We have gradually been compelled to depart from that system as the rates of income tax have increased, and it has become increasingly a personal tax. The personal side of it is represented most completely in the super-tax. I believe that this distinction between the tax on income as it accrues and the personal tax might be developed so as to take taxation to a certain extent off what we can presume to be savings, and throw a little more heavily on to that part of income which we cannot presume with equal likelihood to be savings. I would suggest that if it is desirable to move in that direction we might reorganise our system of income tax, and, instead of having two taxes called income tax and super-tax, have two taxes called 'standard tax' and 'personal tax'; that the standard tax should be like the old income tax and fall upon all income as it accrued, subject, as the old income tax was, to certain total exemptions at the bottom of the scale; and that the personal tax should absorb the fluctuating part of income tax and super-tax and should be avowedly a tax on individuals in proportion to their capacity to bear it. That would have the effect that corporations who are not spenders, except in so far as they pay dividends, would pay only at the standard rate on that part of their income which they put aside and did not distribute. The most obvious cases are insurance companies, where the money accumulates at compound interest, and industrial companies, which retain for further development of their business a certain part of their profits. In both those cases there is strong presumption that the income in question is saved and is not spent. If the standard rate of tax was to be lowered and the loss of receipts in that way was to be made good by regraduating the super-tax and bringing it down to incomes of much lower limit than £2,000 you would be exempting a certain part of income which goes to savings. I think it is difficult to know how much is now saved in that way and how much in other ways, but I am sure that important sums are now saved by corporations rather than by individuals, that is the tendency nowadays, and it is one which it may be worth while to encourage and of which our tax system ought to take account. In the old days, when income tax was at moderate rates and no steep graduation was necessary, there was much to be said for the old system. In the early days of super-tax, when the machinery of super-tax was in its infancy, it would probably have been very difficult to have worked a personal tax of the kind that I suggest. But in the present conditions it merely means an extension of our existing super-tax machinery under a different name, and with super-tax down as low as £2,000 and with further graduation below that point, a large part of our taxation is in effect personal tax, even that part which is collected ostensibly at the standard rate of income tax. We should get clearer and perhaps have greater simplicity in the end if we were to recognise that change, and it would have the advantage that money which accrued in the hands of corporations which could not be spenders, would be exempted.

3881 (MR BELL) *By corporations do you mean limited companies only?* No, I include, for example insurance companies, whether they are limited liability companies or not. But generally speaking, I should make exactly the same distinction as is now made by super-tax; that is to say, my personal tax would fall upon the classes of persons who, if they had large enough income, would now be liable to super-tax.

3882 *I was wondering whether the actual standard tax would fall equally upon a partnership?* What is the present position as regards super-tax?

3883 *Would the same facility for saving be granted to a private partnership as to a limited company for instance?* There are certain marginal cases at present which are dealt with under super-tax lines as carefully as the officials can. I am not very well acquainted with just where they draw the line.

3884 (SIR ALAN ANDERSON) *Private partnerships or the individual partners have to pay super-tax on the reserves held by the partnership.* (SIR JOSIAH STAMP) *And instead of extending the principle of limited companies to partnerships, you would extend the principle of partnerships to limited companies, and say that, in so far as you have limited companies which approximate in their true character to a partnership, they shall be deemed to be partnerships; but because there has been very grave abuse of the distinction between limited company and partnership in the past in regard to super-tax, therefore recent legislation has assimilated all limited companies with a few shareholders, to partnerships.* Perhaps I could answer Mr Bell's question by taking up the point just made by Sir Josiah Stamp. Hitherto the distinction between super-tax and standard tax has been the amount of a man's income, and therefore the arrangements to which he refers were quite distinctly of the nature of evasion. But suppose that the criterion which we have in our mind was whether the money was locked away in a form in which it could not be spent on current expenditure, then we should not object so much to individuals or partners who were in fact behaving in that way imitating the formal company, because they would have met our criterion.

3885 (MR BELL) *That is the only point I wanted to elicit—that they would have just as much advantage by putting to reserve as a limited company would.* I do not like to answer that quite definitely, because it is a technical Inland Revenue point. I should like to do that in so far as it is compatible with preventing evasion of taxation. In all those cases you must not go beyond a point, because it can be abused by those who seek to evade, and that is an Inland Revenue matter on which I am not an expert.

3886 *All I wanted to ask was whether they should be treated as a limited company in every way in which it can be done fairly and rightly?* I should aim at that, but I should have thought that any Inland Revenue authority would say that you would have to be stiffer with private partnerships just as you are now.

3887 *Would that be just?* As just as the present system.

3888 *I should have thought not. If you were going to put a premium upon saving and the holding of reserves it should be done equally with a private partnership as with a company?* It is not done at the present time. I did not raise that point, because I propose no change.

3889 *I mean standard tax, not super-tax?* I am making exactly the same point.

3890 (SIR WILLIAM MCLINTOCK) *There is a distinction between a limited company and a private company formed before 1914 and after?* Yes.

3891 *After 1914 certain private limited companies were treated as partnerships?* Yes.

3892 *This suggestion of yours would mean that all the pre-1914 companies would get off with a lower rate of tax and the amount placed to reserve would not be questioned, whereas in the case of the after-1914 companies, today the Inland Revenue go very exhaustively into all the circumstances of the case?* Yes, but I suggest that these questions are not really relevant to what I am trying to say.

3893 (SIR JOSIAH STAMP) *I think we are drifting rather too much into the technical difficulties of carrying out general principles. I would like to ask you whether something in the nature of a division between the normal tax and the super-tax as they have it in the United States would be possible?* I am inclined to have a somewhat higher standard tax than they have, at any rate at first.

I think it would be too great a change in the existing system to put the standard tax as low as in America. I should suggest 3s. in the £ as the figure.

3894 *That is to say, you would lower the present super-tax down to the class of those who in effect pay at the rate of 3s.* Yes.

3895 *It was started at £5,000, dropped to £3,000, and then dropped to £2,000; with every drop in the level a large number of people come in, and there is an inevitable loss, through evasion, every time?* I think that is the main objection to my proposal. Every tampering with the level of the standard tax leaves more room for evasion.

3896 *The Chairman will remember that the point where super-tax was brought down to a lower level was seriously considered by the Income Tax Commission?* But I think that now the situation is so different from what it was even a very few years ago, we have gone so far in this direction, that if there were other advantages to be gained I would risk this objection; but it is a great objection.

3897 (SIR CHARLES ADDIS) *With regard to the effect of income tax on companies' savings, is it your view that it acts by tempting companies to distribute a larger amount in dividends than they put to reserve?* No, I think it acts by diminishing the amount that they have available for reserve.

3898 *But not in the direction of encouraging increased distribution?* It may a little, but I do not think so.

3899 *Do you think in practice it has had the effect of reducing the amount of reserves?* Yes, I think so.

3900 *We have had evidence given here by Mr Layton that so far as he could judge, the reserves of the companies that he examined all kept pace with the increase in prices. Do you think that was correct?* I should have been surprised that you could get any sound statistical argument on that point, owing to the great changes by amalgamation and otherwise that have taken place in the character of companies in the past 10 years; but in any case it does not follow that the proportion put to reserve before the war was the really correct proportion.

3901 *Is there any real distinction in the position of a shareholder who receives a sum in dividends which might have been put to reserve, and himself invests it in some other industrial security?* I do not quite follow the question.

3902 *Supposing that a company, instead of putting to reserve, pays the amount in dividend and that the shareholder who receives that dividend invests it in some other industrial security?* It does not follow that he will. If he does, it does not make very much difference; but I am inclined to think that the new money for industry is being found more and more out of the reserves of existing companies. The tendency, in the case of a really progressive industry, is to pay the shareholders something to satisfy them and to retain as

301

much as they possibly can in the business for the further expansion of that business. I think that is one of the most healthy ways in which additional capital for business is obtained, and I think that this suggestion of mine would leave more in the hands of the managers of the business, which they could retain in the business without disappointing their shareholders. They could in fact use it as an argument with the shareholders that it brings them within this lower rate of tax if they retain it in the business.

3903 *If you take two classes of shareholders: if you take class A, who receives the amount in dividend, and class B, where the amount is retained by a company and placed to reserve, the distinction is really between borrowed money and compulsory saving. In the case of A, he may save or he may not?* I think the argument is purely psychological. You might say that if you could earn 2s. and give your shareholder 1s., your 20s. shares will then be worth 21s., whereas if you gave him 2s., they would be worth 20s. Therefore your shareholder, by selling 5 per cent of his holding, could be exactly as he was previously; he would have obtained his 2s. But in practice people do not act in that way. If the money is retained in the business, it is much less liable to be spent by the shareholder releasing a portion of his holding than if it is paid to him as dividend; because he looks on the one as capital and he looks on the other as income. There is also a further point. The expenses of raising new capital are heavy, and one of the great advantages of increasing capital by retaining money in the business is that it is a very cheap way by which companies can increase their funds. If they have to issue new shares or borrow in the market, in modern conditions they have to give away a dangerously high sum in order to make a successful flotation. If they retain money in this way it costs them nothing; they have a perpetual regular flow instead of an occasional large but expensive issue.

3904 *The point I wanted to make was this, if I may make it clear. In the case of two shareholders, A and B, the one receives the dividend and the other has it invested for him. Would there be no inequity in taxing the one and exempting the other according to your proposal?* I do not think that any system of taxation is perfectly fair. I do not think that you would increase the existing unfairness. It exists in every case of the super-tax payer at present.

3905 *It seems to me that it would have the effect of encouraging a certain kind of saving, namely, compulsory saving, as against voluntary saving. I do not press that point, but there is a difficulty, I think?* It seems to me that you are imputing to a new system of taxation an inequity that exists at present.

3906 (SIR JOSIAH STAMP) *On that point raised by Sir Charles Addis, there is rather an assumption that super-tax is being lost at the present time on the amount retained by the company. But those sums are due not merely to people with incomes chargeable at a higher rate than the normal rate, but are also due to people chargeable at a lower rate and on the average probably there is not much loss, because there is no repayment to anybody on the money that is invested for them by the company. The shareholder may be hit by having the tax paid at 4s. 6d. in the £, on something for which he is only liable to 2s. 3d., and if you take the whole amount there is no statistical evidence to show that the real rate on the whole lot is higher than the normal rate. The thing is unfair in both directions. On this statistical point about reserves, supposing that the company makes £10,000 profit and looks at its balance sheet and sees that all its assets are intact, and says: 'We will pay £5,000 in dividend and put £5,000 to reserve', and that goes into the business, that is the kind of thing that ought to be encouraged?* That is my suggestion.

3907 *Now supposing the company looks at its assets and says: 'We have got some holdings in Dunlop that have depreciated in value; we must write that asset down', and they deplete their profit and loss account by £5,000, they show £5,000 profit and they pay that away in dividends, apparently they make no reserve, but do they not in effect do exactly the same as the first company?* Yes, I think so.

3908 *Then one way of doing it is to put it into reserve when it is obviously reserve, but we none of us know how large sums out of profits have been saved in the writing down of assets?* No.

3909 *Which makes it almost impossible to judge how much of current profits have been kept intact without distribution. It would seem to show that it is a favourable time, would it not, for an increase in capital when everything slumps in value. By the modern ideas of a balance sheet you compel everybody to put money on one side?* There is a striking instance of that in the case of banks.

3910 (PROFESSOR HALL) *That would apply, of course, to depreciation of plant as well.* (SIR JOSIAH STAMP) *That is a more regular thing, but this seems to show that industry is being particularly hit in the saving of capital at a time when capital values are being depreciated?* (MR KEYNES) Of course it does not always happen that companies do write down assets as much as they should.

3911 (SIR WILLIAM MCLINTOCK) *There are two methods. One company writes down a specific asset and reduces its value, probably they have only written it down to market value and then they hide it up in a big total; another company actually shows the reserve on the other side, and the result is exactly the same for the two companies?* Yes.

3912 *Would you consider there is an essential difference between the one which shows it as a true reserve and the one which writes it down to its market value as a legitimate business expense?* I think the existence of those two methods renders all estimates of amount nearly valueless on this matter.

3913 *I agree. They will have to reform their methods of stating balance sheets for statistical purposes.* (SIR JOSIAH STAMP) *What I want to know is whether you would allow the writing down of capital assets to be charged as a business expense?* (MR KEYNES) I think there is a great difficulty about it, because there is also the question of writing up. If you are to allow companies to write down depreciation of assets as a business expense then you must compel them to write up, and that would involve valuations on the part of Inland Revenue, which would probably be impracticable. I have always regarded the unwillingness of the Inland Revenue to allow writing down as a balancing item against the impracticability of compelling companies to write items up.

3914 (SIR ALAN ANDERSON) *You can practically choose now for a great many things, can you not, whether you will bring in the rise and fall, or whether you will not?* Also it seems to me that if you have writings up and down in accordance with fluctuations in the value of money and include these in income account, you would reach an impossible situation.

3915 (SIR JOSIAH STAMP) *I was going to ask you how you would avoid the appalling mess that Washington [i.e. the United States] has got into the last three or four years?* I do not quite understand the relevance to what I was proposing, because I was not suggesting any change in this particular respect.

3916 *We were on the question of the method of handling reserves in the different kinds of companies. I was wondering if you were going to have differential treatment at all?* Your point relates to the definition of profit. My suggestion does not really touch that.

3917 *You would allow profit to be defined as now?* Yes.

3918 *And you would get over all difficulties about exempting reserves or giving preferential treatment, by charging companies at a low rate of tax?* Yes.

3919 (MR BELL) *What would be the additional tax to the widow who lives in Ryde or the physician who lives in Harley Street? How is it to be made up?* It does not affect his position, because he is at present liable to super-tax.

3920 *I take it that the net result of this proposal would be that companies would be relieved of a good deal of taxation as long as they kept certain reserves intact. How will the revenue make that up?* It would be made up in various ways, partly by a general regraduation which will bring the super-tax limit down and partly by some increase in the personal tax all along the line. But the Harley Street practitioner would not be injured by that any more than any other individual of equal income.

3921 *But individuals would have to find the amounts of which industrial concerns are given the benefit?* Yes, wherever you relieve a particular sort of income from taxation you must make it up on some other sort of income, certainly.

3922 *Do you not fear that that might be a preferential treatment of one sort of people?* It depends how much public opinion was influenced by the desirability of exempting what are certainly savings. I think it may be that the encouragement to savings is rather a fetish sometimes; I do not think it ought to be pushed to its extreme point. But I am assuming that in existing conditions we want to do a little to help savings.

3923 *All sorts of savings equally?* All those that we can encourage without opening doors to evasion, and I think that confines rather narrowly the types that you can assist.

3924 *Would that really be possible in regard to individuals, do you think?* No, I do not think it would.

3925 *Then it would in effect be letting savings of a certain class of taxation off and not letting off another class of savings?* I am inclined, perhaps wrongly, to brush on one side all these minor questions of equity between individuals, because I think that line of argument leads always to abusing a new tax as against an old tax. Every tax that has ever been devised is packed full of these small inequities.

3926 *The inequity seems to me to be a pretty big one?* If these are emphasised it suggests that the new taxes, because they have them, have them more than the old taxes. If we were to go through the old taxes we should find just as many anomalous cases.

3927 (SIR ALAN ANDERSON) *I suppose there is an inherent objection to every new tax. You do not want to change the method of taxation?* There is always an objection to a new system of taxation. One never wants to alter our system of taxation for no reason at all.

3928 (SIR JOSIAH STAMP) *There is no enormous difference in the question of equity between one individual and another and the social value of savings. In your judgement, the social value of savings might be allowed to prevail?* Yes, but I sympathise with Mr Bell's point of view. I think there is a danger of going too far in the other direction.

3929 (MR BRAMLEY) *What would be the effect on the banks? Would your proposal tend to reduce the total amount of savings in the hands of banks, and increase the total amount of savings in the hands of companies?* I do not think so. Do you mean that it would increase the amount of the deposit accounts in banks? The alternative to the money being retained by the companies is that the investor would either spend it or invest it in some other way. Of the other ways in which they can invest it, putting it on deposit at their banks is only one of many.

3930 *The temptation would be to leave more money in the hands of the companies, would it not?* Not so much the temptation as the compulsion.

3931 *That would, of course, reduce the amount of bank deposits, would it not?* It would reduce the amount of money available for investment in other ways, and it is only in so far as interest-bearing deposits at the bank are a form of investment that they would be affected. It would not affect the amount on current account, and I should not think it would much affect the amount held on deposit; but it might.

3932 (MRS WOOTTON) *I understand you do not intend to alter seriously the present graduation of income tax?* No. I think that, if you were to merge super-tax and the fluctuating part of income tax, as I suggest, there are certain adjustments that one would inevitably think it wise to make; there are certain small adjustments which at present arise inevitably out of there being two taxes, which you would take the opportunity of correcting.

3933 *Your proposal is to relieve savings much more than to make any change in general taxation?* Yes.

3934 (MR BOWEN) *Would your proposal mean less revenue?* It would mean less revenue from a particular source, which would have to be made up from other sources.

3935 *Have you in mind what those sources would be?* My idea was that the total receipts from income tax and super-tax would not be diminished unless there were other reasons for diminishing them; that it would be a redistribution between income tax and super-tax payers rather than a relief of those classes; but if there was money which was available to relieve some class or other, personally I think the income tax payers are those who ought to receive it. I think that of the present taxes the income tax and super-tax are the most excessive.

3936 (SIR WILLIAM MCLINTOCK) *Assume that a lower rate of tax is applied to limited companies; they have a bigger sum available then for either distribution or reserve?* Yes.

3937 *If you assume that they pay a larger dividend by reason of the lower income tax, that higher dividend will in turn be subject to the higher rate of super-tax that you suggest?* Yes.

3938 *One may very well off-set the other?* I assume that the companies would to a certain extent increase their nominal rate of dividend.

3939 (SIR JOSIAH STAMP) *You do not think that they would retain in their business the whole of the difference?* No, I do not.

3940 *A great many of them already retain all they want and they would have no use for this money, and they would pay it out as a larger gross dividend?* Yes, and in so far as they paid it out as a larger gross dividend, no revenue would be lost.

3941 (SIR WILLIAM MCLINTOCK) *And the revenue would gain on the higher super-tax?* Yes.

3942 *That would be the tendency, would it not?* I think the tendency would be that a certain amount extra would be retained in the business.

3943 *A portion of it?* A portion of it. All this discussion has been based upon joint stock companies. But the case of insurance companies is very important, because the amount of the additional savings of the country that accrues in the hands of insurance companies per annum is something prodigious, and that part automatically accumulates at compound interest and it is an increasingly large source of savings. If they accumulated at a higher net rate of interest than they do now it would make a very material difference to the amount of savings. I attach more importance to that so far as the magnitude of the additional savings is concerned than I do to the other point.

3944 *Would it increase the bonuses paid by insurance companies?* It would increase them, certainly, if you mean the ordinary type of bonus which is a deferred bonus; it means that the insured person at the maturity of the policy receives a larger sum. If money is accumulating in the hands of the insurance company at a higher rate of interest there is a larger fund to be returned to the policy holder at the end of the period, and that is simply another way of saying that the bonuses are higher.

3945 *In that case no tax would ever be paid on those bonuses?* I do not say no tax; they would pay standard tax.

3946 *Except the standard tax. A limited company must distribute surplus profits at some future date?* Yes.

3947 (SIR ALAN ANDERSON) *Does not an insurance company pay income tax?* It pays income tax, certainly; that is the point of my answer; it would continue to pay standard tax.

3948 *When one takes out a policy one escapes the income tax on the premium?* Up to a certain point. The company pays income tax all the time.

3949 *When you answered about the doctor or the lawyer, the man who is making a personal income, I think you said that he was a hard case, did you not?* I said that he is a hard case now.

3950 *He is no worse off than a private firm now. You say they would be hard cases too?* They are a hard case, too. It is simply that anybody who is liable to super-tax, and who saves out of his income, is in a worse position than a company which saves correspondingly. My proposal slightly aggravates that inequity. But any scheme for helping savings that does not help all savings equally is inequitable in that way. That is an instance of my objection to Mr Bell's suggestions in some of his questions which are along these lines. No way of helping savings would help all savings to an exactly equal extent; therefore an element of unfairness is involved; therefore you must never help savings. This result is the danger of that way of arguing.

3951 (MR BELL) *Still, of course, it is the wish of all of us to be equally fair to all classes if we can. It is not a bad thing in itself to be rather careful?* No, certainly not; I agree with that; but I think that the perfectly fair person has to retire from all forms of action.

3952 (CHAIRMAN) *Will you proceed with the next point in your evidence?* There is the question as to what part of our debt we should be prepared to keep permanently in a short-dated form. I think popular opinion on that is often incorrect, because it is founded on a false analogy with the case of a private individual or of a company. It is clearly advantageous for a company to have its debentures of a long date, so that there may not be any risk of their falling due at a time when the company is embarrassed, or less easily able to raise money. I think the extension of that to the state is a false analogy. I see nothing unsafe in the fact that the amount of short-dated debt falling due for renewal year by year is one figure rather than another figure. My criterion would be determined by the amount of debt which could be kept floating one year with another in a short-dated form at a lower average rate of interest than if it were in long-dated form. I believe that the amount that could be kept floating on that criterion is very large, simply for the reason that there are a large number of holders of funds, particularly banks, to whom it is so advantageous to have debt which is regularly maturing that they are prepared to accept a lower rate of interest on it than on debt which does not mature in that way. In a long-dated debt the lender knows what interest he will receive annually for a long time ahead; he does not know for certain what the market value of his loan will be; in the short-dated debt he knows what the market value will be year by year in the near future; he does not know for certain exactly what rate of interest he will receive. From the point of view of the state it seems to be indifferent in which form they borrow, but there is a certain class of lenders to whom one kind is very much preferable and there is another class to whom the other kind is very much preferable, and I think the division between the two forms of debt ought to be determined by the proportionate appetites of those two classes of investors.

3953 (MR BELL) *In the result, I take it, you agree that there has been an enormous saving to the state by the cheaper form of borrowing on short-term security?* Very great indeed.

3954 (SIR JOSIAH STAMP) *Would you agree that the appetite will vary according as the times are good or bad?* Yes.

3955 *Would you settle it by the period of minimum appetite?* There is a certain difficulty there. It is in the interests of the trading community that the short-dated debt of the Government should be somewhat reduced in good times and somewhat increased in bad times. But those dates may not coincide with the dates at which it is most profitable for the government to convert its debt from one form into the other. You may, I think, have a dilemma sometimes between which objective to follow. If you can fund your debt more satisfactorily in good times, that is the moment to fund rather than in bad times.

3956 *Therefore you would not object to the step taken in reducing the huge floating debt that was frequently coming on the market in 1920 to more manageable dimensions?* No.

3957 *It was a source of great danger at the time, and was in constant competition with the gluttonous demands for money in the industrial market?* I think it was healthy, because it tended to direct new savings into the commercial market rather than into the investment market. It is a characteristic of good times that the new savings of the community ought to be put at the service of trade rather than flow into investments. If the Government at that time is floating long-dated loans to the investor and using the proceeds to repay the market its short-dated loans it does just what is wanted; it brings the new savings of the community into the service of commerce. On the other hand, in bad times, when the demands of commerce are reduced, the opposite is true; but I believe that the fluctuations which would be practicable in the volume of the floating debt as between good times and bad, would not be a very large percentage of the whole.

3958 *Not more than 10 per cent probably.* No, not more than 10 per cent.

3959 (MR BELL) *I am quite clear that there is a fallacy in the argument that a short-term debt is bad, but it seems to have been laid down almost as a financial principle that you must get rid of a short-dated debt of this kind. You are entirely opposed to that?* Yes, entirely opposed to it; indeed, I think if it were carried very far it would put our banking system into an extremely difficult situation. It would be driving bankers into a form of security which is not the most suitable for them.

3960 (SIR CHARLES ADDIS) *Can you make any suggestions as to the amount of floating debt that might be considered permanent?—Is it possible to arrive at an estimate?* It is rather difficult to give a figure, because one does not quite know at what point to draw the line, whether 1929 War Bonds are short-dated debt, whether 1932 Treasury Bonds are.

3961 *Might I take Treasury bills as an instance of floating debt?* I should certainly merge with Treasury bills all the National War Bonds which are of quite short-date—up to 1927/1928. I do not see anything very wrong in the present amount.

3962 *You do not think there is any danger with the amount at the present level?* No.

3963 *That is to say, if a demand were made for money, the Government could always command the situation by raising the interest on short-dated loans?* That is so, but supposing trade was to revive very definitely, I think it would be a sound policy if the Government tried to fund some of it and then was prepared to allow some to be reconverted into short-period debt later on. I do not think they should aim at a much lower figure than the present figure as an average.

3964 (MR BELL) *Might not the existence of the floating debt hamper the Government in any conversion scheme by making it more difficult to raise the cash if the conversion terms offered were not always accepted?* I think that assumes that we are always wanting to have conversion schemes, that the ultimate object of the Treasury is to convert everything. I do not think it would make very much difference. Supposing you had a certain part of the public naturally attracted by long-dated debt and a certain part of the public naturally attracted by short-dated debt, you do not get any rapid change between those two classes of investors, and therefore the market for the long-dated debt would be much the same at one time as at another. In fact by having mopped up all the really short-dated lenders into your short-dated debt, you have a more steady supply of lenders for your long-period debt.

3965 (SIR CHARLES ADDIS) *If the rate of interest on the short-dated debt eventually became the same as on the long-dated debt, would there not be competition?* If that happened, I should say it was a sign that the short-dated debt was getting excessive.

3966 *You would consider whether it was a good opportunity to fund. You would take the two circumstances together?* I think it is inevitable that you should. When the Government has been erring a little in one direction, it would probably be difficult to correct it, because it is just that difficulty which has probably led to the situation which is making the trouble.

3967 *In your view the management of this amount of floating debt would have to be increased and diminished in accordance with the fluctuations in the competition of trade for funds, would involve a certain amount of control?* It would involve a certain amount of intelligence.

3968 *You are not apprehensive as to the degree of intelligence that would be available for controlling credit in that way, are you?* I think it is quite impossible to write down certain rules in a book and then have the Treasury run by clerks from that time onwards by reference to the book.

3969 (PROFESSOR HALL) *I think you mentioned that you convert from short-dated loans to funded loans in times of good trade?* That is a secondary point. I should do that if it was not too expensive.

3970 *Would not that be rather an unfavourable time for funding?* It would; that is the difficulty. The reason for that is that during trade booms, owing to the nature of our credit system, the price of long-dated securities is unduly affected.

3971 (SIR ALAN ANDERSON) *Does it not come to this, that you would go on with the short-dated securities you have got now, unless you found you would save money by converting?* Yes, that is what it comes to.

3972 (SIR CHARLES ADDIS) *In times of commercial expansion do you regard the existence of the floating debt as tending to raise the rate of interest for business purposes?* No, I do not think it does that, but the existence of a floating debt affords an opportunity for diverting savings into the direction of business in the way in which I have indicated. It gives to the Treasury an opportunity, by funding its debt, of getting savings from the public and putting those savings at the disposition of commerce, and if it is practicable to do that, it is a good thing to do; but if it cannot be done, then it cannot.

3973 (CHAIRMAN) *Will you go on to your next point now?* My next point is the one to which I really attach most importance. It relates to times of repayment. I think some debt should be repaid every year in the interests of sound budgeting and sound finance generally. It is a sound principle to have some margin, and the policy of having a sinking fund of a certain amount is a way of insuring that. But when you consider repayments of debt on a larger scale than is required by such considerations, I think again there is a danger of applying the false analogy of an individual who is in debt, who would naturally wish to clear off his obligations at the first possible moment. The effect of paying off debt is to take money from the body of taxpayers and to place it at the disposal primarily of a particular form of investment. If a holder of Government debt is paid off he will probably want to reinvest in something of the same kind. Thus I should say that the main effect of debt repayment at a rapid rate is to divert the surplus resources of the community into the gilt-edged stock market. Sometimes this may be a very right thing to do. If the demand for capital which is offered in that particular form is brisk, then that is a good opportunity to pay off debt. But the policy of paying off debt regardless of the outlet is, I think, a very doubtful one. I think that probably mistakes were made on those lines in the 'nineties, though I do not know the history of that period well enough to be sure. I am clear that if at the present time upwards of one hundred million pounds of debt is repaid annually, that may take a larger part of the surplus of the community and put it at the disposal of the gilt-edged market, than is desirable. But I should look to the criterion of the demand for the outlet for savings in investments of the trustee type rather than to any other criterion in deciding how fast I should repay debt, once I had got a sufficient balance on the right side to satisfy the requirements of ordinary good finance.

3974 (SIR JOSIAH STAMP) *As a corollary to that point we have had the amount of diversion that excessive debt repayment introduces put to us in this form. You draw your taxes from businesses which are progressive but relatively obscure, and you deplete what they would otherwise have had for their development. You direct money by debt repayment, as you say, to the gilt-edged market, which is not big enough or extensive enough to absorb the sums so directed, and they seek the next best thing, which are debentures, and good industrial shares in very large undertakings. Therefore an excessive debt repayment has the effect of encouraging the financing of the largest and best known concerns and discouraging private enterprise?* I think that is true, but I should put even more strongly the point that it has the effect of encouraging colonial investments as against all types of English industrials.

3975 *And even against English debentures?* Even against English debentures; because colonial securities are considered by the public as nearer to the true gilt-edged type than even English industrials are.

3976 (MR BRAMLEY) *The continuation of the interest liability is a question of distribution, not of total wealth of the community?* Provided that interest is being met by taxation on the right class of the community, I do not think that ought to be a determining consideration. It is out of one pocket into another; whereas the other considerations that I have been mentioning have regard to the growth of the aggregate wealth of the community.

3977 (MRS WOOTTON) *What prevents this diversion from correcting itself? What prevents the tendency to invest in gilt-edged securities to straighten it out again?* The fact that there is very imperfect fluidity in the investment market. It is not true that capital seeks the channels of most lucrative investment by itself. It does nothing of the kind. The business of investment is most unsuccessfully carried on, because it is largely conducted by persons, namely, the individual investors, who know nothing whatever about it. It is lack of knowledge.

3978 (SIR JOSIAH STAMP) *It is conservatism too?* It is conservatism, obedience to convention, and lack of knowledge. That is inevitable, and those characteristics exist in the greatest degree in the gilt-edged type of investor. He goes into that class of security precisely because he, rightly, does not like to trust his own judgement. Therefore, you are putting the resources of the community, if you repay debt too fast, into the hands of the class of persons who have least courage and least skill in the utilisation of resources.

3979 (MRS WOOTTON) *There is not a sufficient margin also in the gilt-edged market?* The gilt-edged market is so enormously large as compared with the industrial market that there is not a sufficient margin. I am convinced that there is not a sufficient margin. I am convinced that the disparity in the size of the gilt-edged market and the other markets is much greater than is commonly appreciated.

3980 *Is that lack of fluidity constant, or does it increase and decrease?* I think it varies. At times when the general investing public have suffered misfortunes so that they have no courage, the lack of fluidity is much greater than when they have been having a rather fortunate time and are speculatively inclined.

3981 (MR HICHENS) *It has been put to us in evidence that if, by means, for instance, of a capital levy, we could pay off the whole of the debt and thus relieve the state of some £300,000,000 a year in the way of interest, that*

£300,000,000 would be available for other public purposes, such as education and so forth. Would you regard that as a fallacy or as a fact? The only valid distinction between a capital levy and taxes of the class of the income tax, is that one falls more upon those who hold wealth and the other more on those who earn incomes. That is to say, one is on the existing holders of wealth, the other is on the potential future holders of wealth.

3982 *That is to say, it might re-distribute the burden, it would not affect the magnitude of it?* It would re-distribute the burden in the interests of persons who are now earning their wealth, as against persons who have earned their wealth in past times.

3983 (MRS WOOTTON) *It might be better, might it not, for the state to extend it in certain directions, rather than in others, from a purely psychological consideration?* I think that would be very small, compared with the point that I have mentioned. The evil seems to arise when, in order to make the Budget balance, the rate of income tax upon current effort gets so high as to discourage that effort. I think the evil of discouraging that effort may be greater than the evil of disappointing the expectations of persons who earned their wealth in the past.

3984 (SIR ALAN ANDERSON) *In fact it is better to go on collecting money from income tax, so long as you are not pushing it too far?* Yes.

3985 (MRS WOOTTON) *There is a sort of convention that you ought not to spend out of the National Exchequer more than a certain sum, partly for psychological reasons. If you are relieved of the obligation of spending the amount of the debt interest, it might be possible to divert it to the other objects?* I doubt if that convention would last long if it was divorced from the real burden of taxation. I should not attach much importance to that argument in founding a permanent system of taxation for the country, because those conventions have a very short life. The position now is totally different from what it was a very few years ago.

3986 (MR HICHENS) *Another point of view that was put to us was that the question of debt repayment is not really a very serious matter, that the general public are used to a debt of £6,000,000,000 odd, and that, as it falls due, it will be a matter of no difficulty to replace it; therefore there is no urgency in redeeming the debt?* My view is that there is no urgency to redeem the debt unless the state has other important objects for which it wants the money; that is to say, if it is a question of replacing unproductive debt by productive debt, that may be a very strong reason for reducing the unproductive debt, but if there is no argument of that kind, reducing debt for its own sake I think is an undesirable policy, because it is not really increasing the wealth of the community, it is forcing the surplus of the community into a particular channel, which may not be the channel into which it ought to flow.

3987 (SIR ALAN ANDERSON) *You mean the argument in favour of the reduction of debt is primarily to retain the credit of the state so that it can borrow more if it wants to?* That is an argument which is used.

3988 *That is what you think, is it not: you would not do it, except for the credit of the state?* I would not call it the credit of the state. I would say that if the state has a demand for the money, if the state is itself in the gilt-edged market as a borrower, directly or indirectly, for productive purposes, then in order to make that productive borrowing easier there is a good deal to be said for paying off the debt. But if there is no natural outlet for the sums released by repayment of debt, then it is a mistake to repay debt.

3989 (SIR CHARLES ADDIS) *Supposing the demand for gilt-edged securities, both at home and abroad, was relatively small, the effect would be to drive money into industry, would it not?* The investor would be tempted probably into the second-rate bond, than which there is no worse investment.

3990 *Might there not be also a favourable result in the reaction on rates of interest from the reduction of debt?* It is a roundabout way of producing your result, to take money from industry in the hope that some of it may, by another channel find its way back there.

3991 (MR BRAMLEY) *May I just ask for information on this sentence in paragraph 3 of your paper: 'For example, if the Local Loans Authorities or Borough or County Authorities, are involved in heavy expenditure for housing or public works, which they can only cover by borrowing in the gilt-edged market, then a simultaneous repayment of national debt by the Treasury may be just the right thing to do.' Does that mean that if you could encourage local expenditure proportionately to the repayment of the debt, that would be an advantage?* Perhaps I can illustrate it in this way. I think about two years ago (I am not sure of my exact dates) various local authorities, county and municipal boroughs, and those authorities who borrow through the Local Loans Fund, had big schemes on hand which required large issues by them. At the same date we were in fact repaying Government debt at a very rapid rate. One of those things offset the other. I think it was quite a healthy thing. Money which had been repaid by the Government found an outlet in these loans of local authorities. At the present time, when local authorities have operations on foot on a much smaller scale, the amounts they are borrowing are relatively trifling. An equal repayment of debt therefore at the present time would be less advisable than it was in the circumstances of two years ago.

3992 (SIR CHARLES ADDIS) *You say: 'If the supply of new gilt-edged securities is limited, thus indicating that the demand for capital by borrowers of that type is not extensive, then repayment of national debt on a large scale may be very harmful.' Would you expand that?* Because it forces the surplus resources of the community into a channel where they are not particularly wanted.

3993 (MR HICHENS) *We have been told that there is a psychological effect, that if there is a large Government debt and the Government bondholders are people who are rather apt to look askance at it, money is being wasted by paying interest on the debt, whereas on the other hand if this debt were paid off and the capital were disseminated to industry, the same objection would not quite hold?* I think it is a relic of mid-nineteenth-century sound financial maxims which have extremely little application to the present day. But owing to the fact that the present application is so slight, conventional feelings of that sort gradually disappear. It is unsound to base the policy of the future on the decaying conventions of the past.

3994 (MR BRAMLEY) *I would like to be perfectly clear as to whether the evils arising from repayment of debt arise purely from the process of repayment or whether they are attached to some method of obtaining the means of repayment. Supposing the United States of America were to be inspired with a desire (this is merely supposition of course) to improve the credit of this country and they came along and said: 'We will make you a present of £2,000,000,000 sterling to help you out of debt', and we accepted it and repaid our debt to that extent, would that be a disadvantage to this country?* I think that the advantage of receiving a present of £2,000,000,000 would far outweigh the inconveniences of the financial problem of tidying things up with the proceeds.

3995 *But still, the evils arising from the process of repayment would remain the same, would they not?* I do not think that the evils of repaying £100,000,000 are £100,000,000.

3996 (SIR ALAN ANDERSON) *The evil is that the investors may waste some money?* Yes, the evil is not that you would lose all that £100,000,000, but that the £100,000,000 might not be used quite as well as it might be under other arrangements.

3997 *If the Americans gave us £2,000,000,000, we should have to do something with it?* It depends on what was offering, but here is a great benefit of £2,000,000,000, and however inadvisedly it was used, you would hardly waste all of it.

3998 (MR HICHENS) *At any rate, if the American chose to take some money out of his pocket and put it into yours, you would not mind if a little dropped on the way, whereas you might not think it worth while to change your own money from one pocket to another and lose some of it?* Precisely.

3999 (MR BELL) *There is considerable unanimity I think, in regard to the amount of £50,000,000 for the new sinking fund. All sorts of people say they think that £50,000,000 a year is a reasonable amount to pay off. Is that so, in your judgment?* I should say something round about that figure.

4000 (CHAIRMAN) *Will you pass to your next point?* My next point is closely connected with what we have been discussing. It arises out of the character of the present Trustee Acts. Until 1889 only Consols were available for trustees. During the 'nineties, great trouble began to arise because the amount of funds available for trustee investment was always increasing, whereas the volume of Consols was falling. To meet this certain alterations were made by the Colonial Stock Act of 1900 which greatly extended the range of trustee investments. At that time, the amount of colonial loans was not very great, and it is only comparatively recently that these have become very great. Now the colonies are prepared to borrow practically as much as we are prepared to lend them. The consequence is that if money is available in the gilt-edged market, and there is no new home investment to take off those surplus funds, they almost automatically find their way to the colonies. Thus the diversion of money into the gilt-edged market now creates an unduly strong presumption in favour of its leaving the country. The colonies have socialised a number of services which we have not socialised. Thus the money required for such services in the colonies is easier to borrow than money required for similar services in this country; and in many ways, which I have elaborated in a paper which I think some members of the Committee have seen, the extension of the Trustee Acts so as to cover nearly all colonial government securities, when at the same time the volume of home trustee securities is being reduced, creates a dangerous bias in favour of excessive foreign investment. The conditions which led to the extension of the Trustee Act no longer exist. It would not be wise or practicable to make any change as regards existing trustee securities, but I think that so far as future additions to the list are concerned, the rules ought to be tightened up very much. In a paper that I read lately I suggested that the Treasury should have a certain power of licence. That proposal has been much criticised, and I think there is force in the criticism. I should like to avoid that. I would therefore either abolish the Trustee Acts altogether, for which there is a great deal to be said, or if they are retained, I would allow as new trustee securities only home securities such as prior charges on railways and country and municipal loans, and I should extend the list so as to include a number of public utility services of the type of the Port of London, and so on. I attach considerable importance to this point, though of course if the volume of debt reduction is reduced, it is not so important as it would be otherwise. In any case there is not much prospect of the volume of home Government debt increasing, whereas the volume of investment which seeks an outlet in the gilt-edged market is always increasing. I think it is dangerous, therefore, that the surplus should tend to be drawn off into foreign investment, without more inquiry as to the relative advantage of the different channels of investment than is made at present.

4001 (SIR CHARLES ADDIS) *Do you advocate any control of the market in order to effect that object, apart from the repeal or the amendment of the Trustee Acts?* I am personally not so much afraid of allowing discretion to a central authority as some people are. That is why I originally suggested that the Treasury should have a certain power of licence. I think it is very difficult to define beforehand just what types of securities you will wish to include in the trustee list, and I believe that the Treasury could be trusted to use its discretion wisely. There are many people who believe that all officials and all bankers are devoid of intelligence and that no discretion should ever be allowed to them.

4002 *Would the amendment of the Trustee Act itself, in your judgement, produce any considerable effect? Would it not merely amount to this, that the colonies, who are eager borrowers, would borrow very much the same amount at a slightly higher rate?* I think that the rate would rapidly become somewhat deterrent to them. It would very much encourage them to float as much as they could at home. There are several colonies now where they are rather near the line. Canada is a little across the line. It is now cheaper for Canada to borrow at home than to borrow here; but there is always the danger in a new country where the rates are relatively high, that if you give them the benefit of our trustee rates, which are lower than theirs, you encourage them to borrow outside the country instead of at home. Besides, there is the United States market, which is likely to be attractive to them; and there again an extra half per cent in the London rate for colonial loans would increase the chance of the Americans being able to meet the requirements of the colonies at a competitive figure.

4003 (MR BOWEN) *Have you considered the effect of your proposals upon colonial markets and the effect it would have upon inter-colonial trade or trade between ourselves and the colonies?* I do not think it would have any great influence.

4004 *If the colonies require money—and we are told that they do—do you think this would act as a deterrent to their obtaining money and directly or indirectly affect their prospects of trade with the home country?* That raises the whole question of the use of our own resources. We have a certain surplus available for foreign investment which is best invested in that way. My criticism is not against all foreign investment as such, but a legislative contrivance which gives an undue advantage to it.

4005 *But we are up against public policy in some respects. If we are to encourage the colonies, do you not think it would have a very injurious effect upon colonial trade, if you were to say to our investors: 'You must not invest in colonial investments'?* We should not say that.

4006 *But it would amount to that. It would very substantially restrict their operations, anyhow, and people who had money and who could invest only in gilt-edged securities, would be debarred from the colonial market altogether by your proposals. The colonial market would be open, therefore, only to the other people who had money to invest?* There are some people who think it primarily important to develop the colonies; there are others who think it primarily important to develop good conditions at home. It is a question of the balance between those two ideas. I believe that we ought to pay more attention than we have paid lately to the conditions at home, the return on which, in terms of public welfare, would be quite as great as the return we get from loans to the colonies.

4007 *I should be inclined to agree with you on that, but at the same time in making this distinction you make such a sweeping suggestion here that it would help my view if you would suggest any margin or line of demarcation. How far would it prevent trustees from investing in colonial stock?* The present law is that there are certain stocks to which trustees are limited if they are not specially empowered, but there are a great many investors in the gilt-edged market who are not limited in that way. Many trustees themselves are not limited in that way. It happens that there are now a number of colonial loans which, for technical reasons, because they stand above par and are redeemable within a certain number of years, are not available as trustee investments, and they consequently carry a higher rate of interest. It would not follow from my proposal that no investment would be made in the colonies. It merely means that a special artificial stimulus to investment there would be removed.

4008 *You think that if debt were repaid in any substantial sum above, say, £50,000,000 a year, all that would be directed onto the gilt-edged market again. Could you tell us why you have come to that conclusion?* Not all of it, but if a man holds gilt-edged securities there is a presumption that that is the type of security which suits him. Therefore, if you repay him, there is a presumption that he will reinvest the proceeds in a similar type of security.

4009 *But we have been told so often that there are people who invested in War Loan because of the national security at the time, not because it was a gilt-edged security. Could it be assumed that, if debt were repaid in larger measure than £50,000,000 a year, at least a great portion of the sum so repaid would find its way back into industry?* I should have thought that the proportion of holders of gilt-edged securities who held them for those reasons was now small. That was a strong reason for taking up the loans when issued, but it is rather a muddle-headed reason for going on holding them now. It does no injury to the state if a man sells War Loan. It did give assistance to the state when he subscribed to it.

4010 (SIR ALAN ANDERSON) *With regard to the Treasury having a voice in saying what should be trustee securities and what should not, it does not reflect at all upon one's confidence in the brains of the Treasury, but at first it would put them in an impossible position with regard to the colonies, would it not?* I think that the method would be that the Treasury would decide that over a given period of time a certain amount of loan was to be allocated to colonial borrowers, and they would then call a conference of the various colonial borrowers and arrange the division amongst them. In the case of the Australian Commonwealth, which is much the most important, it would probably take the form of the Commonwealth itself deciding how the amount was to be distributed between the Commonwealth and the various states. I think it would be much simpler to work if all except home investments were cut out, but I think it is going too far to say that the other arrangement is unworkable.

4011 (CHAIRMAN) *Suppose the Australian Government gets £4,000,000 loan from us, how is that £4,000,000 paid? Do they get it in the form of money or goods?* They get it in the form of goods in the end.

4012 *That bears on the point of whether there is an advantage in lending money for the sake of the home trade?* I do not think there is ever any advantage in getting rid of goods just for the sake of getting rid of them. An equal home investment would cause just as great a demand for labour.

4013 *Would there be the demand?* I am assuming that that is so. If there was no eligible home borrower on a sufficient scale then my objection to colonial loans would drop; but my argument is that there are outlets at home which, owing to the character of our organisation, at present do not get their fair chance as compared with colonial loans.

4014 (SIR ALAN ANDERSON) *You say that because of this inequity of the Trustee Act we are unfairly handicapped in favour of the colonies?* Yes, we are handicapping ourselves.

4015 (CHAIRMAN) *What is your next point?* My next point is one which may not interest the Committee at all. I am continuing the same line of argument that I was on before—that the cheapest way of carrying the national debt is to create the type of bond that the investor wants. I gave that as the criterion between short-dated, long-dated and intermediate-dated debt, because there are some people who want their interest fixed and some people who want their capital value fixed. But there is also another class of person, namely, persons who want to be free from risks arising out of variations in the value of money. I do not know how large that market is, but I know that such people do exist, and I think that the state could float a certain volume of bonds economically by catering for that particular class. My proposal would be that the Board of Trade or some suitable body should prepare an index number in accordance with the variations of which the interest and the capital of the loan would be paid. No one would be compelled to subscribe to such a loan except persons who fancied that arrangement. But particularly those, who are connected with corporations which have a very long life, have a natural anxiety on matters of this kind. I might perhaps speak for myself as Bursar of a Cambridge college. The colleges in the past have held the greater part of their property in the form of land. They have also held property, partly manorial dues, which have been fixed in terms of money. In the course of time all their property which was fixed in terms of money has ceased to be of significant value. They have been entirely dependent for their continued prosperity on the fact that their fortunes were not wholly committed to legal tender. Recently for obvious reasons there has been a strong tendency to sell their land and to invest in gilt-edged securities. They are therefore getting into the position, which is dangerous, of having their fortunes in legal tender instead of in real property. I think it is correct to say that in past history every long-lived institution which has had its property in legal tender instead of in real values has been ultimately ruined, because in the long run the value of any legal tender always falls towards zero, if you are considering considerable periods of time. There are other investing bodies, particularly those who are engaged in building up pension funds, who are interested in their fund having a given purchasing power at the end of a considerable period of years. Any pension fund in any part of the Continent of Europe which was invested in gilt-edged securities before the War, has now lost by far the greater part of its value. It has been the case in this country that all funds invested in this way prior to the War have lost a large part of their value. We may hope that that kind of misfortune will not occur in this country in future, but if you are considering a long period nobody can feel sure that it will not. Therefore there are certain investors who would be prepared to take a slightly lower rate of interest in order to insure themselves against that type of misfortune. In think it would be proper for the state to cater for that class, and I think it would also be advantageous to have an official index number of this sort, which could be taken advantage of by other borrowers than the state if they thought fit. The proposal I am making is nearly the same as one which was made by the late Professor Marshall when he gave evidence before the Commission on Depression of Trade in 1886, and again before the Gold and Silver Commision of 1888. I believe the advantages which were claimed for it then are even greater now.

4016 (SIR CHARLES ADDIS) *Would there not be a difficulty in regard to dealings in those bonds? That would depend on their popularity.*

4017 *You would have to make your estimate of what the changes would be in the years ahead?* You could assume that they would have a certain value on the hypothesis that prices would remain the same. As regards the future, you would have to make no more calculations than you have to make at present. Anyone who invests in gilt-edged securities as against ordinary shares, has to make the calculation of whether he thinks over a period of time prices are going to rise or fall.

4018 *You do not think there is much difficulty in regard to dealing with these?* It would be a little less easy to bury your head in the sand.

4019 (SIR ALAN ANDERSON) *And the interest would be settled each year?* Yes.

4020 (MRS WOOTTON) *Do you think there is any prospect of converting any of the existing debt to a bond of that kind?* I think there would be. I think many people would dislike them intensely. The element of variability of money income would not appeal to certain classes; there would be a complication about it; it would be more difficult to understand. On the other hand, I think there are types of investors who would like them very much, and it would depend on the number of such persons when you came to test the market.

4021 (MR BOWEN) *What would be the basis of your index figures?* I do not think it would make very much difference which of the standard types of index number was selected, but I should aim at something rather like the cost-of-living index number, than the wholesale index number; I should prefer a special index number for the purpose.

4022 (SIR CHARLES ADDIS) *You contemplate the issue of bonds for a considerable period of years?* Yes.

4023 (MRS WOOTTON) *May I put a question on another point? In an article which was written by you some time ago, you made a suggestion that instead of devoting sinking fund moneys to repay debt, the Treasury should lay out a sum, possibly £100,000,000 a year, on obtaining productive assets. Would you explain that, and could you at the same time give us your views on the proposal that was put up, that a similar sum should be earmarked for debt reduction or the acceleration of public works?* It is a big question: if you can spare me a few minutes I could develop it. My view is that in modern conditions there has been an insufficient supply of capital at moderate rates for public utility enterprises, which would absorb large sums of money. Owing to the control of profits and rates, and so forth, which is now popular, an investment in a public utility enterprise is very unlikely to yield the investor any unusual gains; he will never be allowed to obtain more than a certain rate of interest. On the other hand, he is not secured against loss. The result is that the inducement to the investment of money in large public utility enterprises is very much less than it was, for example, during the period of the railway boom, when our railways were built. In those days it was realised that it was a speculation, in a sense, but it was hoped that if railways proved a good thing, the investor would make a great deal of money. Supposing that steam locomotion was discovered today, the investor would know that, owing to the control of rates and so forth, he would never be allowed to make anything substantial; and, on the other hand, he might lose his money. I am, therefore, very doubtful whether, in present conditions, the railway system of England could be built by unaided private enterprise. I believe that considerations of this sort stand in the way at this moment of the development of our ports, of our transport system, and of our power system, and that the policy of leaving these to unaided private enterprise is a thing which is no longer practicable. As to the forms in which the state can help, I think there ought to be great variety. In the quotation to which Mrs Wootton referred, I do not mean to suggest that the Treasury should put this amount of money in directly, but that it should facilitate the investment of some such sum in various ways.

4024 *Guarantees?* Guarantees; and I think that a number of experiments might be made as to the best channel for doing this.

4025 (CHAIRMAN) *The Treasury give guarantees now?* We are drifting in that direction; it is already being done. I should like to do it more consciously and on a larger scale. I believe that the public utility enterprise is a thing which as an object of private investment we have killed already by our control of profits, and so forth, and we are liable to suffer because we are now in an interregnum period in which in half of our ideas we have a sort of semi-socialism and in another half of our ideas we still depend upon unaided private enterprise. Public utility enterprise is the sort of thing which particularly suffers in a situation of that kind. This is closely connected with this drift of money abroad to the colonies. In the colonies they have gone faster; they are not in that *interregnum*; the state assists all sorts of things which are not assisted here. I think that is dangerous, and I think that the situation wants looking into. I cannot think that there is so small a need for investment in public enterprise as is actually going on.

(CHAIRMAN) *Thank you very much.*

The witness withdrew.

Keynes appeared before the Committee again on 6 May 1925 to give evidence on a capital levy. His evidence appears as the Appendix to Part II this volume.

Keynes returned to the problems of investing abroad in a brief unsigned note in a Russian debts supplement to *The Nation* of 18 October 1924.

From The Nation and Athenaeum, *18 October 1924*

DEFAULTS BY FOREIGN GOVERNMENTS

The record of defaults by foreign Governments on their external debt are so numerous, and indeed so nearly universal, that it is easier to deal with them by naming those which have not defaulted than those which have.

All foreign Governments which have borrowed any considerable sum on the London market* have been in default in whole or in part on the service of their external debt within the past twenty-five years, with the exception of Chile and Japan. It should, however, be added that the defaults by Peru have been insignificant, and those by Uruguay not very important unless we go back to 1891.

The defaulting Governments include those of all the states of Central and South America, with the above-named two or three exceptions. Other important defaulters within the past twenty-five years include Mexico, China, Egypt, Turkey, Greece, Spain, Portugal, Russia, Austria, Hungary, Bulgaria, and Roumania.

Indeed, it is not an exaggeration to say that it has been very exceptional in the history of foreign investment for a foreign government to keep its engagements.

In addition to those countries which have technically defaulted, there are several other countries which have borrowed externally in terms of their own currency and have then allowed the currency to depreciate to less than half of the nominal value at which the loans were contracted, and in some cases to an infinitesimal fraction of it. The more important countries in this group are Belgium, France, Italy, and Germany.

* The Governments of Scandinavia and Holland, neither of which have borrowed more than relatively small sums, are amongst the exceptions.

When Parliament met at the end of September 1924 the Labour Government faced a vote of censure over its handling of the prosecution of a communist who allegedly had incited mutiny amongst the forces. The Government rejected possible compromises that would have avoided defeat in the House, lost the vote and appealed to the country in a general election called for 29 October. Keynes took no part in the campaign beyond a speech on 25 October at the Corn Exchange in Cambridge in support of the local Liberal candidate F. R. Salter and a widely publicised letter on his behalf.

To F. R. SALTER, *18 October 1924*

My Dear Salter,

I hope you will obtain much support as Liberal Candidate for the Borough of Cambridge. Liberalism has a part to play just as important as in the days of its full strength.

The man who looks ahead ought to vote Liberal. For if Liberalism was to decay, we should be left with one party representing Wealth and Conservatism up against another party representing Labour and Discontent. No Government lives for ever, and I can conceive nothing worse for all of us than a see-saw struggle on class lines between the Haves and the Have-Nots. We shall never get, that way, the evolution of a better society.

But the man who thinks of the tasks immediately ahead of us ought to vote Liberal too. Our most pressing problem is to mitigate unemployment and to raise our standards of output, of housing and of wages. To do this we must increase the mobility of labour between one job and another, organise more skilfully the employment of credit, and direct more wisely the use of our annual savings. (Personally, I attach great importance to improving the equipment of England herself rather than foreign countries.) By reason of their old fashioned dogmas and the class-interests they are compelled to serve, neither Socialists nor Tories are likely to do anything sensible and effective in the near future.

I imagine that the official Labour candidate has no chance of getting in, and that your real opponent is Sir Douglas

Newton. All voters with progressive sympathies, who care about peace and liberty and new ideas and commonsense, should join their forces to put you in against him. Mr Baldwin in his Election Address, has left so many loop-holes for protectionist measures that it will be imprudent for any free trader to vote for Sir Douglas.

There are some people in Cambridge who like stick-in-the-mud for its own sake. Let them vote for Sir Douglas Newton. But let everyone else vote for you.

Yours sincerely,

J. M. KEYNES

After the election returned a Conservative Government with a substantial majority, Keynes looked at the results more generally.

From The Nation and Athenaeum, *8 November 1924*

THE BALANCE OF POLITICAL POWER AT THE ELECTIONS

The statistics of the Election in round numbers, compared with a year ago, can be put in a nutshell, thus:—

(*a*) The number of those entitled to vote was 800,000 more than last year.

(*b*) The number of those who did vote was 2,000,000 more than last year.

(*c*) The Conservatives polled 2,000,000 more, Labour 1,000,000 more, and Liberals 1,000,000 less (after allowing for the constituencies where, this time, no Liberal was standing).

(*d*) Thus of the 3,000,000 new voters and Liberal deserters the Conservatives captured two-thirds and Labour one-third.

As usual, on our present electoral system, the turnover in power has been altogether out of proportion to the turnover in votes; 2,000,000 voters out of 20,000,000 decide the Government of the country. As a broad generalisation, 70 per cent of the electors are steady partymen who can be expected to give the same straight party vote every time. The distribution of this 70 per cent between the parties changes very slowly; at the present time perhaps 28 per cent is Conservative, 14 per cent Liberal, and 28 per cent Labour. Of the remaining 30 per cent, nearly 20 per cent abstain from voting, leaving us with the 10 per cent of wobblers who settle matters. Even the best political tacticians sometimes forget this. They pay too much attention to the party bondsmen and too little to the free men,—the unprejudiced, independent wobblers, who hold the head high and govern us by slightly inclining it to the left or to the right.

Now, owing to the geographical concentration of the strength of Labour in certain parts of the country, particularly in comparison with the Liberals, who are distributed more evenly, Labour's minimum representation is unlikely to fall at any time much below its present figure of about one-quarter of the House of Commons. But, on the other hand, it is, for the same reason, very much more difficult for Labour to obtain an absolute majority of the whole House. For example, if every single voter throughout the country who voted Liberal last week had voted Labour, the Conservative Party would still have had a comfortable working majority of more than fifty seats.

Thus, in order to get an independent majority, the Labour Party would need to capture not only the whole of the Liberal Party, but all the wobblers too. Actually, if the Liberal Party broke up, a considerable portion would join the Conservatives, and thus render the latter almost impregnable in many parts of the country.

What practical conclusions can we draw from this analysis? First, that whilst the Liberal Party cannot expect in future to obtain an independent majority in the House of Commons, it still commands a balancing power which will probably be decisive in one election out of every two.

Second, that it would need exceptional circumstances to give the Labour Party an independent majority,—such circumstances as the combination of several years of Tory misgovernment with a falling standard of life for the mass of the workers. Some sections of the Labour Party would like to stay in the wilderness waiting for the exceptional circumstances. Some day or other distressful economic conditions might yield them a brief opportunity to try extremist experiments. But, on the other hand, large elements in the Labour Party are capable of seeing that social improvements can only come as the result of clear thinking and cool action, and that the tumultuous exploitation of acute distress would give reforms a poor chance to succeed. New social experiments will not get a fair opportunity to prove their worth, unless they can be introduced in times of normal prosperity.

My third conclusion, therefore, is this. We are not likely to see, for many years to come, a progressive Government of the Left capable of efficient legislation, unless Radicals and Labour men stop cutting one another's throats and come to an agreement for joint action from time to time to carry through practical measures about which they agree. Probably not less than 10 per cent of the British electorate are natural Radicals. Their mentality and their feelings and sometimes their class sympathies are distinct from those of the typical Labour enthusiast. Their proper place is outside the Labour Party. They form a nucleus around which from time to time a substantial body of voters will collect. No important reforms will ever be carried in this country without their intellectual, moral, and numerical support.

On 6 November Keynes delivered the Sidney Ball lecture at Oxford under the title 'The End of *Laissez-Faire*'. He gave a revised version of the same lecture in Berlin in 1926 before publishing it through the Hogarth Press.[3]

On 11 December, Keynes travelled to Edinburgh to speak to the local Chamber of Commerce and Manufacturers. His topic was 'The Policy of

[3] It appears in *JMK*, vol. IX, pp. 272–94.

this Country towards Foreign Investments'. Keynes used most of the new material in the lecture in his second contribution to *The Nation* for 1925.[4]

From The Nation and Athenaeum, *17 January 1925*

SOME TESTS FOR LOANS TO FOREIGN AND COLONIAL GOVERNMENTS

Recent columns of *The Nation* have contained several criticisms of the prevailing conventions in regard to loans to foreign and colonial governments. From the investment standpoint each proposition must, of course, be considered separately on its merits. But it may be useful to set out a few of the quite simple general principles which seem to me to govern the matter.

It has been common for writers in the financial press to take the line that, other things being equal, there is a positive advantage in foreign investments as against home investments, because of the stimulus which they afford to our export industries. This is surely mere fallacy. An investment at home provides just as great a stimulus to trade and to employment as an investment abroad. It is not a peculiarity of foreign investment that it should involve, directly or indirectly, the production and sale of goods. On the other hand, so far from there being a presumption in favour of foreign investment as such, there may be, in the present situation of this country, a fairly strong presumption against it. As a rule, an additional foreign investment does not cause, directly and in itself, a corresponding addition to our exports. This is only the case where the borrower expends the proceeds of his loan in purchasing British goods which he would not purchase otherwise. If this is not the case—and frequently it is not the case—the grant of a loan to an external borrower may produce a situation in which, *unless we export more*, our account does not balance. That is to say, market conditions are produced through the state

---

[4] His first on 'Inter-Allied Debts', which appeared on 10 January, is reprinted in *JMK*, vol. XVIII, pp. 264–8.

of the exchanges and the rate of interest which lead us as a country to press our goods more insistently than before on the markets of the outside world. In order to provide for our foreign investment we have to force on these markets a greater volume of exports. And in all probability, in order to do the larger business which is thus required of us, we must be content to sell our exports at a lower real price. Now, there is a certain volume of exportation which we can conduct at prices satisfactory to ourselves. But the more we have to export in order to cover our imports and our foreign loans, the less satisfactory this price will be. There is a great difference between foreign investments which are caused by a previous surplus of exports, which has put the international balance unduly in our favour, and foreign investments which are the result of convention and our investment arrangements and exercise a forcing influence on our exports in order to balance the account.

For these reasons, therefore, there is much to be said in favour of home investments, since they are much less likely to turn the ratio of real interchange with foreign countries against us. When we do lend abroad, the foreign or colonial loan must make out a strong case. In order to justify itself it must be exceptionally lucrative or likely to facilitate British enterprise abroad and the production of commodities of which we stand in need. There are many classes of foreign investment which have manifestly satisfied these criteria in the past. Foreign investments in mines and plantations, for example, must have justified themselves many times over. But it is not foreign investment of this type which is absorbing large sums today. We lend to the Governments of India and the colonies every year something like double the capital which we have put into *all* the coffee, tea, and rubber shares quoted on the London Stock Exchange. The latter investments are individually small; and even the sums which they absorb in the aggregate are trifling compared with the sums which a colonial government will think nothing of borrowing in a day. It is, therefore, mainly loans to foreign and colonial governments which must be examined with a critical eye and be called upon to justify themselves on every ground.

I suggest that there are certain broad conditions which such loans should satisfy, before they can be reckoned as satisfactory investments either for individual investors or in the national interest.

(1) It must be clear that the service of the aggregate foreign debt of the borrowing government is well within its financial capacity even in the event of the supply of new loans drying up and of the service of the existing debt having to be met out of current income. Any case in which a government appears to be borrowing substantially more than the equivalent of the service of its existing debt, and is therefore piling up indebtedness at compound interest, and has been pursuing this course for some considerable time, deserves extra-careful consideration, especially as to whether the whole of the sums borrowed are being invested productively so as to yield a progressively increasing income out of which the ever-increasing service of the debt can be safely met.

(2) It ought to be made a condition of any loan to a foreign or colonial government that there is a specific sinking fund attached to it which operates by drawings or by purchase in the market, so that the capital of the loan will be reduced year by year and be automatically extinguished by the due date. Many recent loans to foreign governments satisfy this criterion. If it had not been for this, the British investor would certainly have fared much worse than he has with his loans to the governments of South America. For, in the absence of a specific sinking fund, the probability of the loan's being repaid at the due date is extremely remote;—it will be refunded and the real repayment further postponed. When we turn, however, to loans to colonial governments we find that they rarely carry a specific sinking fund attached to them. In most cases there is a general sinking fund by which a certain sum is applied out of the budget towards the reduction or avoidance of debt. But this is no substitute.

Such general sinking funds may be applied either to internal debt or to new expenditure. They are a feeble guarantee for the repayment of the foreign lender. At the present time some colonial government loan falls due for repayment every few months, and is almost always refunded instead of repaid. If colonial government loans are to retain their present position in the list of trustee investments, the Treasury should at any rate lay down a regulation prescribing that in every case there shall be a specific sinking fund operating year by year in the market, so as to extinguish the loan to which it is attached by the date of the latter's maturity.

(3) It is relevant to inquire whether the country is borrowing abroad at a considerably lower rate of interest than it is paying at home. Thus British investors, for example, who are prepared to lend to the Commonwealth of Australia at a lower rate of interest than will content the people of Australia for similar loans, are surely in an unsatisfactory situation. There is a strong temptation to the Commonwealth Government, so long as the disparity of rates persists, to borrow abroad rather than at home. As soon as exchange rates have settled down there is an inducement to large British investors to transfer into the internal loans in exchange for the external loans. Moreover, there is no inducement for the gradual repatriation of the external loans into the hands of Australian investors themselves, which in the case of a country gradually growing in wealth is one of the most satisfactory means of discharging the external debt. In such circumstances, therefore, the foreign lender necessarily exposes himself to the possibility of some loss in the capital value of his investment through the tendency of the external and internal rates of interest to come together as time goes on.

(4) Fourth and most important of all, investors must never forget that in the case of external government loans there is no legal redress whatever in the event of default. This is a fact which in the past investors have often enough discovered to their disadvantage when it is too late. All kinds of circumstances can

331

arise when it is no longer to the interest of the external government to treat foreign lenders fairly. The temptation exists as soon as the service of the existing debt is a heavier burden than the benefit which can be derived from any probable future borrowings. This fact must render a loan to an external government a less desirable investment, other things being equal, than a mortgage or a high-class home debenture. Such loans, therefore, can never be regarded as satisfactory to the investor, unless they yield a materially higher rate of interest than can be obtained on the finest home debentures. There is also a further reason for an adequate margin in the rate of interest obtained, which applies, indeed, to all fixed interest investments. In the case of all investments in bonds and debentures there can never be any unexpected profit to compensate for the losses of capital which are bound to occur from time to time, even from the most carefully selected investments. The only fund, therefore, from which a margin can be obtained to average out such losses is in the surplus yield of interest obtainable on the bonds.

Let each investor test for himself his holdings of foreign and colonial government securities in the light of these facts. In the case of foreign government loans the investor has suffered so severely in the recent past that the market price may have fallen in some cases low enough to be tempting;—though it is difficult to be satisfied that the ever-present risk of default has been fully allowed for. I much doubt, however, whether the ordinary run of colonial government securities yield anything like the margin they should, on the above tests, in comparison with our own British Government securities.

If one looks back to pre-war days it is obvious that the conventional attitude towards Austrian and Russian Government loans, for example, was highly imprudent. In the case of Russia, in particular, everyone knew well that she had been borrowing excessively and satisfied none of the above tests. I am not sure that twenty years hence some of our present conventional canons of investment may not seem, in the light of subsequent experience, as ill-advised in their way (though not, I hope and expect, so excessively disastrous) as some of those of the pre-war period are now seen to have been.

With the election of a Conservative Government in October 1924, sterling rose strongly against the dollar on the foreign exchanges, largely for speculative reasons. This rise took it from $4.49 on 31 October to above $4.72 at year's end. In the new year it moved even higher. The rise in the exchange, plus the assurance of a stable Government for a full Parliament, gave the question of Britain's future exchange rate policy a new urgency in official circles and elsewhere. Keynes turned to the issue first on 21 February in his annual review of the speeches of the Clearing Bank chairmen under the title 'The Return Towards Gold'.[5] This article was extensively discussed in the Treasury.

Two weeks later he returned to the issue of currency policy after Bank rate rose to 5 per cent on 5 March.

From The Nation and Athenaeum, *7 March 1925*

THE BANK RATE

In May, 1924, the rediscount rate of the Federal Reserve Bank of New York stood at $4\frac{1}{2}$ per cent. Between then and August, 1924, this rate was reduced by successive stages to 3 per cent. The price level followed suit. In May, 1924, prices had been showing for a year past a declining tendency; but by July, 1924, the index number had turned round, and has been rising ever since. Between July, 1924, and the end of January, 1925, dollar prices rose by about 10 per cent,—a rise which, if it had occurred in pre-war days within an equal period of time, would have been regarded as almost unprecedented and in a high degree dangerous. The cheapening of money, coupled with an 'open market policy' on the part of the Federal Reserve Banks, which made money abundant as well as cheap, was, in vulgar language,

[5] *JMK*, vol. IX, pp. 192–200.

'asking for it'. During the same six months the aggregate credit created by the New York banks increased by the enormous figure of 30 per cent. As well as the above big rise of prices, an investment boom, the largest, measured in volume, ever experienced, duly followed.

In recent weeks a change in 'open market policy', following on some losses of gold and a tendency of the member banks to use more freely their borrowing powers from the central institutions, indicated that the Federal Reserve authorities might be beginning to take notice. On Thursday of last week, February 26th, the New York rediscount rate was raised to $3\frac{1}{2}$ per cent,—a small measure in itself (the rate has never fallen below $3\frac{1}{2}$ per cent in most of the Reserve districts), but indicating which way the wind was blowing.

Throughout the whole of this period the Bank of England rate had stood at 4 per cent. This figure is not strictly comparable with the American rediscount rates, since these usually stand below the market rate, whereas Bank rate here usually stands above the market rate. Nevertheless, the effective English rate has been about $\frac{1}{2}$ per cent above the effective American rate (corresponding to the difference of 1 per cent in the respective official rates). At the same time, the quantity, as well as the price, of credit has been kept almost stationary,—the deposits of the London Clearing Banks stood at the same figure in January, 1925, as in July, 1924, as compared with the increase, mentioned above, of no less than 30 per cent in New York. This did not prevent some rise in our prices sympathetically with the rise in America. But as against their rise of 10 per cent, our rise was only 4 per cent; whilst the dollar–sterling exchange has moved in favour of sterling by 8 per cent.

It is obvious that conditions have been almost ideal for an improvement in the exchange without the necessity for any drastic action on the part of the Bank of England. But if the tendencies in America were to turn round the least bit, even if the position there was to become stationary, it would make a great difference. It is not surprising, therefore, that the Governor of the Bank viewed seriously the movement in New York. A special meeting of the Court was summoned immediately, and the Bank of England's loan rates were raised forthwith by 1 per cent as a prelude to the raising of Bank rate.

This is not likely to be a popular consequence of the policy of a return to the gold standard. But those who think that gold is not the best criterion for the regulation of a credit system are not yet entitled to complain. Though our price level has not risen so much as America's, yet it has definitely risen. The interest on long-dated securities in London is so low, in relation to what borrowers are prepared to pay, that the London market has been unduly attractive to new issues of external loans, with the result that their total volume has tended to exceed the volume of the national savings available for this purpose. The use by the Bank of England of its power of putting on private pressure, behind the scenes, to prevent new issues is dangerous and unsatisfactory, and cannot be permanently effective. Four per cent is probably below the true rate of interest, and there is a presumption, therefore, against the continuance of such a low rate *so long as prices are rising*. There are, therefore, some good and substantial reasons for the Bank of England's action.

The one solid argument on the other side is to be found in the state of employment. The figures for unemployment are actually worse than they were a year ago,—mainly on account of the state of the coal, steel, and shipbuilding industries. This is a reason for being extremely critical of the present governance of our affairs. But although it may be necessary, once a slump has been allowed to occur, to allow to industry the stimulus of a substantial price rise from the bottom of the slump, it is not wise at the phase of the credit cycle which we have now reached, even if it is tempting, to try to cure unemployment by allowing actual inflation. I doubt if a 5 per cent Bank rate, which is not oppressive in itself, will do any measurable harm to employment, provided that the price level shows no tendency to fall. It will do harm in one contingency only—and in that contingency it will do great harm—namely, if the rise in the Bank rate is interpreted by the business world as a prelude to falling prices.

This brings me to the point of real danger. We do not know for certain how to interpret the Bank of England's policy. If the policy is merely to keep our prices relatively stable, to wait for higher prices in America to carry sterling to par, and to proceed after that with the utmost caution and deliberation before committing ourselves to any definite action, then I see but little in a 5 per cent Bank rate to disturb the business world. If the business world could be promised that the Bank of England will do all in its power to protect them from a falling price level, even by lowering the Bank rate if necessary, then they can go ahead in quiet confidence. I agree, therefore, with Sir Josiah Stamp's contention, in the admirable letter which he contributed to Tuesday's *Times*, that industrialists should be given an assurance that no reversion is intended to the discarded policy of deflation, and that it is not the policy of the Bank of England to regard conditions in America and the foreign exchanges as more important than the needs of industry at home.

But if the policy is to restore the gold standard *coûte qu'il coûte* by the end of 1925, then the outlook is not so comfortable. It may well be that $3\frac{1}{2}$ per cent in New York will not do very much to check the incipient boom, and that the recent movement is not to be regarded as a first step by the Federal Reserve authorities to taking the position firmly in hand. But the opposite may also be the case. In this event the early removal of the embargo on the export of gold may involve a heavy sacrifice in the form of increased or continuing unemployment. The maintenance or raising of the Bank rate under conditions of falling prices would be highly injudicious in the present condition of British industry and trade.

Some people think that it is inconsistent to oppose a higher Bank rate at a time when prices have been falling and to support it, at a much later phase of the trade cycle, when prices have been rising. To be sometimes in favour of dearer money and sometimes in favour of cheaper money seems to them like being sometimes a Protestant and sometimes a Roman Catholic. But to think in this way is to overlook the very elements of the argument. What influences enterprise and employment is not the money rate of interest, but the anticipated real rate of profit over the period of the productive process; and this latter is compounded of the Bank rate and the anticipated movement of prices.

The essence of our industrial health, it seems to me, lies in confidence,—that is, in the business world being able to lay its plans free from anxiety lest their anticipated profit will be obliterated by a falling price level. Many writers in the press are arguing that the important risk to avoid is the risk of fluctuations in the American exchange. I think that they see things out of proportion. Only a part of our total production is materially affected by the dollar exchange; and for this part there is no difficulty whatever in insuring the risk very cheaply by dealing on the forward exchanges. On the other hand, almost all producers are affected by the sterling price level, and there is no means whatever of insuring against its movements.

Keynes's suspicions of 7 March that a change in policy was afoot were certainly strengthened by a meeting he attended at the Chancellor of the Exchequer's on the evening of 17 March. At that meeting, Keynes, Bradbury, McKenna and Niemeyer argued about the merits of alternative policies. The next evening, Keynes discussed the issues with the Commercial Committee of the House of Commons. His remarks appeared in *The Nation* for 21 March. The previous day, the Chancellor, Foreign Secretary, the Governor of the Bank and the Prime Minister met and agreed to announce a return to the gold standard at pre-war par in the Budget speech on 28 April.

From The Nation and Athenaeum, *21 March 1925*

THE PROBLEM OF THE GOLD STANDARD

The problem of the gold standard is often discussed as though it was a question of an automatic or self-regulated standard *versus* a managed standard. But this is not the real distinction between the orthodox party and the reforming party. The real distinction is one, not of method, but of object. The essence of a gold standard, in modern conditions, has very little to do with gold itself regarded as a commodity of intrinsic value. Its main object is to establish a uniform standard of currency, which shall be the same over a great part of the world, and which shall be independent of national politics. Unfortunately, these advantages cannot be obtained without the penalty of having to regulate our credit system, with all the far-reaching effects which this exercises over our industry and trade, with reference, not solely or even mainly to our own internal requirements, but to the conditions of credit in the world at large and more particularly in the United States. The main object of monetary reformers, on the other hand, is to evolve a standard of currency regulated primarily by reference to the requirements of the credit system at home and to the stability of internal prices, even when this is only possible at the expense of fluctuations in terms of the standards of other countries, for example, the mark or the dollar. Monetary reformers do not deny the great advantages of an international currency unit. But they think it better to evolve a good standard first (with the hope of universalising it later if possible), thus enabling our own credit system to run smoothly—which they deem almost a necessity for industrial stability; rather than to accept an unsatisfactory international standard, in the hope of improving it later on by organised international co-operation.

But whilst the *objects* of the two schools are thus contrasted, the *methods* of currency management, which each would have to employ to attain its object, are almost exactly the same. A fully automatic and self-regulating metallic standard has not existed in this country since the eighteenth century, and perhaps it was not fully automatic even then. The best, and indeed almost the only, example of such a thing in the twentieth century was the Egyptian currency immediately before the war. Where most of the business of a country is carried on by means of a credit system of the modern type, central management of the currency becomes a necessity. The best example of an attempt under modern conditions to reduce the element of central management to a minimum was to be found in the United States under their pre-war organisation prior to the establishment of the Federal Reserve System. This state of affairs proved so disastrous, particularly in the crisis of 1907, that it became the preoccupation of all thinking American bankers to evolve a managed system.

The course of events in England during the nineteenth century is instructive. The wars of Napoleon brought an inconvertible managed currency for a period of more than twenty years, just as the Great War has brought us the same thing for a period of more than ten years. Then, as now, the management, under the appalling difficulties of war and post-war conditions, was open to criticism. The relation of government finance to inflation and deflation was not fully understood. Then, as now, vicious war finance was allowed to breed inflation and virtuous post-war finance to breed deflation. Then, as now, the orthodox party proclaimed that the one thing necessary was to restore gold convertibility; and a little more than a hundred years ago the deed was proudly done. The results were shocking. We suffered twenty years of successive credit maladjustments and crises, the most disturbed and troubled we have ever known, barely escaping revolution. The growing discontents of the business world culminated in the famous reform embodied in the Bank Act of 1844. The peculiar Act is largely responsible for the myth about our having an automatic gold standard, which persists in the newspapers to this day. The reformers of that time, led by Lord Overstone, perceived that our troubles came from our pretending to have an automatic gold standard whilst really having an unmanaged credit system. Their solution consisted in laying down the principle that, whilst credit-money should still be allowed within limits, it should be made to behave exactly as it would behave if it were actually made of gold. This reform, if it had worked as its authors intended, would indeed have resulted in the virtual abolition of the credit system and the restoration of something very like an automatic gold standard. But in dealing with credit-money, the authors of the reform thought only of banknotes and forgot bank deposits. Thus the effect was not to crush the credit system, but only to drive it from note-issue banking into deposit banking; and the main ostensible object of the Act was quite defeated. The real reform thought only of bank notes and forgot bank deposits. of the Bank of England, and the adoption of the reformers' ideas about the Bank's discount policy, which were not embodied in the Act at all, gradually led to our at last obtaining a managed credit system. On this system, for fifty years, we flourished moderately.

I am afraid that this historical digression has been a little long. I return to my point that the credit system of this country will be a managed system *anyhow*. No one supposes that we can fix our normal gold reserve at (say) 40 per cent of our aggregate note issue and then leave it to the commissionaires of the Bank of England to announce that the Bank rate has gone up or down according as the reserve has fallen below or has risen above the percentage adopted as normal. To avoid sudden and injurious fluctuations, it will be necessary for the Bank of England to exercise the utmost foresight and to take steps long in advance of the actual inflow and outflow of gold, and, on the other hand, to ignore movements of gold when, in their judgement, such movements are due to exceptional and temporary causes. When the Bank Court thinks that it must act, its weapons will be Bank rate and, at times, the purchase or sale of Government securities. A managed currency, which aims at stability of internal prices and of internal credit, will operate in just the same way. The same amount of foresight will be necessary, and the instruments of action will be the same. Nothing will differ except the object. Under the gold standard the object will be to keep the percentage of gold in reserve within a certain number of points above or below a normal figure. Under the stable purchasing power standard the object will be to keep (say) the Board of Trade index number within a certain number of points above or below a normal figure. Apart from the initial difficulty of whatever is unfamiliar, I do not think that any more skill is required to work the one system than to work the other,—because in either case the technical problems, both of prognostication and of control, are essentially the same.

At any rate, on this occasion it is the monetary reformers who are the cautious folk. My concrete proposal is, after all, not very alarming—namely, that we should continue, broadly speaking, under the same legislation and employing the same methods and machinery of management as during the past two years, but with this difference, that we should have as our object the stability of internal prices and the adequacy of internal credit to the requirements of our own trade and industry, instead of the gradual deflation of our prices relatively to those in the United States. The new problem before the Bank of England would not be any more difficult than their present problem.

On the other hand, to declare at an early date that we bind our currency unit irrevocably to gold, is certainly rash. We should not be returning to the pre-war system. We should be taking the risks of a new and unknown predicament. For we should be trying to run a managed credit system disguised as an automatic gold standard, in the totally new conditions created by our indebtedness to America, the concentration of gold in America, and the establishment of the Federal Reserve System in America. Certainly we should no longer call the tune. A movement of gold to or from America, which would drain or swamp us, would be almost unnoticed by them. Certainly conditions in America would play a bigger part in determining our Bank rate and our credit conditions than the needs of our own trade. Certainly we should run the risk of having to curtail or raise the price of credit to our own industries, merely because an investment boom in Wall Street had gone too far, or because

341

of a sudden change of fashion amongst Americans towards foreign bond issues, or because the banks in the Middle West had got tied up with their farmers, or because the American President was dead, or because the horrid fact that every American had ten motor-cars and a wireless set in every room of every house had become known to the manufacturers of these articles. Alternatively, we might be swamped with cheap American money upon which we could not rely.

With our industries in their present struggling condition and employment at its present level, I reckon it of the first importance that we should keep the control of our internal credit system in our own hands. We are not in a condition to stand shocks or storms. I think that we shall make a big mistake if we expose ourselves to them, merely for the convenience—for really it is little more—of a fixed rate of exchange with the dollar. Any important change in the cost of living and the general level of prices, whether up or down, will endanger industrial peace. Every contraction of credit, brought about by the external situation and not required to check an incipient boom at home, will take away from the employer the possibility of expanding, or even of maintaining, the amount of work on hand.

Mr McKenna, after defending the gold standard by pointing out its disadvantages, ended up with the naughty expectation that it will probably depreciate in the long run and so give us a little inflation without loss of apparent respectability. I think that his forecast is very probable. But I am concerned only secondarily with the long run of gold, whether up or down. My pressing concern is the the short-period fluctuations round the mean value, and with losing the control over our credit system, which we might have used, if only we paused to think, for the mitigation of the curses of unemployment and trade instability.

The worst of this controversy is that nine-tenths of it is carried on by people who do not know the arguments on either side. But perhaps that is true of all controversies. Nevertheless, one who is in the minority must make the best he can of what practical politics permit. The leaders of all three political parties have strapped on their blinkers and have decided to see nothing ahead except gold convertibility as our ultimate objective. Let me therefore offer three concrete proposals, not incompatible with their declarations, the adoption of which would reduce the risks I have been describing:—

(1) Whatever happens, the idea of restoring gold convertibility by allowing the existing embargo on the export of gold to lapse on January 1st next is needlessly rash. It would only serve to commit us in advance to do something in circumstances we cannot foresee, which we should not do voluntarily with our eyes open. Those who were in favour of the discarded policy of deflation naturally want to commit us in advance to the possibility of its reimposition. All those, however, who were opposed to the deflation policy of two or three years ago, should carefully avoid this trap. An announcement in advance of the impending removal of the embargo could have only two objects—to commit us to what we should not do with our eyes open, and to assist the immediate return of sterling towards parity by stimulating speculation on the exchanges. The second object is as foolish as the first; for speculation in favour of sterling will be followed by an equal and opposite reaction which will increase our difficulties later. It is desirable, therefore, to pass a Bill continuing the embargo *subject to the discretion of the Treasury* to remove it, when they judge it wise to do so. Is it not clear that the removal of the embargo should be the last stage of the transition—not to be accomplished until after sterling has been maintained at par *de facto* for some considerable time?

(2) The return to convertibility probably involves the amalgamation of the currency note issue with the Bank of England note issue. The terms of the amalgamation present some interesting problems. It would be well to get this question out of the way, before touching the embargo. If this is done, the future convertibility of the new note should be fixed, not in terms of sovereigns, but in terms of bullion. That is to say, the Bank

of England should be liable, not to cash individual notes in sovereigns, but to provide gold bullion against notes in amounts of not less than £1,000 at a time. This would avoid risk of the return of sovereigns into circulation.

(3) The right to send gold to the Mint should be restricted to the Bank of England, and the Bank's price for gold bullion offered by importers should be left to the Bank's discretion. This would enable the normal buying price for gold to be fixed somewhat higher than was the case before the War, above the fixed par of convertibility. It would also leave the Bank discretion not to buy additional gold if, in its judgement, we were in danger of being flooded. I attach great importance to this provision.

There would be room for an interesting Currency Bill on these lines. Being an impenitent economist, I should still be dissatisfied at the slowness of our statesmen to adopt the real cures, which lie to their hand, for some of our present evils. But if I was an industrialist, I should, if these suggestions were adopted, look forward to the near future with less anxiety.

Keynes's remarks before the Commercial Committee were the object of substantial editorial comment. *The Times* on 19 March devoted several paragraphs to the address and drew a correction from Keynes.

To the Editor of The Times, *19 March 1925*

Sir,

The three paragraphs in which your City Editor comments on my recent address to the Commercial Committee of the House of Commons mistake the drift of my argument.

My main concern was with the importance, in present industrial conditions, of retaining full control of our credit system, so as to regulate the supply and the price of credit by reference to our own conditions (including, of course, in these our export trade), rather than in sympathy with the course of events in the United States. Passing all this by, he develops the criticism that a managed stable-price currency would be liable to interfere with our competitive power in the international market. I do not follow the argument by which he reaches this conclusion. In fact, just the opposite is true. A stable-price standard is a much more sensitive instrument than is a fixed exchange standard (e.g., the gold standard) for adjusting a disequilibrium in our terms of international trade. For a movement of the exchange immediately shifts in the required direction the prices of all our exports in terms of foreign money; whereas under a fixed-exchange standard the same result can only be brought about by the long and painful process of altering the whole range of internal prices, loans, and wages, some of which are fixed in terms of money for considerable periods by custom or by contract. As an example of the same principle, Sir Basil Blackett pointed out the other day what great advantages of internal stability India has recently secured by allowing her exchanges to move. In our own case, if the exchange is allowed to fall at the same time that Bank rate is raised, our external competitive power is strengthened during the period of readjustment. But if, when the Bank rate is raised, the exchange is pegged, then our external competitive power is weakened, until the causal train set moving by higher Bank rate, including the lowering of money wages, has been at last completed. Indeed, the real criticism against the stable-price standard is that it is too sensitive in this respect, and I have made suggestions elsewhere (*Monetary Reform*, p. 190 [*JMK*, vol. IV, p. 150]) to remedy this.

Since you head your report of my address 'A Reply to Mr McKenna', perhaps I may repeat what I said to the members of the Commercial Committee—namely, that I agreed with nine-tenths of what Mr McKenna said, and that my purpose was to supplement his exposition and not to correct it. I do not think that he and I differ in any important respect about the risks and inconveniences of a return to a gold standard. But I take less comfort than he does from the thought that in the long run gold will probably depreciate and so give to business men the tonic of a little inflation under highly respectable auspices.

Yours &c.,

J. M. KEYNES

Keynes's letter, when published, produced a comment from the City Editor of *The Times* suggesting that a currency managed to stabilise British prices would undermine Britain's export competitiveness, as current events were proving, and that a return to gold at pre-war parity would be a better course even if it required painful adjustments.

To the Editor of The Times, *20 March 1925*

Sir,

I agree with your City Editor that we have had a managed currency lately. The management, however, has not been directed to establishing a satisfactory state of our own trade and credit 'regardless of the effect on the exchange'; but the opposite. We have been trying to raise the sterling–dollar exchange without sufficient regard to the effect on our own conditions. We have, in fact, succeeded, by attracting American money, in raising the value of sterling, as your City Editor justly points out, above the value to which our export trade is fully adjusted. I agree with him that the disappointing state of trade at this moment is partly due to this policy.

But whilst I quote the success with which recent management of the currency has attained its purpose, as an example of the efficacy of management, it is ironical to have quoted against me the results of a policy, the objects of which are just the opposite of those I advocate.

J. M. KEYNES

Keynes's second letter to *The Times* brought a comment from Wynnard Hooper which suggested that Keynes advocated management of the currency

346

by the Treasury. Mr Hooper opposed such a course and also stated that he believed that price stabilisation was an impossible policy given human nature. Keynes naturally replied the day the letter appeared.

To the Editor of The Times, *25 March 1925*

Sir,

I hesitate to trespass upon your space yet again. This most fundamental problem of modern economic society requires a wider flight of thought and speech than I can expect you to accommodate. Confined within the birdcage of a column, one can but hop helplessly from one small perch to another.

But when Mr Wynnard Hooper gives, with your aid, much prominence to the statement that it is my policy to hand over to the Treasury the future management of our currency, I am compelled to send you a disclaimer. The passage in my *Tract on Monetary Reform*, which Mr Hooper detaches from its context, concludes an argument in which I maintain that he who manages the volume of credit is master, that the note issue merely follows suit, and that, therefore, when credit is managed the note issue needs no management at all and may just as well be left in the hands of the Treasury, who are anyhow entitled to the profit. Mr Hooper is so steeped in the old idea, that the management of the note issue is the essential thing, that he does not notice how I have deposed it by substituting the management of credit.

So far from wishing to diminish the authority of the Bank of England, I regard this great institution as a heaven-sent gift, ideally suited to be the instrument of the reforms I advocate. We have here a semi-independent corporation within the state, with immense prestige and historical traditions, not (in fact) working for private profit, with no interests whatever except the public good, yet detached from the wayward influences of politics. In the last resort, the Cabinet and the Chancellor of the Exchequer must have their way—in the future, as now and always. But it must be the Bank of England which manages our credit system day by day and takes its orders from no one except in the most public way and under public protest. The Bank of England is a type of that socialism of the future which is in accord with British instincts of government, and which—perhaps one may hope—our Commonwealth is evolving within its womb. The universities are another example of the semi-independent institutions divested of private interest which I have in mind. The state is generally sterile and creates little. New forms and modes spring from fruitful minds of individuals. But when a corporation, devised by private resource, has reached a certain age and a certain size it socialises itself, or it becomes an abuse, or it falls into decay. As time goes on not a few of the institutions which a hundred years ago were individualistic experiments are socialising themselves. But none, perhaps, except the Bank of England—and (should I add?) *The Times* newspaper—has yet completed the process. I differ from the immediate policy of the Bank of England; but it is on the greatness and the prestige of this institution, which no one has done more to increase than the Governor who now holds office, that I rest my hopes for the future.

We still pretend to manage our currency as though we did all our business with lumps of sacred metal. But the pretence wears thinner and thinner. Those who advocate the deliberate management of our credit system from the point of view that our credit money represents not gold but the actual working capital of our industries must not be in a hurry; for they are proposing a big change in a sphere where those who must settle the matter are necessarily unfamiliar with the intricate reasons for the change. The reformers are impugning an orthodoxy and must expect, therefore, at this state to be met with 'moral' objections, with 'psychological' prejudices, and with appeals to the immutability of human nature as exhibited in the fashions of today. At present, to debate monetary reform with a City editor (or an ex-City editor) is like debating Darwinism with a bishop 60 years ago. But even bishops—so why not City editors?—move in the end.

J. M. KEYNES

Keynes also attempted to influence opinion in April with a pair of articles entitled 'Is Sterling Over-valued?'.

From The Nation and Athenaeum, *4 and 18 April 1925*

IS STERLING OVER-VALUED?

The chief reasons for anxiety in the near future, on the part of those who advocate an immediate return to the gold standard, depend upon: (1) whether at the present moment sterling is overvalued relatively to the dollar, and (2) whether business confidence and the present high level of prices in the United States are going to continue in a degree which will obliterate the overvaluation of sterling, or, at any rate, prevent the situation from getting worse.

The publication of the latest figures compiled by the Federal Reserve Board of the United States, as to the relative price levels here and in America, goes a little way towards answering the first question. The figures from February, 1924, to February, 1925, are as follows:—

	Great Britain		United States
	In sterling	Converted to a gold basis	
1924 Feb.	180	160	163
Sept.	172	158	156
Oct.	175	161	159
Nov.	176	167	160
Dec.	177	171	165
1925 Jan.	178	175	168
Feb.	178	174	167

Thus, in February, 1924, sterling prices, converted to a gold basis, were three points below American prices; but in February, 1925, they are seven points higher. This means that, between the two dates, the exchange has improved 6 per cent more than the relative price levels justified. The purchasing power parity theory of the exchanges as between two given dates is, for several reasons, not accurate; but these figures do definitely suggest that some overvaluation of sterling is ruling now. The indexes of prices for March, when we have them, will probably show an aggravation of the situation rather than otherwise.

There is, also, other corroborative evidence. The observed result is just what one would have expected as a consequence of the flow of funds from America to London on capital account, which we know to have taken place; whilst the exceptional difficulty which our export trades are finding in competing successfully in the international markets points to the same conclusion. If our exchanges were 5 per cent lower than they are, with our internal price level unchanged, our industries could afford to abate their prices 5 per cent in the international markets. The rise of the exchange, whatever may have been its cause, is at least a part of the explanation of the difficulties of our exporters. I believe that it would be much better for us, as well as much easier, to let our exchange adjust itself to the present level of our prices and our wages, which have now been fairly steady for some time, rather than to run the risk of having to force down the general level of wages by 5 per cent, at whatever cost to industrial peace. The theory, which some journalists put forward, that a return to the gold standard will, in itself, enable our exporters to offer more competitive prices in the international markets, has no reasonable foundation.

The other question, namely, whether the boom in the United States is going to continue, is still most difficult to answer. If prices rise there, then the return to gold may not involve us in any special difficulties in the very near future. But the reaction in Wall Street and the collapse of speculation in the grain markets have caused a definite setback. The prospects are much more uncertain than they were even a month ago. The Chancellor of the Exchequer has therefore done wisely to put off any decision until after Easter. The reasons for moving slowly and cautiously have grown decidedly stronger since the beginning of the year. If we go back to gold and if prices in the United States do *not* rise, we shall be compelled, at all costs, to force down money wages in this country;—which is not an attractive prospect. I do not see why we should gamble on the future course of American prices, instead of waiting to see what happens.

II

The Return-to-Gold Controversy raises two distinct questions. The one relates to permanent arrangements—the ideal currency of the future. The other relates to an immediate practical problem,—namely, whether it is prudent to tie up our price level in a particular way at this particular moment. In *The Nation* of April 4th I gave some reasons for thinking that our present price-level was too high to justify gold parity. I propose now to compare our level of money wages with those elsewhere in Europe. The following are some representative facts.

(i) The January *Bulletin* of the New York Federal Reserve Bank quotes the following daily wages, converted into gold at the current rates of exchange, paid in November 1924, by a large American company which has factories in the various countries compared:—

England	$2.28
Germany	$1.55
France	$1.35 (Paris)
France	$1.24 (outside Paris)
Belgium	$1.14
Italy	$0.96

(ii) *The Economist* for April 11th states that the skilled iron and steel worker receives weekly £1 18s. in Belgium, £1 13s. 7d.

in France, and £2 2s.6d. in Germany; whilst in England the average weekly wage for shorter hours and for the average of skilled *and unskilled* workers is £3 3s.

(iii) In so far as these figures are a measure of higher real wages in England, there is no reason to complain. In the United States, dollar wages are twice what they are in England. But the above unfavourable comparisons—unfavourable from the competitive standpoint—are partly a monetary phenomenon, due to the fact that the current rates of exchange overstate the relative internal value of sterling in terms of its purchasing power over articles of working-class consumption. In other words, if we sell a unit of export for $1, turn it into sterling, pay out the sterling in wages, and consider how much those wages will buy of articles of working-class consumption, as compared with pre-war days, we find that it will buy much less in England than in Germany, France, or Italy. The figures are as follows (the figures for England assuming that sterling is fixed at par):—

	Gold-cost of living (per cent of pre-war)
England	179
Germany	125
France	103
Italy	121

Gold wages are (in round numbers) 50 per cent higher in England than in Germany, and 100 per cent higher than in France, Italy, and Belgium. Real wages are also substantially higher in England, just as they were before the War,—but not nearly so much higher as gold wages are. Thus our difficulty in competing is largely due, not to higher real wages, but to the fact that relatively, the gold cost of living has risen much more in England than in Europe,—which is another way of saying that sterling, measured in its purchasing power over articles of working-class expenditure, is not worth its gold par.

I do not say that the maladjustment is all on one side. Prices in Germany and in Italy, and, above all, in France, are probably destined to rise,—though reparation payments will exercise a restraining influence in the case of Germany. But some of the maladjustment is on our side, so that gold cost of living and gold wages in England will have to fall somewhat, say by 10 per cent, relatively to those elsewhere, to restore equilibrium. I believe, further, that a considerable part of this overvaluation of sterling has taken place quite lately, that is to say, during the past year, as a result of the rapid improvement of the sterling exchange brought about by our monetary policy. It is the success of our monetary policy in using sentiment, more than deflation, to raise the exchange which is at the root of the difficulties of our export industries. Sentiment is a fading flower, and sooner or later we shall be compelled, if we peg our exchanges, to suffer the necessary relative deflation. When this has been accomplished, our export industries will feel better. But during the process we shall all feel very bad indeed. The return to gold may involve reducing money wages by (say) two shillings in the £ throughout industry. Does any one look forward with equanimity to the risk, even a small one, of this result?

There are three ways, and only three, in which we can get back to equilibrium:—

(1) By letting our exchanges fall until they are adjusted with our prices and wages—which would be wisdom;

(2) By gold depreciating abroad and prices not rising at home—which would be luck;

(3) By forcing our prices and wages down until they are adjusted with our exchanges—which would be misery.

The ascetic aspects of the third course have attractions for some. But the average industrialist, banker, or politician is not really anxious to submit us to a further course of deflation and of strikes and unemployment. Some of them are very uneasy. Others, whilst regretting that we have got ourselves into our present dilemma, by cultivating a misguided public opinion at home and abroad about the importance of dollar parity, feel, nevertheless, that it is too late to turn back and that we must now commit ourselves, with the best face we can, to gambling on (2). I admit that it is a gamble which may have a more than even chance of partial success. Nevertheless, most people now appreciate the dangers and the complexities of the case much better than they did a year ago, and sincerely wish that they had not talked so much about the blessings of hurrying back to par. It is in this chastened mood that the British public will submit their necks once more to the golden yoke,—as a prelude, perhaps, to throwing it off for ever at not a distant date.

Keynes's final contribution to the discussion of the issues surrounding a possible return to gold before the Chancellor's announcement came at a meeting of the Royal Statistical Society on 21 April. The paper under discussion was Alfred Hoare's 'The Bearing of Labour Unrest on the Path to be Taken to Sound Currency'[6]. Keynes's comments ran as follows:

From The Journal of the Royal Statistical Society, *May 1925*

Mr J. M. KEYNES said there was so much in Mr Hoare's shrewd and interesting paper with which he agreed that he would like to get out of the way a point with which he did not agree. He doubted the existence of any direct and necessary connection between sound money, or money of any kind, and a budget surplus. It was true that the restriction of credit could be used as an alternative to high Bank rate, and it was true that budget surpluses could facilitate the restriction of credit, but there was no other close connection between the two. The amount of the budget surpluses required for this purpose would be very small, and credit could equally well be restricted by other methods, e.g., by selling to the public securities which now formed part of the assets of the Bank of England or of the currency reserve. If, however, deflation was embarked upon, it would raise the value of money, and he agreed that in this case social justice might justify some taxation of the rentier to compensate the benefit which he would have received through the increased value of money. In order to do that, however, he would have to be isolated from the other income-tax payers, and that would be difficult

---

[6] For Keynes's obituary notice for Hoare, see *JMK*, vol. x, pp. 310–14.

without appearing to discriminate against the holders of Government securities.

The whole question of currency at this stage raised two distinct questions. There was the question of the ideal currency of the future. There was, also, the question as to whether this was the moment for tying up the price level in a particular way. He did not wish to say anything about the first big question, but to follow Mr Hoare in considering, rather, the immediate future of currency in its relation to industrial unrest.

A year or two ago most people agreed that it would have been unwise to have removed the embargo on gold. Mr Mason and Mr Hirst would, perhaps, have been in favour of removing it at any time, but they would have been in a small minority in holding that view. How far had the reasons that used to make the bankers averse to removing the embargo disappeared? The exchange was in fact very near parity, whereas before it was far from parity. At the earlier dates they feared lest the removal of the embargo might necessitate a policy of deflation at home. Was that fear removed by what had happened in the last year or two, or did it still exist? Personally, he believed there was a serious risk still, and he thought that, because the improvement of the exchange, so far as he could judge, had taken place only in part by an alteration of the price level in England. It had taken place to an important extent by influences of a temporary character affecting the normal flow of capital. If the exchange had improved by influences affecting the flow of capital and not by influences affecting the internal price level, this rendered our exports more expensive to the foreigner.

Mr Keynes thought that at the present moment the trouble of the export trade was partly due to the fact that manufacturers were suffering from an improved exchange without the compensation of lower prices at home. What were the special influences affecting capital that had brought about the result? *Firstly*, the changed attitude of Americans towards European investments, and particularly the fact that what Great Britain had said about her future policy gave the American investor a reasonable expectation that he would make a profit on exchange apart from the interest that he would get upon his sterling security. *Secondly*, the embargo exercised by the Bank of England on foreign loans.

On several occasions in the past he had spoken against the scale on which we had become accustomed to lend abroad; but only with the object that its place might be taken by loans at home. An artificial embargo brought about by authority of the central institution, and uncompensated by increased investment at home, played the devil with the export industries, without offering an alternative employment. If it were true that the present level of the sterling exchange had been partly brought about by these influences affecting capital, then it followed that the end of the period of adjustments had not been reached—because these influences affecting capital must be temporary. In that case, the deflation of internal prices required to justify the existing level of sterling exchange was still ahead. If it were to happen that American prices were to rise and the value of the dollar to fall, the adjustment might be brought about without the need for deflation in this country; but in view of the control exercised by the Federal [Reserve] Board, this course of events could not be counted upon.

If there was a risk of deflation in order to control the situation, the arguments for an embargo that held good a year or two ago still existed. There was a serious risk that, if the embargo were removed, prices here would have to be forced down, and that was a prospect which no one had any right to open up. The country was not in a position where we could afford any such thing. In the present condition of the export industries and of employment a policy that might involve the forcing down of money wages by two shillings in the pound all round showed terrifying prospects, and Mr Keynes could see no wisdom in bringing about adjustment by that difficult means rather than by the easy means of adjustment of exchanges to internal prices.

The economic and social difficulties of forcing down prices in this country were so great that there were no advantages to be obtained from an immediate return to the gold standard to justify such a risk. He believed that to be the essence of the whole problem. The whole point was whether or not the country was running the risk of having to force down sterling prices; and if so the date of the removal of that embargo should be undoubtedly postponed.

Chapter 5

THE ECONOMIC CONSEQUENCES OF MR CHURCHILL

With the announcement by the Chancellor of the Exchequer in the House of Commons on 28 April of Britain's return to gold, Keynes's campaign against the gold standard naturally took a new tack. His first comment, which appeared in *The Nation* of 2 May, contained a mistake which he corrected in the next issue.[1]

From The Nation and Athenaeum, *2 May 1925*

THE GOLD STANDARD

Mr Churchill has done what was expected, and the experience of a hundred years ago has repeated itself. With one improvement;—Ricardo's Ingot Plan, rejected then, has been adopted now, and the public are not to have back their sovereigns.

But there is also another improvement,—one of no immediate significance, but perhaps of great importance to the ultimate evolution of our currency. The free mintage of gold has been suspended, and the right to tender gold bullion for conversion by the Mint into legal tender will belong, in future, to the Bank of England only. The Bank of England will be compelled by law to give gold bullion (in bulk) for its notes at the fixed price of £3 17s. 10½d. per oz. standard; it will not be compelled to give notes for gold bullion at a fixed price. Thus our legal tender can never be worth less than its gold parity; but it may, conceivably, be worth more. This wise provision protects us against two contingencies. If, by some unforeseen development in chemistry

---

[1] Keynes's mistake was pointed out to him by several people, including an audience member at an undergraduate lecture in Cambridge, and Hubert Henderson.

or in the mining of gold, or in any other way, gold suffers at some future time a catastrophic fall in value, we shall be unruffled; for our legal-tender money need not follow gold in a precipitate downward course. It also protects us from being flooded with gold from the United States or elsewhere, as the result of prolonged cheap money or of a changed reserve policy or in case of a war in which we are not engaged. I regard this protection as a matter of supreme importance in the new conditions, affecting the world distribution of gold, which now exist. If it were not for this provision, we should be compelled to follow any conditions of unduly cheap money which might occur in the United States, on the penalty of being swamped otherwise with a temporary flood of gold which we could not use and which would be liable to be withdrawn at any time. As it is, we need not accept in unlimited volume short-money overflowing from New York to the demoralisation of our own money market and of credit conditions here.

But, above all, the new law does not prejudice—in the event of gold tending to fall in value (which, in the long run, is much more likely than the opposite contingency)—the further evolution of our currency. It leaves open the possibility of a future régime—if thought and argument and experience tend that way hereafter—in which, as a compromise between old-fashioned principle and new-fashioned theory, we can have a currency of which the gold value cannot fall below its stipulated parity, but which, subject to this proviso, can be managed in the interests of the stability of home prices and the conditions of our own credit. Progress, in this case, can be continued, along such lines as the consensus of opinion may come to approve, without breach of continuity or of contract.

Thus, if we are to return to gold—and, in the face of general opinion, that was inevitable—the Chancellor and the Treasury and the Bank have contrived to do so along the most prudent and far-sighted lines which were open to them.

There is another matter which deserves emphasis. There can

be no doubt whatever of our ability to maintain the gold standard, once our decision is made. The critics of the return to gold have opposed this policy, because it is unwise, not because it is impracticable. We, in Great Britain, have our currency system fully under control; and the recognised instruments of credit management are fully efficacious to maintain sterling in terms of gold at any value within reason which we may select.

Nevertheless, we shall do well to remember that there is no means, in the long run, of maintaining this parity except by so managing our credit as to establish a gold price level here not higher than the gold price levels of other countries. For a time, it is true, there is another method, namely, by influencing the movement of capital; as, for example, by placing an embargo on the issue of new foreign loans in London (which we are doing now), or by paying preferential rates of interest on foreign balances (which we did during the War and for some time afterwards), or by borrowing in the United States (for which facilities are already arranged). These are all means by which the parity of gold exchange might be maintained, in spite of our internal price level being relatively too high. They are attractive, because they obviate, for the time being, high Bank rate and deflation of credit. They are justifiable to meet a temporary emergency—due to a political scare, for instance—or to frighten speculators. But they are dangerous and generally inadvisable, because they only put off the evil day, and, above all, because of their adverse influence on the export trades. For they are simply devices by which the internal price level, multiplied by the rate of foreign exchange, may be maintained at a higher level than will allow the export trades to quote competitive prices on the international market; and they achieve this through enabling us to pay our way by borrowing instead of by exporting. Our export trades are already in trouble because our exchange has been improved rather by the movement of capital than by the adjustment of internal prices. If we must have a gold standard, we had better play the gold standard game according to the recognised rules.

There remains, however, the objection, to which I have never ceased to attach importance, against the return to gold in actual present conditions, in view of the possible consequences on the state of trade and employment. I believe that our price level is too high, if it is converted into gold at the par of exchange, in relation to gold prices elsewhere; and if we consider the prices of those articles only which are not the subject of international trade, and of services, i.e., wages, we shall find that these are materially too high—not less than 5 per cent and probably 10 per cent. Thus, unless the situation is saved by a rise of prices elsewhere, the Chancellor is committing us to a policy of forcing down money wages by perhaps 2s. in the £. I do not believe that this can be achieved without the gravest danger to industrial profits and industrial peace. I would much rather leave the gold value of our currency where it was some months ago than embark on a struggle with every trade union in the country to reduce money wages. It seems to me wiser and simpler and saner to leave the currency to find its own level for some time longer than to force a situation where employers are faced with the alternative of closing down or of lowering wages, cost what the struggle may.

For this reason I remain of the opinion that the Chancellor of the Exchequer has done an ill-judged thing—ill-judged because we are running a risk for no adequate reward if all goes well. But now the decision is made, let us hope for the best. An upward movement of prices in the United States is not improbable. There never was a moment at which 'sentiment', as distinguished from technical conditions, was more important. The public and the business world of the United States are keeping in the form of bank deposits much more purchasing power than they have ever kept in this form previously, and enormously more than their convenience requires. Nothing is necessary to raise prices except that they should spend these funds or invest them in some other way; and there is nothing but the 'sentiment' of these depositors to hinder this. Once the mysterious spring is released which now holds them back, sterling might soon be worth par without any change in the level of sterling prices. It may even happen that our return to the gold standard may be, itself, the impulse which will release this spring of action.

The gold standard party have had behind them much that is not only respectable but is also worthy of respect. The state of mind which likes to stick to the straight, old-fashioned course, rather regardless of the pleasure or pain and of the ease or difficulty of the passing situation, and quite regardless of particular interests and of anything except the public good as they understand it, is not to be despised. How much preferable is this mentality to that of the financiers of France! But it is a state of mind, all the same, whose unsensationalism may deteriorate into an easy, ill-founded optimism and whose conservatism fails to notice how facts and theories are changing. Like other orthodoxies, it stands for what is jejune and intellectually sterile; and since it has prejudice on its side, it can use claptrap with impunity. This is the party of those who, in the words of Dr Johnson, 'without the instigation of personal malice, treat every new attempt as wild and chimerical; and look upon every endeavour to depart from the beaten track as the rash effort of a warm imagination, or the glittering speculation of an exalted mind, that may please and dazzle for the time, but can produce no real or lasting advantage'. Yet good new ideas are the most important thing in the world; and there is no economic field in which they can do more practical good than in that of currency and credit.

From The Nation and Athenaeum, *9 May 1925*

THE GOLD STANDARD—A CORRECTION

In the article which I contributed to last week's *Nation*, I expressed too rashly a commendation of the Chancellor of the Exchequer's 'Bill to facilitate the return to a gold standard'. The repeal of the provision of the Coinage Act, 1870, entitling private persons to demand the coinage of gold bullion, led me to think that the Treasury was wisely providing against our being flooded, at some future time, with redundant gold, which we did not require, to the demoralisation of our currency and credit. But I forgot Section IV of the Bank Charter Act, 1844, which obliged the Bank of England to pay for gold bullion in terms of Bank notes at the fixed price of £3 17s. 9d. per standard ounce. This provision is not repealed. Thus the position remains substantially as it was before. We are to be compelled to accept gold in unlimited quantities at all times, with whatever effects on the value of our legal tender, and even in circumstances where the Bank of England believes it to be contrary to our interests to accept any more.

This unfortunate decision strips away most of the reasons for consolation which I found last week. Unmitigated conservatism reigns at the Treasury. No word has been expressed even in favour of the famous Genoa Resolution and of aspirations towards an internationally managed standard; no word of notice for the theory, which is now as well established as anything can be, that the cure for cyclical unemployment is to be found in the control of credit; nothing indeed that could not have been said fifty years ago. This sterile, hard-boiled mentality may prove short-sighted politically, as well as scientifically. I agree with the orthodox party that the currency requires, more than most institutions, perpetual protection from cranks and from enthusiastic ignorance. Just because almost no one understands it, it must needs rely on prestige and dogma. But ideas in this field are now stirring everywhere; and no economic institution will be secure from ill-judged innovations unless it is progressive and intellectually defensible. The Report of the Committee on the Currency and Bank of England Note Issues will prove, in this respect, but a feeble bulwark, because it ignores or begs most of the important questions. This might have been an historic document. In fact it is somewhat trivial. The object seems to have been to say as little as possible, and the result is perfunctory.

On one matter, namely, the degree of the over-valuation of sterling, I should like to add something to what I have written in *The Nation* previously. The Committee state in their Report that last February, when [the] exchange was $1\frac{1}{2}$ per cent below par, sterling was probably over-valued by a 'significant' amount (let us say x), which they do not attempt to evaluate; and that, therefore, a return to par will not require a deflation exceeding $1\frac{1}{2}+x$ per cent. To bring this about, they cheerfully add, will not involve any 'further danger or inconvenience than that which is inevitable in any period of credit restriction and falling prices'.

Professor Cassel, in an interesting article just published,[2] has been bolder (and more useful) and has attempted to do the arithmetic. He finds that in February the value of x, that is to say, the over-valuation of sterling, was about 4 per cent. This was on the basis of the Federal Reserve Board's index numbers. The same figures for March yield a somewhat better result. But none of these figures are an adequate indication of the disequilibrium;—for the following reason.

The prices of some commodities, namely, the raw materials of international trade, for example, cotton or copper, *always* stand at or near their international price parity; nothing which happens to the exchanges or to credit can make their gold prices materially different in one centre from what they are in another. A further class of commodities, namely manufactured goods

[2] In *The Times* Banking Number for May 1925.

which are imported and exported, cannot move, in any circumstances, very much above their international price parity; for, otherwise, the trade in them is killed. There remains a third class, of which houses, personal services, and railway charges are examples, which, for a time at least, can depart materially from their normal parity with the other two.

Now the purchasing-power-parity theory of the foreign exchanges maintains that, in the long run, even this third class must come into line; because, otherwise, the repercussion of the wage level and of the cost of goods and services, produced in the 'sheltered' trades but consumed in the 'unsheltered' trades, will so impair our power of competing internationally, that either the exchanges must fall or gold will flow out until the internal price level has been forced down all round.

When we are considering how severe a deflation may be required to balance the situation (failing a price rise abroad), the relevant question is how far the prices of the third class of goods are in excess of their normal parity with the first and second class. But the ordinary index numbers are largely made up from the prices of the first and second class, with the result that the disparity of price in the third class is watered down on the average of the three classes taken together. If, for example, the weight given to the third class is only a quarter of the whole, the true disparity may be three or four times as great as the result shown by the wholesale index numbers.

For this reason the cost-of-living index numbers, in which goods of the third class play a much larger part, may sometimes give a better clue to the real situation than the wholesale index numbers, which are made up so largely of the first class. I gave some figures bearing on this in *The Nation* of April 18th.[3] I give below a more complete table of the changes in the gold-cost of living in various countries, as compared with 1913, based on figures published by the Federal Reserve Board.

This table shows that these countries fall into three groups:

[3] Above, p. 352.

January 1925	Gold–cost of living (1913 = 100)
Holland	181
Sweden	179
Great Britain	176
Switzerland	170
United States	158
Canada	149
Australia	148
New Zealand	147
Spain	138
Belgium	137
Germany	124
Italy	123
France	103

the first comprising Great Britain and the other European countries whose exchanges have been restored to their gold parity; the second the United States and the Dominions; and the third the other European countries. It is obvious that the exports of the countries of the first group must be at a serious disadvantage, as compared with 1913, in competing with countries in either of the other groups. It is this table which gives the true picture of our difficulties and our prospects. The Committee on the Currency and the Chancellor of the Exchequer exhibit no sign of having considered it.

When the Chancellor of the Exchequer, Winston Churchill, mentioned Keynes's article of 2 May and its approval of the Government's policy in the course of the second reading debate on the Gold Standard Bill, Keynes also sent a correction to *The Times*.

To the Editor of The Times, *5 May 1925*

Sir,

The Chancellor of the Exchequer quoted me yesterday in the House of Commons as having written that the return to gold had been contrived along 'prudent and far-sighted lines'. I wrote this, unfortunately, under the misapprehension that the repeal of the right to the free mintage of gold would protect our currency from being flooded out in certain contingencies. But I forgot Section IV of the Bank Charter Act, 1844, which obliges the Bank of England to buy gold bullion in unlimited amounts at £3 17s. 9d. per standard ounce. We are therefore, unprotected in a spot where—I had prematurely hoped—a protection had been provided.

I can see no far-sightedness, but, on the other hand, much imprudence in the present circumstances of the world distribution of gold, in maintaining a provision to compel the Bank of England to buy gold bullion without limit at a time when, in the considered judgment of the Bank itself, it may be contrary to our national interests to do so. For this is not a case in which political pressure will influence the Bank contrary to its better judgement.

The Chancellor defended his proposal by arguing that if we were flooded with gold we could use it to pay off our American debt. Mr Churchill has been wrongly advised in this matter. The danger to be avoided is a flood of *temporary* American loans arriving in the form of gold. The Chancellor's proposal to use these funds to pay off our debt to the American Government would amount to replacing a funded debt to the American Government by a debt, repayable at call, to the American money market—an act of obvious folly.

The objection to a gold standard is that it sometimes exposes us to the disadvantages of deflation and sometimes to those of inflation. The first are those which we are risking in the near future; and there is nothing now to be done about it—we must just hope for the best. The second are, in my opinion, the likelier in the long run. Against these we could have guarded ourselves by repealing Section IV of the 1844 Bank Act, and thus giving to the Bank of England a discretionary power to protect our currency from serious depreciation. It is a very great misfortune that the new Bill does not do this.

I am, &c.,

J. M. KEYNES

On 7 May at the annual meeting of the Royal Economic Society there was a discussion of the national debt. Lord Holden was in the chair for the discussion, while the discussants were Keynes, Hugh Dalton, Owen Fleming, R. G. Hawtrey, Alfred Hoare, P. D. Leake and D. H. Macgregor. Keynes's comments ran as follows:

From The Economic Journal, *September 1925*

I see only two reasons for expediting the repayment of debt. The first is to facilitate the raising of funds on behalf of public bodies which require new capital for productive purposes. The second is to increase the amount of the national savings. The first reason does not hold good always, and I do not think that it is valid at the present moment. In 1920, on the other hand, when the housing programme was beginning and public bodies were requiring large sums for investment, I saw no harm but much good in the repayment of the debt. More recently the demand from public bodies has been much diminished. I have argued that the maintenance of a heavy sinking fund at such a time, in conjunction with the provisions of our Trustees' Act, unduly stimulates the flow of capital into the hands of public bodies abroad. I quite foresee a time arising when there will again be an outlet on a large scale for capital at home, and I think it would be good policy to hasten it by governmental activities on a much greater scale than at present. There would then be a reason for converting the dead weight debt into a productive debt. That would be my criterion rather than the repayment of debt as such.

The other ground, namely, the stimulation of saving, was mentioned by Dr Dalton. I quite agree with him that by no means all the money which is taken from the taxpayer in taxes for use in the sinking fund would be saved if those taxes were removed; whereas, on the other hand, almost all the holders of the debt will re-invest their money when they are paid off. If, therefore, there is reason for thinking that saving is on an inadequate scale, that is an argument for the sinking fund. At the present moment, I believe that the heavy rates of taxation

367

militate against activity and the running of risks, and I do not think that the need for additional savings is so urgent as to justify heavier taxation in order to bring about this indirect stimulation of it. There, again, circumstances might change. But these are the two criteria which I should apply in determining the amount of the sinking fund from year to year.

The arguments on the other side seem to me to be partly æsthetic and partly an appeal to the potency of compound interest. For example, the tidying up of the published figures of the national balance sheet seems to make a considerable appeal to some people. Above all, anyone who toys with the national debt can produce a vivid picture of the accumulations of compound interest after a certain number of years. But although compound interest produces the most visible and impressive picture in the case of the national debt, it also works elsewhere in the community, and I would look, rather, to cumulative economic progress by the operation of compound interest in the community at large where it is less directly visible. You do not make compound interest more potent because you take money away from individuals and use it in this particular way. The burden of the Napoleonic wars was taken off our shoulders not by a sinking fund, but by the general progress of the community in the next hundred years. Now I should be very chary of allowing the apparent burden of the national debt to induce me to put on taxation so heavy that it might hold back the general progress of the community.

Another reason which often weighs, I think, is the false analogy between the debt of the individual and the debt of the state. There is no real analogy between the two. An individual's motives for clearing himself of debt may apply to the external obligations of the state; but they can have no application to its internal obligations. I think it would be better, therefore, if we were to confine our attention to the two criteria with which I began.

Keynes's *Nation* article of 9 May (above p. 363) came under attack in the next issue, when a correspondent who signed himself 'Economist' suggested that he had presented a distorted version of one of the arguments used by the Currency Committee by taking sentences out of order and adding his own gloss to the text. Keynes replied.

From The Nation and Athenaeum, *16 May 1925*

I have read the Report again in the light of the above letter, and can discover no misrepresentation. 'Economist's' point seems to be that the Committee's Report consists of a series of entirely disconnected sentences, and that one must not read any one of them in the light of any other. The Committee stated (*a*) that the credit conditions necessary to maintain parity would come about 'automatically and rapidly', and that this would mean no 'further change or inconvenience than that which is inevitable in any period of credit restriction and falling prices',—this being their *only* remark about the method of maintaining parity and its results; (*b*) that in February sterling was overvalued by a 'significant' amount; and (*c*) that, since at that time exchange was $1\frac{1}{2}$ per cent below par, the *extra* adjustment of maintaining parity, in addition to the adjustment under (*b*), would be $1\frac{1}{2}$ per cent. I brought these three statements into logical connection. If this is illegitimate, the Committee's Report is even more incoherent that I thought it was, and also more completely lacking in any discussion of the most important relevant issues. The real questions are: (1) How much is sterling over-valued, [and] (2) by what train of events will adjustment be brought about? Is it 'Economist's' contention that the Committee expressed no opinion whatever on these matters? My own view remains that they did quite clearly express the rather superficial view which I attributed to them. As for 'Economist's' last paragraph, there is not a word in the Report to suggest that the Committee do view credit restriction with serious apprehension, and it was that fact which I wanted to suggest by my word 'cheerfully'.

Later in the month *The Economist* of 23 May, in the course of a review of the materials submitted to the United States Senate's Gold and Silver Inquiry, compared Keynes's contribution (above pp. 289–93) with his letter to *The Times* of 5 May on Mr Churchill's contribution to the second reading debate on the Gold Standard Bill (above, p. 366). It then asked for an explanation of the apparent inconsistency between the documents. Keynes replied.

To the Editor of The Economist, *23 May 1925*

Sir,

In your review of an article, which I contributed last year to *European Currency and Finance*, you ask for an explanation of the discrepancy between my accepting therein the argument that we can get rid of redundant gold by anticipating repayments of American debt and my more recent rebuttal of this argument. There is no explanation—except the following, if this can be considered an explanation.

In the article under review I was considering the absorption of the annual supply of new gold; in my letter to *The Times* I was considering a flow of gold from America as the result of a flood of short loans from New York to take advantage of higher money rates in London. A proposal to check the latter flow by what amounts to using the American short loans to increase the net total of our permanent foreign investment, is obviously both futile and imprudent—as I pointed out. I assume that you agree with this. The objection to the same method in the former case is a little more subtle, and I overlooked it. In this case the method amounts to attempting artificially to increase the flow of our net foreign investment so as to permit the price level here to remain, more or less permanently, below its equilibrium level; in fact, to produce here much the same condition that the Dawes Scheme will attempt to produce in Germany. This might be practically feasible, and would not be open to the same immediate dangers as in the other case considered. Nevertheless, you will, I expect, agree—as I now admit—that this also is objectionable and unsound in the long run.

Yours, &c.,

J. M. KEYNES

In *The Economic Journal* for June 1925, Keynes returned to both the Report of the Committee on the Currency and the Gold Standard Act in two brief notes.

From The Economic Journal, *June 1925*

THE COMMITTEE ON THE CURRENCY

Report of the Committee on the Currency and Bank of England Note Issues. (Cmd. 2393.) 1925.

This Committee was appointed by Mr Snowden on June 10, 1924. At the outset the Committee's reference was limited to the question, 'Whether the time has now come to amalgamate the Treasury Note Issue with the Bank of England Note Issue, and, if so, on what terms and conditions the amalgamation should be carried out.' They heard witnesses about this from June to September, 1924. But at some later date—probably in January 1925—the Committee decided to interpret their task so as to include the general question of an immediate return to the gold standard. They did not, apparently, at this second stage of their proceedings, hear any witness except the Governor of the Bank of England.* In the end this broader issue became the main topic of their Report, and the ostensible subject of their terms of reference is relegated to a few sentences in the last two pages.

The Committee was a strong one, consisting of Lord Bradbury, Mr Gaspard Farrer, Sir Otto Niemeyer and Professor Pigou.† But one cannot say the same of the Report. Their attitude seems to have been that, since a return to gold was in any case

---

* The Committee state that 'proposals for substituting the price level of commodities in general for gold as the regulating principle of the currency have been fully and carefully explained in evidence before us'. Amongst the small number of witnesses examined I am the only one named who is known to be an advocate of this principle. When I appeared before the Committee, however, the only question on which I was invited to give evidence was that of the amalgamation of the two note issues. My evidence-in-chief was wholly directed to this matter, as also was most of my cross-examination, though wider issues came in a few times incidentally. There is no indication what the evidence was, which is referred to in the above sentence, or from what quarter it came.

† Mr Austen Chamberlain, who was the Chairman at the outset, resigned on accepting office as Foreign Secretary.

inevitable, it was useless to examine the objections and indiscreet to contemplate the difficulties. Consequently the less said the better (the Report could be printed *in extenso* in eight pages of *The Economic Journal*), and it was wiser to utter a few conservative banalities than to tackle large questions. But the reader must also feel, as he reads, that the Committee lacked intellectual interest in their subject, and were convinced from the start that there was little to be said on the subject which had not been said a hundred times already.

The result is that the Report amounts to next to nothing, and is more remarkable for its omissions than for what it contains. Two matters which they thought it worth while to discuss were the objection that the restoration of parity is technically impossible, which no serious authority has ever maintained, and the idea of fixing the exchange at 4·79 (the rate existing last February) rather than at 4·86, which no one has ever proposed. Amongst the points, on the other hand, which they thought not worth mentioning, I pick out the following in particular.

1. They dismiss without argument both the proposals for a devalued sovereign and those for a managed currency. This rules out most of the major problems, especially the importance of price stability, the future prospects of gold prices and the possible subordination of our credit system to that of the United States. Nevertheless, since a serious consideration of these questions would have led them far afield, the Committee's decision, to limit itself to the practical problems arising out of the proposal for an early restoration of gold, is intelligible.

2. But neither do they mention the proposals for international co-operation in the regulation of credit, so as to avoid cyclical price movements, which the Geneva [*sic*] Conference blessed in a famous resolution and of which Mr Hawtrey is the foremost advocate. One might have expected that they would have coupled their advocacy of a return to gold with a warning against its possible vagaries and a plea for an organised scheme to mitigate them. But not a word; not a hint even that gold is, or

could be, or ought to be, itself a managed currency. *A fortiori*, the Committee do not mention the possible connection between the working of the gold standard and the credit cycle, and between the latter and unemployment. They show no awareness of the fact that the connection between the management of the currency and the trade instability, of which unemployment is a leading symptom, is the main argument in favour of a managed currency, whether or not on a gold basis, advanced by its advocates.

3. No one was in favour of restoring gold convertibility a year ago—for the reason that to tie the sterling price level to the gold price level would have involved too violent a disturbance of the former. If we contemplate making the restoration shortly, the question for those who direct practical policy is to know how much disturbance it would involve now. It is not an easy question to answer, but it is impossible to act prudently without trying to answer it. The Committee produce no arguments and no figures and content themselves with the conclusion that 'we must still be prepared to face a fall in the final price level here of a significant, though not very large, amount, unless it should happen that a corresponding rise takes place in America'.

They do not tell the Chancellor of the Exchequer that this question of the parity between the internal price level and the external price level is really a question of the parity between one set of internal prices, namely, those of which the sterling price × the sterling exchange is *always* at or near the world price, and those of which the sterling price × the sterling exchange is not sensitive to the prices of similar goods and services elsewhere; and that it is partly the same problem as that of the disparity between the prices in what have come to be known as the 'unsheltered' industries and those in the 'sheltered' industries. An improvement in the sterling exchange necessarily lowers all the 'unsheltered' prices, and if this is unaccompanied by forces tending to depress the 'sheltered' prices to an equal extent, those who produce in the 'unsheltered' industries are in obvious difficulties, because they are selling at the unsheltered price level and, in part at least, buying and consuming at the sheltered price level.

It is not easy to measure the amount of the discrepancy between the two sets of prices. But it is certainly not measured by comparing the index number of wholesale prices here with a corresponding index number in America or in Germany. For such an index number is largely made up of unsheltered prices, which are necessarily, whatever happens, nearly the same in both index numbers; and the effect is to water down and to obscure any disparity between the movements in the sheltered prices here and elsewhere.

My own guess is that, compared with 1913, sheltered prices here are, at the present rates of sterling exchange, perhaps as much as ten per cent too high in comparison with the unsheltered prices, and that the injury thus caused to the competitive position of our exports in the international market is aggravated by the fact that in Germany, France, Belgium and Italy the sheltered prices are fully ten per cent too low. I base this guess mainly on the cost-of-living index numbers and the price-of-exports index numbers.

At any rate, whatever the answer, this is the essence of the practical problem; and a Report which ignores it is not to the point.

4. Assuming that there is some disparity between the two sets of prices, the next question must be directed to the causal process by which equilibrium can, or will, be restored. There are three alternatives:—

(1) the unsheltered prices may be raised relatively to the sheltered prices by a rise in world prices;

(2) the unsheltered prices may be raised relatively to the sheltered prices by a fall in sterling exchange;

(3) the sheltered prices may be lowered relatively to the unsheltered prices.

The first of these alterations is outside our own control—it may, quite likely, come to our rescue, but to depend upon it is a gamble. The second is that which I should have preferred as being calculated to restore equilibrium with the least possible disturbance to the course of production and to industrial peace. If we reject this and decide, on the other hand, to aggravate the disparity by *raising* sterling exchange, we are bound to consider by what causal process the third alternative can be brought about.

The Committee have made no attempt to analyse the facts; but, in so far as they discuss the matter at all, they contemplate that the necessary readjustments can be achieved by raising Bank rate. *How* this will come about—that is to say, by what intermediate steps—they give no indication. Do they mean that, by raising Bank rate and by curtailing credit sufficiently, unemployment can be intensified without limit until, even in the unsheltered industries, wages move downwards? If so, one is bound to admit the theoretical possibility. If not, what precisely is the causal process which they envisage?

I suspect that their conclusions may be based on theories, developed fifty years ago, which assumed a mobility of labour and a competitive wage level which no longer exist; and that they have not thought the problem through over again in the light of the deplorably inelastic conditions of our industrial organism today.

But I suspect also a further confusion of ideas. High Bank rate has two distinct sets of consequences—one, its effect on the international flow of capital provided it is high *relatively* to the rate elsewhere, and the other its effect on the internal credit situation. Now the efficacy of high Bank rate—from the purely financial point of view—for preserving the parity of the gold standard largely depends upon the first set of consequences. If Bank rate is made *relatively* high, the inflow of capital is stimulated and the outflow is retarded. If this tendency is set up strongly enough, the gold parity and the financial equilibrium are completely protected—at least for the time being—and there may be little restriction, if any, of internal credit. But, in this case, the industrial disequilibrium may remain—because the greater the success of the Bank rate in producing the first set of consequences, the less is its success in producing the second.

For how would the process work out in practice? The high Bank rate is just as oppressive to the unsheltered as it is to the sheltered industries; and since the former are already working on a narrower margin of profit, it is they which are likely to go under first. Thus the high Bank rate *may* produce equilibrium (I do not say that it *must*)—not permanently, indeed, but for a longish time—by the progressive destruction of our weaker export industries and, at the same time, making good the deficit thus caused in our trade balance by diminishing, to the necessary extent, the net outflow of capital. Foreign investment provides a sluice, the due regulation of which by means of Bank rate can maintain the internal price level, for years together, either above or below the level outside—limited, nevertheless, in one direction by the volume of available savings, and by the other to the extent that we can live on our capital, or on what we should otherwise save. Since our available balance for new foreign investment has been, even since the War, of the order of £200,000,000 a year, we have this wide margin with which to provide for the closing down of of our export industries and the support of those who were previously employed in them.*

Now the Committee are half aware of this possibility and of the objections to it. They strongly deprecate the use of foreign credits for the support of the exchange. But they do not seem to notice that a high Bank rate, in so far as it attracts foreign short-loan money to London, does exactly the same thing.

The objections to the drastic restriction of credit at home are so pressing and so obvious in the present state of trade and employment, that there will always be a strong temptation to

---

* To avoid misunderstanding, let me add here what I have argued elsewhere, that, in any case, I should like to see some transference of resources from the export trades to capital developments at home, and the use of the above-mentioned margin to finance the latter. But to bring this about satisfactorily would require quite a different policy from the above.

the Bank of England to redress any adverse movement of gold to the maximum extent by attracting foreign money and to the minimum extent by restricting home credit. The recent declarations of the Chancellor of the Exchequer and the action of the Bank of England (at the time of writing) in squeezing up the bill rate, which is what counts in attracting foreign money, whilst leaving other rates unchanged, which are what matter to home credit, already point in this direction. And this is only natural, because the return to gold presents us with an unpleasant dilemma—the attraction of foreign money, which is admittedly unsound, or the restriction of home credit, which is deservedly hateful.

These few remarks go only a little way towards elucidating the problem. But we have a right to expect that the authors of a Report which recommends a high Bank rate as the panacea should present some sort of an account of how they expect their remedy to do the trick.

5. Ricardo recommended an appreciable margin between the buying and selling prices for gold, namely £3 17s. 6d. for the former and £3 17s. 10½d. for the latter. Sweden during the war took precautions to protect herself from a flood of redundant gold. The Genoa scheme for international credit control would be much facilitated if each country was responsible for its own stock of gold and was not free to unload its surplus at any time and in any quantity upon its neighbours. There are indeed many reasons—too many to discuss here—for reserving to ourselves, at this stage, some discretion to protect our currency against undue expansion. I attach very great importance to the Bank of England being relieved of the obligation to buy gold at a fixed price. Certainly the choice is of grave significance. But the oracle is dumb—the Committee do not mention it.

In presenting this Report at the same time as his Budget speech, the Chancellor of the Exchequer declared that 'it contains a reasoned marshalling of the arguments which have convinced His Majesty's Government'. From such a description one would expect an historic document which, whether one agreed with it or not, would take its place in the line of famous memoranda which have moulded our currency policy in the past—at any rate an armoury of up-to-date arguments in favour of old-fashioned expedients. But we find instead a few pages, indolent and jejune.

THE GOLD STANDARD ACT, 1925

The following comments may be made:—

1. After an interval of more than 100 years, Ricardo's Ingot Plan (first outlined in 1811) is, in effect, adopted by Section 1 (2) of the new Act. Ricardo's ingot was to contain twenty ounces troy of fine gold.* In these larger days the size is raised to 400 ounces—worth nearly £1700. Dr Bonar's most interesting article on Ricardo's proposals (*Economic Journal* (1923), Vol. XXXIII, p. 281–304) is worth re-reading in the light of the new Act.

2. The repeal of the right of members of the public to present gold for mintage (Section 1 (1)(c)) is not so important as it appears at first sight, because Section 4 of the Bank Charter Act, 1844, remains in force. This section runs as follows:—

'All Persons shall be entitled to demand from the Issue Department of the Bank of England, Bank of England notes in exchange for gold bullion, at the rate of £3 17s. 9d. per ounce of standard gold...'

Thus we are not to follow (at present) the precedent set by Sweden of reserving to ourselves a discretion not to accept unwanted gold in unlimited amounts. Nor are we to have the limited protection recommended by Ricardo of widening the limits between the buying and selling prices (he suggested £3 17s. 6d. for the former).

3. The new obligation placed on the Bank under Section 1 (2)

* Under the temporary clauses of the Resumption Act, 1819, the Bank was liable to redeem its notes in ingots of 60 ounces. Particulars of actual transactions under these clauses and also an illustration of Ricardo's ingot are given in *The Economic Journal* (1923), vol. XXXIII, p. 291.

to provide gold bullion by weight instead of sovereigns by rate avoids the slight uncertainty which used to exist as to the exact gold points owing to the possibility of the sovereigns obtained being below full weight. The points now depend solely upon interest, freight and insurance. The freight rate outwards has been recently raised to 5s. per cent. On this basis and at current interest rates Messrs Samuel Montagu and Co. put the gold export point at \$4.843 to the £. The gold import point is stated to be in the neighbourhood of \$4.90.

4. Convertibility from, and into, gold is limited to Bank of England notes. Currency notes remain legal tender, but are made absolutely inconvertible. Thus there is no way of obtaining gold for export except by acquiring Bank of England notes.

5. The Chancellor of the Exchequer announced that he had arranged borrowing powers under Section 2 of the Act with the Federal Reserve Board up to \$200,000,000, and with Messrs J. P. Morgan up to \$100,000,000. No charge will be made for the former if it is not used. For the latter a commission of $1\frac{1}{4}$ per cent is to be paid for the first year and half that amount for the second if the credit is not used. Thus £375,000 will be paid if the credit is not used at all.

Keynes returned to currency matters in *The Nation* on 13 June with a brief article on sterling.

From The Nation and Athenaeum, *13 June 1925*

THE ARITHMETIC OF THE STERLING EXCHANGE

The arithmetical effect on the foreign exchanges of the maintenance of a higher rate of discount in London than in New York is often overlooked. The following note is an attempt to indicate it.

In New York 90-day bank bills are discounted at $3\frac{1}{4}$ to $3\frac{3}{8}$ per cent. In London the discount rates on similar bills expressed in sterling are $4\frac{3}{8}$–$4\frac{7}{16}$ per cent; and it is reported that American banks can obtain somewhat higher rates, say $4\frac{1}{2}$–$4\frac{5}{8}$ per cent, on sterling bank deposits. So long as funds are available in New York in the hands of lenders who are indifferent where they hold them and look only to the yield obtainable after allowance for any exchange risk, this difference in interest rates must be approximately reflected in the premium on forward dollars, as compared with spot dollars, i.e., dollars for delivery against sterling at a future date must be worth about 1 per cent per annum more than dollars for delivery against sterling now. This is in, fact, the case, dollars for delivery in three months being 1 cent per £ (i.e., $\frac{5}{6}$ per cent per annum) dearer than spot dollars.

This difference between spot and forward rates of exchange corresponding to differences in interest rates, is now familiar. But it has not been noticed by writers in the financial press that, so long as confidence is felt in gold convertibility, the *forward* rate cannot fall below the gold-export point, and, there, that the spot rate must *exceed* the gold-export point by the amount of the premium on forward dollars.

In the above illustration, dollars three months forward have been taken,—chiefly because this is a date for which comparisons are easy and dealings active. This indicates that the spot exchange must be *at least* 1 cent per £1 above the gold-export point. But the same argument can be applied to a six months' transaction. Six months' sterling bank bills in London are discounted at $4\frac{5}{8}$–$4\frac{11}{16}$ per cent, and six months' dollar bank bills in New York are discounted at $3\frac{1}{2}$–$3\frac{5}{8}$ per cent. Thus dollars six months forward must be worth about 2 cents per £1 more than spot dollars; yet, as before, sterling six months forward must be worth at least gold-export point. Hence in so far as six months' transactions are practicable, the spot exchange for sterling in terms of dollars must stand at least 2 cents per £1 above the gold-export point.

In so far as the same disparity of interest rates applies to securities of longer date, and provided that suitable securities are available, the same argument continued would prove that the spot exchange for sterling must stand at least, as high as the gold-*import* point. The longer the date, however, the greater is the obstacle offered by such items as income tax and commissions. Moreover, the actual disparity between the rates of interest in the two centres is less in the case of somewhat longer-dated securities. Indeed, certain types of bonds, e.g., foreign government bonds, are cheaper in New York than in London. Even so, however, an effective difference of 1 per cent per annum in the rates of interest for periods up to six months is so great that one would expect, in anything like normal circumstances, that the exchange would certainly exceed the gold-export point by more than $1\frac{1}{2}$ cents per £1, which is its approximate level at present, and would probably approach the gold-import point. I have not examined pre-war records in detail, but I do not recall any occasion analogous to present conditions in which sterling interest rates could stand so high above dollar rates without drawing gold.

What requires explanation is, therefore, not that exchange should be so good as 4.86, but that it should be so bad. Owing to the operations of the forward exchanges, the rate of exchange, which can be considered favourable, is not absolute, but is relative to the effective difference in discount rates. If discount rates in London and New York stood at approximately the same level, then an exchange of 4.86 would probably indicate a satisfactory situation. But that it should, in present circumstances, be no higher than this shows either that New York distrusts sterling bills or that New York is, in fact, investing so heavily in this form already that, without distrusting sterling, the New York banks do not care to put any more eggs than they are, in fact, putting into this particular basket.

This last alternative is the probable explanation of the facts. The current level of the exchange, taken in conjunction with the difference of interest rates, suggests that the balance of ordinary payments is running so heavily against sterling that the proceeds of the full amount of bills, which America is prepared to take in response to the rate of interest, are absorbed in settling the account. The comparative stability round 4.86, which has been maintained lately, may be explained by the fact that at any rate below 4.86 the attraction to American banks to remit balances to London is very strong, whilst each movement of $\frac{1}{2}$ cent above 4.86 materially lessens the inducement.

If Great Britain's balance of international payments was level apart from borrowing in America, a difference of 1 per cent in the discount rates might be expected to attract gold from New York. Dear money in London, relatively to New York, *must* keep the sterling exchange above the gold-export point, until our credit is gone or our borrowing power exhausted. But the tremendous efficacy of this policy in supporting the exchange operates primarily by causing us to borrow in New York—just as much as though we were drawing on a loan from Messrs Morgan.

Soon after this article appeared Keynes began to think of approaching the subject on a more substantial scale. His first forum was the Committee on Industry and Trade which was set up during the summer of 1924 under the chairmanship of Sir Arthur Balfour. Sidney Webb had asked Keynes to be a member of the Committee on 24 July 1924, but he had declined.[4] Early in November 1924 the Committee asked Keynes to give evidence to it, but he asked to be excused until the Committee's investigations had become better defined. With the return to gold, however, he offered to give evidence

---

[4] His letter of 24 July 1924 declining Webb's invitation ran as follows.

Dear Mr Webb, One's natural inclination, on receiving such an invitation as is conveyed to me in your letter of to-day's date is to accept. But on reflection I feel great doubt whether I should do well to serve on the proposed Comm^ee. I am alarmed by the vagueness and wide scope of the proposed field of enquiry and sceptical as to the capacity of the usual type of Committee to deal with it usefully. The general upshot is, I suppose—Are the prospects of British Trade good or bad? There are some detailed aspects of this which certainly call for enquiry. But they are, in the main, difficult questions of fact which could only be tackled by a very small Committee of specially qualified persons with a good number of full-time investigators working under them. If—as I assume to be the case—this is to be a fairly large Comm^ee of the usual type, mainly composed of representatives of various points of view who will take evidence, I doubt if they will obtain within a reasonable period of time results proportionate to the labour involved. So very reluctantly and with many apologies, I must beg to be excused. Yours sincerely, J. M. Keynes.

on 15 May. He finally appeared before the Committee on 9 July, prepared to expand on the memorandum which he had submitted in May.

From the Committee on Industry and Trade, Minutes of Evidence

COMMITTEE ON INDUSTRY AND TRADE

THIRTY-FIFTH DAY
Thursday 9 July 1925

Present:

Sir Arthur Balfour (*Chairman*)

Mr John Baker, M.P.	*Secretary:*
Mr F. A. Hargreaves	Mr W. Carter
Sir Norman Hill, Bart.	*Assistant Secretaries:*
Sir John S. Hindley	Mr W. L. Buxton
Mr David Landale	Mr A. R. Fraser
Sir Peter Rylands	
Sir Hubert Llewellyn Smith	

Mr J. M. Keynes, called and examined

16,434 (CHAIRMAN) *Mr Keynes, you have given us a memorandum?* Yes.

Memorandum submitted by Mr J. M. Keynes

16,435 1. The purchasing-power-parity theory as stated by modern economists is very much the same thing as the parity between prices etc., in what are called the sheltered trades and those in the unsheltered trades. That is to say, a maladjustment of the internal price level in relation to the external price level mainly shows itself in the relations between those in the sheltered and unsheltered industries.

2. The prices of some commodities, namely, the raw materials of international trade, for example, cotton or copper, *always* stand at or near their international price parity; nothing which happens to the exchanges or to credit can make their gold prices materially different in one centre from what they are in another. A further class of commodities, namely, manufactured goods which are imported and exported, cannot move, in any circumstances, very much above or below their international price parity; for, otherwise the trade in them is killed. There remains a third class, of which houses, personal services, and railway charges are examples, which, for a time at least, can depart materially from their normal parity with the other two.

3. Now the purchasing-power-parity theory of the foreign exchanges maintains that, in the long run, even this third class must come into line; because, otherwise, the repercussion of the wage level and of the cost of goods and services, produced in the 'sheltered' trades but consumed in the 'unsheltered' trades, will so impair our power of competing internationally, that either the exchanges must fall or gold will flow out until the internal price level has been forced down all round.

4. When we are considering how severe a deflation may be required to balance the situation (failing a price rise abroad), the relevant question is how far the prices of the third class of goods are in excess of their normal parity with the first and second class. But the ordinary index numbers are largely made up from the prices of the first and second class, with the result that the disparity of price in the third class is watered down on the average of the three classes taken together. If, for example, the weight given to the third class is only a quarter of the whole, the true disparity may be three or four times as great as the result shown by the trade index numbers.

5. For this reason the cost-of-living index numbers, in which goods of the third class play a much larger part, may sometimes give a better clue to the real situation than the wholesale index numbers, which are made up so largely of the first class. I give below a table of the changes in the gold cost-of-living in various countries, as compared with 1913, based on figures published by the Federal Reserve Board:—

January 1925	Gold cost of living (1913—100)
Holland	181
Sweden	179
Great Britain	176
Switzerland	170
United States	158
Canada	149
Australia	148
New Zealand	147
Spain	138
Belgium	137
Germany	124
Italy	123
France	103

6. This table shows that these countries fall into three groups: the first comprising Great Britain and the other European countries whose exchanges have been restored to their gold parity; the second the United States and the Dominions; and the third the other European countries. It is obvious

that the exports of the countries of the first class must be at a serious disadvantage, as compared with 1913, in competing with countries in either of the other two classes.

7. There are two alternative ways of bringing about restoration of equilibrium. What may be termed the sheltered prices may be left as they are, whilst the foreign exchange may be allowed to fall somewhat, with the result that the unsheltered prices can rise and yet remain in the same relation to world prices as before. Or, alternatively, we may fix the exchange, thus tieing the unsheltered prices to world prices, and committing ourselves to a policy of somehow or other forcing down the sheltered prices (that is to say, unless the remedy comes about through a general rise of world prices). During the period when [the] exchange has been fixed and before sheltered prices have been forced down, the export trades feel the full blast. For they have to pay sheltered prices for much that they consume, yet cannot secure more than the unsheltered world prices for their products.

8. Failing a general rise of world gold prices which will raise the unsheltered prices, the great question now before the country is by what process of adjustment the sheltered prices can be brought down to the level of the unsheltered prices. On this point I have no satisfactory solution to offer to the Committee. It is not obvious by what peaceful method a general reduction of wages in the sheltered industries is to be brought about. Apparently the official policy is to bring to bear Bank rate and credit restriction in the event of disequilibrium reacting, as it must do in the long run, on our balance of trade. But the worst of this instrument for this particular purpose is that it falls with equal weight on the unsheltered as on the sheltered industries; and since the profits in the former show a narrower margin than those in the latter it is more likely to bring about a restriction of activity in those innocent industries rather than in those which it is necessary to attack. It is not obvious that the high Bank rate and credit restriction will bring about the necessary readjustment except by a process so long and so painful that the country as a whole would certainly not readily accept it.

16,436 *I understand, however, that you wrote it two months ago and would like to make a new statement to the Committee. Do you want to read your new statement?* No. I have notes, but I have not anything written out.

16,437 (MR BAKER) *May I ask how far it will differ from the memorandum we already have, if at all?* It will be in amplification of it. I propose to direct myself to the question of unemployment in its present phase and its relation to monetary policy. It seems to me that the diagnosis of the present state of unemployment is absolutely plain. The remedy is another matter. Unemployment is in its serious aspect confined to our export industries. There is not much abnormal unemployment in those of our industries which make entirely for home purposes. Rather paradoxically this great depression in the export industries is not combined with a general world slump. The conditions outside this country are not on the whole bad. You can find particular quarters of the world, such as China, where there are obvious difficulties in trade, but on the whole I should have said that the general trade situation in the world was fair to good. In the United States it is quite abnormally good. They are doing excellent trade on a level keel without any signs of inflation, and I see no recent evidence that trade is particularly bad anywhere in the British Empire. What we have to explain therefore is the combination of great depression in our main export industries with reasonably good trade in the world at large and reasonably good trade in our own home industries. I believe the explanation of this to be as plain as a pike-staff. We have raised the value of our money internationally during the past year by about 10 per cent, without materially altering either the wage level or the cost of living in this country. That means that our export industries receive in terms of sterling 10 per cent less than they would have received in similar circumstances a year ago, whereas what they are having to pay in wages, and what they can justifiably be called on to pay in wages having regard to the cost of living, is exactly the same as it was a year ago or at any rate not much changed. The result is that this margin of profit is converted into a loss.

I have prepared a table which seems to me to put the matter in a straightforward way. I have taken the cost of living in the United States, the cost of living in the United Kingdom, and the level of wages in the United Kingdom, and I have converted these into gold value; I have made the correction for the sterling exchange during the time it was below par and have modified the amount of that correction in accordance with the improvement in the exchange recently. If members of the Committee would not mind taking down a small number of figures I think I can make it clear. In March 1924 we were in very close equilibrium with the outside world. The cost of living in the United States in 1924 was 156. (I might say that all these figures are as compared with the pre-war figure of 100.) The cost of living in the United Kingdom was 157. The level of wages in the United Kingdom was 155. This is in terms of gold, of course.

16,438 (CHAIRMAN) *What was the level of wages in the United States?* There is no good index number of that. The date I have given you is March, 1924, when as I say there was almost perfect equilibrium. By June, 1924, the position was still much the same; the cost of living in America had fallen to 154, in this country it had fallen to 150, and wages had improved slightly to 157. So that an improvement of real wages had taken place, but we were still not out of equilibrium to any appreciable extent with the United States.

16,439 *Our trade was desperately bad both in March, 1924, and June, 1924?* It was very much better than now, and people were in an optimistic state of mind about the prospects.

16,440 *Was it better in actual figures?* The unemployment figures were much better, and the trade returns were much better.

16,441 *A shade better?* I am discussing the reasons for the abnormal unemployment and the worsening which has taken place in the past year. I think most people a year ago looked to an improvement. My own view a year ago was that things were decidedly taking a turn for the better, and there was no sign that our export trade had abnormal difficulties in competing—any more than they had for some little time past. By October the exchange had begun to improve as a result of the talk about the restoration of the gold standard, and we were beginning to get out of equilibrium, but not seriously. In October the cost of living in the United States was 157, while in this country it had risen to 162, and wages here were 164. By December most of the mischief had been done; the anticipation of the restoration of the gold standard had caused a big improvement in the exchange and by that date the United States cost of living was 158, our cost of living was 174, and our wages 172. By March of the present year the American cost of living was 158, ours 176, and wages 177. In April the American cost of living was still 158, our cost of living 172, and wages 178. For May and June I have not yet got the American figures, but I believe that they are practically unchanged. Our cost of living has remained unchanged, and with the correction for the exchange the figures for May and June are the same as for April, that is to say 172. Wages, for a full working week and making no allowance for short time, have risen a little to 180 in May, and 181 in June. The total result of this is that if you take the rate of wages and do not allow for short time there has been an improvement in real wages. Wages were a little below the cost of living in March of last year, and now they are nine points above. To that extent you may say that wages have been moving in the wrong direction apart from the external situation, but the main thing is that whereas our cost of living and wages were in equilibrium with the United States last March, they are now 10 or 11 per cent higher.

Of course the result is inevitable when that happens. We have improved our exchange 10 per cent, but we have not altered our cost of living, we have not altered our level of wages. If there had been a boom in [the] price level in America that might have lifted us out of our difficulty, but things on the whole there have run pretty level, and the result is therefore what we see. The position is aggravated by the fact that while we are on the wrong side in excess of the United States, taking the United States as the norm, European countries are very much below the United States. In the case of

Germany she is not so much below as she was, but she is still very much below; the stabilisation of the mark has been gradually resulting in an increased cost of living. The cost-of-living figures for Germany are as follows:—In March, 1924, 107; in June, 1924, 112; in September, which is roughly comparable with October, 116; in December, 123; in March, 1925, 136; in April, 137. April is the last figure available. That means it is not easy for Germany to pay quite such low money wages as she could before. Her cost of living has been raised 30 per cent, and her wages not so much, so that her material conditions have been worsening. That means that German wages will have to rise sooner or later. But Germany is still able to give a money wage which is 30 per cent below our money wage, and yet leave German workmen as well off in relation to pre-war as ours are. Their cost of living is 30 per cent below ours, and therefore their money wage may be 30 per cent below ours without the German workmen being badly off.

When you come to France it is more striking still. I do not altogether trust the French figures. I have not made a complete table, but it will be quite easy to follow without a complete table. Taking for example March, 1925, which is the latest date I have, the gold cost of living in France was 94, that is to say, actually less than pre-war.

16,442 (SIR PETER RYLANDS) *I took some figures out of Montagu's weekly report which gives about 110 for France. They fluctuated between 111 and 112, I think?* My figures are taken from the Federal Reserve Bulletin, which is always convenient for this purpose, and corrected for the exchange. My figures are for Paris. Possibly his are for other parts of the country.

16,443 *It may be that in the industrial parts of France it was a little different?* I say I do not trust these figures. I think they are too low to be true. I think your figure of 110 is much more plausible than my own figure of 94, and I would willingly substitute yours for this purpose.

16,444 *The figures I have got, translating them at the average rate of exchange, are 112 in May and 111 in April, 114 in March, and 116 in January?* I readily accept that. I think that is more plausible than mine. At any rate the cost of living in France, whatever the figure you take, is not very much above pre-war. The consequence is that there also they can take a money wage far below ours without their standard of living being actually depressed. I think, therefore, that our difficulties are fully explained by the fact that the gold equivalent of our money wages has been forced by the return to gold out of equilibrium with the rest of the world, and as our cost of living has also been forced out of equilibrium, though not quite to the same extent, it is very hard to force a reduction in the money wage until you have first forced a reduction in the cost of living—the two dovetail into one another.

When the return to the gold standard was being discussed two questions arose: the question of the merits of gold as an eventual standard, and the wisdom of doing it at the moment. I argued very hotly that a decision to return to gold at that moment involved as its corollary reducing money wages throughout the country 10 per cent, and I did not perceive by what *modus operandi* we were going to achieve that result. Therefore I thought this act to be an extremely foolish one until we had thought out by what means we were going to alter the internal price level, because nothing can be more certain than that a country cannot alter the external value of its money without altering the internal value. I thought it particularly dangerous because it aggravated the pre-existing situation. In the case of Germany when they stabilised the mark they were very much below the world level, so that it was not a specially dangerous thing for them to do. They could stand a relative rise of their money values; in fact it would help them towards equilibrium rather than otherwise. The evidence was that even a year ago having regard to everything that has happened since the war, the difference in our investing power and so forth, our internal money values were too high. In order to be in true equilibrium with the rest of the world we already had to reduce the money cost of living and the money standard of wages.

16,445 (CHAIRMAN) *Before the gold question arose at all?* Before the gold question arose at all. So that it was not, as in the German case, something which would tend to compensate a deviation in the other direction from equilibrium; it was something which was calculated to aggravate the existing disequilibrium. It is for this reason that the results have been so rapid and so very marked. There was no initial friction to overcome; it merely accelerated a movement that was already tending to take place.

16,446 *Should there be no compensating advantage in purchasing our foodstuffs abroad?* A certain amount.

16,447 *That will come?* That does come. Our cost of living has fallen 4 points converted into gold, and I should predict that that will go further, for I do not think that we yet have the full benefit of that.

16,448 *Then you come to the point of sheltered industries?* Even in the case of imported food, by the time it reaches the consumer very many home services have entered in in the way of transport, and retail delivery, and one thing and another, and if they are at a high level the benefit of purchasing the prime material at the ports at lower sterling prices has been watered down to a great extent so that you do not get anything like the full benefit in reduced cost of living.

16,449 *Apparently from what you say, in March 1924, before the question of the gold standard arose, we were living in a fool's paradise that could not be maintained in any case?* But that was a result of anticipation of a gold standard.

16,450 *You think so?* I think almost entirely. There had been an enormous movement of funds from America to this country to take advantage of the return of the gold standard which we had been announcing was going to take place. Anybody over there, who believed our announcements, had a profit in his pocket.

16,451 *That was a year ago last March?* Not a year ago: last March.

16,452 *At that time we were living under conditions where we could not do the world's trade on account of our cost?* I believe at that time we were out of equilibrium, but not seriously.

16,453 *We could not do the world's trade on account of our cost, and therefore it is not possible that the return of the gold standard has aggravated this point; it had to be faced in any case?* I think 10 per cent over the whole country is a very big amount; 2s. in the £ in any man's wages is a very big thing. I think that in March, 1924, we had overcome a very large part of the pre-existing disequilibrium which had existed earlier. I believe that if we had kept the exchange adjusted to our position at that date and had not raised expectations of a return to the gold standard, and had had easy money, we could have gone a long way towards abolishing unemployment by now. Things were favourable at that moment. I quite agree with you that we are not in equilibrium, that we are still on the wrong side, and it is very hard to measure how much that was. In my opinion 10 per cent is very big; 2s. in the £ reduction in a man's wages is a thing you can only achieve after a great row. It is not a thing you can slip into without anybody noticing it very much. The decision of the Government to return to gold was *ipso facto* a decision to reduce everybody's wages 2s. in the £. Therefore it was a decision to have a row with every industry in turn.

I regard that as the first stage of the diagnosis. How has the improvement of the exchange actually operated? It operates first of all by our export industries being in difficulties, and by unemployment in our export industries. That reduces our favourable balance of trade. The Bank of England then feels it necessary to counteract that unfavourable balance of trade. Their methods of counteracting it have been two: first of all by an embargo on foreign investment, which has recently been extended to colonial investment as well, and partly by offering rates of interest in London which attract loans from New York. The Bank of England has been creating a monetary situation in which the rate of interest for three or six months' money is 1 per cent per annum more than it is in New York—an absolutely unprecedented situation. So long therefore as an American banker believes that the gold standard is going to be maintained, and that he will be able to take his money away again without loss, he can get 1 per cent per annum more by lending his money in London than in New York. In fact, the gold standard has made our credit so good that we no longer have any need for exports! Credit is only useful to the borrower, not the lender; it is not usual to inquire very strictly into the credit of the lender; it is only on the assumption that we are a borrowing country that we need think about our credit being good. But our credit is so much improved that we have no difficulty in borrowing in New York whatever sum we require to make good the deficiency in our exports caused by unemployment in our industries.

16,454 *That is only a temporary method?* That is only temporary, and is obviously unsound in the long run. The Bank of England has no difficulty in preserving equilibrium for the time being partly by the embargo on foreign investment which reduces the amount we send out of the country, partly by attracting American money which increases the amount which comes into the country. That is one way or another a method of living on our capital, and is therefore unsound in the long run. The Bank of England therefore has to consider other measures to bring down the internal price level so that in the long run we shall be able to live, not by borrowing, but by exporting again.

What methods are open to the Bank of England to bring down the internal price level? There is really no method which does that to any large extent except the restriction of credit, and while that has not gone very far as yet, there are symptoms that there has been some restriction of credit. If the position goes on as at present and we are to continue with bad export trade, that restriction of credit will probably be intensified, if one correctly follows the policy of the Bank of England. How does the restriction of credit bring down internal prices? It brings down the prices of certain raw materials possibly by making it difficult for holders to carry them, and therefore compelling them to throw them on the market. But that is not the main feature, because it is not the price of raw materials that is the trouble. They are at the world price already. The trouble is the cost of wages and the cost of retail distribution, the cost of freight charges and so forth.

16,455 *And railway transport?* I include railway transport in freight charges. Restriction of credit does not directly affect this. The way it works is by limiting the opportunities of offering employment. That is to say, the method of the Bank of England is to intensify unemployment until the workers are prepared to accept lower wages. So that our policy has been first of all to produce a situation in which we were condemned to reduce wages 10 per cent and then finding that that does not happen of itself, as, of course, it could not, the only method open to us (the old-fashioned method of producing equilibrium) is deliberately to intensify unemployment until wages do in fact fall. That is the old theory of the Bank rate for bringing about equilibrium. Unemployment, one should remember, is produced in two ways, partly by exports being non-remunerative, and partly by credit being in short supply. I should say that up to this present stage it is the first of those factors which is the more important. The second factor, however, has been quite important; the embargo on foreign loans in particular, by restricting the capacity of borrowers to place orders has undoubtedly operated, and also the fact that new borrowers find it not easy to raise money, and that new issues are difficult to arrange, and so forth. All that tends to restrict opportunities for employment, and to intensify unemployment. So that as far as I understand the official policy of the Treasury and the Bank of England—though it is only a half-conscious policy—it is to intensify unemployment until wages do come down; and I think the Government in the recent debates, instead of apologising for what happened, ought to have pointed with pride to the comparative success of their methods up to date in that they had produced additional unemployment to the extent of 25,000, that that had already produced a greater willingness to accept lower wages, and that one would hope it would be sufficient to do the trick, or if it was not we should have to continue intensifying unemployment until willingness to accept lower wages was still more apparent than now.

16,456 *But the necessity for an alteration in our cost of production existed long before the return to the gold standard?* I do not think that it existed to any important extent.

16,457 *Trade was intensely bad at the end of 1923 and in 1924?* Yes, but my belief is that we had, given a continuance of easy money, turned the corner in 1924.

16,458 *But we had unemployment in 1922 and 1923 which was worse than even today?* It is only saying that the exchange was already too high at that date.

16,459 *No doubt you will deal directly with the alternative policy and tell us what you think might have been done?* The alternative policy would have been to have kept your internal price level steady because of the immense difficulties of altering it, and allowed your exchange to adjust itself to that.

16,460 *And adjust itself by trade?* Adjust itself by trade. My own opinion is that it was not so far from adjustment. The exchange would always have brought about true equilibrium and would have brought our internal prices to a competitive level with the outside world.

16,461 *We will say that from 1921 even we have not been in a competitive position?* If you go back as far as that we were in a world wide slump. I think that there was a certain period of time during which we, in common with the United States, were suffering from a cyclical depression which was a reaction from the previous boom.

16,462 *It was exaggerated by cost of production?* It was very violent, but it was a more or less normal experience. It was not that we were out of relation to the rest of the world, but that there had been a general disequilibrium between the different factors of production all over the world. America by their monetary policy emerged from that in the course of a year or two.

16,463 *Theirs was a much simpler problem?* Yes it was simpler.

16,464 *They did not owe money?* That is so; it was a bit easier for them. But we by our own policy aggravated the difficulties of our own situation, and that culminated in the policy of the last year. When one comes to the objection to what I interpret the official policy to be, I think that the great difficulty of producing a fall of prices by the intensification of unemployment is that when things reach a certain point the Government is inevitably pressed to do politically things which defeat its own object. On the one hand it will be having a tight credit policy at the Bank of England, and as soon as that tight credit policy begins to produce its effects those effects are so unpleasant politically that the Government begins to take other steps which counteract its own policy; so that you get the process of adjustment spun out much longer.

The next difficulty seems to me to be that you cannot reduce all wages simultaneously by the method of internal pressure as you can by the exchange. If all wages could be reduced simultaneously the cost of living would fall too, and real wages would very likely be very little lower than they had been before, and the working classes would not have suffered; so that if there was any machinery by which you could reduce all wages simultaneously the objections to the policy that I have been outlining would not be very serious. But that is not practicable. The difficulty I see is that those workers who are first asked to accept a reduction have a legitimate grievance because if you ask workers in a particular trade to accept a reduction they have no guarantee that the cost of living will fall and you are in the first instance, until it has fallen, throwing on them a reduction of their real wage against which they can legitimately protest.

16,465 *The reduction should be national really if it were possible?* I do not think you could do that. It is a wide question of course. The other difficulty is that the pressure that you exert falls on the weakest industries first, where unemployment is already greatest. Those industries are generally speaking the industries in which wages are already relatively low, industries where you cannot legitimately ask them in relation to other people's wages to accept less. The paradox is that you want to reduce wages first in those industries where there is least unemployment.

16,466 (SIR PETER RYLANDS) *Are those industries which would least affect the cost of living?* I think if you could put down railway charges, if you could put down retail trade charges, if you could reduce the wage of bakers—

16,467 *But those are not the wages you are talking about. Are you not talking about the wages of the iron and steel workers, and people like that?*

16,468 (CHAIRMAN) *Those are the wages you are talking of as being the least able to bear it?* Those are the wages least able to bear it. The leading instance is the coal industry.

16,469 (SIR PETER RYLANDS) *They would have the least bearing on the cost of living?* They would have the least bearing on the cost of living. They have very little effect on the cost of living and it is rather unjust to expect them to accept a reduction.

16,470 (SIR JOHN HINDLEY) *Do you say coal is one of the things that has least bearing on the cost of food?* It has very little. I do not remember its exact order in the Board of Trade's index number, but its position is not high.

16,471 *Surely from the point of view of transport it has some bearing?* It has some bearing certainly; all these things have some bearing; but it has very little bearing compared with the wages of bakers and other producers for retail, for example.

16,472 (CHAIRMAN) *The point will develop, I think, as we go on. Your point is the cost of food transport compared with the cost of manufactured goods transport, and coal for industry. It will have a big effect on the latter, of course?* The wages index that I am quoting, if it is of interest to the Committee to know what industries it is based on, consists of the wages of bricklayers and labourers, engineering fitters and labourers, dock labourers, railwaymen, woollen workers, cotton workers, miners and agricultural labourers. It is a very wide index.

16,473 *Have we not a totally new situation, which you refer to in your memorandum, in the existence of the higher wages in what are commonly called the sheltered industries?* That is my point precisely. It is the wages in the sheltered industries which are the problem, whereas the wages on which you are bringing pressure to bear are in unsheltered industries which are very likely quite reasonable already until the wages of the other industries may be brought down. If you could reduce the wages in sheltered trades that would reduce the cost of living and then you could then legitimately ask the colliers to take a lower wage.

16,474 *The trouble about the sheltered wage is that it is very largely tied up with special considerations, local considerations, and so on?* They are very difficult to get at, because if an industry has not any more than a normal unemployment it is very hard to see what pressure you can bring upon them to make them reduce their wages. Your instrument of unemployment tends to attack industries at the wrong end of the scale which are comparatively innocent ones. Why did the Bank of England and the Treasury make what I consider this mistake—because I think that throws light on the matter.

I think they made it for two reasons. In the first place they miscalculated the degree of disparity by attending to the inappropriate index number. They attended, I believe—I gather this from the not very clear remarks in the Report of the Committee on Currency [and Bank of England Note Issues]—to the wholesale index numbers. That is a point I deal with in my memorandum. If you want to know the disparity of English home prices it is perfectly useless to take prices of raw cotton in Liverpool, because the price of raw cotton in Liverpool is always the same, when corrected for the exchange, as the price of raw cotton in New York. It must be. The wholesale index numbers are largely made up of the international raw materials which are always at equilibrium, so that if you take that type of index number the disequilibrium you are searching for is very much watered down, and it will appear to be of the order of 2 or 3 per cent when it is perhaps really of the order of 10 per cent. What you ought to look at is the wages index number, the cost of living index number, and the Board of Trade index number of prices of our manufactured exports. Those three things give you the best clue. They would all have led to a conclusion of the order of 10 per cent as being the disequilibrium on the basis of gold parity. But I think the Treasury and the Bank of England have been influenced entirely by the Board of Trade wholesale commodities index number, and that showed a trifling disparity of the order of 2 or 3 per cent. I think that was the first part of their mistake.

I think the second part was that they believed there was some automatic or magical way in which high Bank rate would reduce wages, averting their attention from the fact that the only way in which it could do that would be by intensifying unemployment. I think they did this because they had not re-analysed the facts in the light of modern conditions. They were depending upon the orthodox theory of economic text-books, and that orthodox theory assumed mobility of labour and competitive wages. The way the argument ran was this. If the export trades get into trouble and there is unemployment, there will be a movement of labour from the export trades into the other trades which will bring down wages in the other trades by the competition of these other men offering themselves. The orthodox theory of the text-books assumed that when there is unemployment in the coal industry some of the colliers offer themselves as bakers, and this brings down wages in the baking industry, and so the conditions are very quickly averaged out between all industries, and you cannot have for any length of time this disparity between unsheltered industries and sheltered industries. That is to say they assumed that labour is free to move from industry to industry and from place to place, and that an unemployed man can get himself occupation by offering to work for a lower wage than the standard wage in one of the relatively prosperous industries.

16,475 (MR HARGREAVES) *By displacing another workman?* By under-cutting, and therefore with the result of bringing down the wages in the other more prosperous industries.

16,476 (MR BAKER) *It does not alter unemployment, but the wage rate?* It alters the wage rate. That theory has no relation to the facts at all, however. It is impossible of course for a collier to offer himself as a baker below the standard wages of bakers, that cannot in fact happen, partly because of the power of the trade unions in preventing the cutting of rates by the competition of unemployed labour from other industries, partly because the dole has reduced the extreme pressure to find employment elsewhere, and partly because labour for two reasons is very much less mobile both between places and industries. The reason it is less mobile between places is due partly to the condition of housing. A man has a house in the place where he has been employed, and it is a rash and dangerous thing for him to give up that house to go and seek employment in another part of the country where very likely he will not be able to get a house. The fact that he has a house in one place and no security of getting a house in another place pins him down and so limits his capacity to rove about and find employment elsewhere. The other thing—and I think it is an unavoidable and permanent factor—is that during a considerable part of the nineteenth century we were increasing at a rapid rate; everything was on a general crescendo, just as in the United States now; everything was increasing at the rate of 3 per cent per annum or something of that kind. That meant that when a given industry was too large and another industry too small you did not force a man out of the industry that had too much labour into the other, but you just stopped taking new men in for a certain period of time, and with the rapid general progress going on, the slack would be taken up not so much by driving men out of the industry as by simply stopping the intake for a bit. Then it was very much easier to bring your industry into equilibrium by just not taking on new hands—which you can do when the whole economic machine is stepping forward at a great pace—than by actually discharging men. One sees that illustrated in the case of railways. During the period when the railways were being rapidly extended, supposing the railway companies found themselves with redundant staffs they could right the situation by not taking on new men and using their redundant staff on new sections of line. If they are not opening new sections of line, if they find themselves with redundant staffs, there is no way of dealing with the situation except by sacking men. That is much more difficult both practically and humanly than stopping new men from coming into the industry. So that the old assumption about the mobility of labour and about the way in which a fall of wages in one trade would be reflected in others, in my opinion no longer holds good except in the very

long run. I think it may be true that in the very long run it does operate.
In the course of years low wages in unsheltered industries will react on the
wages of sheltered industries, but it will not react quickly. Therefore the
hypothesis on which the old theory was based as to the way in which you
could bring about equilibrium between the internal value of your money and
the external value of your money no longer holds good. I do not think that
the authorities realised that we are now in a situation in which a forcible
change in the internal value of money is extraordinarily difficult. We are in
something much more like medieval conditions in which it was so difficult
to change the internal value of money that when you were in disequilibrium
with the external value you had what was called a debasement of currency,
leaving internal prices the same and allowing the external value of your
money to fall. The orthodox nineteenth-century theory of keeping the
external value of your money to a certain gold parity, and making the internal
value of your money follow suit, did not work badly in the conditions of that
age; but of course they never tried in that age a forcible disturbance of 10
per cent. The change in the value of our money relatively to the value of
other people's in any given period of time never approached that. So that
they never set themselves so difficult a problem. Apart from that the
conditions in which such a solution would work were much more nearly
fulfilled than they are now. I therefore regard our present situation as the
dilemma necessarily brought about by the monetary policy of the past year.
We have committed ourselves to a policy of reducing wages 2s. in the £,
unless something turns up in the external conditions of the world, without
having any idea whatever as to the *modus operandi* by which that reduction
of wages can take place.

16,477 *Had we not already locked ourselves up long before?* Not as long as
our exchange could fluctuate, because we could always make the external
value of our money what we liked. I do not know that there is any easy
solution out of the difficulty. There seem to me to be three alternatives when
I come to possible policies. One would be to allow the exchange to fall, which
is the only wise course, but one which I suppose it is certain will not be taken.
One must rule that out because it is impossible for the existing authorities
to reverse the policy which they have adopted so recently. That is the first
policy. The second policy is to intensify unemployment without limit until
wages fall—which is the theory, as I understand, of the Currency Committee's
Report—and the Bank of England has taken tentative steps in that direction.
The objection to that seems to me to the probability, indeed almost the
certainty, that political influences will interfere to prevent the completion
of this long before it has reached its logical conclusion. The third policy is
to pursue what, strictly speaking, is the unsound policy of gambling as it were

on the chance of something turning up of an unexpected kind—which might quite well happen—which would pull us out of our difficulties as, for example, an inflation in America which was not accompanied by an inflation here—something which would diminish the value of American money and therefore revive our export industries and so bring back the necessary equilibrium. The third course is essentially unsound. It is the course which we are half pursuing now, viz., that of not following the sound policy to its logical extreme, but borrowing a good deal from abroad and hoping something will turn up. This gambling policy might take various forms. We might do our utmost to try to engineer something like an internal boom, flinging sound finance to the winds by programmes of capital expenditure and so forth, which would allow costive industries to discharge some of their labour into the booming internal industries. We could abandon all restriction on credit, we could remove the embargo on foreign loans, and when these various unsound policies produced their inevitable effect on our exchanges, when they began to cause a drain on the Bank of England, we could meet that by using our American credits and borrowing in America. That is to say, we could use our American credits to engineer a boom at home, and easy credit, and all the rest of it.

16,478 (SIR NORMAN HILL) *And lend abroad?* And lend abroad. Do something utterly unsound in the hope, as so often happens, that something would turn up; that the impulse we were setting going at home towards prosperity would in fact, in some way which we could not predict, take up the slack.

16,479 *But not in a permanent way?* Not in a permanent way, simply in the hope that we could carry on this policy for sufficient time to give us some chance of assistance from one of the innumerable things happening that one cannot foresee.

16,480 (CHAIRMAN) *Which of the sound principles do you suggest?* I think that the only sound policy is the first one, but I cannot conceive that the Government would so quickly reverse the policy it has undertaken. It is not practical politics.

16,481 *Will the Government be able to resist the first policy at all, if in effect we cannot do our export trade?* It is very hard to say. What I think is very likely to happen is that the Government will try a mixture of the second and third. The Bank of England will try to have a 'sound' policy and will greatly intensify unemployment, and the Government will neutralise all the things the Bank of England is doing by other things in the opposite direction, so that we shall not get the benefit of either thing. And we shall probably keep that state of things going for some considerable time, when either the unemployment will become so unpleasant that it will lead to a political upheaval which might result in a complete change of policies, or the present situation will drift on sufficiently long and in the end an adjustment will be brought about and then our troubles would be relatively over. Because these troubles are not eternal; they are troubles that exist during the period of maladjustment. If you could get the cost of living down, then people are not worse off than previously. It is simply the difficulty of seeing how that is to be achieved in any reasonable space of time.

16,482 *But our difficulty in exports is not competition with America, it is competition with the depreciated currencies like France?* Not entirely; it is aggravated by them. Until the improvement in exchange we could compete with United States coal in Canada and South America. The effect of the improvement in exchange has just made the difference that American coal has been brought to a level with ours. We are charging 10 per cent more for our coal than previously; the sterling price is 10 per cent heavier to a Canadian purchaser than it was before the improvement of the exchange. That just has the effect of letting in the American coal. It is very difficult to follow out all its consequences. It operates sometimes less than 10 per cent and sometimes more. Unquestionably the thing has been aggravated by the fact that apart from Germany the other continental exchanges have been working in an opposite direction, so that even if we had stopped where we were we would have been suffering some difficulties.

16,483 *We are bound to suffer, so much depending on our exports?* I think it is useless to pretend you can raise your exchange 10 per cent leaving your wages and cost of living where they were and not experience the effects on export industries which we are experiencing. The thing is a logical predictable consequence. While it is perfectly true we have many other troubles—and because we have other troubles this was a particularly dangerous thing to do in that it aggravated the existing bad situation—yet it is useless to avert one's eyes from the effect of the new policy of last year which has so much aggravated the whole situation. That is what I wanted to say.

16,484 (MR BAKER) *On the question of trade you say the United States of America trade is good?* Yes.

16,485 *It might be probably on the whole, but you would not call the iron and steel trade good when they are only working to 70 per cent of capacity?* In America?

16,486 *Yes?* Their 100 per cent is a very fictitious figure. They had some easiness in their iron and steel industry in the spring, but I should have said relatively speaking iron and steel in America was in very good order if you take as a rough test the prices of iron and steel shares on the New York stock exchange.

399

16,487 *Have they not gone down recently?* On the whole they stand high.

16,488 *I thought they had fallen?* They had a slight setback, but only slight, and part of that has now been recovered.

16,489 *With regard to your typewritten proof you seem to have modified that very considerably by what you have said in your oral evidence. I thought you were one of the people who were wanting a reduction in wages in the sheltered trades; I am not in favour of a reduction in wages. Also on another page you say you have no remedy to offer I think. You have given up your suggestion of dealing with the currency?* No, that is my first remedy, but I regard that as not practical politics at the moment. I still offer that for what it is worth, but I feel at the moment there is not much chance of its being acted on.

16,490 *I thought I had quite a number of questions to ask, but it seems to me from what you have said this morning your views are so much in consonance with my own feeling about the situation that I have not any questions to put to you.*

16,491 (SIR PETER RYLANDS) *I should just like to emphasise the point made with regard to the manner in which our internal value of the £ is below the external value. From what I understand you to say that arises from the lag in the effect of the fall in the price of imports on which the cost of living depends so far as affected by internal costs of manipulation?* It is partly that lag, but I think it is much more that those imported foodstuffs and so forth form only a certain proportion of the items that make up the cost of living.

16,492 *But supposing the wages all fell immediately, the internal value would remain the same as the external value?* Yes.

16,493 *But there is a lag; they do not fall until the cost of living falls?* And the difficulty is that the cost of living cannot fall until they fall.

16,494 *That is what I mean by the word 'lag'. There is a lag in the effect on the cost of living, and so upon wages, and wages not going down until the cost of living falls you get that disparity which you pointed out to the Committee was about 10 per cent. I take it that a somewhat similar phenomenon was going on in this country during the year or two preceding when the value of our £ was even then rising. I think I am right in saying that the exchange on New York was about 3.40 in about 1920?* You have to take in conjunction the movement of the exchange and the movement of American prices. You have to compound the two, and I have not in my mind the result of that composition.

16,495 *Very likely there was some tendency of the same sort going on even before March, 1920?* My memory of the figures is that we have gone through a series of waves in which we were in adjustment and out of adjustment, and the moments when we were out of adjustment were when America was exporting capital very freely. The effect of the large exports of capital by America was to put the exchange more in our favour than our position really justified. During the phases when America was exporting heavily we were suffering in a less degree the same difficulties as now. There were intermediate periods in which we were not suffering in that way.

16,496 *If anything there might have been the same tendency, broadly speaking, as now?* At certain dates, but I would not commit myself to the dates without looking up the matter.

16,497 *Turning to the Continent where there has been a steady depression of the currency at the rate of about 10 per cent per annum, the lag operating in the other direction has brought about the persistence of a higher value of the franc internally than externally.* Yes.

16,498 *With the result that today the internal value of the franc is, if . anything, little more below the world's parity than the £ is above it?* Yes, but I should say a good deal more below in the case of France, and about the same in the case of Germany.

16,499 (SIR HUBERT LLEWELLYN SMITH) *Do you mean now in Germany?* Yes. Germany was, of course, very much below. I mean now in Germany.

16,500 (SIR PETER RYLANDS) *The Chairman says he thinks, and I must say I think, we are suffering most from Belgian and French competition in the iron and steel trade today. I take it that the cost of living in Belgium is not remotely different to the cost of living in France?* It is rather higher.

16,501 *You have given the figure of 137, which looks rather higher than anything I have seen.*

(SIR HUBERT LLEWELLYN SMITH) *That only shows that the Belgian cost of living has gone up compared with itself in 1913. The French cost of living must also be compared with itself. It has not any kind of comparison with the cost of living in Belgium.*

(SIR PETER RYLANDS) *You mean the index number may be based on something different.*

16,502 (SIR HUBERT LLEWELLYN SMITH) *It simply shows the percentage changes on the basic value of the French cost of living in 1913 and the Belgian cost of living in 1913?* Relatively to itself the gold cost of living in Belgium in May of this year was 131. That is very near to the figure you mention. That is to say, it is very near the German. It is not so serious as the French. It is more on the German level than the French level.

16,503 (SIR PETER RYLANDS) *There is no doubt that the wages in Germany and France are reflected more than the cost of living in this figure?* Yes.

16,504 *And measured in gold they are indubitably very much lower than those in this country?* Yes, without the real wages being particularly low.

16,505 *I take it you will agree that that is very largely responsible for [our] inability to carry on our export trade in the iron and steel industry at all events in competition with Belgium?* I do not know sufficiently about those trades to know how far Belgium in particular was responsible. I should have been inclined to think that France, Belgium, and Germany all played their part in that. If you say Europe, I agree. I dare say you are right about Belgium, But I cannot answer that on my own knowledge.

16,506 *It comes home to us every day of the week, of course. You have no policy to suggest at all that this Committee, for instance, could recommend, except a gamble?* Well, it is for the Committee to say what they could recommend.

16,507 *But you are here to help us, I take it, to come to some decision. You are not really in a position to suggest anything practicable?* Well, I say these are the three alternatives: to let the exchange go, to follow the policy of dear money and the intensification of unemployment, and, thirdly to hope that something will turn up and live rather a free life in the meantime. What I think will happen will be a compromise between the last two.

16,508 *I suppose it is an economic fact that this disbursement of about £1,000,000 a week in unemployment benefit and pensions and high Government expenditure, does create considerable activity in the home trade and help the sheltered industries?* Certainly.

16,509 *That in itself tends to strengthen the position of the sheltered industries and helps them to maintain their present rates and profits and remunerations?* Undoubtedly. That is one of the reasons why the old-fashioned repercussion of wages in one industry on wages in another does not have its full effect. Supposing the unemployed were not receiving the dole, retail trade would become so bad that there would be a tendency for wages to fall in the industries connected with retail trade.

16,510 *Can you hold out the slightest hope that the Continental position will improve from our point of view within anything like a reasonable time?* I think it will slowly tend in a direction favourable to us. I believe particularly in Germany there is a considerable chance of a rise in prices and wages.

16,511 *Belgian prices have fallen very materially during the last month, and manufacturers are not interested, and the country is not much interested in what is going to happen in five years' time, but we want to know whether there is any hope, do you think, that the internal value of the franc will rise during the next eighteen months?* If I was to predict at all I would predict that the movement would be in the right direction from our point of view.

16,512 *But you are not prepared to predict anything very violent or rapid?* I believe our own cost of living and wage level will tend to fall in the next six months. I think the pressure already put on will have some consequences, and I think that money wages in Continental countries will tend to rise, so that I should anticipate that there will be a smaller gap six or nine months hence than now. But I do not feel optimistic about the very big difference that exists being covered.

16,513 *I notice according to the Board of Trade returns the adverse balance of trade rose from £76,000,000 in 1923 for the first five months to £166,000,000 in 1925?* That is the visible balance of trade.

16,514 *That is the visible adverse balance. Do you think that is really covered by [in]visible exports, or do you think it is provided by balances left in this country, or other methods which might be described as living on our capital?* It is difficult to say. I wish I felt more confident about the Board of Trade invisible items. I do not know how they are compiled, but I think they are, to a considerable extent, corrections made on the best information available of previous estimates; so that if you start from a wrong basis the whole thing may be wrong. I think that the original estimates of invisible items on which the Board of Trade started may have been rather too low. On the other hand, whether they make enough allowance for the extraordinary fall in shipping income, for example, I do not know again. I think it would be very useful if the Board of Trade could compile an estimate which is as detailed as the American estimate. I think the American estimate is immensely better because it has a much firmer statistical basis than the Board of Trade estimate. The Board of Trade estimate is a good enough guess, I think—as good a guess as anybody could make who is having mainly to guess. Thus I do not put enormous faith in those figures, though I cannot provide any better ones myself. The other thing I would say is, that looking at it from quite another point of view, namely, on the basis of what amount of American money has come into this country, I should guess, without being able to stand cross-examination on the subject, that American money may have been coming in at the rate of, say, £50,000,000 a year.

16,515 *In deposit or sterling?* In the purchase of sterling bills, of one shape or another. If that is true, since this is the main item which makes up any deficit, it follows arithmetically that our invisible plus items fall short of our visible minus items by £50,000,000 a year. But I would not ask the Committee to attach any importance to that guess.

16,516 *But the figure of £166,000,000 in five months strikes the ordinary person as rather alarming. Do you not think it is at all alarming?* I think it is alarming, but I am very cautious about these figures. There are so many things to take account of. For example, take the rise in the price of rubber. A great part of it is directly or indirectly owned by Englishmen. That is a huge item. I only give that as an example of the things which one has to look out for. One must be very careful before one can be certain. But I agree with your suggestion that the position is alarming.

16,517 *So far as we are not in a position to make up a favourable balance of trade there is a reaction, I understand from what you say, upon the amount of business likely to be placed in this country by the borrower?* Yes.

16,518 *So that that is another adverse factor?* Yes.

16,519 (CHAIRMAN) *I would like to have a little further discussion with you on the question of what I call the locked-up position which you depicted to us. You say we have totally different conditions today. We have trade unionism very strong, the lines of demarcation between industries very clearly defined, the difficulty of transferring labour from one industry to another, accentuated by the housing question, and also by the 'dole', the unemployment benefit, and so on. How long are we going to be able to carry on in such a locked-up position?* It is very hard to say. There is one extraordinary instance I should like to mention to the Committee.

16,520 *I include the sheltered trades in what I call the locked-up position?* Yes. I think one most extraordinary fact—no doubt it is familiar to you—is that the number of men employed in the coal industry is as great as two years ago and the increased unemployment is due to new men having entered the industry in the last two years. That is partly due to the fact that there is a tendency for the localisation of the coal industry to move. South Yorkshire is employing more men than ever before; South Wales and Northumberland are declining. It does not happen that the South Wales and Northumberland miners move to the South Yorkshire coalfield; they remain in their former localities on the dole; and new labour from the agricultural population of South Yorkshire is drawn into the South Yorkshire mines. So that you have a case there which is very extraordinary, because it is not a difficulty of moving from one industry to another, but it is a difficulty even of moving from one coalfield to another.

16,521 *Of course, what might ease up our locked-up position would be if other countries were locked-up in the same way?* I do not know. Would that help it?

16,522 *That is a dreadful solution, but it is one that is contemplated?* I think it might aggravate our situation.

16,523 *But it is one that is contemplated a great deal by certain sections of the community?* Supposing the European steel industry were in a great state of depression and supposing their men were unable to obtain work in their country, it would intensify the situation rather than help it.

16,524 *I think it would myself, but it is advocated by many people that if other countries were in exactly the same position that would be of benefit to us?* No, I think it would intensify our situation.

16,525 *If we adopted your policy and let the exchange fall, how would that remedy the disparity between sheltered and unsheltered wages?* Because the export price level would rise to the internal price level. It would take the form of an increased demand for our exports; the export trades would have no difficulty in paying a level of wages as good as the internal wages.

16,526 *Would not there be a danger of the sheltered trades rising with them?* There might be a tendency in that direction.

16,527 *That would not help to reduce our cost of production?* If our exchange falls 10 per cent our gold level of wages falls 10 per cent on that same day.

16,528 *With regard to the Trade Facilities Act, do you think that has been a good method of trying to increase employment?* It all depends what one's policy is. If one's policy is to increase unemployment by dear money and then to prevent that by using the Trade Facilities Act to counteract its consequences, the thing is an absurd contradiction. I do not think there is any place for the Trade Facilities Act simultaneously with restriction of credit by the Bank of England.

16,529 *And the same with the Export Credits scheme?* The Export Credits scheme in the same way. Personally I rather like those schemes.

16,530 *You like them as temporary schemes?* I like them as temporary schemes. I would like to stimulate in all sorts of unsound ways a general state of prosperity in the hope that I could get a cumulative wave of prosperity going which would lap up the slack. I do not believe you can ever get straight by depressing things. I think there is always a lot of unused capacity in the country, and that prosperity is cumulative, and I would like to create unsound artificial prosperity in the hope that it would prove cumulative. But I do not like suggesting that because I admit fully it is only a temporary expedient and is essentially unsound.

16,531 *With regard to the Dawes Report, we have had a good many representations made to us by various industries some saying that it is beneficial and some that it is very detrimental. What is your view of its effect generally on the industries of this country?* I do not think it has had much effect yet, because Germany has not had an export surplus and she has met all her obligations under the Dawes Report out of money borrowed from the rest of the world. The Dawes Report begins to come into effect from next year onwards, and I think the way in which it will operate, if it is successful which I much doubt, will be by keeping the money level of wages in Germany down either at their present level or below it. We have been assuming so far that in Germany, as in Belgium, there is and there will be a tendency for wages to rise towards the international level. The Dawes Report will try to prevent that from happening and in so far as it is successful it means that the low level of money wages in Germany will be perpetuated.

16,532 *Of course it must bring great pressure on Germany to export and produce?* That is its whole object.

16,533 *In that connection what about the hours question, which must have a big effect on the question of production?* What matters is the money wage per effective hour.

16,534 *That means the production per hour really?* Yes.

16,535 *That will press the Germans into working longer hours, will it not?* I think very likely so, but of course how far you can press a country by external influence I do not know. Before long you make political difficulties, and every political party puts the blame on the foreigner, and the breaking point comes before long.

16,536 *The evidence we have had is that at the present time people in Germany, Belgium and France are showing great willingness to work longer hours individually, quite apart from any control from the top. That is bound to have a very big effect on our situation if it is continued, is it not?* Yes, I think it is. I have always thought that the stimulation of German exports was bound to be adverse to us owing to the fact that their staple exports overlap so very considerably with ours.

16,537 *On the other hand, there is the point that Germany in prosperity was practically always importing up to £80,000,000 more than her exports pre-war?* Yes, but under the Dawes Scheme the notion is to stimulate the exports without stimulating the imports. If you stimulate the imports you again defeat yourself. If Germany was an agricultural country it would all be different. Supposing the pressure on Germany was to cause her to export foodstuffs at low prices the effect on us would be quite different from what it is.

16,538 *On the question of subsidies to industry, do you think the provision of subsidies is any remedy for the present situation?* I must ask what is the concurrent policy. I think to restrict credit on one side and give subsidies on the other side is to get the worst of both worlds.

16,539 *What about the fiscal system? Is your reply to that the same?* It seems to me that protective measures must worsen the situation because the export industries must be injured by them. The effect of protection is to make the disparity between internal and external prices move further in the direction which is already on the wrong side. I can imagine protection being a remedy for some things, but as a remedy for this it seems unthinkable.

16,540 (SIR HUBERT LLEWELLYN SMITH) *I was unfortunately detained at another Committee, so that I have not heard everything you have said. In your memorandum, and I think in your argument, you rely a good deal, do you not, on these figures of the cost of living, for those reasons given?* I do, yes.

16,541 *Those figures are given in the Federal Reserve Bulletin, and in the April, 1925, number of the Federal Reserve Bulletin there is a very complete account of the sources from which they are drawn. You are probably familiar with it?* Not very. I am not an expert on the value of these statistics.

16,542 *I wanted to ask whether you had any occasion to test their comparability?* I said earlier, I think before you came in, that the French figures in particular I distrusted. They seem to me to be lower than they really should be.

16,543 *There are in fact, as we have had in evidence, omissions, and very*

406

notable omissions, of important articles, and there is the insertion of others which do not materially affect the cost of living? Then in the case of Germany the basis of compilation has been changed I think twice, which is always dangerous. If you are comparing for a period over 18 months, which was what I was doing, I think they are much more reliable than if you are comparing with pre-war. Also the differences are so large that there is room for considerable error without affecting the argument.

16,544 *I am not dealing with your argument, but I may say I have recently been trying to use these same figures and they fill me with a great deal of distrust. I wondered whether you were acquainted with an inquiry which the Ministry of Labour made periodically, based rather on a different system?* Before the War?

16,545 *No, since the war. It has now been handed over to the International Labour Office. They bring the local prices to bear upon the standard consumption of articles which are included in our own cost-of-living index. It has the disadvantage that you are estimating the cost of living in a European country on the false assumption that the workman consumes the same articles in the same proportion as the British workman; but having once got over that obviously incorrect assumption it has the advantage that you are absolutely standardised?* I do not like that method. I should distrust that method. You will remember there were some inquiries made by the Board of Trade before the war which did more than any other inquiries I have seen to confirm the theoretical point as to the objection to doing that. I remember the results, which came out about 1907, of those inquiries were that if you took the English diet, the cost of living was cheaper in England than in Germany; and if you took the German diet the cost of living was cheaper in Germany than in England.

15,546 *In the use I made of the results I found I had to allow quite a number of points for that error. We can in some cases measure it, because now the International Labour Office is continuing that inquiry and has taken a number of different standards. They have taken the British standard, and they have taken the Central European standard; France and Belgium is another group, and Southern Europe is another—though how well they have done it I do not know. They have worked out for those standards the figures that our Ministry of Labour used to work out here, so that you can make a comparison. I only wanted to ask whether you thought that those figures were comparable?* One of my difficulties is that I am not interested in the cost of living except as an indication of the sheltered prices level. Even if I knew the index of the cost of living quite accurately, still that would only be an approximate index to what I am after.

16,547 *I did for a kindred purpose try to estimate what was the difference between the real wages estimated by internal prices of articles of ordinary consumption and the gold value of wages. It was very much the same as your problem. I do not know whether I was right, but I got hold of France, Germany and Belgium, and I got an indication of about 15 points difference, London being 100?* That is 15 per cent then.

16,548 *It is 15 per cent on the London scale, but supposing Paris was only 60, it would be a good deal greater percentage. So I called it 15 points. I think these figures will give a good deal more discrepancy—more like 20 or 25. It is only a matter of statistical interest, But I made it a little less. I suppose you would compare it with the United States figure, would you, of 158 for gold?* It does not look to me so very different.

16,549 *It is interesting because they are based on a different set of figures?* Germany seems to me to be about 12 per cent (I am doing it very roughly), which is not very far from your figure.

16,550 *Without committing yourself to anything, you would not be surprised to find a figure of about 15 points?* Not at all. My French figures give more than that, but as I say I distrust the French figures.

16,551 *I distrust the figures too. They include paraffin, which no French workman uses nowadays, and they have left out coffee, which is an article of universal consumption.*

16,552 (SIR NORMAN HILL) *As I understand the general picture that has been put to this committee is that the War has affected radically our export markets, more especially in regard to the development of domestic production in the other countries. I understand that this is the picture that is put to us?* That is not the picture that I particularly have been putting today.

16,553 *I may not have fully appreciated the evidence, but the picture that I have got in my my mind from what we have heard is that many of our old customers are now busily producing what they used to get from us, and there is every likelihood of their going on producing; and that therefore our manufacturing industries are having to study new methods with the object of producing different articles, perhaps specialised articles, and finding new markets. That is the kind of picture?* I think there is something in that, but I should be more inclined to believe that the test is price. I believe that at the right price we could still find very big markets for our goods.

16,554 *Yes. It has been emphasised by a great many industries that there is still a demand but they are beaten in price. If that is the kind of problem that we have before us am I right in understanding from what you have told us that of your three plans Nos. 1 and 3 are temporary expedients?* No, I do not think No. 1 is particularly temporary. No. 1 is really maintaining our price level steady, and letting the exchange adapt itself to other people's price levels. That I should be prepared to continue permanently.

16,555 *But you are maintaining it steady in equilibrium with the States?* No. I would keep the price level in England at whatever it is, and maintain it at that level.

16,556 *No matter what happened in any country?* Yes.

16,557 *That would be a permanent policy?* Yes.

16,558 *Abandoning the gold standard altogether?* Yes.

16,559 *You would have nothing more to do with it?* Well, substantially it is abandoning it. I would have various provisions for preventing rapid movements of the exchange that had no real significance. I would not allow us to be blown about by every breath of wind. To that extent I would still be interested.

16,560 *If we had to abandon the gold standard policy do you think we should be all more comfortable in this country?* I ought to explain I have not been directing myself today to the ultimate merits of the gold standard. Everything I have said today would be consistent with the gold standard being the best standard. What I have been arguing against is linking ourselves to gold at a moment when it means a 10 per cent change in our price level.

16,561 *That is why I thought you were rather putting it forward as a temporary expedient?* Suppose the value of gold was to alter 10 per cent, the particular objections I have been raising today would cease to operate.

16,562 *You mean if it altered today.* I also take the view that from a permanent point of view there are objections to gold, but those are quite distinct from the particular point I have been urging today, all of which might have been urged by somebody who believed the gold standard was the ideal one.

16,563 *The third policy you mentioned was entirely an expedient?* Yes. I should like to say that quite apart from this money question my own view is that owing to changes in the external world such as you have been indicating, probably our export trades will be permanently on a lower scale in relation to population than they were in pre-war days. And I think we should do well to have a transference of labour to some extent from the export trades to non-export trades, and balance our reduction of exports by investing less capital abroad and more capital at home. As we happen to be a country which exported capital we have room to reduce our exports very materially and yet have plenty to pay for our necessary imports, merely by reducing our exports of capital and using more at home. So that my long-period policy would be the gradual transference of labour from export industries and a large programme of capital expenditure at home, which would absorb the savings which had previously found an outlet abroad.

16,564 *If you went in for that policy, or if you stuck to our policy of pushing our exports anywhere and everywhere as far as we could in the altered conditions, there will have to be a very big transference of labour?* Our exports are at present 20 per cent below pre-war, so I think a good part of it has been effected, but still I agree it is a fairly large transference.

16,565 *We are 20 per cent down in our exports, and you have explained that our unemployment is not fluid and is not adjusting itself. There are a great many gaps in a great many directions?* Provided we could have capital programmes at home and easy money conditions at home, I believe that it would be easy to make a beginning at absorbing that labour in home industries.

16,566 *Absorbing it in some home industries, but not the industries in which they had been working under the other policy of exports?* To a certain extent you would be stimulating the same industries, but making them slightly alter the class of article they produce. If we had any of the great schemes that have been proposed for capital development at home that would certainly stimulate the employment of labour in the coal industry and in the iron and steel industry because they would require the products of those industries.

16,567 *And possibly in directions quite different from the centres from which you were working the export trade in coal or iron?* To a certain extent, but it would not be like turning colliers into bakers.

16,568 *But you would have to solve what you say is now impossible, namely to get the superfluous miners of South Wales shifted to Yorkshire?* Yes, but if there is an intake for labour the business of transfer is not an insuperable difficulty. What I think is so extraordinarily difficult is to absorb labour out of industries when the other industries are not wanting any labour. You must first of all create a condition of demand for labour in the other industries.

16,569 *Because of the unemployment benefit and such things as that, you put forward the point that now labour is not fluid even in its own industry?* Yes.

16,570 *And because of the housing problem?* Yes, but I think that would be greatly mitigated if there was a big demand for labour. To give an example of the kind of way in which it would work; if there was a big demand for labour the growing up population would be attracted only to industries that were in a sound condition, so that the coalfields in South Yorkshire would have to take active steps to transfer labour from other districts in order to get the labour they want. As it is, they pursue the line of least resistance and take in young men out of the growing up population.

16,571 *If we were working under your third policy it would be with the hope of bringing about the results you have indicated in your second policy?* Partly that, and partly, as I say, that various things might turn up which I cannot specify.

16,572 *And make it not so necessary?* Something might happen to the price level in America, or all sorts of things, that would make the situation less acute all round.

16,573 *If the unexpected does not turn up we shall have sooner or later to work under your second policy, shall we not?* Or under my first.

16,574 *We have had some very interesting evidence of what is happening in France, and we are told that there everybody is very eager to work and trying*

*to make money, not much caring how long they work; there is no unemployment
and everybody is very very busy indeed. Now if we take your first policy and
we do what France has been doing since the War, is that a permanent policy?
Shall we go on existing like that?* I am not quite sure how you interpret my
first policy. As I say, the first policy I outlined in my original remarks was
a policy of letting the exchange adjust itself to the existing price level.
Suppose that something happened to the value of gold so that it was also
adjusted to gold, then comes the further question whether we are to adhere
to gold as a permanent standard or not. I am against gold, but for different
reasons from those. So that my first policy has two branches, one of which
would be permanent and the other not permanent.

16,575 *Does it differ from the French policy?* Certainly. The French policy
has not been to keep their internal prices steady. Their index number has
risen 100 points in a year and a half.

16,576 *They have not kept it steady because of what?* Because they have
been inflating.

16,577 *You say keep it in equilibrium but do not inflate?* Do not inflate
seriously.

16,578 *Keep it in equilibrium with the rest of the world?* No; keep it in
equilibrium with itself. Keep it at the same level that you find it. I mean
if our cost of living is 172, to have a state of affairs where it can remain
permanent[ly] at 172 or thereabouts.

16,579 (CHAIRMAN) *When you say do not inflate seriously, what do you
mean?* I say that because the world 'inflation' is used so very ambiguously.
It is used sometimes for something which produces a rise in prices, and it
is used sometimes for easy monetary conditions which may or may not
produce an effect on prices. I feel it desirable to ease out credit conditions
at this juncture perhaps a little rashly, and as soon as it began to have an
important effect on prices I should draw in again. I should not allow it to
go to any distance, but in view of the special conditions at the moment I
should be prepared to be a little rash in the way in which I opened out credit
facilities in the first instance.

16,580 (SIR NORMAN HILL) *I am afraid I do not quite follow all that you
are putting to us. Is it right that sooner or later you are going to do what you
say is so hard for political reasons—which you dealt with under your second
policy? That is where we shall have to come to, is it not?* I think that we must.
It is not the same problem. The one problem is not to divert labour out of
the export industries, but to reduce wages in the other industries, so that
the cost of living will fall, so that you can reduce wages in the export
industries to a level at which you can support the existing condition of those
industries. That is quite a different policy from the policy of the transfer

of labour from export industries into other industries. That second policy of the transference of labour from export industries into sheltered industries you would have to bring about by some stimulation in internal conditions that might be rather unsound at the outset. That would be the way of doing it. The method of facilitating transference would be to make home industries boom. But if your object was to depress the internal trade in order that exports could survive, then the policy would be to depress internal industries. So that these two things really lead to the opposite conclusions.

16,581 *I was speaking as to the second policy and not as to the third policy. Let things alone and then pressure from the unemployed will bring down wages?* I think I have become confused as to which you mean by my second and which by my third.

16,582 *Was not your possible policy to leave things alone until wages come down?* But that is quite a different policy to the policy which I have been mentioning more recently, in my cross-examination by you. That is aiming at transference. If I had my way completely I should not regard the stability of the exchange as important, but, all the same, I should be aiming at a transfer from the export industries to the home industries by stimulating the latter.

16,583 *What was worrying me in my own mind was, can we avoid bringing down wages? Taking the world as it is, must we not either work longer or take less for the same hours? Is that the position?* It depends whether you are taking about gold wages or sterling wages. We have to bring down gold wages, but whether we have to bring down sterling wages depends on the exchange.

16,584 *It is what we get for the wages?* What we have actually done is to raise gold wages 10 per cent in the last year. I say that is the source of all our troubles. But there is often a confusion as to whether one is talking about gold wages or sterling wages. I suggest a policy by which gold wages can fall compatibly with sterling wages remaining the same.

16,585 (SIR HERBERT LLEWELLYN SMITH) *That is No. 1 policy?* Yes.

16,586 *That is the one which you say was hopeless?* Yes. That is the best policy.

16,587 (SIR NORMAN HILL) *Do you think that we can carry on [in] the world without reducing the standard of living here?* Yes.

16,588 *And without working harder?* I think the discussion is getting confused. Part of our difficulty may be that we have to consider the standard of living. I have not been addressing myself to that particular problem because I do not think the aggravation of the situation in the last year is due to that. That is part of our pre-existing difficulty. What I have been directing myself to this morning is not to our real wages being unduly high, but to the disparity between the value of money in this country and its value outside. Suppose the cost of living came down to the external cost of living, then wages could come down without any fall in the standard of life. In my original table it is not the discrepancy between 172 and 181 which I am dwelling on; it is the discrepancy between the 172 and the 158. The other is a separate argument.

16,589 (CHAIRMAN) *The 158 is the American figure?* Yes. In so far as it is purely a monetary phenomenon it may be cured without any bad effects whatever on real wages.

16,590 (SIR NORMAN HILL) *What you suggest by your first plan which you favour would enable the people in this country to go on living as we have been living since the war without working harder?* I think it is very hard to say. I cannot see any reason why we should not live just as well as we have been doing, if we went about it the right way.

16,591 *Without working any harder?* Without working any harder, provided we *all* worked. You see, I think that the whole situation changes enormously if you get things going, if you get full time worked everywhere and full employment everywhere. I think that would probably improve our conditions sufficiently to enable us to maintain our existing standard of life. I think that our existing standard of life is too high with unemployment and the rest of it as it is, but I am not clear, if our policy was wise in other directions, that there is any need for reducing real wages in this country.

16,592 (MR LANGDALE) *According to the cost-of-living and wages figures which you have given us, in March, 1924, the cost wages were 155, and in June, 1925, they were 181. That is a difference of 26 points?* Yes.

16,593 *The difference in the cost of living is only 15 points?* Yes.

16,594 *So that there is about 11 points margin. Wages might be reduced by 11 points without the figures being in any worse position than they were before?* Yes.

16,595 *That is about 6 per cent. That is a good load off the 10 per cent, is it not?* I was not thinking of that. There is more than 10 per cent between 158 and 181. I agree if these figures are reliable it would appear that at a time when money wages ought to have been coming down they positively have been going up.

16,596 *That has had nothing to do with the return to the gold standard has it?* No, I should not think it has.

16,597 *With regard to another point you refer to, you said that business in the outside world was fairly satisfactory. Those who are engaged in the export in this country to India and China find that the cost of production in Lancashire is too high?* As I said, I thought it was a question of price, but I should also regard China as being subject to particular conditions.

16,598 *China at the moment is in an unsatisfactory condition?* I have not heard any evidence to make me think that India is otherwise than normally prosperous at this moment.

16,599 *There is no doubt that the price of Lancashire goods is too high for eastern people. If Lancashire wishes to increase her export, or merely to do as much an export trade as before the War, her prices will have to come down?* My argument was that it was a question of price—the price we have to ask for exports in order to equal the internal cost—rather than any deep-seated serious lack of prosperity in other countries.

16,600 *Do you think we would be able to maintain this trade, or increase it, with the present 181 per cent of cost wages in this country?* As long as the level of gold prices outside this country remains what it is I think it is impossible. That is my argument.

16,601 *The wages will have to come down?* The question is by what *modus operandi*, by what course or process, will they come down? I say it is dangerous to put ourselves into a situation when they have to come down, because the only way of bringing them down is by intensifying unemployment until they do come down. If the business world takes the view that we are committed to this, and they must come down, then it ought to welcome unemployment, because that is the only way of doing it. It ought to do all it can to increase unemployment until wages do come down.

16,602 *Unemployment will be increased if your manufactures are too dear for you to sell?* Yes, but I think it is no good regarding that as an Act of God; it is the consequence of your own policy. I say, if that happens, you will have done it on purpose, because you must be assumed to will the consequences of your acts.

16,603 *That is due to your paying too high wages?* But you would not be paying too high wages if you had not improved the exchange by 10 per cent. When you willed that you would improve the exchange by 10 per cent, you ought to have willed at the same to reduce wages 10 per cent. There is no method of doing as you propose except by intensifying unemployment.

16,604 *You increased money wages 10 per cent?* You increased gold wages 10 per cent. You have not altered money wages very much. The effect of the improvement of the exchange is to increase gold wages 10 per cent.

16,605 *And to make your food cost low?* Yes.

16,606 *Generally speaking, you think you can maintain this 181 per cent above pre-war?* No, I do not, not if external gold prices are at their present level and the exchange remains at its present level. I do not think we can maintain gold wages at 181 if the external value of gold is somewhere in the 150's.

16,607 (SIR JOHN HINDLEY) *Do you suggest that we are really in a position to set the standard of living?* Who do you mean by 'we'?

16,608 *The country?* But we do not.

16,609 *As an industrial country depending very largely on exports, must we not follow rather than try to set the standard?* But the standard of living is not the same in the United States and in China. It is not the same everywhere. Our standard of living, I quite agree, must depend upon our own productivity, and we cannot set our standard of living independently of our productivity. But I do not think there is any law by which our standard of living must necessarily follow the standard of living in other countries.

16,610 *Do you think it is reasonable to compare the United States with Great Britain?* No, I do not think we can expect to have as high a standard of living as they can.

16,611 *As far as the United States is concerned her exports are more or less a luxury?* I would rather say that her essential exports are not nearly such a large portion of her total trade.

16,612 *Her prosperity is really dependent on her internal trade?* To a much greater extent.

16,613 *To a very much greater extent?* But our prosperity depends on our internal trade much more than people think.

16,614 (SIR PETER RYLANDS) *In discussions about the gold standard, I have heard people say that the argument in favour of returning to the gold standard was that it would lighten the burden of our debt to America, and cheapen the cost of things that come in. What would you say about that?* That is pure rubbish.

16,615 *Perhaps you would explain, because I think I am right in saying it is a very popular idea that by improving the exchange with America it lightens the burden of our debt and reduces the cost of things?* It lightens the burden of our debt in terms of sterling but not in terms of goods and services. The debt is fixed in gold and the burden of it depends upon what quantity of goods [and] services is equivalent to that amount of gold.

16,616 *The fact being that international trade is the exchange of units of effort and not of currency?* Yes, otherwise we could go on raising our exchange for ever until our external debt was nothing at all.

16,617 (CHAIRMAN) *The question of the importation of food is important in relation to the cost of living?* If everything comes down in proportion you are exactly as you were.

16,618 *Where are you to begin?* The restoration of the gold standard by lowering the sterling price of food does not do us a pennyworth of good if the value of sterling has been altered correspondingly.

16,619 (MR BAKER) *When we have this reduction in wages how much better off will the country be relatively—never mind the workers for the moment—than we were before we started reducing?* Not a penny the better off.

16,620 *All the fuss is to leave us where we were? Yes, that is the best that can happen.*

16,621 *If you looked at the matter so far as cotton is concerned, could you tell us the margin of difference between the reduced price of raw cotton and the increased price of cotton goods abroad if we raised the price abroad 10 per cent?* I have not worked it out. I think that the figures are worked out in certain publications of the cotton trade.

The witness withdrew.

Before he appeared before the Committee on Industry and Trade, Keynes offered *The Times* a series of articles on the consequences of the return to gold. On 8 July the editor of *The Times* accepted the series subject to his seeing the final version. On seeing them he wrote to Keynes.

From GEOFFREY DAWSON, *16 July 1925*

My dear Keynes,

I am rather embarrassed by these articles. They are extraordinarily clever and very amusing; but I really feel that, published in *The Times* at this particular moment, they would do harm and not good. Whether you like it or not, the gold standard has now been restored beyond all hope of recall. This being so, it seems to me that the only thing to be done is to make the best of it. I do not in the least mind publishing criticism of the Government in this or any other respect; but three solid articles seem to me to be rather over-doing it. Mill, to whom I showed the articles last night, suggested that you should be asked to cut them down into one. Personally I am against this, as I am sure would you be, for perhaps I appreciate their merits as a literary performance better than he does. But I really am reluctantly driven to the conclusion that I cannot take them as they stand, and that you had better let them loose elsewhere.

Yours sincerely,
GEOFFREY DAWSON

Keynes then offered the articles to Lord Beaverbrook, the proprietor of, amongst other newspapers, *The Evening Standard*.

To LORD BEAVERBOOK, *17 July 1925*

Dear Beaverbrook,

I have written three articles, under the general title of 'Unemployment and Monetary Policy' and the sub-titles of I.

416

The Diagnosis. II. The Policy of the Bank of England, and III. The Alternative Courses for the Government. The first two of these articles are, I think a little under 1,500 words, the third could, if absolutely necessary, be reduced to the same length. But it would be difficult, and it stands at present at about 1,800 words.

I offer you these for publication in *The Evening Standard*. It would, I think, be essential in view of the continuity of the argument that they should be published fairly quickly one after another—all three, that is to say, within about a week.

If you are interested in the proposal in principle I can send you copies of the articles to-morrow morning. In my opinion they are good journalism and are matters of popular interest. I think they would provide you with good texts worth developing in *The Express* and *The Standard* for some little time to come. The thesis of the first article is that Winston's policy has committed us to reducing everyone's wages 2/- in the £. The thesis of the second article is that the Bank of England's policy of credit restriction is a policy of bringing about the above result by deliberately intensifying unemployment. The third article makes two suggestions for treating the situation in a different way, compatibly with remaining on the gold standard.

Could you let me know about it as soon as possible. I shall be available on the telephone—Museum 3875. I suggest a fee of £50 for each article.

Yours sincerely,
[copy initialled] J.M.K.

Beaverbrook accepted the offer and *The Evening Standard* published them on 22, 23 and 24 July. Keynes expanded the articles into a pamphlet which the Hogarth Press published less than a week later under the title *The Economic Consequences of Mr Churchill* (*JMK*, vol. IX, pp. 207–30). Chapters I, III and V of the pamphlet correspond to the original newspaper articles.

Once publication of the articles began, Keynes continued his correspondence with Dawson.

To GEOFFREY DAWSON, *23 July 1925*

Dear Dawson,

As you may have seen, I have been printing a slightly abbreviated version of the articles which I sent you in *The Evening Standard*. I am also publishing an enlarged version as a pamphlet next week, under the title of *The Economic Consequences of Mr Churchill*. I will of course send you a copy of this for review in the ordinary way.

I don't quite agree with the implication of your second letter, namely that the only purpose of my articles is to write against the gold standard. My final conclusions were directed towards a remedy which was compatible with the gold standard. And I am sure we shall never find a remedy in the present state of affairs until, to some slight extent, we face the facts and admit what the real causes are. My object in the first two articles was to bring this out clearly.

I appreciate of course that what I was saying was not really compatible with the line which *The Times* is taking, yet I cannot but think that it may prove difficult as time goes on to keep up the bluff that the return to gold standard has nothing to do with our troubles with any sort of plausibility. However, I daresay that the best way is that I should write you a letter on the matter from time to time if, as heretofore, you will be able to find room for it.

Yours sincerely,
[copy initialled] J.M.K.

From GEOFFREY DAWSON, *26 July 1925*

My dear Keynes,

Many thanks for your letter. Yes, I saw the articles in *The Evening Standard* and shall look forward to the pamphlet.

Perhaps I did not make my meaning quite clear in rather a hurriedly dictated letter. Glad as I always am to see your extremely brilliant and amusing contributions in *The Times*, I felt that the publication of three long articles, even if accompanied by a leader in a different sense, would identify us rather too much with an attitude that we have always hitherto resisted. On the whole I think that an occasional letter is a better alternative.

Yours sincerely,
GEOFFREY DAWSON

Keynes's articles led to comments in the press and several flurries of correspondence. The earliest came when the City Editor of *The Morning Post* published a lengthy discussion of his articles on 27 July. Keynes picked him up on one matter.

To the Editor of The Morning Post, *29 July 1925*

Sir,

My attention has been called to a lengthy criticism of some articles of mine in your City Page on Monday. On the main issue I must refer your readers to my pamphlet, *The Economic Consequences of Mr Churchill*, which has just been published. But your City Editor makes one small slip which, perhaps, I ought to point out. He wrote: 'Because we are not out for debate with Mr Keynes, but only for the clarification of the situation, we shall not assert that price levels may not, at times, be affected by monetary policy, in which connection, however, it would have been better if Mr Keynes had made fuller acknowledgment of our cost of living having latterly tended to fall below the American level.'

But in the very article criticised I pointed out that a year ago the gold cost of living was 157 here and 154 in America; whereas the latest available figures are 180 here and 158 in America. Since I am not out for debate, I will not do more than assert that 'at times' 180 is greater than 158—indeed, just about as often as price levels are affected by monetary policy.

I must also state what your City Editor must surely know well, that to assert that the management of the currency in this country prior to the readoption of gold had my approval, is a gross travesty of my opinions. I criticised it repeatedly and vehemently.

It is typical of the silliness and utter lack of intellectual standards with which this controversy is carried on by City Editors, that, because I am in favour of managing the currency with a view to stability of prices, I am, therefore, supposed to be in favour of managing it with a view to instability of prices—sometimes I am said to have favoured deflation, as in your City columns, and sometimes inflation, as in the City columns of some of your contemporaries.

Yours, &c.,

J. M. KEYNES

The publication of *The Economic Consequences of Mr Churchill* coincided with two other events. One was the announcement of his engagement to Lydia Lopokova. Another was the publication of the Report of the Commission of Inquiry into an industrial dispute in the coal industry which had become more pronounced with the return to gold. The Report contained an addendum by Sir Josiah Stamp which argued that the recent difficulties in the industry were related to the exchange appreciation involved in the return to gold. The links between the pamphlet, the Report and Keynes's engagement are clear in the following letters.

From SIR JOSIAH STAMP, *28 July 1925*

My dear Keynes,

My *very heartiest congratulations*. Matrimony was all you needed to make you as near perfect as it's possible to be without being a nuisance.

I shall be delighted to lunch on Saturday.

Many thanks for the pamphlet, which is excellent in every way.

I was *most loth* to write my Coal addendum—it went against my grain to be embarrassing in any way to the Powers, but I didn't see how I could *honestly* escape it.

Yours

J. C. STAMP

From LORD BEAVERBROOK, *31 July 1925*

My dear Keynes,

Many thanks for sending me your pamphlet—which naturally possesses great interest for me—and for the additional figures in your letter. You have had a very good press—even from the newspapers which do not agree with us—and deservedly so. But the ranks of the unorthodox are being recruited rapidly—Sir Josiah Stamp being the latest to stampede. I think your 'unemployment' argument against the Bank of England policy, to which you gave prominence in your *Evening Standard* articles, has gone home.

I was delighted to see the news of your engagement in the press. Matrimony will bring you with a bound from youth into early middle age, and since, being older than you are, I already consider myself middle-aged, I am selfish enough to be glad at anything which reduces the disparity between us and brings you into my own class! I wish you every happiness.

Yours sincerely,
BEAVERBROOK

The link between unemployment and the gold standard certainly went 'home' as Beaverbrook put it, for the next month brought three powerful attacks on Keynes's position, as well as controversy elsewhere in the press and in the House of Commons. One came in the form of a long letter to *The Times* from Sir Henry Strakosch, the South African banker, which took issue with Keynes's views, while the other two came slightly later in the form of a long article in *The Financial News* by Lord Bradbury, Chairman of the Committee on the Currency and Bank of England Note Issues and an article in the *Westminster Bank Review* by Walter Leaf, chairman of the Westminster Bank. Keynes replied first to Strakosch.

To the Editor of The Times, *31 July 1925*

Sir,

Sir H. Strakosch's comments on my pamphlet *The Economic Consequences of Mr Churchill*, to which you give prominence today, are a nice example of the capacity to find 'good in everything'.

Sir H. Strakosch points out that on a previous occasion sterling rose to within sight of parity at a time when our internal price level did not justify it. This movement culminated at the date at which he begins his table—namely, December, 1922, to March, 1923. Our situation then, as he justly remarks, was very similar to what it was this spring. We were suffering accordingly and our unemployment figures were much as at present. If, at that date, we had restored the gold standard, the results would probably have been just what they are now. Since, fortunately, we did not make that mistake, we were able to recover equilibrium by a fall in the exchange without any marked disturbance, as Sir H. Strakosch also points out, to our own prices and wages. As a result of this our costs became adjusted to the international level, our unemployment figures fell by nearly half, and by the middle of 1924 it really seemed to most of us that we had turned the corner and were on the way to good times again. Then began the last and most fatal campaign to restore sterling parity. By the end of 1924, as Sir H. Strakosch's table shows, the exchange had again reached a level too high in relation to the internal value of money, and between December, 1924, and March, 1925, we worked ourselves into the same dangerous disequilibrium as a year [sic] before. This time, however, we have cut ourselves off from the exchange remedy and have left ourselves with no alternative but to beat down the level of wages. Hence our present tears. But why Sir H. Strakosch imagines that this little piece of history demonstrates 'the outstanding virtues of the gold standard' I have no idea.

His letter raises another hare more worth hunting. He points out that for two and a half years sterling wages and cost of living here and the dollar cost of living in America have been moderately steady, while the exchange has fluctuated sharply. If only we had had the gold standard all this time, he goes on to argue, the exchange would have been stable too and we should have enjoyed the best of every conceivable world! This is surely an extreme example of the fallacy that you can alter the exchange without altering prices. Professor Cassel has given reasons for the view that the fluctuations of the exchange during this period corresponded to the fluctuations in the volume of foreign investment by the United States. If the exchange had been fixed we should have been compelled in self-protection, even after the initial adjustment had been made, to have had alternately very cheap money and very dear money in London. Does Sir H. Strakosch think that this would have had no consequences?

The argument serves to bring out clearly the essence of our difference of opinion. I hold that in modern conditions wages in this country are, for various reasons, so rigid over short periods, that it is impracticable to adjust them to the ebb and flow of international gold-credit, and I would deliberately utilise fluctuations in the exchange as the shock-absorber. Sir H. Strakosch, believing that any other course is 'more appropriately called repudiation', would make exchange stability at 4.86½ the central object of policy and would leave prices and wages to be the shock-absorbers. In this case he must put up from time to time with unemployment and trade disputes and worse; but, looking as usual at the bright side of things, he will doubtless contrive to see even in these the final demonstration of 'the outstanding virtues of the gold standard'.

Yours &c.,

J. M. KEYNES

Strakosch replied to Keynes's letter, suggesting that the experience of the previous five years did not support Keynes's position and that unstable exchange rates were likely to be a greater source of internal instability than the gold standard. The City Editor of *The Times* went further when in commending Sir Henry's letter to his readers he suggested that the logical conclusion of Keynes's policy was either hyper-inflation on the German scale or inflation as in France and Italy. Naturally Keynes replied.

To the Editor of The Times, *5 August 1925*

Sir,

I am an advocate of managing the currency in the interests of the stability of prices and wages. Those who are opposed to this policy think it good tactics to represent me as being in favour of managing it at random. Some of them say that I am in favour of managing it as in this country before the restoration of gold parity, that is, in the interests of deflation; in your City page today I am represented as an inflationist, and the management of the German mark after the war as the 'logical conclusion' of my proposals; and Sir Henry Strakosch seems to think that every inconvertible currency which has ever existed is an example of what I recommend. It is obvious that rational controversy is impossible with those who, whether from intellectual deficiency or emotional excess, are unable to distinguish between the policy of keeping the value of money steady and the policy of depreciating it to nothing.

To bring the issue back to the practical problems of the moment, and with the object, not of settling the gold controversy, but of elucidating it, let me ask the supporters of the official policy how they answer the following questions:—

1. Are we supporting the exchange by artificial interference with the export of capital and by borrowing in New York?

2. If so, how does this differ from the policy which we used to contemn the French?

3. Is it necessary (failing the depreciation of gold abroad) for the restoration of our financial equilibrium in these circumstances that money wages generally should be reduced?

4. If so, what steps are proposed with the object of reducing money wages?

5. If the limitation of credit facilities and the maintenance of dear money are the methods proposed, how do they achieve the object by deliberately intensifying unemployment?

6. In general, how are the working classes to be induced to accept lower money wages except by the pressure of lock-outs and unemployment?

7. If it is politically impossible (as in the case of the coal industry) to force money wages down by these methods, where are we going to end?

8. Would it be equally necessary to reduce money wages if the dollar exchange stood at 4.40 (as it did a year ago) instead of at 4.86 (as it does now)?

If the official party will face these questions fairly, and answer them frankly, we may begin to escape from the Monkeyville atmosphere in which our gold fundamentalists have enveloped us.

Yours faithfully,

J. M. KEYNES

Early August 1925 also saw Keynes giving a lecture 'Am I a Liberal?' (*JMK*, vol. IX, pp. 295–306) to the Liberal Summer School in Cambridge (on 1 August) and marrying Lydia Lopokova in London on 4 August.

Keynes's reply to Lord Bradbury's criticism of *The Economic Consequences of Mr Churchill* came on 18 August.

From The Financial News, *18 August 1925*

OUR MONETARY POLICY

It is a comfort to the author of *The Economic Consequences of Mr Churchill*, after reading a good many criticisms of his pamphlet, to see Lord Bradbury's contribution to *The Financial News*, which lifts the subject once again on to the level where rational controversy is possible. But the worst of Lord Bradbury's article is that it stops just when it is becoming most interesting.

If it is true that sterling prices are too high, then, he says, 'there are only three conceivable remedies—the reduction of sterling prices, the increase of our competitors' gold prices, or making the £ worth less than $4.86...If he (Mr Keynes) will not have the first and cannot have the second, he is inevitably thrown back on the third.' Quite true. Lord Bradbury argues, further, that the second alternative may not come off, owing to the United States successfully managing its currency in the interests of price stability and thus preventing a price rise. I agree. I think it an unreliable expedient, and I, therefore, coupled it with a second proposal, which Lord Bradbury ignores, for reducing wages, &c., 5 per cent all round.

But what is Lord Bradbury's solution? He, apparently,

accepts the first alternative, namely, 'a credit policy which will reduce sterling prices'. This, indeed, is the correct course for all members of the orthodox party. In this case I ask for a reply to the central issue raised by my pamphlet—How is he going to do it? I argued in my pamphlet that there was no way except through credit restriction; that this method was socially disastrous in [the] process and socially unjust in the result; and that it was probably politically impossible. The coal subsidy and the reduction of the Bank rate to $4\frac{1}{2}$ per cent have gone some considerable way, since I wrote my pamphlet, to confirm the truth of the last of these contentions.

I admit that the old prescription for curing an internal price level, which is too high, by dear money and credit restriction would certainly do the trick, if it could be carried to its logical conclusion. But I maintain that in modern conditions the medicine is so nasty that the patient cannot be induced to swallow it. Therefore, to embark on a policy which assumes that medicine on the old prescription *can* be administered is not sound statesmanship.

To embargo foreign loans and to reduce the Bank rate to $4\frac{1}{2}$ per cent is *not*, whatever else it may be—as, I think, Lord Bradbury will admit—the old prescription.

Our high money costs of production have turned the balance of international payments against us. Failing the application of the old prescription, we can only maintain the exchange by borrowing and by interfering with the normal export of capital. The Bank of England effects this by embargoing foreign issues even to the extent of requiring old loans maturing here to be paid off out of funds raised elsewhere, and by making special arrangements with the central banks of Holland and of the Union of South Africa to assist her with gold and with the New York Federal Reserve Bank to buy sterling bills.

Since we still have reserve resources and our credit is good, the Bank is able, in these and other ways, to raise very large sums for the support of the exchange, at a rate, I should guess, of not less than £100,000,000 per annum, which is enough to make good the wastage of nearly 500,000 men in unemployment. The Bank of England and the Treasury are not allowed, for political reasons, to execute the correct gold standard policy. Therefore, to keep up gold appearances they have to submit to expedients which in old days would have shocked Lord Bradbury out of his skin.

Does Lord Bradbury applaud this state of affairs? If not, should he not denounce the subterfuges of the Bank of England? And where does he think it will all end?

At the end of the month he wrote a long letter to *The Times* concerning Walter Leaf's article in the *Westminster Bank Review*.

To the Editor of The Times, *28 August 1925*

Sir,

Dr Leaf's recent article on Price Levels in Relation to Monetary Policy indicates that it is desirable to restate the problem from the beginning.

Goods and services fall into groups according to the sensitiveness of their gold prices to those of similar things elsewhere.

First come the staple raw materials of international commerce, of which wheat, cotton, copper, and export grades of coal are good examples. These must necessarily adjust themselves rapidly to changes in the international price level. Where there is a highly organised market, as in the case of cotton, the adjustment takes place within a few minutes. Let us call this Class A.

Next come (Class B) the articles on which the working classes spend their incomes, the price of which is measured by the index numbers of the 'cost of living'. Food makes up 60 per cent of these, and wholesale food is largely composed of Class A articles. Thus an improvement in the exchange soon tends to lower the sterling cost of living somewhat below what it would have been otherwise; but not, at first, to the full extent—perhaps, at a guess, to half the extent—of the improvement in the exchange.

Next come money wages (Class C). Where there is a cost-of-living sliding scale, these will respond to a fall in the cost of living. But there is no automatic force to make them fall on the average as much as the cost of living. As a rule, there is no means of bringing down money wages except by the pressure of unemployment and trade disputes.

Next come various other types of home expenses which do not respond at all, in any direct way, to the improvement in the exchange and to the fall in the price of Class A articles. Railway freights, postage, insurance, local and Imperial taxes, debenture interest are examples of these, which we will call Class D.

Lastly come manufactured articles (Class E), the cost of which is mainly made up of the costs of the A, C, and D expenses which the manufacturer incurs. If Class A expenses are a large proportion of the whole, the manufacturer can cut his prices materially. But in so far as Class C and D expenses enter in he can only cut his prices, in advance of a price fall in these classes, by reducing his margin of profit. Those manufacturers whose goods are neither imported nor exported on a large scale (which we will call E_1) are under no compulsion to reduce their prices in advance of a fall in their costs of production. Those, on the other hand, who are subject to international competition fall into two classes—those whose products are of a kind of which a largely increased supply of sufficiently identical quality *cannot* be quickly obtained from elsewhere (which we will call E_2) and those whose products *can* be quickly obtained from elsewhere (which we will call E_3). Thus the E_1 manufacturers are best placed, whilst those E_2 manufacturers whose A costs are in a large proportion of the whole are next best placed, and the E_3 manufacturers whose C and D costs are a large proportion of the whole are the worst-placed. Our textile manufacturers are an example of those in a middle position. Our coal, iron and steel, and shipping industries are examples of the worst-placed class.

Now our problem today consists in the failure of the prices in Classes C and D to respond to the increased exchange value of sterling, and in the fact that until the prices in Classes C and D have fallen to the price level of Class A, the prices in Classes B and E are also maintained, in varying degrees, too high. It is these facts which constitute the 'overvaluation of sterling'. It is self-evident that a rise in the exchange value of sterling reduces the sterling cost of what we *buy* abroad below what it would have been otherwise. The question is whether it has affected adversely the gold price at which we can produce what we *sell* abroad. The 'overvaluation of sterling' consists in a rise in the money cost of what we produce for export above its equilibrium value. How then, does Dr Leaf seek to disprove the 'overvaluation of sterling'? He takes the index numbers of wholesale prices in England, which are largely made up of Class A articles, compares with them similar index numbers in the United States, and finds that the two are fully adjusted—as they nearly always must be. At the same time he ignores the prices in Classes B, C, D, and E—which are the sole cause of trouble. I have contended that our difficulties have arisen because the price of coal, for example, has fallen with the improvement in the exchange, whereas wages and other home costs have not fallen. Dr Leaf thinks that he can disprove this by producing figures which confirm my contention that the prices of coal and other articles in Class A have indeed fallen with the improvement in the exchange, and by ignoring the level of wages and other home costs. It would seem that Dr Leaf does not know what the controversy is about. This suspicion is confirmed by another passage in which he states that the importation of gold into London, as the result of dearer money here than in New York, proves that sterling is undervalued.

We do not possess index numbers specially compiled with the

object of indicating the price changes in each of my groups. But we have index numbers which are fairly satisfactory for the purpose. For Class A the usual wholesale commodity index numbers, whilst not ideal, since they include some articles which are not Class A, are reasonably reliable—the Board of Trade index here and the Bureau of Labour index in the United States being the most carefully compiled. (Dr Leaf's comparisons of various wholesale indexes vary according as they contain more or less Class A Articles.) For Class B we have the Ministry of Labour cost-of-living index, and for Class C Professor Bowley's wages index. For Class D we have nothing. As regards Class E, we have nothing for E1, but for E2 the Board of Trade's index of prices of manufactured exports is tolerable, and for E3 there is the Board of Trade's index of raw material exports (chiefly coal) and the Chamber of Shipping's index for shipping freights. What do these several indexes show?

In June, 1924, when the sterling exchange was 12 per cent below par, the indexes, converted into gold, were as follows (1913 = 100):—

(Converted from sterling into the equivalent gold value)

United States Wholesale index	Great Britain					
	Wholesale index	Cost of living	Wages	Manufactured exports	Materials for exports	Shipping freights
145	143	150	157	164	154	110
A	A	B	C	E 2	E 3	E 3

These figures indicate that Class A was, as usual, nearly adjusted to the outside world; that world shipping freights were already seriously depressed; and that prices in Classes B, C, and E2 were already on the high side. Thus, as I said in my pamphlet, we had a serious problem, even when sterling exchange was 12 per cent depreciated, in the relatively high level of prices in Classes B and C, and E2—which already showed itself in unemployment and depressed exports. (The allegation that I attribute all our troubles to the gold standard is a myth in my case, as Sir J. Stamp has shown it to be his. I expressly limited this influence to the worsening of our position during the past year. Indeed, a prominent part of my argument was directed to showing that the return to gold was particularly rash just because we already had other troubles which we could not afford to aggravate.)

What had the position become in June, 1925, with the exchange at par?

United States Whole-sale index	Great Britain					
	Whole-sale index	Cost of living	Wages	Manu-factured exports	Materials for export	Shipping freights
157	158	173	180	191	156	101
A	A	B	C	E 2	E 3	E 3

Thus the wholesale index was still adjusted; Class E3 had been compelled to abate its prices by almost the full extent of the improvement in the exchange, and in the case of freights by considerably more, the shipping industry having to support not only the exchange burden, but also an aggravation of the depression in the international freight level. On the other hand, the divergence of the prices in Classes B, C, and E2 from those in Class A was seriously aggravated.

In June, 1924, the ratios of the price levels in the British A, B, C, and E2 classes respectively to the American wholesale index were 99, 103, 109 and 113 per cent. If we consider the abnormally low costs in certain European countries, and the impairment of our position through the war, this was sufficiently serious. It was, therefore, rash to adopt an exchange policy, the first effect of which would certainly be to increase the discrepancy and to widen the gap to be bridged by painful social adjustments. The result of such a policy is that in June, 1925, the same ratios had become 101, 110, 115 and 122 per cent. I believe that the last two of these ratios are about 10 per cent higher than they need have been if, during the past year, we had concentrated on stability of internal prices and had left the exchange to look after itself. However that may be, it is these high figures which are at the root of our troubles. In the United States there is evidence that the corresponding ratios have fallen, rather than risen, during the past year. As regards Europe, the B and C ratios have fallen in France, Italy, and Belgium, and have risen in Germany; but in all these countries they are still much below 100.

When I wrote my pamphlet on *The Economic Consequences of Mr Churchill*, I did not foresee that such plain and evident matters—namely, that our relative money costs are too high and that the return to gold parity has aggravated this—would be denied. The exact percentages are open to dispute; but I believed, and still believe, that the main facts are incontrovertible. Perhaps I should have learnt from my experiences after the Treaty of Versailles what passionate moral indignation a statement of economic truth can provoke. Nevertheless Dr Leaf's assertion, that sterling is actually undervalued, still takes my breath away.

Lord Bradbury has truly pointed out in an article in *The Financial News* that there are three remedies open to us:—(1) a reduction in sterling costs; (2) a rise in our competitors' gold costs; (3) a fall in the sterling exchange; though one might add (4) a permanent reduction in the volume of our foreign investment such as would render a complete return to our former favourable international balance of trade permanently unnecessary. If (1) proves politically impracticable, if (2) does not occur, and if (4) is by itself inadequate, I have no doubt that sooner or later (3) will become inevitable. But since it is very unlikely that this third alternative will be accepted except as the result of bitter experiences, it seemed worth while to make suggestions for a remedy on the lines of (1) and (2). The orthodox remedy is, of course, to bring about (1) by means of credit restriction. I argued in my pamphlet that this method would be socially disastrous whilst it was going on and socially unjust in its results, and also that it was probably impracticable politically. I suggested, therefore, that we should aim at an all-round 5 per cent reduction of money wages by agreement pending a fall in the cost of living, and that we should, at the same time, release gold in the hope of raising prices elsewhere. The first of these suggestions has been ignored by my critics. I daresay that it is not practical politics. Nevertheless since it is very probable that we shall remain on the gold standard for the present, I suggest that it is our business to seek a remedy along the lines either of (1), (2), or (4).

What in fact are we doing? The coal subsidy and the reduction of Bank rate indicate that the authorities have abandoned, for the present, the attempt to reduce sterling prices. Mr Churchill, in the House of Commons, even has the audacity to represent himself as a defender of the present level of money wages against my nefarious plans to reduce them. Meanwhile the Governor of the Bank of England, converted at last to the methods of his *confrère* at the Bank of France, exercises his ingenuity to cover our adverse trade balance by preventing the export of capital and by borrowing abroad. The last named policy may be a first half-unconscious step in the direction of (4), that is to say, a permanent curtailment in the scale of our foreign investment. But the right way to achieve this result cannot be, in the long run, by means of an embargo, but by the deliberate organisation of investment at home, resulting in an increase in the rate of interest, at which foreign borrowers can sell their bonds here, above the corresponding rate in New York, and, above all, by the organised transfer of labour out of the export industries.

What we need, expressed in one sentence, is to reduce our C and D gold costs relatively to similar costs elsewhere. The mistake which we have made in raising the exchange, also expressed in one sentence, is that we have increased the amount of the necessary reduction by at least 10 per cent, without any plan as to how to effect the reduction.

If I was in authority but was committed to the gold standard, I should try to get some help from each of the remedies (1), (2), and (4). I should do what I could, short of restricting credit (which might be very little) to reduce prices in Classes B, C, D, and E. I should export as much gold as possible with a view to raising prices elsewhere. I should take steps, other than the embargo, such as an alteration of the Trustee Act and the encouragement of expensive new capital projects at home, to reduce the existing pressure towards overseas investment. I should try with might and main to shift labour out of the export industries (especially coal). And, in the face of a hard task, rendered much harder by muddleheadedness, I should trust, for the rest, to luck, and hope for the best.

But it will be difficult for the authorities to apply any remedies at all if, like Dr Leaf and Mr Churchill, they deny the existence or the nature of the disease.

I am yours, &c.,

J. M. KEYNES

On 3 September, two days before his letter on Leaf appeared in *The Times*, Keynes went off to Russia to meet Lydia's family and to act as the official representative of the University of Cambridge at the Bicentennial Celebrations of the Academy of Sciences held in Leningrad and Moscow between 5 and 14 September. While in Moscow Keynes gave two lectures, 'The Economic Position in England' and 'The Economic Transition in England'. These appear below.[4]

THE ECONOMIC POSITION IN ENGLAND

1. Money wages in England are 80 per cent higher than before the War. The cost of living of the working classes is 73 per cent higher. Thus real wages have improved about 4 per

---

[4] The second has strong parallels to 'Am I a Liberal?' (*JMK*, vol. IX, esp. pp. 303–6).

cent. Since working hours have been somewhat reduced, and since the intensity of work is also—according to most observers—less rather than more, the position of the working class is improved.

2. At least this is the case for those who are in work. The black spot is the large proportion of unemployment. From 10 to 12 per cent of the workers are without employment, including near 1 million adult male workers. Even the position of these, however, is much better than it would have been in similar circumstances before the War; for a married unemployed worker receives from the state about 40 roubles a month.

3. The unemployment is not equally distributed throughout industry, but is concentrated in those trades which compete for their markets with foreign goods—in particular shipping, shipbuilding, coal, iron and steel, engineering and textiles. In those industries which depend on the home market and supply goods to satisfy the very considerable purchasing power of the working classes, the position is entirely satisfactory. For example, in the building industry the whole of the productive capacity is employed; and the tobacco industry, the beer industry, the artificial silk industry (which makes the stockings which every English factory-girl and shop-girl now wears) are making greater profits than ever before.

4. The explanation of this situation is the obvious one—with sterling at gold parity, British prices and wages are too high relatively to world prices. I reckon that British wages would have to fall nearly 20 per cent to be in equilibrium with those in France, Germany, Italy and Belgium, and nearly 10 per cent to be in equilibrium with the world situation as a whole. The problem how to bring about this reduction is as much a political as an economic problem. Not much progress has been made as yet towards its solution.

5. The result is that the industries of the country fall into two groups—what are called the 'sheltered' industries which are exceedingly prosperous and comfortable and the 'unsheltered'

435

industries which are in great distress. The high prices of the goods produced by the prosperous 'sheltered' industries make wages and other costs in the 'unsheltered' industries so high that the latter are handicapped in competition with their foreign rivals.

6. This disequilibrium between the two groups is the fundamental problem for Great Britain; and this problem has been gravely aggravated by the restoration of the gold standard. A year ago sterling was 12 per cent depreciated compared with gold, and this depreciation provided a sort of bounty to the export industries. Now, when sterling is at par, the 'sheltered' industries maintain the same prices and wages, whilst the 'unsheltered' industries, which sell for export, realise 12 per cent less in sterling for what they sell than they realised when sterling was depreciated. The result has been to reduce some of them almost to bankruptcy.

7. The correct remedy would be a fall of wages in the 'sheltered' industries. But since employment is good in these industries and the trade unions strong and determined to accept no reductions, it is very difficult to put pressure on them. On the other hand, in the 'unsheltered' industries, where the pressure of unemployment and bad trade exists in a high degree, the wages are already relatively low, so that these industries have a good case before public opinion and in justice for not suffering a further reduction.

8. The first example of an attempt to reduce wages—namely in the coal industry—has had a surprising result. This industry is the most exposed of all the 'unsheltered' industries. Accordingly the mine-owners were able to prove that if they continued to pay the present wages they would become bankrupt. On the other hand, the mine-workers were able to prove that, if the wages were lowered, their standard of life would be unjustly reduced below the standard in other industries. The other trade unions supported the mine-workers and declared that they would order an almost general strike if the Government insisted

436

on the reduction. The Government, at a loss to know what to do, made the surprising decision to appoint a Commission to examine the case, and meanwhile for the Government themselves to pay the difference between what the mine-owners offer and what the mine-workers demand! This costs the Government at present about 20 million roubles a month.

9. The disequilibrium naturally results in brisk imports and reduced exports, thus impairing the balance of payments. This is being temporarily remedied by the Bank of England in two ways—partly by bank credits from America, and partly by prohibiting the financiers of the City from making new foreign loans. This prohibition now extends even to loans to other parts of the British Empire. This state of affairs also has its reaction on Russia and makes impossible what would in any case be difficult, namely new loans to Russia.

10. There is one other aspect of the case which has its application to Russia, namely the growth of population. The high level of unemployment and the difficulty in transferring labour out of the unprosperous industries into the prosperous industries is not a little due to the excessive growth of population and to the fact that the number of younger workers entering industry every year is much greater than the number of old workers going out. I believe that the poverty of Russia before the War was due to the great increase in population more than to any other cause. The War and the Revolution reduced the population. But I am told that now again there is a large excess of births over deaths. There is no greater danger than this to the economic future of Russia. There is no more important object of deliberate state policy than to secure a balanced budget of population.

11. In conclusion I emphasise that the economic problem of England is essentially a problem of solid and economic disequilibrium and not primarily a problem of poverty or of a lack of technical capacity to produce wealth.

14 September 1925

THE ECONOMIC TRANSITION IN ENGLAND

Great Britain, not less than Russia, is suffering an economic transition in the early stages of which we are now living. An American economist, Professor Commons, one of the first to recognise the nature of this transition, distinguishes three epochs, three economic orders, upon the third of which we are entering.

The first is the epoch of scarcity, whether due to inefficiency or to violence, war, custom or superstition. In such a period there is the minimum of individual liberty and the maximum of communistic, feudalistic or governmental control through physical coercion. This was, with brief intervals in exceptional cases, the normal economic state of the world up to (say) the sixteenth or seventeenth century.

Next comes the era of abundance. In a period of extreme abundance there is the maximum of individual liberty and the minimum of coercive control through government; and individual bargaining takes the place of rationing. During the eighteenth and early nineteenth centuries Europe won its way out of the bondage of scarcity into the free air of abundance, and in the latter nineteenth century this epoch culminated gloriously in England in the victories of *laissez-faire* and historic liberalism. It is not surprising or discreditable that the veterans of the Liberal Party cast backward glances on that easier age.

But England is now entering on a third era, which Professor Commons has called the period of stabilisation and has truly characterised as the actual alternative to Marx's communism. In this period, he says, there is a diminution of individual liberty, enforced in part by governmental sanctions, but mainly by economic sanctions through concerted action, whether secret, semi-open, open or arbitrational, of associations, corporations, unions and other collective movements of manufacturers, merchants, labourers, farmers and bankers.

The extremes of this epoch in the realm of government are

Fascism on the one side and Leninism on the other. For my part, I accept neither. Yet state socialism offers no middle course, because it also is sprung from the presuppositions of the era of abundance, just as much as *laissez-faire* individualism and the free play of economic forces. Therefore I direct all my mind and attention to the development of new methods and new ideas for effecting the transition from the economic anarchy of the individualistic capitalism which rules today in Western Europe towards a régime which will deliberately aim at controlling and directing economic forces in the interests of social justice and social stability. I still have enough optimism to believe that to effect this transition may be the true destiny of a New Liberalism.

It happens that England has today in the position of her coal industry an object lesson of the results of the confusion of ideas which now prevails. On the one side the Conservative Government is pursuing an orthodox nineteenth-century policy based on the assumption that economic adjustments can and ought to be brought about by the free play of the forces of supply and demand. They still assume that the things, which would follow on the assumption of free competition and the mobility of capital and labour, actually occur in the economic life of today.

On the other side not only the facts, but public opinion also, have moved a long distance away towards the epoch of stabilisation. The trade unions are strong enough to interfere with the free play of the forces of supply and demand; whilst public opinion, albeit with a grumble and with more than a suspicion that the trade unions are growing dangerous, supports the trade unions in their main contention that coalminers ought not to be the victims of cruel economic forces which they never set in motion.

The idea of the Conservatives, that you can, for example, alter the value of money and then leave the consequential adjustments to be brought about by the forces of supply and demand, belongs to the days of fifty or a hundred years ago when trade unions were powerless, and when the economic juggernaut was allowed to crash along the highway of progress without obstruction and even with applause.

The orthodox economics, which we have inherited from the nineteenth century, assumes a high degree of fluidity of the economic organism. It depends on what I would term the *principle of diffusion*—the principle that, when any disturbance is introduced at any point in the economic organism, it diffuses itself fairly rapidly through the whole organism until a new position of equilibrium has been reached. It has always been admitted that the economic organism is partly rigid and that friction may delay the process of diffusion. But it has been supposed that the organism has sufficient fluidity and mobility to allow the principle of diffusion to be a good working hypothesis.

That a great measure of diffusion still takes place, I do not deny. But the ease and rapidity of diffusion is—in England at least—much less than it used to be. I put this down to three main influences:

1. A rapidly progressive community possesses much more mobility than a stationary or slowly progressive community. In the case of the former equilibrium can be restored by (for example) a particular industry growing more or less fast. It is much easier to retard the rate of growth than actually to drive capital and labour, which are already in an industry, out of it. I attach immense importance to this. I do not think that Englishmen sufficiently realise to what an extent their nineteenth-century methods depended on the fact that the country was living in a continuing economic crescendo. The orthodox economic assumptions work much better in the United States than in England precisely because in the United States the crescendo of progress still continues.

2. The growth in the power and authority of the trade unions both to maintain wages and to exclude the entry of new labourers into a trade.

3. The growth of a sort of humanitarianism, exemplified in the 'dole' to the unemployed, which interferes with the natural pressure of economic forces on individuals.

These influences have, between them, introduced a considerable degree of rigidity into the British economic system. Yet the authorities still frame their policies on the assumption that a high degree of mobility and diffusion still exists. Hence our tears and troubles.

It is not an accident that our first difficulties, which will last long and take many different forms, should centre about monetary policy. For no feature of our pre-war system depended more fundamentally on the principle of diffusion than did our pre-war gold standard regulated by means of Bank rate. The first and most important step, in my judgement, is to establish a new monetary system based on a stable level of internal prices, which will not ask from the principle of diffusion more than it can perform.

But this is not the only item in my new economic programme. I believe that there are many other matters, left hitherto to individuals or to chance, which must become in future the subject of deliberate state policy and centralised state control. Let me mention two—(1) the size and quality of the population and (2) the magnitude and direction of employment of the new national savings year by year.

Some of you in Russia will not agree with me in seeking help in these matters from a reformed and remodelled Liberalism, which above all, shall *not*, if my ideal is realised, be a *class* party. Leninism—so it seems to me—is at the same [time] a persecuting religion and an experimental technique. Capitalism too is at the same time a religion, which is much more tolerant, however, than Leninism is, and a technique which, from having been experimental, is now perhaps in danger of becoming obsolescent. On the religous side it is not for me, who am a free-thinking heretic, to speak. But the experimental technique is necessarily a matter of most high interest. We in the West will watch what you do with sympathy and lively attention, in the hope that we may find something which we can learn from you. For we too have new problems to solve.

15 September 1925

On his return from the Soviet Union Keynes wrote three essays under the title 'Soviet Russia'. These appeared in *The Nation* for 10, 27 and 24 October before the Hogarth Press published them in December under the title *A Short View of Russia* (*JMK*, vol. IX, pp. 253–71).

Keynes's return also brought a renewal of his agitation over official financial policy. On 12 October he journeyed to Manchester to speak to the Manchester Branch of the Federation of British Industries the next day. Two days later his speech appeared in *The Manchester Guardian Commercial*.

From The Manchester Guardian Commercial, *15 October 1925*

Mr Keynes said that if the Treasury and the Bank of England had listened to the advice which the Federation of British Industries had pressed on them at frequent intervals during the past three years employment today would have been exceedingly good. The F.B.I. had been all through not only moderate and reasonable in its officially expressed policy, but right.

We may also differ about the cure [continued Mr Keynes], but we cannot differ about the character of our difficulties. It is no longer true that there is a world depression. The United States has never in its history experienced such unmitigated prosperity as at the present day. It is not true that our principal customers are abnormally impoverished, unless it be in China. Home trade is good on the whole. Wheat, sugar, cotton, copper, steel, oil, and coal—to take some of the commodities which to us are the most important in the world—are in abundant supply. It is not true that we are technically inefficient. We are not backward in the new industries—artificial silk, motor-cars, oil-driven ships, electrical engineering. In all those things we hold our own with the whole world. The foundations for prosperity exist.

The reason why unemployment does not diminish and

certain industries are half-bankrupt lies in the fact that our manufacturing costs of production, measured in gold, are higher than those of our chief industrial competitors. That is the result of our having used financial devices to fix the gold value of sterling at a value above that which, in fact, it has measured by its command over home services.

These excess costs of production may be divided into two parts. One part is due to the fact that the real wages of our workers are higher than those in the rest of Europe. The other part is because our cost of living, when converted into gold at the current rate of exchange, is higher than the corresponding cost abroad, so that we have to pay our workers higher money wages before they are dead level with wages elsewhere. Thus the second factor has nothing to do with the efficiency or inefficiency of capital or of labour, but is just a symptom of monetary maladjustment.

So far we all agree. But when we come to the cure, one can distinguish three schools of opinion. The first school I will call the pious school. The pious school thinks that the monetary factor is not very important one way or the other. It stresses the high level of taxation and the high real wages of our workers, their relatively short hours, and their tendency to ca'canny. In its hysterical moments it is occupied with something said to be prevalent in this country which it calls Communism. According to this school, there is very little that the Government can do except to economise drastically in its own expenditure. Apart from Government economy there is nothing to be done except to exhort everybody in terms of copybook maxims. We must forget party differences, we must all pull together, we must work much harder, employers and employed must be at peace, those whose wages are relatively high must be willing to reduce them for the benefit of others, and the old country will pull through yet.

The ablest representative of this school in the daily press is, perhaps, the City Editor of *The Morning Post*. Gentlemen who write to the newspapers belong to this school more often than not. So does Mr Baldwin, except in the matter of governmental economics—about which as a sensible man he has no illusions. The first leader in today's *Times* is a perfect example of this philosophy. All the same, this school, I am afraid, though vocal and more than respectable doesn't cut much ice. In practice its precepts boil down to demands for reduced Government expenditure and reduced real wages. Now, though it is not good manners to cast doubt on such admirable sentiments, I do doubt whether these measures are practicable and even—in general—desirable. I do not believe that important economies in Government expenditure are possible except in the fighting services—while the latter, though desirable, are not compatible with our present foreign policy of guaranteeing distant frontiers against the Turk, and of undertaking to defend Germany disarmed against France in the plentitude of her military power—two steps in the highest degree imprudent.

As for our real wages, while they are higher, I am glad to say, than in the rest of Europe, they are not so high as in the United States. I am not convinced that they are higher on the average than we can afford. Ca'canning is a degrading and antisocial practice. Wages are too high in particular grades and particular industries relatively to others. But I sympathise with the working classes in resisting a general reduction of real wages. I am sure that no material reduction is possible in the near future without engaging on a social struggle of which no one could foretell the outcome.

The second school is the strait-laced school. This school recognises the existence of monetary disequilibrium and would like to cure it by carrying out, pretty ruthlessly the orthodox rules of the pre-war gold standard. If British prices are relatively too high, this means that credit is relatively too abundant. If the markets for capital and goods are left perfectly free and unrestricted, as they ought to be—so runs the teaching of this school—gold will flow out and credit will be restricted until equilibrium has been restored. This may involve temporary sacrifices, but they are necessary and worth while.

The ablest exponent of this philosophy in the daily press has been the distinguished and well-informed City Editor of *The Manchester Guardian*. Now the fault of this school is that it depends too much on applying to new conditions rules which were drawn up with a view to old conditions, without considering in sufficient detail how they will work out in these new conditions. The only method by which the high Bank rate and credit restriction can lower prices is, so to speak, by deliberately organising a depression. These measures aim at depriving the business men of sufficient cash for carrying on at the existing level of prices; and rely on this to effect the necessary reduction of prices.

Now in conditions of boom or incipient boom it is necessary and desirable to use this method to damp down business enthusiasm. But at a time of depression deliberately to organise more depression simply breaks the heart of the employer of labour. Moreover, when it is wages which which the policy aims at reducing, it may, in modern conditions of organised labour and impaired mobility of labour, merely produce the depression without bringing about an adequate reduction of prices. The reason why we are still full of unemployment when the rest of the world is recovering from the depression of 1921 is because for three years past whenever business was raising its head the Bank of England has seized the opportunity to restrict credit and so organise a depression with a view to lowering prices in the interests of the dollar exchange. When the adjustment has at last been affected, this school will have done its worst and its best for the time being. But, meanwhile, the consequences of this policy are disastrous. Indeed another five years of this policy might bring us to the edge of revolution, if revolution is ever possible in this country.

The third school I will venture to call the sensible school. It has included the Federation of British Industries, Mr

445

McKenna, Sir Alfred Mond; and the leading weekly newspapers, *The Nation*, *The New Statesman*, and *The Spectator*. I even notice a slightly greater wisdom in the weekly *Manchester Guardian* than in the daily. This school believes that prosperity is more important than the dollar exchange, that prosperity is cumulative, that prosperity by allowing production up to capacity and full-time employment may enable us at the same time to pay present real wages and, nevertheless, reduce our costs. This school, therefore, would set itself in every possible way to organise prosperity instead of depression, would stimulate new capital developments of every kind, would encourage the business world to launch out, and would give it the confidence and the credit to do so.

Up to the date of the reintroduction of gold convertibility this spring, it was easy to combine these aims with an absolutely sound financial policy. It is not so easy now. The prosperity policy will probably lead in its early stages to a loss of gold, perhaps on a large scale, and we must be prepared to take no notice of this, which would, in normal times, be incompatible in the long run with a sound gold-standard policy. It involves a risk. Nevertheless, the risk should, I think be taken. Having made the mistake of returning to the gold standard before we were ready for it—the only remedy is to be found in not taking the gold standard too seriously for the time being.

In classifying the schools of opinion I have not yet placed the authorities of the Bank of England—for that reason that I simply do not know where they stand. At one time I thought that they belonged to the strait-laced school. But their latest actions no longer bear this out. Lenin and Mussolini have at least explained what they were at. But our despots are dumb. The veiled prophetess of Threadneedle Street speaks in the riddles of Bank rate, the City reverently accepts her word, but no one, it seems, has any idea what the old lady really means.

The recent policy of the Bank of England is capable of two opposite interpretations. The Bank of England may wish quite deliberately to lose a certain amount of gold in order to have a good excuse for curtailing credit once again, and for raising the Bank rate to 5 per cent after an interval. The object of the recent recoil of Bank rate may be *pour mieux sauter*.

On the other hand, it may mean that at last the Bank has come over to the sensible school, that the object of the present cheap money is to revive trade, that we can rely on a continuance of cheap money until trade does revive, that gold will be allowed to flow out on a large scale if necessary without any restriction of credit ensuing, and that the Bank's resources in America will be used if they are needed. If this is the policy, our prospect may be fairly bright.

Take Manchester for example. If Lancashire was producing up to capacity, would it not be possible to reduce costs materially, without any reduction of wages? Is this not a better programme than to curtail credit in the hope that the resulting unemployment will lead to a fall in real wages? Cheap money is a dangerous thing. Cheap money in the right conditions can work wonders. I would run the risk of cheap money at the present juncture. With abundant cotton plus abundant credit is not a remarkable revival in the textile industries perfectly possible?

It may be that the Bank of England has no steady or thought-out policy at all, but lives empirically day by day—by cunning rather than science. It is absurd that we do not know. For the immediate future of this country depends on the answer. The premature return to gold renders what I call the prosperity policy more difficult and more risky than it would have been otherwise. I urge, all the same, that the Federation of British Industries should use its influence to make sure that it is the prosperity policy and not the suicide policy which wins the day.

The Guardian Commercial's report of Keynes's speech led to two further letters from Keynes.

To the Editor of The Manchester Guardian Commercial, *17 October 1925*

Sir,

In your otherwise excellent report of my speech at the F.B.I. luncheon, Manchester, the other day, you attributed to me the dreadful expression 'ca'canning'. I did not know how to pronounce the word, and I did not know its derivation, but I did, I think, know how to spell it. The mistake had, however, the result of bringing me from a correspondent the whole story. I send it to you in case there may be some others amongst your readers besides myself who learn something from it.

My correspondent writes:—

This is made up of two words 'calling' spelt in Scotch cain and the und [*sic*] canny, a word which as a good Englishman you no doubt apply to all Scotchmen, good and otherwise. Ca'in is the participle of the verb to call and 'canny' is an adjective. The phrase you should have used was therefore 'ca'in canny'. Further 'a' in *Ca'in* is pronounced as in *calling*.

I would only add that the last sentence is to me ambiguous. Am I to pronounce *ca* as *car* or as *caw*?

I am, etc.,

J. M. KEYNES

To the Editor of The Manchester Guardian Commercial, *26 October 1925*

Sir,

I am afraid that I am still in error about 'ca'canny'. My letter which you published last week has brought me another correction from a further correspondent, who writes this time as follows:

The verb in *to ca'canny* has nothing to do with the word to call (vocare—spelt also *ca* in Scots). In this phrase it means to work, drive or knock—e.g. my mither ca's the mangle. In the well known Scotch song beginning, 'Ca' the yowes to the knowes', the word is used in the sense of *drive*—not *call*, i.e. 'Drive the ewes to the knolls'—(and I your lover will go with you). A Scots expression puns on the two meanings:—Ye can ca' me (call) what ye like if ye dinna ca' (knock) me ower (over)'.

I am, etc.,

J. M. KEYNES

The Manchester Guardian's and *The Commercial*'s City Editor's comments on Keynes's speech drew two more letters.

To the Editor of The Manchester Guardian, *19 October 1925*

Sir,

Your City Editor argues today that my recommendation to maintain Bank rate at 4 per cent, in spite of the loss of gold, is somethat risky. No doubt this is so. But the policy of last spring has produced a situation in which *no* course is open to us against which there are not considerable objections.

He, I understand, advocates dearer money and the restriction of credit if the outward flow of gold continues. May I ask him whether he advocates this in order to tempt back the American balances which have been flowing away, or in order to curtail credit at home in the hope of reducing prices? If his object is the former, could we not attain the same end, namely, short-period borrowing from New York, by using the Bank of England's credits with the New York Federal Reserve Bank, leaving our own Bank rate where it is in the interests of trade recovery? If, however, his object is the latter, may I ask him to particularise a little the causal train by which he thinks dear money and credit restriction will lower prices?

We agree, I think, that the trouble is the high level of British costs of production when expressed in terms of gold. Will dear money cure this, except by the process—as I expressed it the other day—of organising depression; that is to say, of increasing losses and bankruptcies amongst employers and unemployment amongst workers, in the hope that both parties will eventually abate their demands under the overwhelming pressure of their

449

misfortunes? In what way will dear money and credit restriction tend towards a lower cost of production, unless it be thus?

If this is the way in which dear money does its job, isn't it sensible not to be strait-laced?

Yours, &c.,

J. M. KEYNES

To the Editor of The Manchester Guardian Commercial, *2 November 1925*

Sir,

Your City Editor's account of my opinions published last week is one to which I cannot, for several reasons, conveniently reply in an adequate manner within the limits proper to correspondence. In a few respects he misrepresents me. In other passages he raises solid and important arguments.

Yet most of this is really irrelevant to the essential difference between us, which is something broader. He stands firm on the past; I am trying to grapple with the future. He thinks that we have nothing to do but to follow the good old rules. I think that things have changed, and that the presumptions as to fact, upon which his rules depend, no longer hold. I am doubtless wrong and rash in many matters, and will be corrected by experience. But I am trying with all my wits, now in this direction and now in that, to face up to the new problems, theoretically and practically, too. Your City Editor is blind as a bat—so it seems to me—to the shifting scene, though so much abler than the other bats. For this reason, what he writes is—except from the debating standpoint, which one can always enjoy—to me absolutely uninteresting and unsignificant. I know it all before-hand; for I was brought up on it and taught it for years. If only I could convert him, not to my opinions and recipes, but to my state of mind! Then, whether we agreed or not, we should be able to discuss with exhilaration and with profit the difficulties ahead. So I appeal to him to step out of his coffin, discard his strait-laced shroud, and join the ranks of the living.

Yours, &c.,

J. M. KEYNES

The remainder of the year brought one more letter from Keynes's pen—not on the gold standard. In June 1924 Keynes had taken part in a deputation to the Prime Minister to lobby against the authorities' proposals to commute tithes (see *JMK*, vol. XII). The deputation was not successful.

To the Editor of The Times, *21 November 1925*

Sir,

As the Bursar of a college which is one of the largest owners of impropriate tithe, I have followed closely the proceedings on the Tithe Bill. In my opinion the feature of the Bill which deserves the closest attention is the method of valuation which the Government have seen fit to adopt.

Tithe is at present a form of real property of which the annual value in terms of money fluctuates in a way which cannot be foreseen with certainty. It is proposed to compel the owners by legislation to accept in lieu of it a fixed money annuity. With one class of owners, the clergy, an agreed bargain has been reached, in which rating concessions play an important part. With another class, the lay rectors, amongst whom are the Colleges of Oxford and Cambridge, no agreed bargain has been reached.

The question has arisen, therefore, how to fix the amount of the money annuity, failing agreement. The Colleges have proposed that the question of valuation should be submitted to an independent arbitrator, who would hear evidence. The course taken by the Government has been to ask the opinion of a single authority, of much eminence, but not an expert in this particular matter, and to whose appointment for this

451

purpose the disadvantage (or advantage) attached that the Government knew beforehand what his opinion would be, since they had obtained it on substantially the same matter a year previously. This gentleman has not heard evidence from the parties concerned; nor has he based his decision on the present net annual value of the property in question. He has looked into the future and has decided that the value attached to tithe must be calculated by reference to what its value would be on the assumption, which he deems reasonable, but which the owners dispute, that the prices of corn will fall rapidly during the next 15 years to their pre-war level.

The method of arriving at a fair figure is a question of some general importance, because several other analogous transactions are on the programmes of the various political parties—e.g. coal royalties, the coal mines themselves, railways, rural and urban land under Mr Lloyd George's schemes. Suppose, for example, that the same method were to be applied in fixing a money annuity receivable by landlords in lieu of future rent. Let us suppose that the decision is left to the judgement of a single individual, the bias of whose opinion is known beforehand. Let us suppose further that this individual expects agricultural prices to fall steadily to two-thirds of their present level, and calculates the annuity on the basis of what rents would be if this assumption is realised. Would not landlords feel aggrieved at being expropriated from a considerable part of the present value of their property on the ground of a disputed and unverified expectation that something might be going to happen some years hence which would cause rents to fall? Might they not reasonably demand that such a settlement should be preceded by an open and impartial examination of their case?

Compulsory expropriations of property in return for a fixed money annuity are very much in the air just now. Whether the valuation embodied in the Tithe Bill is right or wrong in itself, have the Government seriously considered the nature of the precedent which they are setting? As a Bursar I am disgusted at a measure which, as I believe, robs the Colleges of Oxford and Cambridge of expectations worth £100,000 or so. As an economist I realise that the establishment, by a Conservative Government, of a precedent of this kind, which may be much quoted and often acted on in future, is a matter of more importance. The passage of this Bill and the light way in which our complaints as to its justice have been handled by Ministers mark, I think, an important transition in the attitude of public opinion towards property rights. It means that, in future, property will be liable to expropriation not at an arbitrated figure, but at such price as may seem to the Government of the day to be convenient on broad political grounds. For my own part, I believe that expropriations of particular forms of property may become increasingly necessary in the public interest; but I believe also that the mode of fixing the compensation payable in such cases should partake of the attributes and formalities of the public administration of justice—which have been conspicuously lacking in this case.

Yours, &c.,

J. M. KEYNES